Windows™ 3.1 QuickStart

Ron Person

Karen Rose

Windows 3.1 QuickStart

Copyright © 1992 by Que® Corporation

Library of Congress Catalog No.: 91-61975

ISBN: 0-88022-730-3

94 93 92   6 5 4 3

Interpretation of the printing code: the rightmost double-digit number is the year of the book's printing; the rightmost single-digit number, the number of the book's printing. For example, a printing code of 92-1 shows that the first printing of the book occurred in 1992.

Windows 3.1 QuickStart is based on Microsoft Windows 3.0 and 3.1.

Screen reproductions in this book were created using Collage Plus from Inner Media, Inc., Hollis, NH.

Publisher: Lloyd J. Short

Acquisitions Manager: Rick Ranucci

Product Development Manager: Thomas H. Bennett

Managing Editor: Paul Boger

Book Designer: Scott Cook

Production Team: Jeff Baker, Claudia Bell, Scott Boucher, Brad Chinn, Michelle Cleary, Denny Hager, Carrie Keesling, Phil Kitchel, Bob LaRoche, Laurie Lee, Jay Lesandrini, Anne Owen, Juli Pavey, Caroline Roop, John Sleeva, Kevin Spear, Bruce Steed

About the Authors

Ron Person has written more than twelve books for Que Corporation, including *Using Excel 4 for Windows,* Special Edition; *Using Windows 3.1,* Special Edition; and *Using Word for Windows 2,* Special Edition. Ron is the principal consultant for Ron Person & Co. He has an M.S. in physics from The Ohio State University and an M.B.A. from Hardin-Simmons University.

Karen Rose is a senior trainer for Ron Person & Co. She has written five books for Que Corporation, including *Using Windows 3.1,* Special Edition; *Using Word for Windows 2,* Special Edition; *Using WordPerfect 5*; and *Using WordPerfect 5.1,* Special Edition. Karen teaches Word for Windows and desktop publishing for Ron Person & Co. and has taught for the University of California, Berkeley Extension, and Sonoma State University.

Ron Person & Co., based in San Francisco, has attained Microsoft's highest rating for Microsoft Excel and Word for Windows consultants—Microsoft Consulting Partner. The firm helps corporations nationwide in consulting and developing in-house programming and support skills with the embedded macro languages in Microsoft Excel, Word for Windows, and other major Windows applications. The firm's macro developer's courses have enabled many corporations to develop their own powerful financial, marketing, and business analysis systems in a minimum amount of time. If your company plans to develop applications using Microsoft's embedded macro languages, you will gain significantly from the courses taught by Ron Person & Co. For information on course content, on-site corporate classes, or consulting, contact:

Ron Person & Co.
P.O. Box 5647
3 Quixote Ct.
Santa Rosa, CA 95409
(415) 989-7508   Voice
(707) 539-1525   Voice
(707) 538-1485   FAX

Product Director
Kathie-Jo Arnoff

Production Editor
Barbara K. Koenig

Editors
Cindy Morrow
Pamela Wampler
Laura J. Wirthlin

Technical Editors
Jerry Ellis
Greg Perry
Don Roche Jr.

*Composed in ITC Garamond and
MCPdigital by Que Corporation.*

Acknowledgments

Windows *3.1 QuickStart* was created through the work and contributions of many professionals. We want to thank the people who contributed to this effort.

Thanks to everyone at Microsoft Corporation. Their energy and vision have opened new frontiers in software—software that is more powerful, yet easier to use. Microsoft Windows has changed the face of computing. Thanks to Christie Gersiche for keeping us in touch and informed.

Thanks to the software consultants and trainers who helped us write *Windows 3.1 QuickStart*.

Robert Voss, Ph.D., applied his knowledge of many Windows programs to the chapters on Windows accessories, Windows Graph, and the Microsoft applets. Again, Robert has done a conscientious and in-depth job. Robert is a senior trainer in Microsoft Excel and Word for Windows for Ron Person & Co.

Don Roche Jr. is the DOS and Windows expert who wrote the chapter on working with DOS programs under Windows. Don is a very experienced technical writer and computer consultant in Austin, Texas. Don does technical writing and support for corporations.

Doug Bierer contributed the networking portions of the book. Doug is a Certified Netware Instructor and Engineer (CNI/CNE). He's been working with Netware, Banyan, and LANtastic for approximately seven years. Doug currently works for Vitek Systems Distribution, Systems Education, in Sacramento.

Ralph Soucie, long time contributing editor to *PC World* and author of a popular book on Microsoft Excel, is a Microsoft Excel consultant. Ralph works out of Tualatin, Oregon. Ralph contributed extensively to the chapters on Program Manager and File Manager.

Matt Fogarty is the talented artist who drew the pictures of the guitarist and the pelicans (using Paintbrush), and the horse race and the old man's character study (using Microsoft Draw). Matt is a student at Santa Rosa High School in Santa Rosa, California.

Technical editing was done by Don Roche Jr., Greg Perry, and Jerry Ellis; however, the responsibility for any errors that may have slipped through their knowledgeable gaze lies solely with us.

The skillful pens of our editors ensure that our books are consistent and easy to read. That they succeed in their jobs is evident by the comments of our corporate clients on the quality and value of Que books.

Kathie-Jo Arnoff, Product Director, managed the lightning-fast process of getting *Windows 3.1 QuickStart* into print. Kathie-Jo has designed and managed our books before and always produces excellent results.

Barbara Koenig, Production Editor, worked with us daily to ensure that we didn't get too far behind schedule and to give us feedback on style and content. We're grateful to Barbara for asking questions that helped clarify the material, and for editing with such a subtle pen that we couldn't tell whether our words had changed—we only knew they sounded great.

With the rush of consulting, training, and book development going on in our office, we could not have kept our heads above the diskettes and client folders were it not for our assistant, Wilma Thompson.

Trademark Acknowledgments

Que Corporation has made every effort to supply trademark information about company names, products, and services mentioned in this book. Trademarks indicated below were derived from various sources. Que Corporation cannot attest to the accuracy of this information.

1-2-3 and Lotus are registered trademarks of Lotus Development Corporation.

Adobe Type Manager is a trademark and PostScript is a registered trademark of Adobe Systems, Inc.

Ami Professional is a trademark of SAMNA Corporation.

COMPAQ Deskpro 286 is a registered trademark of Compaq Computer Corporation.

CorelDRAW! is a trademark of Corel Systems, Inc.

dBASE is a registered trademark of Ashton-Tate Corporation.

DCA is a registered trademark of Digital Communications Assoc., Inc.

DeskJet and LaserJet are registered trademarks of Hewlett-Packard Co.

Linotronic is a registered trademark of Linotype-Hell Co.

Mace Utilities is a registered trademark of Paul Mace Software, Inc.

Microsoft and PowerPoint are registered trademarks and Windows is a trademark of Microsoft Corporation.

Microsoft Paintbrush is a trademark of ZSoft Corporation.

Microsoft TrueType is a registered trademark of Apple Computer Corporation.

MultiMate and WordStar are registered trademarks of Wordstar International Corporation.

Norton Utilities is a trademark of Peter Norton Computing.

PageMaker is a registered trademark of Aldus Corporation.

PC Tools is a trademark of Central Point Software.

Q+E is a trademark of Pioneer Software.

Quicken is a registered trademark of Intuit.

SideKick is a registered trademark of Borland International, Inc.

SQL is a trademark and Personal System/2 is a registered trademark of International Business Machines Corporation.

Vopt is a trademark of Golden Bow Systems.

WordPerfect is a registered trademark of WordPerfect Corporation.

Contents at a Glance

Table of Contents

Introduction

Welcome to *Windows 3.1 QuickStart*. Whether you are a novice with computers or are familiar with DOS programs, this *QuickStart* provides one of the easiest and fastest ways to master the Windows revolution.

You will find that Windows 3.1 makes personal computers more accessible, even to first-time computer users, and moves you further up the productivity curve. Controlled studies, surveys, and the experience of thousands of students have shown that Windows programs help new users learn more quickly and help experienced users become more productive. Aside from increasing your productivity, Windows and Windows programs are more fun to use than character-based DOS programs.

Who Should Use This Book?

Consider *Windows 3.1 QuickStart* your personal instructor. Because the step-by-step instructions include only the most important concepts, your learning isn't obstructed by a cloud of side issues. The numbered steps and concise explanations get you into the program and through your work without much page turning, rereading, or index flipping.

What you learn in *Windows 3.1 QuickStart* carries over to Windows programs such as Microsoft Excel, Microsoft

Word for Windows, and Aldus PageMaker, because all Windows programs work in a similar way. After you learn the basics, you're well on your way to understanding any new Windows program. The *QuickStart* not only gets you going quickly, but also gives you a head start on learning any Windows programs.

If you're an experienced personal computer user but are not familiar with Windows, you will find *Windows 3.1 QuickStart* an excellent way to come up to speed quickly. When you need more detailed information, you can turn to the Help menu found in Windows programs and to Que's line of Windows books, including *Using Windows 3.1*, Special Edition; *Using Excel 4 for Windows*, Special Edition; and *Using Word for Windows 2,* Special Edition.

How To Use This Book

Each chapter in this book follows the same format. First, new commands or procedures are briefly described, and then numbered steps guide you through the required mouse actions or keystrokes. The numbered steps make it easy for you to follow the procedures without losing your place. Throughout the procedures, illustrations are provided to show how the screen (or a similar program's screen) should appear. Some procedures are followed by short notes that describe important tips or cautions in using basic features of the program.

Many of the free programs that come with Windows will help you understand how other Windows programs operate. In this book, the following chapters are the most important chapters for learning about different types of Windows programs and for learning how to work with multiple programs:

Chapter	*Purpose*
Chapter 1 An Overview of Windows	Gives you the "big picture" about how Windows operates.
Chapter 3 Operating Windows	Shows you how to use Windows menus and dialog boxes.
Chapter 4 Editing, Copying, and Moving in Windows	Teaches you the basics of using all Windows programs.

Chapter	Purpose
Chapter 11 Using Windows Write	Explains how to enter and edit text in any Windows program while you use a simple word processing program.
Chapter 12 Using Windows Paintbrush	Shows you how to draw with a bit-mapped drawing program.
Chapter 19 Integrating Multiple Programs	Explains how to run multiple programs and how to pass data between them.
Chapter 20 Running DOS Programs	Explains how to run one or more DOS programs under Windows.

As you use *Windows 3.1 QuickStart*, you may want to do the following:

- *Skim* through a descriptive chapter to learn about features that may be useful to you later.
- *Scan* the table of contents at the front of the book when you aren't sure what you want to locate.
- *Search* the index at the back of the book when you know the specific word or command you want to learn about.
- *Experiment* with ideas you find in this book.
- *Guide* yourself as you work with the Help information found in the Help menu of most Windows programs.

How This Book Is Organized

Windows 3.1 QuickStart shows you how to operate Windows and the free programs that come with it. The book contains chapters on sharing data between programs designed for Windows, including Microsoft Excel, Microsoft Word for Windows, and Aldus PageMaker, and on sharing data between DOS programs such as Lotus 1-2-3 and WordPerfect.

Chapter 1, "An Overview of Windows," illustrates how Windows can improve your work and helps you decide which features are most important to the way you work.

Chapter 2, "Getting Started," explains how to start Windows and describes its capabilities on different computer systems.

Chapter 3, "Operating Windows," covers the important concepts used in all Windows programs. You learn how to control window sizes, operate menus, select from the choices in dialog boxes, and enter and edit data. What you learn in this chapter applies to all Windows programs.

Chapter 4, "Editing, Copying, and Moving in Windows," teaches you the basics of working with all Windows programs. You learn how to open, close, and save files, and how to copy and paste text, numbers, and graphics within documents and between programs.

Chapter 5, "Grouping Programs and Documents," explains how to use the Program Manager to keep related programs and documents together so that you can easily find and use them.

Chapter 6, "Managing Files," explains how to use the File Manager to copy and erase files, create directories, and format diskettes—all the disk-maintenance problems that were tough and time-consuming under DOS but now are easy under Windows.

Chapter 7, "Customizing Your Work Area," shows you how to customize Windows with your own color schemes and "draw-it-yourself" desktop patterns. The chapter even discusses more mundane topics, such as how to add a new printer.

Chapter 8, "Controlling the Printer," describes how Windows programs store print jobs in a spooler while the jobs are waiting to print. This feature enables you to keep working in Windows while the Print Manager manages printing.

Chapter 9, "Managing Fonts and TrueType," describes how you can take advantage of Windows' new TrueType font management technology to get more fonts from your printer and better-looking fonts on-screen.

Chapter 10, "Using Object Linking and Embedding," explains how you can link files together and how to start one program from within another.

Chapter 11, "Using Windows Write," shows you how to use an executive word processing program at the same time that it teaches you how to enter and edit text in any Windows text-oriented program.

Chapter 12, "Using Windows Paintbrush," describes an enjoyable and colorful Windows program that introduces you to drawing in Windows. Paintbrush works the same way as, and with a toolbox similar to, many of the powerful drawing, design, and drafting programs designed for Windows.

Chapter 13, "Creating Macros," shows you how to make recordings that duplicate your keystrokes and mouse actions—a great way to automate repetitive tasks.

Chapter 14, "Using Desktop Accessories," reviews the personal productivity programs that come free with Windows, including the Clock, Calculator, Calendar, Cardfile database, Terminal, and Notepad. These small pop-up programs are convenient to use while you use other Windows programs.

Chapter 15, "Using Microsoft Draw," teaches you how to use a handy drawing program that comes free with programs like Microsoft PowerPoint.

Chapter 16, "Using Microsoft Graph," describes a program that quickly and easily creates attractive charts and that comes free with programs like Microsoft Word for Windows.

Chapter 17, "Using Windows Applets," overviews several mini-programs that come free with some Windows programs. Included are WordArt for creating logos and Equation Editor for writing equations.

Chapter 18, "Using Multimedia," introduces you to a new concept in Windows—multimedia. With the Windows multimedia tools, you can produce and present computer "events" made up of multiple media forms, including both video and audio components. You also can use these tools to access any of the commercially available multimedia packages, such as animated stories and on-line reference libraries.

Chapter 19, "Integrating Multiple Programs," brings you into the next generation of personal computers. You learn how to run multiple programs and how to copy and paste data and graphics from one program to another. You even learn how to link Windows programs together so that they pass data automatically.

Chapter 20, "Running DOS Programs," explains how to run multiple DOS programs, such as Lotus 1-2-3 and WordPerfect, and how to customize Windows so that your DOS programs run efficiently.

Appendix A, "Installing Windows 3.1," helps you install Windows and its desktop programs.

Appendix B, "Summary of Windows Shortcuts," lists the most useful shortcuts in Windows 3.1 and a few of the free programs.

Appendix C, "Help, Support, and Resources," directs you to sources for getting help with Windows and Windows programs.

Conventions Used in This Book

With Windows, you can use the mouse, the keyboard, or shortcut keys for most operations. Throughout the chapters, keyboard and mouse techniques are provided.

To select a command option by typing its underlined letter or by pressing its shortcut key, you may need to use a key combination. In this book, a key combination is joined by a comma or a plus (+) sign:

Combination	Keystrokes
Alt, *letter*	Press Alt, release it, and then press the letter key.
Alt+*letter*	Hold down Alt, press the letter key, and then release both keys.
Ctrl+Ins	Hold down Ctrl, press Ins, and then release both keys.

When you use the mouse to operate Windows, you can perform four kinds of actions:

Action	Explanation
Click	Place the mouse pointer on the item you want to affect, and click the left mouse button.
Double-click	Place the mouse pointer on the item you want to affect, and click the left mouse button twice in rapid succession.
Drag	Place the mouse pointer on the item you want to affect, and hold down the left mouse button as you move the mouse.
Shift+Click	Hold down Shift and then click the item.

Text you are instructed to type appears in a **bold blue** typeface. Text displayed on-screen, such as a prompt or message, appears in a special typeface.

An Overview of Windows

1

Windows is leading a revolution in personal computers. The Windows revolution makes people more productive with less work, yet Windows is easier to learn and use than DOS. This chapter shows you why Windows is fueling this revolution.

Windows is an environment surrounding the *disk operating system* (DOS). DOS enables computer programs to run on your computer. Before Windows, computer operators were faced with remembering difficult DOS commands. Operators also had to learn such programs as Lotus 1-2-3 and WordPerfect, which shared no common menu structure or operating techniques. Much practice was necessary to become proficient in DOS-based programs, and hard work was required to master the power hidden inside them.

Windows eliminates these problems. It masks DOS, doing away with arcane DOS commands and improving the way DOS uses memory. Programs designed specifically for Windows—such as Microsoft Excel, Aldus PageMaker, and Microsoft Word for Windows—share common menus and operate the same way. Learning one program, therefore, helps you learn other Windows programs. And because pull-down menus and pop-up dialog boxes make all options available to beginners and experts, Windows programs are more accessible to all users—everyone moves up the productivity curve.

Key Terms in This Chapter

Desktop	The screen background area on which windows and icons containing programs are displayed.
Document	The data on which a program works. A document may be the data in a spreadsheet program, a letter in a word processing program, or a chart in a drawing program.
DOS	The disk operating system that coordinates hardware and software actions. DOS is the foundation underneath Windows.
Environment	The collection of objects, commands, and rules composing the work space in which Windows and Windows programs work.
Graphical user interface (GUI)	A visual environment that helps you control computer programs more easily and with more consistency.
Icon	A pictorial representation of a command, program, or document.
Window	A rectangular area on-screen that encloses one specific program or one specific document.

Learning Faster with Windows

People are visual creatures. Most of what we learn comes through our sight. We remember best what we can place in a unique location, not what we tag with a text name.

Windows programs use what is technically known as a *graphical user interface*, or GUI (pronounced "gooey"). A GUI takes advantage of the visual way that people are accustomed to working and in which most people prefer to work.

Like the programs designed for Windows, a GUI uses pull-down menus. Many of the various Windows programs have the same menus, many of which are even in the same locations.

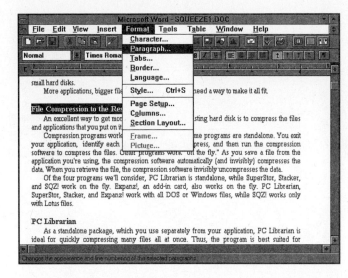

For example, when you choose Format from the menu bar in a Word for Windows 2.0 window, the Format pull-down menu appears.

Selecting a command in a pull-down menu from a Windows program produces a dialog box if the command requires additional information.

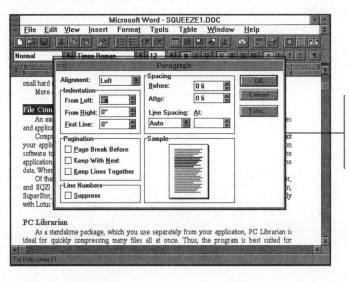

All choices or options for the command are available in the dialog box.

1

You don't need to move down through 10 or 12 layers of menus, as some DOS programs require. Because all your choices or options are immediately visible or are visible in a list that appears for that choice, a beginner and an expert have the same access to the program's features. Windows programs make their power accessible, not hidden beneath layers of menus.

Windows also uses *icons*, or small pictures, to represent items you can quickly identify. For example, the simple drawing program that comes with Windows, called Windows Paintbrush, contains a memorable toolbox that needs little explanation.

The toolbox on the left side of the Paintbrush program contains icons that represent the drawing tools.

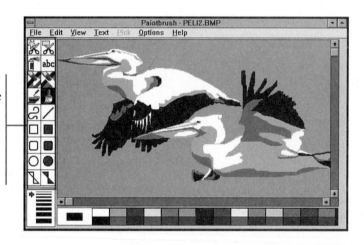

The Program Manager makes it obvious which icon to select to start different programs.

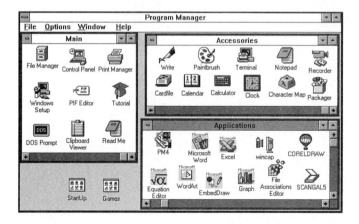

With Windows and Windows programs, you can control programs the way you prefer. You can use a mouse-driven pointer while you are learning or drawing, use the keyboard during data entry, or use shortcut keys for speed. Many people first learn with the mouse and then use both the mouse and the keyboard as they become two-handed masters.

Sharing Operating Methods

Learning one Windows program helps you learn other Windows programs. Not only are the operating methods the same in different Windows programs, but many of the menus and commands are identical.

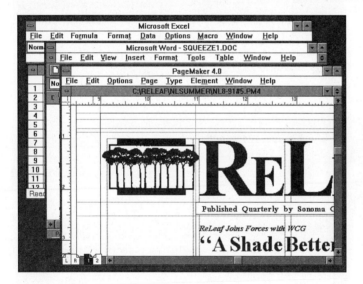

Many menus and commands—such as File, Edit, Format, Window, and Help—are in the same locations and perform the same functions in different Windows programs.

Using the Windows Desktop

The Windows desktop, which runs multiple programs, is a metaphor for the desktop on which you're used to working. Each Windows program can fill the screen or fit into a window. DOS programs fill the screen, unless you are running Windows on an 80386 or 80486 computer.

Running programs in separate windows enables you to see what is happening in other programs and to switch to other programs quickly.

1

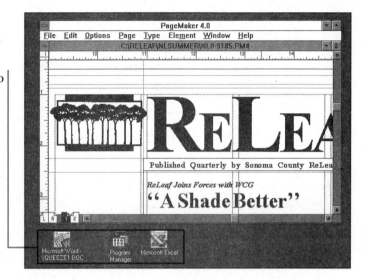

When you want to save space on the desktop, you can shrink a program's window so that it becomes an icon at the bottom of the desktop.

Running Multiple Programs Simultaneously

You can load multiple programs in Windows and quickly switch from one program to another—even if they are a mix of Windows and DOS programs. If you run Windows on an 80386 or 80486 computer, you can even request that programs you aren't currently working in continue to run in background windows.

For example, you can run WordPerfect for DOS and Microsoft Excel (a Windows program) at the same time.

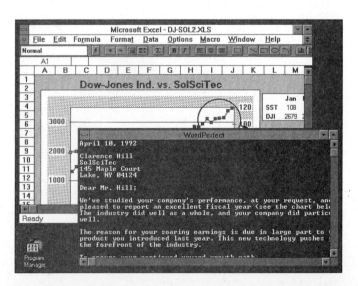

Copying and Pasting Text and Graphics between Programs

Windows makes it easy to copy text or graphics from one program to another. You can copy and paste text, numbers, or graphics between programs designed for Windows. You can even capture an image of the screen and paste it into Windows programs. If you are using DOS programs, you can still copy and paste text and numbers between programs, saving typing time and eliminating the chance for typing errors.

You can link together many Windows programs so that changes you make to one program's data automatically change the data in the other, linked Windows programs. Therefore, separate programs from different manufacturers can work together and share data as though they were a single program.

The program PackRat, for example, is a personal information manager that stores names, addresses, phone numbers, appointments, and notes. Word for Windows is a high-performance word processing program.

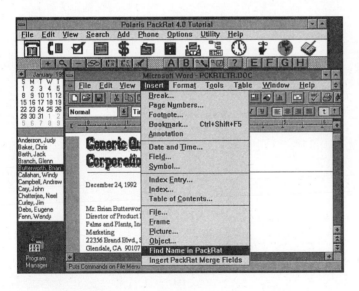

Although these two programs are made by different companies, you can write letters in Word for Windows and let PackRat retrieve the name and address from its database of people you contact.

1

Using the copy and paste capabilities of Windows, you can integrate text, graphics, and captured computer screens into a single document, such as this training tutorial created in Aldus PageMaker.

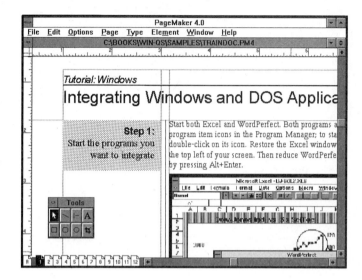

Running DOS Programs under Windows

You don't have to leave behind DOS programs, such as DOS versions of Lotus 1-2-3 and WordPerfect, when you run Windows. Although these programs were originally designed to run under DOS, Windows adds new capabilities to them.

You can run WordPerfect for DOS at the same time you're running other programs, and even copy and paste text and numbers between programs.

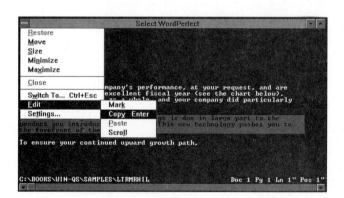

Remember that the active DOS program fills the entire screen—unless you are running Windows on an 80386 or 80486 computer. On an 80386 or 80486 computer, you can run DOS programs so that they fill the screen or fit into a window.

Making Better Use of Memory

Programs designed for DOS 4.0 and earlier were restricted to using no more than 640K of memory. Such programs either left out features to stay small or were slow because they continually had to retrieve pieces of the program from disk.

Windows breaks that 640K memory limit. Programs designed for Windows aren't restricted to using 640K, which means faster operation for large programs and almost unlimited memory for data. In fact, if you run Windows on an 80386 or 80486 computer, information that doesn't fit into memory spills over onto your hard disk—making your hard disk an extension of memory.

Getting Help When You Need It

Windows programs are easy to use because they offer an extensive Help feature. Word for Windows, for example, includes almost 200 pages of Help information that is on the hard disk and available to you while you work.

Many Windows programs contain help about commands and procedures, such as how to create a form letter.

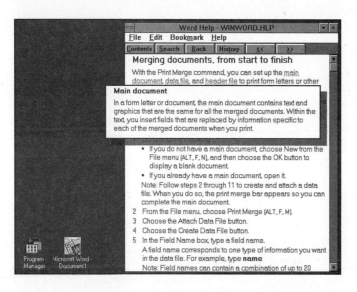

Selecting underlined words or phrases in the Help window displays a definition or opens another Help window.

1

Help files in many Windows programs use a feature known as *hypertext*. Hypertext enables you to jump quickly from one Help topic to another. For instance, if you are looking at a Help file in Word for Windows that shows how to build a mailing list, you might see the phrase <u>Printing form letters or other merged documents</u> underlined in the explanation. Clicking the underlined phrase takes you immediately to a window that explains what File Print Merge is. You also can backtrack to an earlier action, search for help by key words, and print the Help information.

Taking Advantage of Windows Features and Programs

In addition to providing the features already discussed, Windows comes with programs and tools that make using your computer easier.

The Program Manager displays icons that represent the programs and data documents you work with most frequently.

You can group your programs together, and you can start them by choosing an icon in the Program Manager instead of typing the program's name.

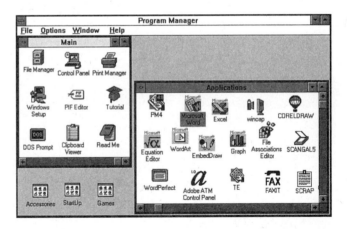

Another helpful program is the File Manager. Using the File Manager is much easier than using arcane DOS commands for organizing your hard disk and copying, erasing, or moving files.

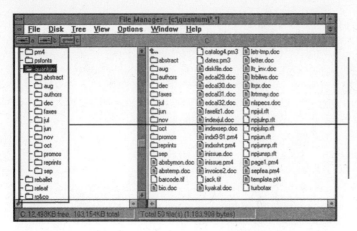

The File Manager displays a tree-like structure that shows how files and subdirectories are arranged on your hard disk.

A third program, the Control Panel, enables you to customize many features within Windows, such as the desktop background, colors, printer connections, and mouse operation.

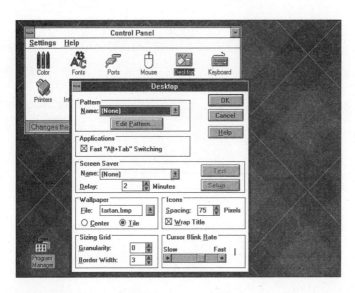

Customizing the desktop background and window colors can make your computer a little more friendly and a lot more personal.

Windows provides many other accessory programs. These include Windows Write (a simple word processor), Windows Paintbrush (a drawing program), and Windows Terminal (a communications program). Another program included with Windows and described in this book is the Print Manager. It enables you to continue working in a Windows program while the Print Manager controls the printer and a list of documents that you want to print.

1

In some documents, you may want to embed objects. For example, you may want to embed a chart in a report you're writing using the Word for Windows word processing program. Using Windows' new *object linking and embedding* (OLE) technology, you can embed the chart in your report and then, from within Word for Windows, edit the chart in the same program you used to create it.

Summary

Now you know why Windows is causing a revolution in the way people use personal computers. Windows programs—and DOS programs running under Windows—are easier to use, which means that advanced programs are more accessible to everyone. Windows makes your personal computer more enjoyable to use.

This chapter covered the following important points:

- Windows provides consistent menus and operations in Windows programs.
- You can copy and paste text and graphics between Windows and DOS programs.
- You can load or run multiple programs at the same time.
- You can customize your work area to fit the way you like to work.
- The Program Manager and File Manager enable you to manage your programs and hard disk more easily.

Now that you are familiar with what Windows can do for you, put it to work. Chapter 2 shows you how to get started. If you are new to Windows, read Chapter 3, "Operating Windows." What you learn in that chapter applies to all Windows programs.

After you learn the basic concepts of operating Windows programs, you will want to learn about the Program Manager, discussed in Chapter 5, and the File Manager, explained in Chapter 6. From there, take a look at the table of contents, and explore topics that look interesting.

Getting
Started

If you are new to personal computers or if you are new only to Windows, this chapter will help you get started. Step-by-step, it shows you how to start and exit Windows. You learn about the different parts of the Windows display and the purpose of the mouse and the keyboard in Windows. The Help feature is discussed in Chapter 3, "Operating Windows."

If you have any experience with personal computers or with Windows, some of this material may be familiar to you. After you feel comfortable with the parts of the Windows environment, you can move to the next chapter to learn basic Windows operations. Chapter 3 supplies detailed instructions for starting programs, controlling windows, and using pull-down menus and dialog boxes.

Starting Windows

Understanding the Windows desktop

Understanding the parts of a window

Using the mouse

Using the keyboard

Closing documents, programs, and windows

2

Key Terms in This Chapter

Program window	A window that contains a Windows or DOS (non-Windows) program. Multiple program windows can be open at one time.
Document window	A window that contains a document and is displayed within a program window. Some programs enable you to open multiple document windows.
Control menu	A menu that appears as a hyphen or a long bar at the top left corner of each program or document window, enabling keyboard users to move, size, or close windows.
Mouse pointer	An on-screen pointer that moves as you move the mouse on your desk. You use the mouse and mouse pointer to select text or objects, to choose menu commands, and to move, size, or close windows.
Program Manager	A Windows program that helps you group together other programs and documents so that you can find and start them easily.

Starting Windows

This section shows you how to start Windows from your hard disk. Before you start Windows, you must install it. Refer to Appendix A for instructions on how to install Windows.

Follow these steps to start Windows from the hard disk in your computer:

1. Make sure that the drive door of each floppy drive is open.
2. Turn on your computer.
3. If necessary, respond to the prompts for the date and time.
4. When the `C:\>` prompt appears, type WIN and press ⏎Enter.

If you have followed the Windows on-screen installation instructions and let the installation process modify your AUTOEXEC.BAT file, you can use the preceding instructions to start Windows from any directory on your hard disk.

2

Note: You cannot run Windows from a diskette-only system unless that system is on a network.

Starting Windows in Different Modes

Unless you indicate otherwise during start-up, Windows runs in the mode that best fits your computer's configuration. You may, however, have a reason for wanting Windows to start in another mode. The two modes available are *standard mode* and *386-enhanced mode*. Standard mode is for 80286-based computers and 80386- or 80486-based computers with less than 2M of memory. Even if your 386 or 486 PC has more than 2M of memory, standard mode is preferable because it manages memory better than 386-enhanced mode. The 386-enhanced mode takes advantage of advanced features available on an 80386- or 80486-based PC with more than 2M of memory.

Note: Windows 2.x programs may not run under Windows 3.x If you are not sure whether a Windows program is made for Windows 3.x, start the program under Windows 3.x. A warning box is displayed if the program was made for the earlier Windows. Contact the program's manufacturer for the Windows 3.x updated version.

To start Windows in a specific mode, type one of the following commands at the DOS prompt:

WIN/S   To start in standard mode

WIN/3   To start in 386-enhanced mode

You can see the mode in which your computer is running by opening the Program Manager and choosing the Help About Program Manager command. The Program Manager is described in Chapter 5, "Grouping Programs and Documents."

Starting a Program and Windows Simultaneously

You can start a program when you start Windows. For instance, to start Windows and simultaneously start Word for Windows, type the following line at the DOS prompt:

WIN WINWORD

Then press Enter. The WIN portion of this command starts Windows, and the rest of the command tells Windows which program to run. (If this technique

2

does not work, Windows cannot find the program; therefore, you must type the program's complete path. For example, if the program you want to start—WINWORD.EXE—is located on drive C in the WINWORD directory, type **WIN C:\WINWORD\WINWORD.EXE** at the DOS prompt.)

You can start a Windows program and also load one of its documents when you start Windows. For example, to start Windows and to start Microsoft Excel with the worksheet BUDGET.XLS loaded, type the following line at the DOS prompt:

    WIN C:\EXCEL\BUDGET.XLS

In this example, the BUDGET.XLS worksheet is located in the C:\EXCEL directory. Because files ending with XLS are *associated* with Microsoft Excel, the Microsoft Excel program starts and then loads the BUDGET.XLS file. Every program provides its own file extension; files with this extension are automatically associated with the program. In Chapter 6, "Managing Files," the discussion of the File Manager describes how to associate other data files with a program.

If you want a specific program to start every time you start Windows, you can add the program's icon to the StartUp window in the Program Manager. Refer to Chapter 5 to learn how.

Understanding the Windows Desktop

Windows programs run on a screen background known as the *desktop*. The programs and their documents appear on-screen, like reports lying on your desktop. Your Windows desktop may contain multiple Windows or DOS (non-Windows) programs. Each program appears in its own window or fills the screen.

Two types of windows appear on the desktop. A *program window* contains the program itself. The menu bar that controls the Windows program is always at the top of the program window and below the title bar. In Windows, you can have several program windows open at one time. (A DOS program must fill the screen when Windows is in standard mode.) A *document window* may appear within some program windows. Document windows contain the data or document on which the program works.

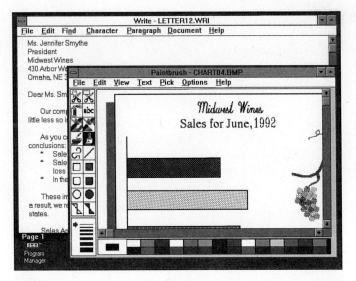

Some Windows programs, such as Windows Write and Windows Paintbrush, display only one document at a time within the program's window.

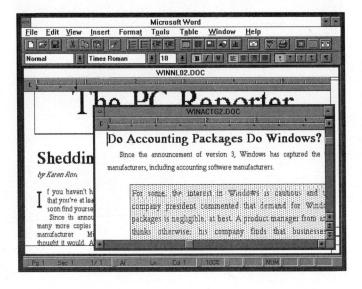

Programs like Microsoft Excel and Word for Windows can have more than one document window, enabling you to work on multiple letters, worksheets, charts, or databases at once.

Understanding the Parts of a Window

A window is built from parts that enable you to change the window by moving, sizing, or scrolling it. To understand directions given further in this book, you must be able to identify the various parts of a window.

Illustrated in this section are the different parts of a program (or document) window. The window elements are the same for all Windows programs. In this example, Word for Windows is on the upper portion of the Windows desktop in a program window. The smaller document window, internal to the Word for Windows window, contains a single document. The small icons—miniature pictures—at the bottom of the screen represent programs that are not in windows.

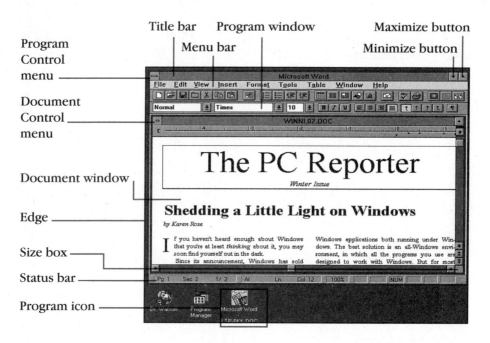

Table 2.1 describes the parts of the window shown in the illustration.

Table 2.1
The Parts of Program and Document Windows

Window Part	Description
Program window	A window that contains a program.
Document window	A window within a program window that contains the document on which you are working.
Program icon	A program reduced to an icon.
Program Control menu	A menu that controls a program window's size, location, and position relative to other program windows.
Document Control menu	A menu that controls a document window's size and location.
Title bar	A bar containing a program or document title, or both.
Menu bar	A bar containing a program's pull-down menus.
Status bar	A bar containing menu descriptions, prompts to action, or document status.
Maximize button	An icon that increases a window to a full screen.
Minimize button	An icon that shrinks a program window to a pictorial representation (icon) at the bottom of the screen.
Edge	A window edge you can move with the mouse to resize a window.
Size box	A moveable corner you can use to resize the right and bottom window edges.

2

2

If a document window fills the inside of a program window, or if a program window fills the screen, a different icon appears at the top right corner of the program window. The Restore icon restores a full-screen program or document into the window it previously occupied.

Document Control menu   Restore icon

This example shows the same document; however, the Word for Windows program window fills the screen, and the document window fills the inside of the program window.

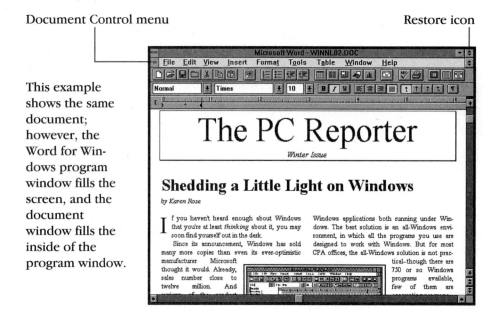

Note: When a document window fills the inside of a program window, the Document Control menu in many programs changes its location from the top left corner of the document window to a position left of the File menu.

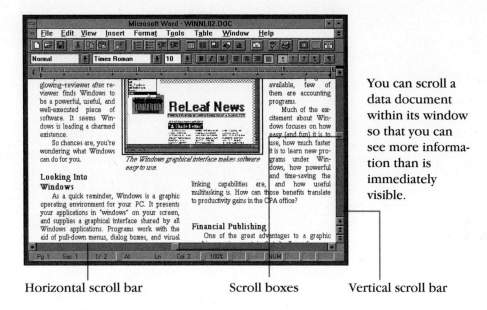

You can scroll a data document within its window so that you can see more information than is immediately visible.

Horizontal scroll bar   Scroll boxes   Vertical scroll bar

Use the following parts of a window to scroll a document:

Window Part	Description
Horizontal scroll bar	Scrolls data sideways through the window.
Vertical scroll bar	Scrolls data vertically through the window.
Scroll box	Shows the horizontal or vertical position of the data displayed in the document window, relative to the entire document.

Understanding the Program Manager

When Windows starts, it displays the Program Manager, which contains group windows and group icons. Each of these groups contains a collection of programs or data you use to get a specific type of work done. If you group together work-related programs and data, starting programs and their associated data documents is easier. You can start a program by choosing the icon that represents the program.

The Main group is a collection of programs that comes with Windows. Inside the Main group window are program item icons, each of which represents a program or a program and its associated data document. Activating a program item icon, as explained in Chapter 5, starts the program for that icon and loads an associated data document if you have defined one.

Windows programs already running are displayed in their own windows or as icons at the bottom of the screen.

Program Manager window

Group window

Program item icon

Group icon

Icon of open program

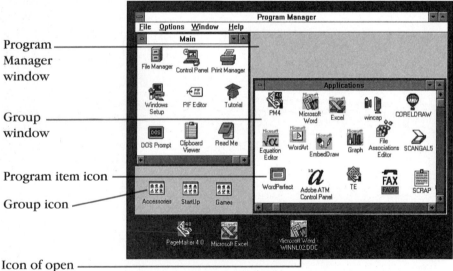

Note the following window parts of this illustration.

Window Part	Description
Program Manager window	A program window containing group windows and group icons.
Group window	A window within the Program Manager that contains program item icons.
Group icon	A small representation of a closed group window.
Program item icon	An icon that starts a Windows or DOS program and possibly an associated data document.
Icon of open program	An icon representing a running program that has been minimized to an icon.

Other groups that come with Windows are shown as group icons at the bottom of the Program Manager window. The Accessories group contains small desktop programs, including an executive word processing program, a calculator, a clock, and a calendar. The Games group contains two games. The StartUp group contains programs that start up whenever you start Windows. You may see other group icons within the Program Manager window that were added during installation or by a previous Windows operator. Programs already running are displayed as icons outside the Program Manager window, such as the Microsoft Word, PageMaker 4.0, and Microsoft Excel icons shown in the preceding illustration. If a document is open within a program already running, that document's name appears with the program icon, as shown in the Microsoft Word icon.

Note: You can easily create your own group windows and program item icons (you learn how in Chapter 5). You also can customize your Windows desktop so that it automatically displays the group windows you want when you first start Windows. As a result, your own Windows desktop probably looks somewhat different from the screens shown in this chapter—but the elements of each Windows desktop are the same.

2

Using the Mouse

You can control Windows and programs designed for Windows with the mouse, keyboard, function keys, shortcut keys, or a combination of these. A few graphically oriented Windows programs require a mouse for drawing or positioning objects. Using the mouse is the easiest and most natural way to learn Windows and Windows programs. If you are new to Windows, begin by using the mouse; later, if you want, you can make a transition to touch-typing your commands or pressing shortcut keys (key combinations).

Note: Do not feel that you must use either the mouse or the keyboard exclusively. Use them together for more efficiency and productivity.

The mouse you are using has two or three buttons; you can use either type of mouse with Windows. The mouse serves two purposes: to make selections from pull-down menus and pop-up dialog boxes; and to select text or objects you want to delete, move, or modify.

Hold the mouse in a relaxed but firm grip with two fingers resting on the buttons, the head under your palm, and the tail (wire) pointing in the same direction as your fingers. When you press a mouse button, do not move the mouse. Just relax and comfortably click the button.

Do not choke the mouse. Relax!

As you move the mouse on your desktop, a pointer on the Windows screen moves accordingly. The pointer is often shaped like an arrowhead but may change shape depending on the pointer's location on-screen. If you find that you aren't moving the pointer accurately when you use the mouse, check how you are holding the mouse. Make sure that the tips of your fingers are on the buttons and that the wire runs parallel to your fingers.

Note: The left mouse button is usually the only button you press. If you are left-handed, refer to Chapter 7, "Customizing Your Work Area," for an explanation of how to customize Windows to swap the left and right mouse buttons.

Using the Keyboard

With Windows and Windows programs, you can use the keyboard for typing, choosing menus and commands, and selecting options from pop-up dialog boxes. In addition, many Windows programs have shortcut keys (key combinations) that reduce multiple-keystroke or mouse-keystroke combinations.

Windows uses the following areas of the keyboard (you may find slight variations on your keyboard):

- The function keys, labeled F1 to F12 at the top of the IBM Enhanced Keyboard (or F1 to F10 at the left of the IBM Personal Computer AT keyboard)

- The alphanumeric, or "typing," keys, located in the center of the keyboard (these keys are most familiar to you from your experience with typewriter keyboards)

- The numeric and cursor-movement keys, found at the right side of the keyboard

The following illustration shows the IBM PC AT keyboard:

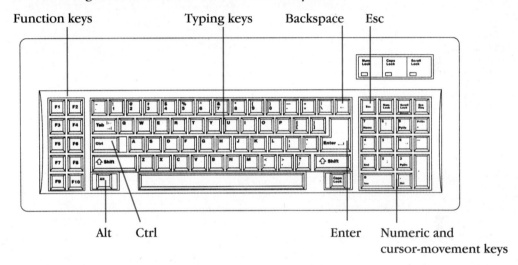

This illustration shows the IBM Enhanced Keyboard:

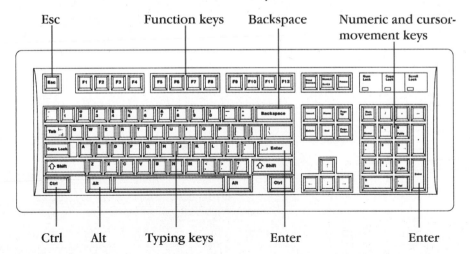

Function Keys

2

Many Windows programs use function keys in combination with other keys. In some programs, each function key can carry out four tasks when you use it by itself or with another key. In Windows, the function keys or their combinations provide shortcuts for commands you can choose from the menu. You should use the menus to select commands as you are learning, or if the command you want to select is one you use infrequently. Use shortcut keys after you become experienced.

You use the following keys in combination with the function keys:

Shift

Alt

Ctrl

Key combinations are shown in this book with a plus sign (+) between the keys—for example, Alt+F4. To use this combination, you hold down the Alt key and then press the F4 function key. After you press the function key, release both keys.

Note: In many Windows programs, shortcut keys are shown on the right side of pull-down menus, next to the commands they duplicate.

Keys that should be pressed in a specific order but not held down during the key sequence are shown with commas between the keys—for example, Alt, T, P.

Alphanumeric Keys

The alphanumeric keys work similarly to those on a typewriter. A critical but easily overlooked difference between typing with a typewriter and typing in a computer program is that you do not need to press the Enter key to end lines at the right margin. When you type text and reach the end of a line, the text automatically "wraps" to the next line.

You can use the Enter key as a carriage return at the end of a paragraph. You press Enter to insert blank lines in your text, such as the lines that separate paragraphs. You can use the Enter key to complete commands or dialog boxes you have selected in Windows programs.

The Shift, Alt, and Ctrl keys are part of the alphanumeric keyboard. The Shift key creates uppercase letters and other special characters, just as it does on a typewriter keyboard. You also can use Shift, Alt, and Ctrl with the function keys as shortcut key combinations that duplicate menu commands. Pressing the Alt key by itself activates the menu bar.

Cursor-Movement Keys

The *insertion point* is the blinking vertical line in Windows programs that marks the location on-screen where the next character you type will appear. In DOS programs, the insertion point is called a *cursor* and appears as a blinking underline character or a reverse-video (highlighted) character.

Use the keys marked with arrows at the right side of the keyboard to control the movement of the insertion point or cursor. When you press an arrow key, the insertion point or cursor moves, if possible, in the direction indicated by the arrow on the key. Most programs enable you to use the Home, End, PgUp, and PgDn keys to move around in the document.

Arrow keys are located on the number keys on the numeric pad at the far right side of the keyboard (duplicating the arrow keys on the enhanced keyboard). When you activate the Num Lock key (as indicated by a light on some keyboards), pressing keys on the numeric pad produces numbers. You press the Num Lock key to alternate between numbers and arrow keys on the numeric pad.

Note: Windows enables you to customize the flashing rate and the movement rate of the insertion point. See Chapter 7, "Customizing Your Work Area," for the procedures to make these changes.

Closing Documents, Programs, and Windows

When you close a document window, program window, or Windows itself, you clear open data documents from the computer's electronic memory. If you need to use these documents again, you must save them, which makes a magnetic recording of your documents on a diskette or your hard disk. (Later, you can open these magnetic recordings, called *files*, and your documents will reappear on-screen.)

Note: When working with a Windows program, if you close a document window, the program asks whether you want to save the changes you made to the document. When working with DOS programs, be careful; some programs close immediately, without asking whether you want to save changes to the document. In these DOS programs, you must remember to save the document before exiting the program.

33

Closing a Document Window

Some Windows programs, such as the File Manager, Word for Windows, and Excel, can contain more than one open document window. Microsoft Excel is used in the following illustrations to show how to close document windows. To close the topmost document window, follow these steps:

1. Click the File menu, and then click the Close command.

   Or press Alt, F, C.

In this example, the File menu is pulled down in the topmost document window.

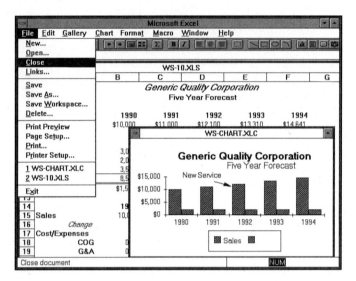

In some programs that don't allow you to open more than a single document at once, the File menu does not contain a Close command. In that case, usually you close the document by starting a new file (File New) or by opening an existing file (File Open) or by exiting the program (File Exit).

If you have changed the document since you opened it, a dialog box appears before the document closes.

2. Click the Yes button to save and then close the document, the No button to close without saving, or the Cancel button to ignore the Close command.

   Or press Y to save and then close the document, N to close without saving, or Esc to cancel the Close command.

If you have previously saved the document, the program saves it under the same name.

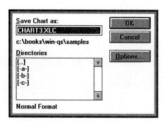

If you have not yet saved the document, another dialog box appears, prompting you to type a file name.

A default file name, such as CHART3.XLC, may appear. You can type a new file name over the default file name. Use the Del (Delete) or Backspace key to correct errors in typing. If a blank file name box appears, simply type the file name in the box.

A file name consists of a root name of one to eight characters. When you name a file, you must observe the file-naming guidelines of your operating system (MS-DOS, DR DOS, or PC DOS). For example, MS-DOS file names can be one to eight characters, with no spaces, periods, or other punctuation marks (although symbols such as the pound sign or ampersand are allowed). After you name and save a file, the file name appears in the title bar of the document's window.

2

Many programs add their own three-character extension to your file name. You can add your own extension if you prefer, separating it from the root name by a period (.). When you later open a file, however, most Windows programs list only the files that contain their own extensions; therefore, letting your program assign the extension is better than adding your own.

File names can contain the following characters:

Letters	a to z
	A to Z
Numbers	0 to 9
Symbols	- (hyphen)
	_ (underscore)
	! (exclamation point)
	@ (at)
	# (pound)
	$ (dollar)
	% (percent)
	^ (caret)
	& (ampersand)

Use a symbol as the first character in a file name to make the file name appear first in a list of file names.

File names cannot contain the following elements:

Blank spaces (use a valid symbol instead)

The symbols *, +, and =

More than one period

The following file names are valid:

BDGT_JUN.XLS

!PROPSL.DOC

LTR08#12.DOC

However, the following file names are invalid:

BDGT JUN.XLS (blank space used)

\PROPSL.DOC (backslash used)

LTR08.12.DOC (extra period used)

2

A second way to close a document window is to activate the Document Control menu (Alt, hyphen) and choose the Close command. You also can press Ctrl+F4 to close the active document window.

Closing a Program Window

When you close a program's window, you also close the document windows within it. When you close a Windows program, you are prompted to save documents that you have changed.

Note: Closing the Program Manager window exits Windows.

PageMaker is used in the following illustrations to show how to close a program window. To close the topmost program in Windows, follow these steps:

1. Click the File menu, and then click the Exit command.
   Or press Alt, F, X.

In nearly every Windows program, the File menu contains a command for exiting the program.

2

If you have
changed your
documents since
you opened
them, a dialog
box appears for
each document.

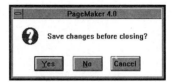

2. Click the Yes button to save and then close the document, the No
   button to close without saving, or the Cancel button to ignore the
   Close command.

   Or press Y to save and then close the document, N to close without
   saving, or Esc to ignore the Close command.

If you have previously saved the document, the program saves it under the
same name. If you have not yet saved the document, the program prompts
you to enter a file name for the document. The preceding section describes
valid file names.

You close windows containing DOS programs by saving any documents you
have changed and then exiting the DOS program. When you exit the DOS
program, its window closes. Chapter 20, "Running DOS Programs," contains
more information on running and exiting DOS programs.

A second way to close a program window is to activate the Program Control
menu (Alt, **space bar**) and choose the Close command. Or you can press
Alt + F4 to close the program window.

Exiting Windows

Windows is under the control of the Program Manager. When you close the
Program Manager window, you exit Windows.

Follow these steps to exit Windows:

1. Exit all DOS programs, using their normal exit or quit procedures.
2. If the Program Manager window is visible, click it to make it the
   topmost window, or press Alt + Tab⇄ until the Program Manager is in
   the topmost window.
3. Click the File menu and then click the Exit Windows command, or
   press Alt, F, X.

4. If you made changes to documents in open programs, you are prompted to save the changes before exiting Windows. As explained in the preceding sections, you may be asked to type a file name for each document you have not yet saved.

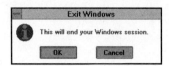

The Exit Windows dialog box appears.

5. Click OK or press ⏎Enter to exit Windows; click Cancel or press Esc to return to Windows.

A second way to close Windows is to activate the Program Control menu in the Program Manager (press Alt, space bar) and choose the Close command. You also can press Alt+F4 to close Windows.

Summary

This chapter helped you get Windows started, described the different parts of a window, and showed you how to quit Windows and its programs.

The following important points were covered in this chapter:

- The Program Control menu is a square icon to the left of the program's title bar. The Program Control menu controls the program window, and you use it to exit the program.

- The Document Control menu is a square icon to the left of a document window title. If a document window fills the program window, the Document Control menu appears as a hyphen or a long bar to the left of the File menu. The Document Control menu controls the document window.

- The menu bar is always below the title bar in Windows programs. A menu pulls down from the menu bar when you click a menu name with the mouse, or when you press Alt and then press the underlined letter in the menu name.

- You start Windows by typing **WIN** at the DOS prompt and then pressing Enter.

2

■ You exit Windows by quitting DOS programs and choosing **File Exit Windows** in the Program Manager. You are asked whether you want to save the documents you have changed in Windows programs that are still open.

Now read Chapter 3, "Operating Windows," to learn how to operate Windows and Windows programs. What you learn in Chapter 3 applies to all Windows programs, giving you a good head start in understanding any new Windows programs you use.

Operating Windows

Compared with most DOS character-based programs, Windows programs are easier and more natural to learn and operate. With Windows programs, you benefit from decreased learning time, fewer mistakes, and an easier transition from one Windows program to another. In fact, studies show that people who use graphical interfaces such as Windows use three times as many programs in their daily work as people who use character-based programs. Windows programs can make you more efficient, productive, and valuable at work.

What you learn in this chapter will help you to operate any Windows program. The skills you learn here carry over to other programs.

This chapter shows the three methods of controlling Windows and Windows programs: the mouse, the keyboard, and shortcut keys (key combinations). The mouse is the primary method because it makes learning new programs easier. The keyboard works well for touch-typists who prefer not to take their hands off the keyboard. And shortcut keys improve everyone's speed.

After learning how to choose menus, select commands from the menus, and select options from pop-up dialog boxes, you learn how to control the location, size, and status of windows that contain programs.

Finally, you learn how to use one of the most important features of Windows programs: the Help commands.

3

Key Terms in This Chapter

Pointer	The on-screen symbol you control with the mouse and use to select items and commands.
Mouse button	The button on the mouse that, when pressed, selects the item on which the pointer is located.
Dialog box	A window containing options that appears when a command needs additional information before it can be executed.

Working with the Mouse and the Keyboard

Most Windows programs work equally well under mouse or keyboard control. The mouse makes learning and searching through program menus easier. A mouse is also invaluable in using graphics programs. In time, you will find that using the mouse and the keyboard together is the fastest and most efficient way to work.

Using the Mouse

The mouse pointer changes appearance on-screen. Usually the mouse pointer appears as an arrow or an I-beam. Other pointer shapes are described throughout the chapter. The basic shapes of the mouse pointer are as follows:

Mouse Shape	*Function*
Arrow	Selects or chooses menus, commands, or options.
Two-pointed arrow	Resizes windows and selected objects or borders in some programs.
Four-pointed arrow	Moves selected objects in some programs.
Cross hair	Draws graphics objects in graphics programs.
Hourglass	Waits while the program works.
I-beam	Moves the insertion point (cursor) or selects text you want to edit.

For most tasks, you press the left mouse button. If you prefer to press the right button, however, you can use the customizing features described in Chapter 7, "Customizing Your Work Area," to swap the left and right buttons.

You use four types of mouse actions:

Action	Meaning
Click	Put the mouse pointer on an item and press the left mouse button.
Drag	Put the mouse pointer on an item, hold down the left mouse button, and move the mouse.
Double-click	Point to an item, rapidly press the mouse button twice, and release it.
⇧Shift+Click or Ctrl+Click	Hold down ⇧Shift or Ctrl as you click. You use ⇧Shift+Click in many Windows programs to select more than one item. You use Ctrl+Click to select multiple nonadjacent file names in a list.

To click an item, follow these steps:

1. Move the mouse so that the tip of the mouse pointer (usually an arrow) is on the menu name, command, dialog box option, graphics object, or text that you want to select.

2. Quickly press and release the mouse button.

To drag across text or to drag a graphics object, follow these steps:

1. Move the mouse so that the tip of the mouse pointer is on the object or at the beginning of the text. (While on text, the pointer appears as an I-beam.)

2. Press and hold down the mouse button.

3. While holding down the mouse button, move the mouse. If you are dragging a movable graphics object, the object will move.

Selected Text

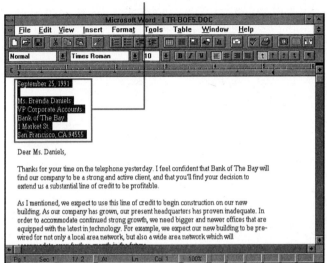

3

If you are selecting text, a highlighted area encloses the text over which you move the pointer.

4. Release the mouse button.

Using the Keyboard

In addition to typing text and numbers, you can use the keyboard in Windows programs to choose from menus, select commands, and select options from dialog boxes.

To choose a menu and select a command in the current Windows program, follow these steps:

1. Press Alt.
2. Press the underlined letter in the name of the menu you want.

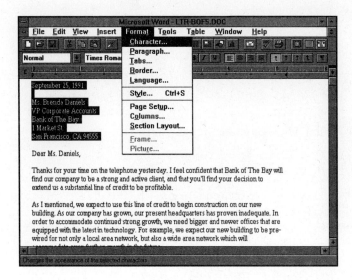

3

Pressing Alt and the underlined letter of a menu name pulls down that menu.

3. Press the underlined letter of the command you want in the menu.

   If you do not want to choose a command from the menu, press Esc. Press Esc a second time to move the mouse pointer back into your document.

Shortcut keys can save you steps by bypassing menus, commands, and actions and immediately producing a result. Shortcut keys usually combine the Shift, Alt, and Ctrl keys with a function key (F1 to F12) or an alphanumeric key.

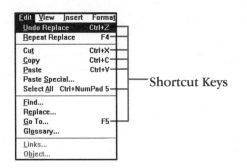

Shortcut Keys

Many programs display the most frequently used shortcut keys on the right side of the pull-down menus.

3

To help you learn to use the keyboard to work with menus and dialog boxes, you should understand how certain keystrokes are indicated in this book:

Key(s)	Action You Take
Alt, *letter*	Press Alt, release it, and then press the under-lined letter in a menu name.
Alt+*letter*	Hold down Alt as you press the underlined letter in an option name within a dialog box.
letter	Press the underlined letter to execute the command in a menu.

Two other keys have important uses. The Enter key executes the selected command or dialog box. The Esc key backs out of the current menu or dialog box without executing it.

Controlling Menus and Dialog Boxes

Learning how to operate one Windows program puts you well on your way to operating other Windows programs. The menus, commands, and dialog boxes in all Windows programs operate similarly, and many commands—such as File, Edit, Format, Window, and Help—are exactly the same in different programs.

Dialog boxes appear after you select certain commands. A dialog box enables you to see every available option.

As you begin to use Windows programs, keep in mind one of the most important concepts in Windows programs:

Select, then do!

In all Windows programs, you make changes by first selecting text, worksheet cells, or graphics objects, and then doing something to them with a command or a shortcut key combination.

As you work with menus and dialog boxes, you should understand how the following terms are used in this book:

Term	Meaning
Choose	To choose a menu or to complete a dialog box. Click the menu name and then the command, or press Alt, *letter*, *letter*.
Select	To select a command in a menu, to indicate on-screen the item you want to affect, or to specify an option you want to use. Click the option name or type its underlined letter.
Deselect	To remove the selection from an item on-screen. Click anywhere outside the selection, or press any arrow key.

3

Choosing Menus and Commands

Menus display the commands available in the program. Menu names always appear in a menu bar at the top of each program window.

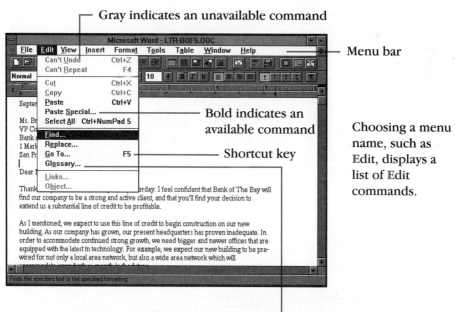

Gray indicates an unavailable command

Menu bar

Bold indicates an available command

Shortcut key

Choosing a menu name, such as Edit, displays a list of Edit commands.

An ellipsis indicates that a dialog box will follow

You choose commands from all Windows programs the same way. Many programs use similar commands for similar actions—a practice that makes learning multiple Windows programs simpler.

To choose a menu and then select a command with the mouse, follow these steps:

1. Put the tip of the mouse pointer on the menu name and click the mouse button.
2. Put the tip of the mouse pointer on the command and click the mouse button.

To choose a menu and then select a command with the keyboard, follow these steps:

1. Press [Alt] and then release it to activate the menu bar.
2. Type the underlined letter in the menu name you want to choose.
3. Type the underlined letter in the command you want to select.

Note: Press Esc to back out of menus or dialog boxes or to return to your document from the menu bar. Pressing Esc cancels the current menu, dialog box, or edit action. Many Windows programs have an Edit Undo command. Undo undoes the last command you executed. With the mouse, you can back out of a menu by clicking the menu name a second time. To back out of a dialog box, click Cancel.

Selecting Options from Dialog Boxes

Some commands need additional information before they can perform an operation. On a pull-down menu, the names of these commands are followed by an ellipsis (...). For example, the command Format Number in Microsoft Excel requires the numeric or date format you want to use or create. When you select Number from the Format menu, a list is displayed from which you can choose existing predefined or custom formats. Also displayed is a text box in which you can type new custom formats.

In the following Word for Windows screen, the Open dialog box illustrates a text box in which you type a file name. The scrolling list boxes enable you to change directories or select file names.

Text box ——— List box ——— Command buttons

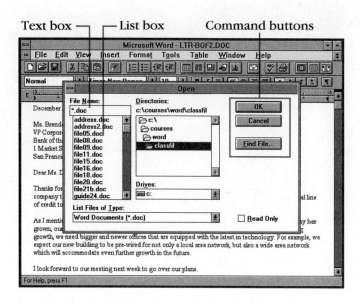

The Open dialog
box in Word
for Windows
is similar in
all Windows
programs.

3

The Microsoft Excel worksheet's Edit Paste Special dialog box illustrates two
groups of option buttons and individual check boxes that enable you to
indicate how you want pasted numbers to interact with numbers already in
the worksheet.

Option buttons ——— Command buttons

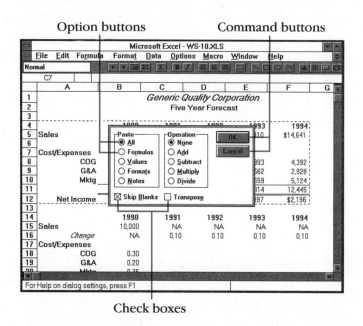

The Edit Paste
Special dialog box
in Excel shows
special pasting
options.

Check boxes

In character-based programs, you have to move through as many as 12 layers of menus to see all of the available options. Most dialog boxes, however, display all possible options for a command, which means that Windows programs give beginners and experts quick access to the full power of the program. No options are hidden. (A few dialog boxes include a second dialog box you can use to select advanced options.)

Dialog boxes contain different items designed to help you enter data or select options for a command. Table 3.1 lists the items in a dialog box and describes their uses.

Table 3.1
Dialog Box Items

Item	Description
Text box	A data-entry area for text, data, or numbers.
List box	A list of predefined data-entry items, options, or existing files or directories.
Option button	A round button that specifies an option. You can select only one button from a group; the selected button is filled.
Check box	A square box that specifies an option. You can select more than one check box; an X in the check box indicates that the option is selected.
Command button	A large rectangular button that executes or cancels a dialog box. Some command buttons display another dialog box.

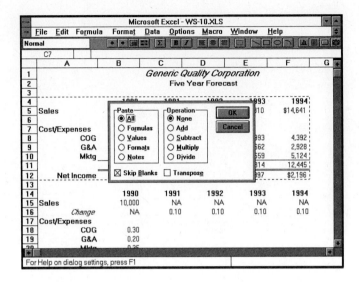

In this dialog box, the All option button is selected from the Paste group, and the None option is selected from the Operation group.

3

With the mouse, click another option button in the same group to select a new option and to deselect the original option.

With the keyboard, press Alt+*letter* to select an option (where *letter* is the underlined letter for each option button). A dashed line surrounds the active option button. Move the selection to another button in the same group by pressing any arrow key.

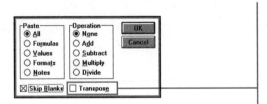

In this dialog box, the Transpose check box is empty, which means that this option is deselected.

With the mouse, click a blank check box to select it. Click the check box a second time to remove the X and deselect the check box.

With the keyboard, press Alt+*letter* to select a check box (where *letter* is the underlined letter for the check box). Each time you press Alt+*letter*, you toggle the check box between selected and deselected. If a check box does not contain an underlined letter, press Tab until the check box is enclosed in a dashed line and then press the space bar.

3

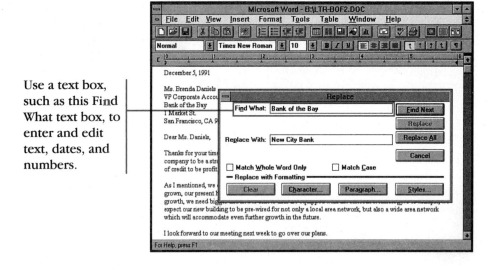

Use a text box, such as this Find What text box, to enter and edit text, dates, and numbers.

With the mouse, activate the text box by moving the mouse pointer (I-beam) to the location where you want to type or edit; then click the mouse button. This procedure places the flashing insertion point in the text box so that you can enter new text or edit existing text. Press the left- or right-arrow key to move the insertion point backward or forward. Press Del to delete the character to the right of the insertion point, or press Backspace to delete the character to the left. To select multiple characters, position the mouse pointer immediately in front of the first letter you want to select, click and hold down the mouse button, and drag across the text you want to select. Then use the editing techniques described in the section "Editing Text" in Chapter 4.

With the keyboard, activate the text box by pressing Alt+*letter* (where *letter* is the underlined letter in the name of the text box). Type new text or edit the existing entry. Again, use the editing techniques described in the section "Editing Text" in Chapter 4.

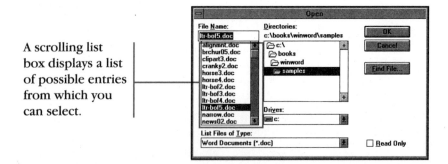

A scrolling list box displays a list of possible entries from which you can select.

With the mouse, scroll through the list by clicking the up or down arrow at the right side of the scroll bar. Make large jumps through the list by clicking in the gray area of the scroll bar. Drag the white square (*scroll box*) in the scroll bar to new locations for long moves. Click once on the item you want to select. The selected item in the list is highlighted.

With the keyboard, select the list box by pressing Alt+*letter* (where *letter* is the underlined letter in the name of the list box). If the list box is separated from the text box containing the underlined letter, press Tab to activate the list box. After activating the list box, press PgUp, PgDn, or the up- or down-arrow keys to move through the list. The selected item in the list is highlighted.

3

Drop-down icon

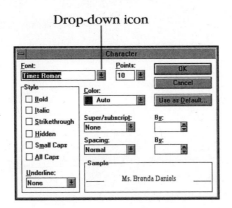

A special type of list box, a drop-down list box, is a text box with a down arrow at the right end of the text box.

A drop-down list box conserves space by not showing the full list until you request it.

With the mouse, you can display the drop-down list box by clicking the drop-down icon at the right end of the text box. When the scrolling list appears, select the item you want by clicking it.

Drop-down list

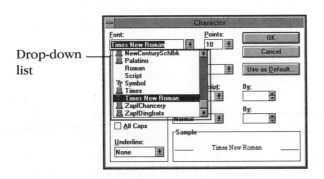

The selected item in the list is highlighted.

53

3

With the keyboard, select the list box by pressing Alt+*letter* (where *letter* is the underlined letter in the name of the list box). After you activate the list box, press Alt and then press the down-arrow key to make the drop-down list appear, if it has not already appeared. Press PgUp, PgDn, or the up- or down-arrow keys to move through the list. The selected item in the list is highlighted.

Command buttons complete or cancel a dialog box or display an additional dialog box. Choosing OK completes the dialog box, accepting all the selections you have made; choosing Cancel backs out of the dialog box, canceling your selections.

Some command buttons, such as the Tabs button in the Word for Windows Paragraph dialog box, enable you to "tunnel through" to the dialog box of another command. The *tunnel button* in this example tunnels through to the Tabs dialog box.

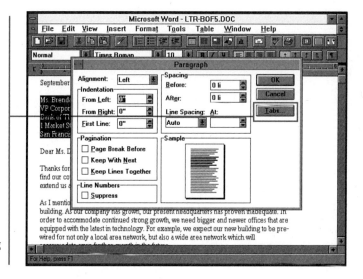

With the mouse, choose a command button by clicking it.

With the keyboard, press Enter to choose the command button enclosed in a bold rectangle (usually the OK command button). Press Esc to choose the Cancel button. Choose tunnel buttons by pressing Alt+*letter* (where *letter* is the underlined letter for the button).

Note: In some dialog boxes, double-clicking an option button or a list item selects that option button or item and simultaneously chooses the OK command button.

Operating Menus in DOS Programs

When you are operating a DOS (non-Windows) program, use
operating procedures and keys you use in that program. Althoug
such as Lotus 1-2-3, WordPerfect, and dBASE operate under Windows,
menus and control keys remain the same. These DOS programs do not take
on the pull-down menus, dialog boxes, or other features of a program designed for Windows. (You can, however, use a special Windows menu in a
DOS program to copy an object in the DOS program and then paste it in a
Windows program. For details, refer to Chapter 19, "Integrating Multiple
Programs," and Chapter 20, "Running DOS Programs.")

Controlling Window Positions and Sizes

Just as you move papers on your desk, you can move and reorder program
windows on your screen. In fact, you can resize windows, expand them to full
size, shrink them to small icons to save space, and restore them to original
size.

The topmost program window is the active window. It contains the program
in which you are currently working. This section shows you how to make a
program window the active window.

The following keystrokes are useful in controlling windows:

Key Combination	Explanation
Alt + Tab	Activates the next program, opening any icon to display its window. Until you release Alt, you see a small box containing the next program's name.
Alt + Esc	Activates the next program window or icon, but does not open closed windows.
Alt, space bar	Selects the Program Control menu on the active program.
Alt, -	Selects the Document Control menu on the active document.

If you can see several windows on-screen, you can use the mouse to activate a
window by clicking the window. You can double-click an icon to open it into a
window.

Moving a Window

You can move a window to any location on-screen. By moving a program window or document window, you can arrange your work on-screen just as you would on your desk.

To move a window with the mouse, follow these steps:

1. Activate the window by clicking its title bar or edge.
2. Point to the window's title bar.
3. Press and hold down the mouse button.
4. Drag the window to its new location by moving the mouse as you continue to hold down the mouse button.
5. Release the mouse button when the window is where you want it.

To move a window with the keyboard, follow these steps:

1. Activate the window by pressing Alt + Tab⇄ or Alt + Esc until the window you want to move is topmost.
2. Choose the Program Control menu by pressing Alt, **space bar**.

   Or choose the Document Control menu by pressing Alt, -.
3. Select the Move command (either click the Move command or press ↓ until the Move command is highlighted, and then press ↵Enter).

A four-pointed arrow appears, and the window borders turn gray.

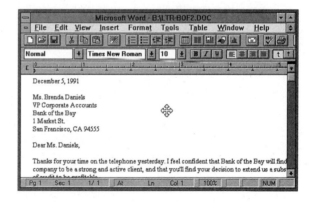

4. Press the arrow keys to move the shadowed borders to the place where you want the window. As soon as you press an arrow key, the four-pointed arrow changes back to an arrow pointer.
5. Press ↵Enter.

Note: You cannot move a window that is maximized to occupy the full screen. To move a maximized window, first restore it to a smaller size (see the upcoming section on "Restoring a Full-Screen Program or Document into a Window").

Changing the Size of a Window

Changing the size of a window enables you to position and size program and document windows so that you can see more than one data area. Copying and pasting data between programs is therefore much easier. To change the size of a window, you drag one or more window edges to a new position, or you use a Control menu command.

With the mouse, change the size of a window by following these steps:

1. Activate the window by clicking its title bar or edge.
2. Move the pointer to the edge or corner of the window you want to size. When the pointer is correctly positioned, it changes into a two-pointed arrow.
3. Press and hold down the mouse button and drag the two-pointed arrow to move the edge of the window.
4. Release the mouse button.

With the keyboard, change the size of a window by following these steps:

1. Activate the window by pressing Alt + Tab↹ or Alt + Esc.
2. Choose the Program Control menu by pressing Alt, **space bar**.
   Or choose the Document Control menu by pressing Alt.
3. Select the Size command. A four-pointed arrow appears in the center of the window.
4. Press the arrow key that points to the window edge you want to move. For example, press → to indicate that you want to move the right window edge. A two-pointed arrow appears over the edge you want to move.
5. Press the arrow key that will move the window edge in the direction you want. For instance, if you want to move the right window edge to the left, press ←.
6. Press ↵Enter. To return the window edge to its original position before you press ↵Enter, press Esc.

Note: You cannot size a window that is maximized to occupy the full screen. To size a maximized window, first restore it to a smaller size (see the up coming section on "Restoring a Full-Screen Program or Document into a Window").

3

Filling the Screen with a Window

Sometimes you will want the program to fill the entire screen, especially when you are working with only one program. In programs that contain multiple document windows, such as Microsoft Excel and Word for Windows, you can make a document fill the entire area within the program window. This feature is useful if you want to see the largest area of a worksheet or letter.

To use the mouse to make a window fill the screen, click the up-arrow button at the top right corner of the program or document window.

Program maximize button

Document maximize button

This up-arrow button is known as the *maximize button*.

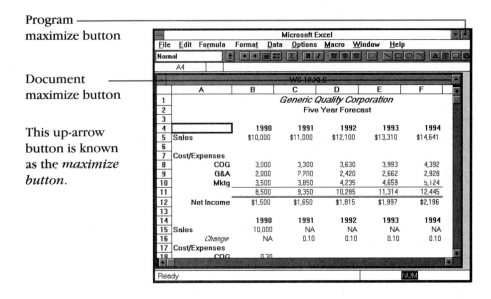

To use the keyboard to make a window fill the screen, follow these steps:

1. Press ⎡Alt⎤, **space bar** to choose the Program Control menu.

   Or press ⎡Alt⎤, ⎡-⎤ to choose the Document Control menu.

2. Select the Maximize command.

Note: Some Windows programs contain a single document. In these programs, you cannot maximize the document because it already fills the major portion of the program's window.

Restoring a Full-Screen Program or Document into a Window

Often you can see more easily what you are doing, such as cutting or copying text between program windows, if both programs are in windows smaller than the full screen. In this case, if one of the programs fills the entire screen, you must restore it into a smaller window.

To use the mouse to restore a full-screen program into a sizable, movable window, click the two-pointed arrow located at the top right corner of the program window.

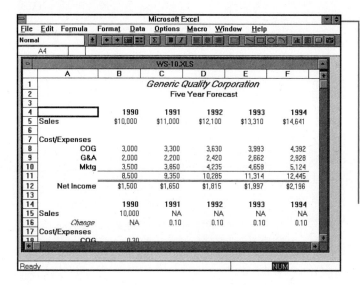

This two-pointed arrow is the *program restore button*. It reduces a full-screen Windows program into a smaller window.

To use the keyboard to restore a full-screen Program into a smaller window, follow these steps:

1. Press (Alt), **space bar** to choose the Program Control menu.
2. Select the **Restore** command.

In programs that can contain multiple documents, a document can fill the program window or be in its own smaller window. To use the mouse to restore a maximized document into a smaller window, you can use one of two methods. The method you use depends on the program's design.

Document _____ restore button

If the program shows a *document restore button*, like the two-pointed arrow shown in this Microsoft Excel document, click it to restore the maximized document.

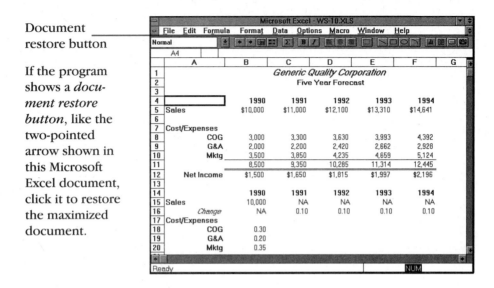

If the program does not show a document restore button, follow these steps:

1. Click the Document Control menu.

The Document Control menu appears as an icon to the left of the File menu.

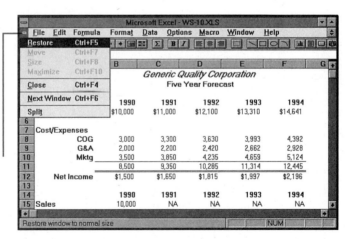

2. Click the Restore command.

Note: The Document Control menu may change position. When the document is in a window, its Control menu is at the top left of the document window. When the document is maximized to fill the inside of a program, the Document Control menu for some programs appears to the left of the File menu.

To use the keyboard to restore a document window of either design, follow these steps:

1. Press ⟨Alt⟩, ⟨-⟩ to choose the Document Control menu.
2. Select the Restore command.

Reducing a Window to an Icon

When you need to work with a large number of programs at one time, you may want to reduce some of them to icons. A program icon contains the program and its document; however, they require less space on-screen, and you can quickly open them into a window or full screen.

Note: If you are operating Windows in 386-enhanced mode, DOS programs can continue to run even when they are icons.

Minimize buttons

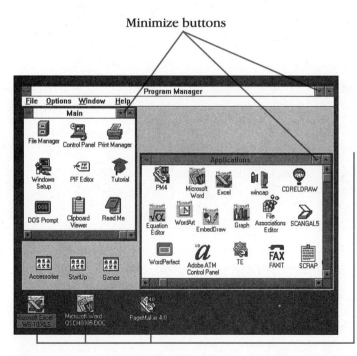

You can shrink programs such as Microsoft Excel, Word for Windows, and Aldus PageMaker and arrange them as icons.

With the mouse, shrink a window to an icon by clicking the down-arrow button located on the right side of the program's title bar. This arrow is known as the *minimize button*.

With the keyboard, shrink a window to an icon by first choosing the Program Control menu (press Alt, space bar) and then selecting Minimize.

Note: Most document windows inside a program window cannot be reduced to icons. Exceptions are document windows in the File Manager and the Program Manager.

3

Restoring an Icon into a Window

Restore an icon into a window by double-clicking the icon; alternatively, press Alt+Tab until you see the icon's name, and then release the Alt key.

If you want to select an icon but not restore it, press Alt+Esc until the icon is selected; then press Alt and then space bar to display the icon's Control menu. Choose any of the Control commands, such as Restore, Maximize, or Close.

Note: To use the keyboard to restore an icon to its original size quickly, press Alt+Tab until the icon is selected. When you release Alt+Tab, the icon restores itself into a window.

Moving an Icon

You move an icon with the mouse by positioning the pointer on the icon, holding down the mouse button, and dragging the icon to the new location. Release the button when the icon is where you want it moved.

To move an icon with the keyboard, first select the icon by pressing Alt+Esc until it is selected. Next, choose the Control menu by pressing Alt and then space bar. Select Move. Press the arrow keys to reposition the icon. Finally, press Enter when you are finished moving the icon.

Using the Task List To Arrange Icons and Windows

The Task List is a Windows feature that is always available to help you switch between programs or arrange windows and icons in predetermined patterns.

T...
you ...
the desk...
background o...
when you press
Ctrl + Esc.

To use the Task List to arrange windows or icons, follow these steps:

1. Display the Task List by double-clicking the desktop background or pressing Ctrl + Esc.

2. Choose one of the options listed in table 3.2. Either click the appropriate button in the Task List dialog box or press Alt + *letter* (where *letter* is the underlined letter for the button).

Table 3.2
Task List Dialog Box Options

Option	Action
Switch To	Activates the selected program in the Task List.
End Task	Exits the selected program in the Task List.
Cancel	Backs out of the Task List. You also can press Esc.
Cascade	Arranges open windows in an overlapping cascade, from top left to bottom right.
Tile	Arranges all open windows to fill the screen with equal-sized windows.
Arrange Icons	Arranges all program icons along the bottom of the screen.

Switching between Programs

When you have many programs running, you need an easy way to switch from one program to another. Remember that the topmost program window with a solid title bar is the active window, the one in which you are working.

3

Switching with the Mouse or the Keyboard

With the mouse, you can activate a window, or bring it to the top, by clicking that window. Be careful not to click a part of the program's window that will issue a command. You can activate a program icon by double-clicking the icon.

With the keyboard, you have two choices of key combinations to activate another program's window: Alt+Tab and Alt+Esc. Pressing Alt+Tab cycles through program windows quickly; only a box containing the program's name is displayed. When you see the name of the program you want, release the Alt and Tab keys. Pressing Alt+Esc cycles through program windows and icons also, but more slowly; each window must be completely redrawn before the next window appears.

Switching with the Task List

If you are using the mouse or the keyboard and must switch among many programs, you may want to use the Task List. The Task List shows you which programs are currently loaded.

You can activate any program you want by choosing it from the Task List.

To activate a program from the Task List with the mouse, follow these steps:

1. Double-click the desktop background to display the Task List.
2. Double-click the name of the program you want to activate.

To activate a program from the Task List with the keyboard, follow these steps:

1. Press Ctrl+Esc to display the Task List.
2. Press ↑ or ↓ to select the name of the program you want to activate.
3. Press ↵Enter.

A third way to display the Task List in many programs is to choose the Program Control menu (Alt, space bar) and select the Switch To command.

Getting Help

Windows programs have Help information to guide you through new commands and procedures. In some programs, the Help files are quite extensive.

They tell you about parts of the screen, the actions of commands, and the step-by-step procedures to complete specific tasks.

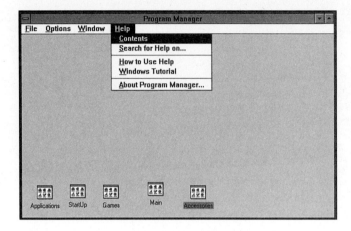

3

To get help in Windows programs, choose the **H**elp menu by clicking **H**elp or pressing [Alt], [H]; then select one of the Help commands.

From the **H**elp menu, you can select commands that provide help with using the Help feature or the operating procedures; that provide an index of specific topics; and that enable you to search for information about a specific topic. Choosing one of these commands displays a Help window.

To get help about how to use Help in the Program Manager, choose the **H**elp menu and select the **H**ow to Use Help command. Or, after the Help window is displayed, press Help (F1).

Note: In many Windows programs, pressing F1 immediately displays the Help window.

Help programs may differ slightly from one Windows program to another and between older and newer versions, but most Windows programs contain variations on three methods of controlling the Help program:

Method	Description
Menus	At the top of the Help window are the menus to control the Help program.
Buttons	Under the menus are buttons for listing the contents of the Help file, searching for a specific subject, going back to the previous subject or help screen, and choosing from a list of the Help subjects you have most recently viewed.

continues

Method	Description
Hypertext words	The text in a Help screen contains underlined words or phrases. Choosing a word or phrase with a solid underline moves you to that topic so that you can learn more about it. Choosing a word or phrase with a dotted underline pops up a window containing a short definition.

Locating a Help Topic

Command buttons are located under the menus of some Windows Help programs, enabling you to browse through topics or find specific topics quickly.

Choose a command button by clicking it or pressing Alt+*letter* (where *letter* is the button's underlined letter).

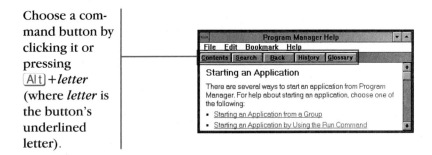

Table 3.3 describes the Help buttons displayed in the Program Manager Help screen and two buttons (<< and >>) that many other Help programs use.

Table 3.3
Common Help Buttons

Button	Description
Contents	Displays the contents of the program's Help file. Choose one of the listed subjects to jump to that subject.
Search	Displays a list of key words and phrases in the program's Help file. You can type or select a word or phrase to jump to that subject.

Button	Description
Back	Displays the most recent subject you viewed. You can continue choosing Back to review subjects you already have viewed, until you get to the Contents screen.
History	Displays the last 40 subjects you have viewed, with the most recently viewed subject at the top of the list. You can return to a subject by double-clicking it.
Glossary	Displays an alphabetized list (glossary) of terms used in the Help program. You can select a term to display its definition. (Not all Help programs use this button.)
<<	Displays the preceding subject in a series of related subjects. You can continue choosing this button until you reach the first subject in the series. The button is dimmed if no previous subjects exist.
>>	Displays the next subject in a series of related subjects. You can continue choosing this button until you reach the final subject in the series. The button is dimmed if no further subjects exist.

3

Viewing Help's Contents

To get an overview of your program or to see what subjects are contained in the Help file, you can list the Help file's contents. To view the contents, choose the Contents button.

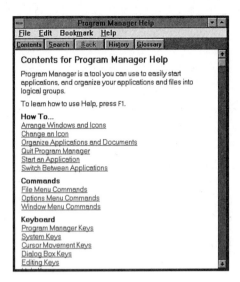

3

In the Program Manager's list of contents, subjects are divided into three categories: How To, Commands, and Keyboard.

The subjects listed in the How To category describe how to perform functions in the Program Manager. The subjects listed in the Commands category describe how the commands in the Program Manager's three menus work. The subjects in the Keyboard category describe how to use key combinations and specific keys. To jump to any of these subjects, click the subject, or press the Tab key to select the subject you want to display and press Enter.

Searching for Help on Specific Topics

In the Help program, you can select the Search button when you want to search for help on a specific topic. In the Program Manager, for example, you can follow these steps to search for topics related to starting applications:

1. Click the Search button to display the Search dialog box.

   Or press Alt + S to display the Search dialog box.

2. In the Type a word text box, type **applications, starting.**

   Or click the down arrow in the scroll bar until applications, starting appears in the list; then click that phrase.

   Alternatively, press Tab⇕ to move into the list, and then press ↑ or ↓ to select applications, starting.

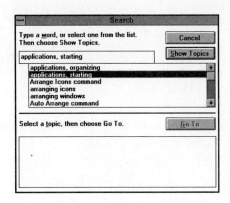

In this Search dialog box, applications, starting is selected as the search topic.

3

3. Click the **S**how Topics button at the top right corner of the dialog box.

Or press [Alt] + [S] to show the topics (or press [↵Enter]).

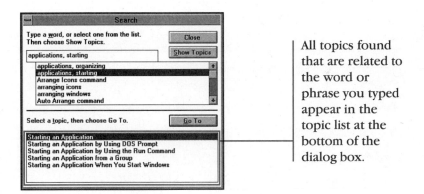

All topics found that are related to the word or phrase you typed appear in the topic list at the bottom of the dialog box.

4. In the Select a topic text box, click the topic you want to read.

Or press [↑] or [↓] to select the topic you want to read.

5. Click the **G**o To button to go to the topic.

Or press [Alt] + [G] to go to the topic (or press [↵Enter]).

Pressing Shift+F1 displays context-sensitive help in some Windows programs. Pressing Shift+F1 when a dialog box or error box appears gives you help about that box. In some Windows programs, pressing Shift+F1 first changes the mouse pointer into a question mark. If you then click a command or a particular part of the screen, the program displays information about that command or that portion of the screen.

Jumping to Another Help Topic

Within the Help text are underlined *hypertext* words or phrases that enable you to jump quickly to related information. Two kinds of underlines are used for hypertext words and phrases in Help text:

3

Underline	*Action You Take*
Solid underline	Click the word or phrase underlined with a solid line to jump to that topic. With the keyboard, press ⎯Tab⎯ or ⎯Shift⎯+⎯Tab⎯ to select the word or phrase, and then press ⎯Enter⎯ to jump to the selected topic. Choose the **B**ack button (or the << button in some programs) to return to the previously displayed topic.
Dashed underline	Point to a word or phrase underlined with a dashed line, and then click the mouse button to display the definition (click a second time to close the definition). With the keyboard, press ⎯Tab⎯ or ⎯Shift⎯+⎯Tab⎯ to select the word or phrase, and then press ⎯Enter⎯ to display the definition. Press ⎯Enter⎯ a second time to close the definition.

Marking Help Locations for Easy Reference

In some Windows programs, when you find a Help topic that you may want to return to again, you can put a bookmark on it, just as you use a bookmark to mark a location in a book. You can then return to a topic that has your bookmark. You can use more than one bookmark in a Help file.

To put a bookmark on a Help topic, follow these steps:

1. Display the Help topic on which you want to put a bookmark.
2. Choose the **B**ookmark menu and then select the **D**efine command.

The Bookmark
Define dialog box
appears.

3. Select the Bookmark Name text box (if it isn't already selected) and
   type a bookmark name of your choice. Notice that the bookmark name
   that first appears in the text box is the title of the current topic; you
   can accept this title as your bookmark name.

4. Choose OK or press ⏎Enter to attach your bookmark to the specified
   topic.

To return to a bookmark in a Help file, use these steps:

1. Choose the Help command in the Windows program.

2. Choose the Bookmark menu by clicking it or by pressing Alt + M.

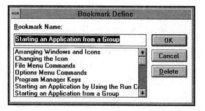

This list of
bookmarks shows
that several topics
have bookmarks.

3. Click or type the number of the bookmark to which you want to
   return.

   If more than nine bookmarks are shown, click More at the bottom of
   the menu or press M. From the Go To Bookmark list that appears,
   select the bookmark you want to go to, and then choose OK.

The Help window displays the topic containing your bookmark.

To remove a bookmark, first choose the Bookmark menu and then select the
Define command. Next, click the bookmark's name in the list or press Tab to
move to the list. Press the up- or down-arrow key to select the name. Finally,
choose the Delete button to delete the bookmark, and then choose OK or
press Enter.

Adding Your Own Notes to Help

Besides marking Help topics with bookmarks, in some Windows programs you can attach your own notes to Help topics. Custom notes are helpful in programs such as the File Manager, where, for example, you may want to remind someone how to make hard disk backups with the File Copy command. Not all Windows programs have the capability of attaching custom notes to the Help topics. The accessory programs and utilities that come with Windows—such as Write, Paintbrush, and File Manager—include this capability.

Paper-clip icon

A Help topic with an attached custom note has a paper-clip icon next to the topic's title.

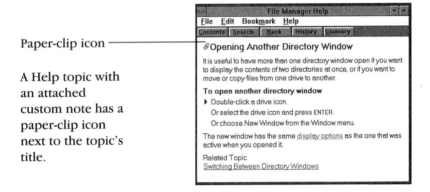

To attach your own note, or annotation, to the Help topic currently displayed, follow these steps:

1. Choose the Edit menu and select the Annotate command.

When the Anno- tate window appears, the insertion point is in the Annotation text box, ready for you to type.

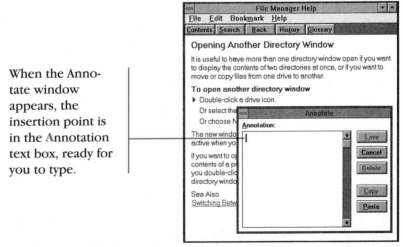

2. Type the text you want to attach to the topic.

This example shows the Annotation text box after a note has been attached to the Help topic Opening Another Directory Window, found in the File Manager.

3. Choose Save to attach the annotation to this Help topic.

You can paste text into the Annotation box from the Clipboard by choosing Paste (in this way, you can copy text from another program and paste it into your annotation). You can copy your annotation by choosing Copy (in this way, you can then paste the text of your annotation into another program).

To read a previously attached note, display the topic and click the paper-clip icon next to the topic's title, or press Alt and then select the Edit Annotate command.

To delete an annotation, display the topic containing the annotation, choose the Edit menu, and select the Annotate command; or click the paper-clip icon and then choose Delete.

Using Other Help Features

Not all Windows programs contain the same Help features, menus, or buttons. Some additional Help commands are listed in table 3.4.

Table 3.4
Other Help Commands

Command	Action
Edit Copy	Copies the information in the active Help window to the Clipboard. You can then switch to the program where you want to paste the information, and choose **Edit Paste**.
File Open	Opens a selected Help file of another program.
File Print Topic	Prints the current Help topic to the default printer.
File Print Setup	Sets up a selected printer or changes the printer settings.
File Exit	Exits the Help program.

Recovering from a Crash

Your computer rarely encounters an internal instruction that it doesn't understand or that conflicts with another instruction. For this and other reasons, your program may "crash," or stop working. When this happens, you generally see a message on-screen advising you that the program has encountered an unrecoverable error.

Though crashes occur rarely, they are the best reason for you to save your important documents frequently. (Earthquakes happen rarely, too, but it's best to be prepared.)

Fortunately, if your program crashes, it doesn't mean you have lost everything. Often you can recover from a crash by shutting down only the program that crashed. In many cases, you won't have to turn off your computer or restart Windows. You lose the data in the program that crashed (unless the program has a file-recovery utility, as do Word for Windows and other programs), but you shouldn't lose data from any other programs that were running at the same time.

If you encounter a message advising you that your program has terminated, press these keys:

   Ctrl+Alt+Del

You are prompted with a message offering you three alternatives. The first is to press the Esc key, which exits the message box. If you don't think your program really crashed, you can try pressing Esc to return to your program. If it doesn't work (and it probably will not), press Enter to exit the program and return to Windows. If that doesn't work, you must reboot your computer.

Follow these steps to recover from a program crash:

1. When you get a message advising you that your program has terminated, press Ctrl + Alt + Del. (Hold down Ctrl and Alt, and then press Del.)

2. To close your program (and lose what you were working on), press ↵Enter. If this works, you will return to Windows. Restart your program and continue working.

3. If you encounter another error message (rather than returning to Windows), press Ctrl + Alt + Del again to restart your computer. You will lose unsaved data in any programs that were running when the crash occurred.

Summary

This chapter covered the most important information you need to operate Windows and Windows programs. You learned how to use both the mouse and the keyboard to choose menus, select commands, and select options from dialog boxes. You saw how to switch between programs and how to change the size and position of windows on-screen—all under mouse or keyboard control. Finally, you learned how to get help information about using menus and commands.

The following important points were covered in this chapter:

■ The mouse pointer's shape tells you what you can do at specific screen locations.

■ You select text or graphics items, choose a menu, and then select a command to affect what you have selected.

■ You choose menus, commands, or dialog box options by pointing to them with the mouse pointer and clicking the mouse button.

■ You choose menu or dialog box options by pressing Alt and typing the underlined letter in the menu or option name. When a menu is pulled down, you type the underlined letter of the command you want to execute.

After you learn how to use Windows menus, commands, and dialog boxes in one Windows program, you will know how to use them in any Windows program.

To learn how to start and use your Windows programs, see Chapter 4, "Editing, Copying, and Moving in Windows."

3

Editing, Copying, and Moving in Windows

4

One of the greatest advantages to working with Windows is that all Windows programs work in a similar way. Every program has a title bar at the top that tells you the name of the program and the name of the document you're working on; every program has a menu bar; every program has a window around it that works in a predictable manner.

But the similarities go even deeper. Not only do all Windows programs have a menu bar, but all menu bars contain certain commands that are the same in every Windows program. And in all programs that include typed text, the basic techniques for editing text are identical. In this chapter, you learn common Windows commands, and you learn how to edit text in any Windows program. Selecting text so that you can copy or cut it is one of the most important skills you can learn.

Another feature shared by Windows programs is the Clipboard—a temporary storage area that holds text you copy or cut. Because the Clipboard is shared by all Windows programs, you can duplicate or move text in many ways: within a single document; between different documents in the same program; and between different programs. You can even copy and move text between Windows programs and DOS programs (such as Lotus 1-2-3 and WordPerfect) running in Windows.

Key Terms in This Chapter

Copy   An operation that stores in the Clipboard a duplicate of selected text or graphics from a program.

Paste   An operation that inserts the information in the Clipboard into the active program at the current insertion point or cursor.

Cut (Move) An operation that removes selected text or graphics from a program and stores the text or graphics in the Clipboard. You can use the Cut operation also to *move* text or graphics.

Clipboard An area of memory reserved to hold text or graphics that you cut or copy.

Starting Programs

Programs in Windows share many common features. They operate similarly, supporting both the mouse and the keyboard. They look alike, with features in one program window similar to those in another program window. And you start them all the same way—directly from an icon in the Program Manager. You can use either the mouse or the keyboard to start a program.

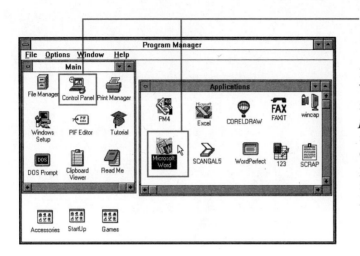

Program item icons

Programs in Windows are represented as *program item icons*, which are contained in program windows in the Program Manager.

4

To use your mouse to start a program, follow these steps:

1. Start Windows and activate the Program Manager. (If Program Manager appears as an icon, double-click the icon to open the Program Manager window.)

2. Click the program window containing the program you want to start. (If the program window appears as an icon, double-click the icon to open the program window.)

3. Double-click the program item icon that represents the program you want to start.

To use your keyboard to start a program, follow these steps:

1. Start Windows and activate the Program Manager. (If Program Manager appears as an icon, hold down [Alt] and press [Tab⇆] repeatedly until you see a box on-screen containing the name *Program Manager*. When you release [Alt], the Program Manager icon opens into a window.)

2. Press [Ctrl]+[Tab⇆] to activate the program window containing the program you want to start. (If the window appears as an icon, press [↵Enter] to open the icon into a window.)

3. Press any arrow key to activate the program icon item representing the program you want to start. (The active program item icon appears highlighted.)

4. Press [↵Enter], or choose the File menu and select the Open command.

Editing Text

With the exception of some shortcut keys, the text-editing techniques described in this section work in all Windows programs and in the text boxes within the dialog boxes displayed by these programs.

Whenever you position the mouse pointer over an area of text that can be edited, the pointer appears as an *I-beam*. This shape indicates that you can edit this text if necessary.

4

Insertion point   I-beam

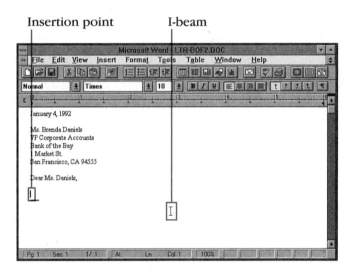

The *insertion point* is the flashing vertical line in text, indicating where text editing or typing will occur.

With the mouse, edit single characters in text by following these steps:

1. Move the I-beam between the characters where you want to locate the insertion point.

2. Click the mouse to position the flashing insertion point between the characters.

3. Do one of the following:

   • Press Del to delete a character to the right.

   • Press ⬅Backspace to delete a character to the left.

   • Type characters at the insertion point.

With the keyboard, edit single characters in text by following these steps:

1. Press the arrow keys, PgUp, or PgDn to move the flashing insertion point between the characters you want to edit.

2. Do one of the following:
   - Press [Del] to delete a character to the right.
   - Press [◆Backspace] to delete a character to the left.
   - Type characters at the insertion point.

With the mouse, edit multiple characters by following these steps:

1. Move the I-beam to the first character you want to edit.
2. Hold down the mouse button and drag the I-beam across the characters you want to edit.

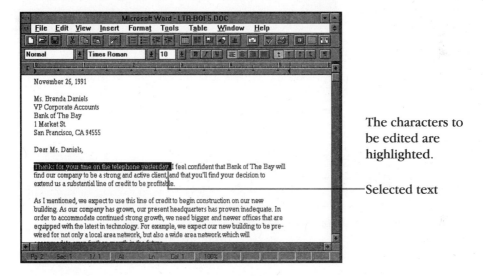

The characters to be edited are highlighted.

Selected text

3. Do one of the following:
   - Press [Del] to delete the selected characters.
   - Press [◆Backspace] to delete the selected characters.
   - Type new characters to replace the selected characters.

With the keyboard, edit multiple characters by following these steps:

1. Press the arrow keys, [PgUp], or [PgDn] to move the flashing insertion point next to the first character you want to edit.
2. Hold down [◆Shift] and press an arrow key to move the insertion point; the text over which the insertion point passes is selected. Hold down [◆Shift] and [Ctrl] together to select entire words as you press [←] or [→].

3. Do one of the following:

- Press ⌨Del to delete the selected characters.
- Press ⌨⬅Backspace to delete the selected characters.
- Type new characters to replace the selected characters.

To deselect text with the mouse, click anywhere in the text. To deselect text with the keyboard, press PgUp, PgDn, or an arrow key.

4

Some Windows programs include shortcuts for editing text. These shortcuts may work in some parts of the program, such as body copy or a formula bar, but not in other parts, such as a dialog box. Experiment to find the shortcuts that help you. Table 4.1 lists shortcuts you can use for editing in many Windows programs.

Table 4.1
Common Editing Shortcuts

Action	*Result*
Double-click	Selects the word under the I-beam.
Click, ⌨⇧Shift+Click	Selects all text between the first click and the ⌨⇧Shift+Click.
⌨⇧Shift+⌨← or ⌨→	Selects the next character to the left or right.
⌨⇧Shift+⌨↑ or ⌨↓	Selects the preceding or next line.
⌨⇧Shift+⌨PgUp or ⌨PgDn	Selects text from the insertion point to the top or bottom of the page or screen.
⌨⇧Shift+⌨Home	Selects text from the insertion point to the beginning of the line.
⌨⇧Shift+⌨End	Selects text from the insertion point to the end of the line.
⌨Ctrl+⌨⇧Shift+⌨← or ⌨→	Selects a word each time you press ⌨← or ⌨→.

Copying and Moving in Windows Programs

Nearly all Windows programs contain the commands Cut, Copy, and Paste on the Edit menu. These commands enable you to cut or copy information you have selected in one place and paste it somewhere else. You can use these techniques to copy and move information either within a document, between documents, or between programs.

Because copying information between programs is fairly new, you at first may not think of many ways to use the feature. But as you work more with multiple programs, you will find that copying and pasting between programs saves you time, eliminates typing errors, and gives you the chance to use programs together as though they were part of a single program.

An important part of the copying and moving process is the *Clipboard*. Like a writer's clipboard, the Clipboard is a Windows program that holds information so that you can copy or move it from one place to another—within *and* between programs.

To refresh your memory about switching between programs, refer to Chapter 3, "Operating Windows."

Copying and Moving Text

You can copy or cut text from a Windows program and paste the text into any other Windows or DOS program that accepts your keystrokes. You can use the same technique to copy or move text within a Windows document or between Windows documents. To copy and move text between Windows documents or programs, or within a document, follow these steps:

1. Select the text you want to copy or move.
2. Choose the Edit menu and select the Copy command if you want to copy text.

   Or choose the Edit menu and select the Cut command if you want to move text.
3. If you are copying or moving between programs, activate the other program by clicking its window, or by pressing Ctrl + Esc and selecting the program from the Task List. Open the document into which you want to move or copy the selected text.
4. Position the insertion point where you want the text to appear.
5. Choose the Edit menu and select the Paste command.

Copying and Moving Graphics or Screen Images

Copying and moving graphics within and between Windows programs uses a nearly identical process to copying and moving text. To copy and move graphics or screen images within or between Windows programs, follow these steps:

1. Select the graphics you want to copy or move. If you want to capture an image of the screen, skip to step 2.

Scissors tool ⌐ ⌐Pick tool ⌐Selected graphics area

4

You can select graphics in different ways. In some programs, such as Windows Paintbrush, you use a *lasso* or *scissors* to draw around the area you want to copy.

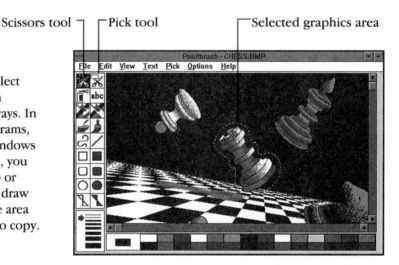

Other programs, such as CorelDRAW!, display *handles* to indicate a selected graphics object.

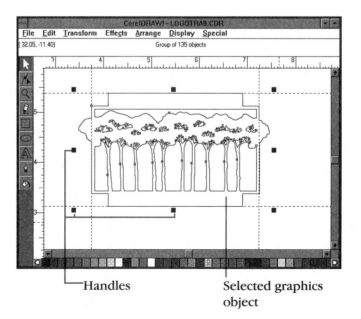

Handles

Selected graphics object

2. If you want to copy a graphic, choose the Edit menu and select the Copy command. If you want to move the graphic, choose the Edit menu and select the Cut command.

   Or capture the entire screen as a graphic image by pressing PrtSc. Press Alt + PrtSc to capture only the active window as a graphic image. (You will not see a change on-screen.)

3. If you are copying or moving between programs, switch to the program in which you want to paste the image: click the program's window, or press Ctrl + Esc and select the program from the Task List. Open the document into which you want to copy or move the selected graphic.

4. Position the insertion point or graphics placement tool where you want the text or graphics to appear.

5. Choose the Edit menu and select the Paste command.

4

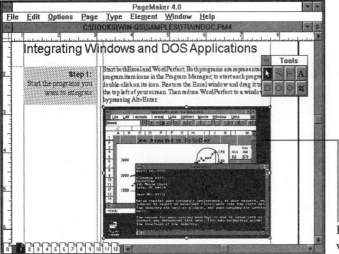

Pasting a screen image of a program such as Microsoft Excel into PageMaker or Word for Windows is an excellent way to create training materials or documentation.

Pasted image of window

Note: If the Print Screen key does not work on your keyboard, you may have an older keyboard. Try Alt+PrtSc or Shift+PrtSc as alternatives. (The Print Screen key may be named PrtScrn or PrtSc, depending on your computer.)

The screen images you capture by pressing PrtSc or Alt+PrtSc have the same resolution as your monitor. CGA monitors have the lowest resolution, EGA monitors have higher resolution, and VGA or Super VGA monitors have even higher resolution.

Note: You may find that after you copy a graphic image from one program, the Paste command in the other program is gray on the Edit menu. The two programs use different methods of drawing graphics, and you cannot copy and paste between them. Check the documentation in the first program for alternative methods of copying, such as holding down the Shift key while you choose the Edit menu. You may then see alternative copying commands.

4 Copying and Pasting in DOS Programs

DOS programs can use the copy-and-paste capability provided by Windows, but they have some limitations. For example, you cannot paste graphics into a DOS program. And if you are running Windows in standard mode, you can capture only a full screen of text, not a selected portion of text. For more information on running DOS programs under Windows, refer to Chapter 20, "Running DOS Programs."

Moving text and objects in DOS programs is different from moving them in Windows programs. To move within a DOS document, use the program's own techniques. In DOS programs running under Windows, you don't have a Cut command, as you do in Windows programs. To move text from a DOS program running under Windows, you must copy and paste it using the Windows technique, then delete it from the DOS program using the program's own technique.

Copying When Windows Is in Standard Mode

If Windows is running in standard mode and you want to copy from a DOS program, you must copy the entire full screen of text. If you are using an 8088, 8086, or 80286 computer (or if you started Windows by typing WIN/S), you are in standard mode.

To copy the entire contents of the DOS screen while in any Windows mode and on any type of computer, follow these steps:

1. Scroll or position the screen to show what you want to copy.
2. Press PrtSc.

Note: If the Print Screen key does not work on your keyboard, you may have an older keyboard. Try Alt+PrtSc or Shift+PrtSc as alternatives. (If it still doesn't work, deselect PrtSc and Alt+PrtSc as reserve shortcut keys in the PIF Editor; see Chapter 20 for details.)

If the DOS program is in text mode, you will copy the text on-screen. If the program is in graphics mode, you will copy an image of the screen. Although you cannot edit the text of a screen image after you paste it, you can paste the image as a graphic into such programs as Word for Windows, Windows Write, and PageMaker. Screen images are extremely useful for training and documentation.

Copying in 386-Enhanced Mode

4

In 386-enhanced mode, you can run DOS programs in windows rather than full screen. Running DOS programs in windows enables you to see multiple programs and copy selected text from the screen. Or you can copy the entire graphics screen. You can use either the mouse or the keyboard to copy in a DOS program that is running in a window. (Remember, the DOS program must be running in a window—not full screen—to copy selected text.)

With the mouse, copy selected text from a DOS program by following these steps:

1. If the DOS program is running full screen, put the program in a window by pressing [Alt]+[↵Enter]. (Press [Alt]+[↵Enter] a second time to restore the DOS program to full screen.)

2. Click the Control menu icon at the top left corner of the window, and choose the Edit command.

3. Select the Mark command.

4. Select the text you want to copy by pointing to a corner of the area you want to select, holding down the mouse button, and dragging across the area.

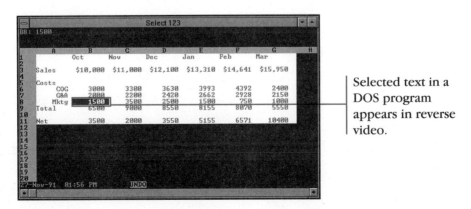

Selected text in a DOS program appears in reverse video.

5. Click the right mouse button to copy the selected text to the Clipboard.

6. Follow the appropriate set of instructions for pasting, as described in the next sections of this chapter.

Note: While you are selecting text or graphics with the mouse, the title bar of the program changes to show the word *Select*. You cannot paste or use the program while you are selecting. Press Esc to return to program control.

4

With the keyboard, copy selected text from a DOS program by following these steps:

1. If the DOS program is running full screen, put the program in a window by pressing Alt + ↵Enter. (Press Alt + ↵Enter a second time to restore the DOS program to full screen.)

2. Press Alt+**space bar** to open the Control menu.

3. Choose the Edit command.

4. Select the Mark command. Notice the rectangular cursor that appears at the top left corner of the screen.

5. Press the arrow keys to move the cursor to the top left corner of the area you want to copy.

6. Press and hold down ⇧Shift and then press the arrow keys to select the text you want to copy.

7. Press Alt+**space bar** to open the Control menu; then choose Edit and select Copy Enter.

To copy a graphics screen from a DOS program that is running in 386-enhanced mode, press PrtSc or Alt+PrtSc. The entire screen or window is copied to the Clipboard.

Pasting from a DOS Program into a Windows Program

You can paste text or graphics from DOS programs into Windows programs; however, only Windows programs designed to work with graphics will receive graphics.

To paste text or graphics from a DOS program into a Windows program, follow these steps:

1. Activate the receiving program by clicking its window, or by pressing Ctrl + Esc and choosing the program from the Task List. Open the receiving document.

2. Position the insertion point where you want to paste the text or graphics.

3. Choose the Edit menu and select the Paste command.

Pasting Text into a DOS Program

You can paste only unformatted text into DOS programs. Two methods of pasting are available, depending on whether the DOS program you are pasting into is full screen or in a window.

To paste text into a DOS program that is full screen, follow these steps:

1. Activate the receiving program and open the receiving document.

2. Position the program's cursor where you want the pasted text to appear.

3. Press Alt+Esc to return to Windows and minimize the DOS program to an icon. (If the program can run only full screen, minimizing the program to an icon is the only way you can access the Control menu.)

4. Open the Control menu on the DOS program's icon by clicking the icon, or by pressing Alt+Esc until the icon is selected and then pressing Alt+space bar.

5. If you are running in standard mode, choose the Paste command.

   As soon as you choose Paste, the program icon expands and fills the screen. You will see the text on-screen, just as though you had typed it.

   If you are running in 386-enhanced mode, select the Edit menu and then choose Paste. (If you're running in 386-enhanced mode, however, you should be able to run the DOS program in a window by pressing Alt+↵Enter. Pasting into a window is easier than pasting into a full screen. See the following set of instructions.)

6. Delete any unnecessary text that you may have included in the copy.

To paste text into a DOS program that is running in a window, follow these steps:

1. Position the program's cursor where you want the pasted text to appear.

2. Open the Control menu by clicking it or by pressing Alt+space bar.

3. Choose the Edit menu and select the Paste command.

4

Even though WordPerfect and Lotus 1-2-3 are DOS programs, you can use Windows to copy numbers from 1-2-3 and paste them into Word-Perfect.

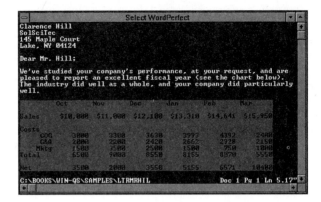

Using the Clipboard To View and Save Cut or Copied Data

When you cut or copy information, Windows stores it in a special part of memory called the Clipboard. The information stays in the Clipboard until you clear it or until you cut or copy new information. You therefore can repeatedly paste the same item until you clear or change the Clipboard.

With the Clipboard Viewer program, located in the Main group window, you can view the Clipboard contents, clear the Clipboard, and save and retrieve Clipboard contents. This last feature is convenient because you can make a library of different clippings you want to use repeatedly, or a set of clippings you want to send to someone through a diskette or electronic mail.

Viewing Clipboard Contents

To see the contents of the Clipboard, choose the Clipboard Viewer icon from the Main group in the Program Manager.

You can see the current clipping in the Clipboard's window. Use the scroll bars to move the window's contents if you want to see more. The contents may look out of proportion, but they readjust after you paste them.

4

Saving and Retrieving Clipboard Contents

You can save and retrieve Clipboard contents to use them later or to use them on a different computer. You also can create libraries of files on-disk that contain clippings you use frequently.

To save the contents of the Clipboard to a file, follow these steps:

1. Choose the File menu and select the Save As command.

2. Choose a new directory from the Directories list, if needed (however, if you save the file in the Windows directory, as proposed, you won't have to switch directories the next time you want to open the file).

3. Type a file name in the File Name text box. The Clipboard saves the file with the extension CLP.

4. Choose OK or press ⏎Enter.

To retrieve Clipboard contents saved to a file, follow these steps:

1. Save or paste the current Clipboard contents if you do not want to lose them—a retrieved clipping replaces the current Clipboard contents.

2. Choose the File menu and select the Open command.

3. If the file containing the Clipboard contents is located in a different directory, select the directory from the Directories list box and press ⏎Enter.

4. Select the file from the File Name list box or type the file name in the File Name text box.

5. Choose OK or press ⏎Enter.

Clearing the Clipboard To Regain Available Memory

Large clippings may take up a great deal of memory. To delete the Clipboard contents and regain memory, display the Clipboard Viewer window, choose the Edit menu, and select the Delete command.

4

Summary

This chapter describes one of the most important features of Windows: copying and moving data within and between programs. When you use only Windows programs, you find that you can use programs together as though they were a single program. Even if you use DOS programs, you can reduce the amount of retyping you do and the number of typing errors you introduce into the transferred data.

The following important points were covered in this chapter:

- You can start a Windows program by double-clicking its icon in the Program Manager.

- Many editing techniques are the same in all Windows programs.

- To copy text or graphics to another program, select what you want to copy, choose Copy from the Edit menu, switch to the other program, and choose Paste from the Edit menu.

- To move text or graphics from a Windows program, select what you want to move, choose Cut from the Edit menu, switch to the other program, and choose Paste from the Edit menu. To move text or graphics from a DOS program, choose the Mark command from the Edit command in the Control menu, select what you want to move, choose Copy Enter from the Edit menu, switch to the other program, choose Paste from the Edit menu, and then return to the DOS program and use DOS techniques to delete the text or graphics that you moved. You can move your selection to a Windows or a DOS program.

- Windows programs accept pasted text or graphics. DOS programs accept only pasted text.

■ The Clipboard Viewer program, found in the Main group of the Program Manager, enables you to view, save, retrieve, or delete the contents of the Clipboard.

Now that you are familiar with how to operate Windows programs and how to copy and paste between programs, you should turn to Chapter 20 to learn how to run DOS programs. If you work with more than one Windows program or if you want to see how Windows programs are designed to work together, turn to Chapter 19. It explains how you can tie Windows programs together so that they pass data between themselves automatically.

4

Grouping Programs and Documents

In this chapter, you learn how to start programs and documents with the Program Manager, and how to group programs and documents to fit the way you work. The Program Manager helps you keep programs and their associated documents in groups where you can easily find and start them.

Most people group programs and their data documents together by job type. You may want to group programs and data together into accounting, electronic mail (E-mail), and report-writing groups. If you have a set of tasks you must do daily, you may want to create a group window that contains the programs, along with their documents, that you use each day. Within a Daily Business group window, for example, you can assign program item icons that represent each program and document you need in your daily work.

The Program Manager is the first program that opens when you start Windows. Within the Program Manager are many group windows or group icons. These groups either were created automatically when Windows was installed or were added by an operator after the installation of the program.

Note: Closing the Program Manager exits Windows. Before Windows quits, you are prompted to save unsaved documents in Windows programs.

Understanding the Program Manager

Creating groups of programs you use regularly

Customizing group windows

Quitting the Program Manager and Windows

Key Terms in This Chapter

Program Manager	A program that helps you start frequently used programs and documents.
Group window	A document window that contains icons you use to start programs and any associated documents.
Group icon	An icon that represents a group window.
Program item icon	An icon within a group window that represents a program or a program with an associated document.

5

Understanding the Program Manager

The Program Manager contains windows and icons that help you quickly find and run programs and documents you use frequently.

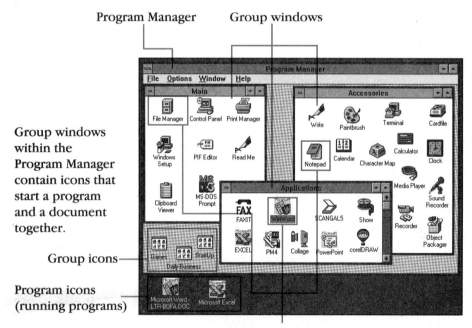

Program Manager

Group windows

Group windows within the Program Manager contain icons that start a program and a document together.

Group icons

Program icons (running programs)

Program item icons

After you start a program, it runs in its own separate window or appears as an icon at the bottom of the Windows desktop.

Table 5.1 describes the items in the Program Manager window.

Table 5.1
The Program Manager Window

Item	Description
Group window	A document window within the Program Manager that contains icons you use to start programs and documents. You can create group windows to group together programs you use at the same time or that contribute to the same job.
Group icon	An icon that represents a closed group window. Choosing the group icon displays the group window.
Program item icon	An icon within a group window that starts a program and, optionally, one of its associated documents. A program item icon is not the program, but only a start-up icon; therefore, you can have the same program item icon in more than one group window.
Program icon	An icon that appears on the Windows desktop (outside the Program Manager window) and that represents an actual running program. Program icons are not the same as program item icons, which you use only to start programs.

Windows comes with four sets of group windows that include the free programs that come with Windows. During installation, Windows automatically creates an extra group window to hold the programs you have on your hard disk. At any time, you can create your own custom group windows and program item icons.

The following group windows come with Windows:

Group Window	Description
Main	Includes programs and tools to help you control printing; set up printers, plotters, and modems; customize the desktop; and manage files.
Accessories	Includes desktop programs that come with Windows, such as a simple word processing program, a drawing program, a calendar, and a calculator.
StartUp	Includes programs that Windows activates immediately upon starting.
Games	Includes two games, Solitaire and Minesweeper.
Applications	Includes any applications (programs) Windows detects on your hard disk.

You can create custom group windows, such as this group called Daily Business, for the programs you use together or that you use for a specific job.

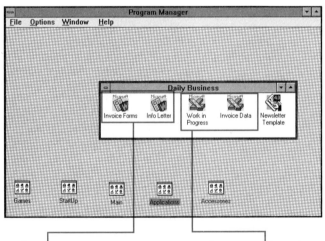

Word for Windows program item icons   Excel program item icons

The Daily Business group window shown here contains programs such as Microsoft Excel, Word for Windows, and PageMaker, as well as one document associated with each of them. When you double-click a program item icon in the group window, the program starts and loads the document associated with that particular program item icon. For this reason, you see several Word for Windows icons; each contains a different associated document.

Each program item icon represents a specific task. Program item icons in the Daily Business group window have been given names such as Invoice Forms,

Info Letter, and Work in Progress. When you create your own work groups and program item icons, you can name each one according to the task it performs.

Controlling the Program Manager

The Program Manager is always on-screen in a window or is represented as an icon at the bottom of the screen, giving you quick access to programs and documents. The Program Manager is also the route through which you exit Windows.

5

Opening Group Windows

To start a program with the Program Manager, you must first activate the Program Manager to make it the topmost window. When the Program Manager window is active, you can see the group windows and group icons it contains. To open a group window that is reduced to an icon, double-click the icon or press Ctrl+Tab until the icon is selected, and then press Enter. If the group window you want is already open, click it to make it active, or press Ctrl+Tab until it is highlighted (some of the open group windows may be on top of other group windows or group icons, hiding them).

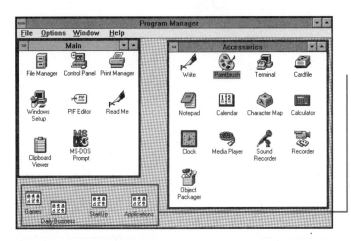

Group icons are usually located at the bottom of the Program Manager window.

If you can see the Program Manager window but it is partially hidden by another window, click it to bring it to the top. Or, if you can see the Program Manager icon, double-click it to restore it to a window.

Alternatively, press Alt+Tab until the Program Manager window or icon is selected (or until the name *Program Manager* appears in a box on-screen); then release both keys.

You also can activate the Program Manager by selecting its name from the Task List. To activate the Task List, double-click the desktop background or press Ctrl+Esc.

Starting Programs from a Group Window

When you open a group window, you see program item icons. Each icon represents a program and its associated data document. Some program item icons may start a program without loading an associated document.

With the mouse, start a program that is within the active group window by double-clicking the program item icon.

With the keyboard, select an icon and start its program by following these steps:

1. Press Ctrl + Tab↹ until the group window or icon you want is selected. If you are selecting a group icon, you must press ↵Enter to open the window after the icon is selected.

2. Press one of the arrow keys to select the program item icon you want.

3. Press ↵Enter to start the program and document represented by this icon.

Note: If you attempt to start a program with the program item icon but the program does not start, or if the program starts but an error message appears, check the program item properties for that program item icon. The name or directory path to the program or document files may be incorrect. Files may have been moved, renamed, or erased. Refer to the section "Redefining Groups and Program Items," further in this chapter, to learn how to correct these problems.

Arranging Group Windows and Icons

You can arrange group windows and icons manually as described in Chapter 3, or you can use commands in the Program Manager to arrange them.

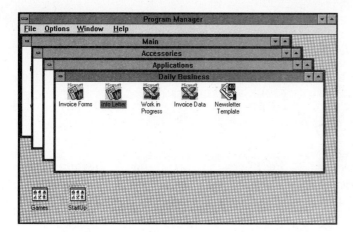

If you want a *cascading* arrangement of overlapping windows, choose the Window menu and select the Cascade command.

5

Cascading windows are useful when you want multiple windows open, but each window contains a large number of program item icons. When you have too many windows to fit in a single cascade, Windows creates a second cascade offset from the first.

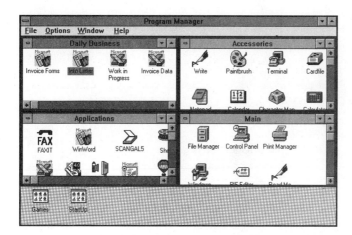

If you want a *tiled* arrangement so that you can see a portion of all open group windows, choose the Window menu and select the Tile command.

Tiled windows fill the screen with all open windows. Tiling is useful when you need access to the program item icons from multiple groups, and each group holds only a few program item icons.

To arrange the program item icons within a group window, select the group window by clicking it or pressing Ctrl+Tab until the window is active. Then choose the Window menu and select the Arrange Icons command. If you want

Manager

ige icons automatically whenever you activate a window,
ns menu and select the Auto Arrange command. A check
ide the Auto Arrange command when it is on. Choose Auto
urn it off.

....y Changing the Program Manager to an Icon

The Program Manager window and its group windows are like any other windows. You can use the techniques described in Chapter 3 to move and size the windows or to change them to icons or restore them to windows. An additional feature of the Program Manager, however, is that it can reduce itself to an icon whenever you start a program with a program item icon. This reduction gets the Program Manager quickly out of the way and gives you more room on the desktop.

To reduce the Program Manager to an icon whenever you start a program (unless the program starts as an icon), choose the Options menu and select the Minimize on Use command. Minimize on Use shows a check mark when it is selected. To turn off this command, choose it again. You can minimize the Program Manager also by selecting the Minimize button at the top of the screen.

Customizing Your Own Group Windows

You don't have to keep your programs only in the Applications group. You can create your own groups, putting together programs and associated documents you use for a specific job or at a specific time.

Note: Each program item icon refers to one program and either one associated data document or no associated data document.

Creating Your Own Group Windows

Before creating group windows, think about the tasks you perform each day. Divide them into related groups, such as writing proposals, managing a project, or contacting clients and sending follow-up letters. Each of these groups of tasks can become a group window. Within each group window, you can add program item icons that start programs and open documents.

To create your own group window, follow these steps:

1. Activate the Program Manager window.
2. Choose the **F**ile menu and select the **N**ew command.

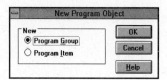

The New Program Object dialog box appears.

3. Select the Program **G**roup option.
4. Choose OK or press ↵Enter.

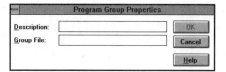

The Program Group Properties dialog box appears.

5. Select the **D**escription text box (it may be selected already) and type the title you want for this group window. Do not make an entry in the **G**roup File text box. The Program Manager automatically creates a GRP file extension for the group you are creating.
6. Choose OK or press ↵Enter.

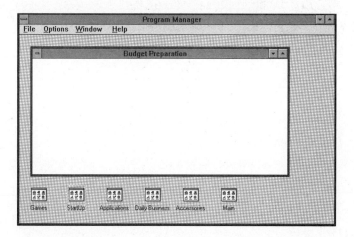

The new group window you create remains open on-screen.

If you are immediately going to add program item icons to the window, leave it open. The following section describes how to add the program item icons that start programs.

Adding Program Item Icons to a Group Window

After you create a new group window, you will want to add to it the program item icons that start programs and open documents.

Note: Microsoft recommends that you do not include more than 40 program items in a group. A large number of program item icons in a group window defeats the purpose of using the Program Manager for quick and easy program start-up.

To add program item icons to a group window, follow these steps:

1. Activate the group window in which you want to add the new program item icons. (Click the window or press Ctrl + Tab⇥ until it is on top.)
2. Choose the File menu and select the New command.
3. Select the Program Item option from the New Program Object dialog box that appears.
4. Choose OK or press ↵Enter.

The Program Item Properties dialog box appears.

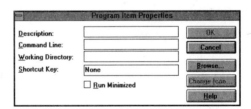

5. From this dialog box, select the Description text box (it may be selected already) and type the title for the program item icon.
6. Select the Command Line text box and type the path name, file name, and extension of the program for this item.

   If you are unsure of the path name or program's file name, choose the Browse button to display the Browse dialog box.

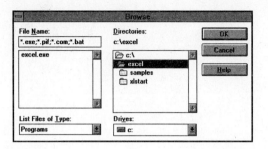

The Browse dialog box contains scrolling list boxes from which you can select the directory and file name of the program you want to start.

From the Directories list, select the directory containing the program you want. (To go to a higher, or parent, directory, choose an open folder above the directory you are in currently.) Select the program's file name from the File Name list. Choose OK or press ↵Enter. The path name and program name appear in the Command Line text box of the Program Item Properties dialog box.

7. If you want a data document (such as a spreadsheet, letter, or data file) to open with the program, type a space after the file name, followed by the path name and file name of the document. A completed command line, in which the program and document are in separate directories, might look as follows:

```
C:\EXCEL\EXCEL.EXE C:\BUDGETS\JUNE.XLS
```

8. In the Working Directory text box, enter the directory you want activated when you start this program (your program then defaults to this directory when you open or save files).

9. In the Shortcut Key text box, enter the shortcut key or key combination you want to press to activate the program (the program must be running).

   For example, if you assign the shortcut keys Ctrl+Shift+B to the June Budget program item icon, you can press Ctrl + ⇧Shift + B to activate the June Budget window, if it is running.

10. Normally, Windows chooses an icon to represent the program item you are creating. If more than one icon is available to represent the item, the Change Icon button becomes bold. Choose the Change Icon button to display the Change Icon dialog box.

5

In the Change Icon dialog box, you can select an icon to represent a program.

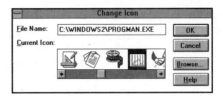

In the File Name text box, enter the Windows path, followed by the program name PROGMAN.EXE. Choose OK or press ↵Enter to display a variety of icons, and then click the icon you want. Choose OK or press ↵Enter to return to the Program Item Properties dialog box.

11. Select the Run Minimized option if you want the program to minimize to an icon upon start-up.

12. Choose OK or press ↵Enter to display your new program item icon in the group window.

The Program Item Properties dialog box displays your entries for the new program item.

In this example, the June Budget program item appears as a graph icon.

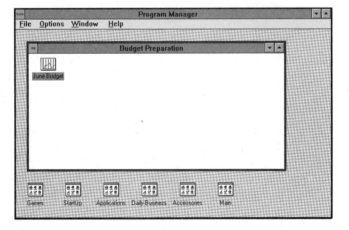

5

Note: By default, the Browse dialog box initially lists only program files (files with the extensions EXE, COM, BAT, or PIF). To see all the files in the directory, select the All Files option from the List Files of Type list box. You may need to create a program information file (PIF) for DOS programs that will not run with the automatic PIF settings. PIFs are explained in Chapter 20, "Running DOS Programs."

Redefining Groups and Program Items

After you gain experience with group windows and program item icons, you may want to change the names you have assigned them. Additionally, you may want to change the document associated with a specific program item icon.

To change the title of a group window, follow these steps:

1. Select the group icon whose name you want to change (you cannot change the name of an open group window).
2. Choose the File menu and select the Properties command.
3. Select the Description text box and type a new title.
4. Choose OK or press ⏎Enter.

To change the title of a program item icon or to change the program or document started by that icon, follow these steps:

1. Activate the group window containing the program item icon you want to change.
2. Select the program item icon.
3. Choose the File menu and select the Properties command.
4. Change the icon title in the Description text box, or change the program file name or document file name in the Command Line text box.
5. Choose OK or press ⏎Enter.

If you have used Windows Version 3.0, you may notice that some of the group and program names look different. Version 3.1 limits the width of names on-screen by *wrapping* the text to additional lines. This word-wrap feature is helpful because it can create names up to three lines (40 characters) long; however, you may have to shorten some of the group and item names to avoid obscuring other icons beneath them in the window.

5

Deleting a Program Item Icon

As your job changes or as you become more familiar with Windows and group windows, you may want to keep a group but move or delete a program item icon within that group. To delete a program item, follow these steps:

1. Activate the group window containing the program item icon you want to delete.
2. Select the program item icon you want to delete.
3. Choose the File menu and select the Delete command, or press Del.
4. Choose Yes when prompted to verify the deletion.

Note: This procedure removes only the icon from the group window. The program and data file remain on-disk.

Deleting a Group

If you no longer use any of the program items in a group window or you find the group window unnecessary, you can delete the entire group from the group window. To delete a group, follow these steps:

1. Select the group icon for the group you want to delete. (Do not select an open window.)
2. Choose the File menu and select the Delete command, or press Del.
3. Choose Yes to verify that you want to delete the group.

Note: Deleting the group removes the group window and its program item icons from the Program Manager window. The program files and data files remain on-disk.

Moving and Copying Program Item Icons

As you become more familiar with your work habits in Windows, or as your job changes, you may have to change groups, which may mean copying or moving program items between groups. You also may find that one program item would be useful in more than one group window (you can use it repeatedly for different jobs). Don't re-create the program item in the multiple groups; instead, move or copy the existing program item to other groups where it is needed.

With the mouse, you can move a program item icon to another group window by dragging the program item icon onto the destination group window and

108

then releasing the mouse button. You also can drag a program item icon onto a group icon, but you have no control over where the program item icon will be positioned within the new window.

With the keyboard, follow these steps to move a program item icon:

1. Activate the group window containing the program item icon you want to move.

2. Use the arrow keys to select the program item icon you want to move.

3. Choose the **F**ile menu and select the **M**ove command.

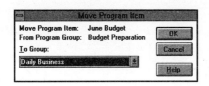

The Move Program Item dialog box appears.

4. Press ⟨Alt⟩+⟨↓⟩ to open the drop-down list box.

5. Press ⟨↑⟩ or ⟨↓⟩ to select the name of the destination group window.

6. Choose OK or press ⟨↵Enter⟩ to move the program item icon.

With the keyboard, copy a program item icon to another group window by following these steps:

1. Activate the group window containing the program item.

2. Press the arrow keys to select the program item icon you want to copy.

3. Choose the **F**ile **C**opy command.

4. Press ⟨Alt⟩+⟨↓⟩ to open the drop-down list box.

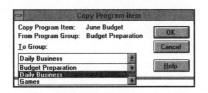

The drop-down list box appears in the Copy Program Item dialog box.

5. Press ⟨↑⟩ or ⟨↓⟩ to select the destination group name from the drop-down list box.

6. Choose OK or press ⟨↵Enter⟩

5

With the mouse, move or copy a program item icon to another group window by following these steps:

1. Arrange the two group windows so that both are visible.

2. Activate the group window containing the program item you want to copy.

3. To move the program item icon, drag it to the new group window. To copy the program item icon, hold down Ctrl and drag it to the new group window.

4. Release the mouse button.

5

Quitting the Program Manager and Windows

Be careful when quitting the Program Manager. When you close or quit the Program Manager, you also quit Windows.

When you are ready to quit Windows, follow these steps:

1. Save the data in your programs by using the File Save As command for each program. You do not need to quit the programs; they close when you quit Windows.

2. Activate the Program Manager.

3. Choose the File menu and select the Exit command.

The Exit Windows dialog box displays immediately before you exit Windows.

Note: If you want Windows to restart with the same arrangement of group windows in the Program Manager window, choose the Options menu and select the Save Settings on Exit command before you exit Windows.

110

Summary

In this chapter, you learned that the Program Manager acts as a central coordinator for programs. It eliminates your need to search through disks and directories to find and start a program and program document. Instead of searching, you can open the Program Manager and start a program (or a program with a document) by double-clicking the icon that represents the program. You can create program item icons that start a program and document. By grouping program item icons together and storing them in a group window, you can easily find and start programs and documents related to a specific task.

Some important points covered in this chapter are the following:

5

- ■ Four group windows come with the Program Manager: Accessories, Main, Games, and StartUp. During Windows installation, you can choose whether the installation program will also create an Applications group window.

- ■ You can start a program by opening its group window within the Program Manager and then double-clicking the program item icon that represents the program.

- ■ You can add program item icons to an open group window by choosing the File menu, selecting the New command, and selecting the Program Item option. You are then asked for a title for the icon and the location of the program that the icon represents.

- ■ You can change the names of group icons or program item icons and what they represent by selecting the group icon or program item icon you want to change, choosing the File menu, and selecting the Properties command.

From here, you can move to any of the chapters that describe how to operate Windows or DOS programs. Chapter 6, "Managing Files," explains how easily you can manage your disk files when you use the File Manager instead of DOS commands.

Managing
Files

6

The File Manager in Windows is a well-designed tool that acts like an office manager. It helps you organize your files, manage your disks, copy and erase files, and start programs.

You can maintain your files and directories more easily with the File Manager than with DOS commands. For example, with the mouse, you can copy all the files in a directory to a diskette by dragging the directory's icon onto the diskette drive icon and releasing the mouse button.

**Understanding
the File Manager**

**Selecting and
opening files and
directories**

**Controlling File
Manager windows
and displays**

**Managing files
and directories**

**Using drag and
drop**

**Managing
diskettes**

**Starting programs
and documents**

Key Terms in This Chapter

Memory	The electronic part of your computer where work and calculations are done on programs and data. The contents of the memory disappears when you turn off the power.
Disk	A hard disk or diskette device that magnetically stores programs and data. Data and programs on-disk do not disappear when you turn off the power. A hard disk is inside your computer and stores tens of millions of characters. A diskette is a flexible plastic disk that stores approximately one million characters.
Data	The information you create with the help of a computer program. Each type of program has its own unique way of saving data. Data for Windows programs is often referred to as a document. Data stored on-disk is stored in a file.
Program or *application*	Instructions that tell the computer how to operate and what to do when you give a command. For example, programs tell a computer to do word processing at one time and accounting at another time.
Storage	A mechanical part of your computer where data and programs are kept magnetically for long periods while the computer is off. Storage places also are referred to as disk drives, hard disks, or diskettes.
File	A collection of data or program information stored magnetically on a diskette or hard disk. A file is similar to a letter or report within a filing cabinet.
File name	A name by which you can find, open, or manage a file.
Directory	A method of segmenting a disk so that files and programs can be grouped together by type or category. Directories are similar to the drawers of a filing cabinet.
Subdirectory	A directory within another directory. Subdirectories are similar to folders within a drawer of a filing cabinet.
Directory tree	A diagram showing how directories and subdirectories are related.

6

Understanding the File Manager

Before you can understand the File Manager, you should understand how a computer keeps data while you work on it and how it stores data for long periods of time. After you understand the File Manager, managing your disks and the files they contain is much easier.

Understanding Storage, Memory, Files, and Directories

Your computer does all its calculations and work in electronic memory. Electronic memory is called RAM—*random-access memory*. RAM is where the computer program and Windows reside as they work; it is also where the data you are working on resides. If the computer loses electrical power, the data, program, and windows are lost from memory. Because electronic memory is limited in size and is volatile, the computer needs a way to store large amounts of data and programs for long periods of time.

6

Computers use magnetic storage to store programs and data for long periods of time or while the power is off. Magnetic-storage media can be *diskettes,* which are removable and don't contain much space, or *hard disks,* which are internal to the computer and have vast amounts of space. A *disk drive* reads data from a disk and writes data to a disk. Diskettes are identified by the drive letters A and B. Hard disks may be identified by the drive letters C, D, and so on. When you load a program or a data file, the computer places into electronic memory a copy of the information stored on-disk. If power is lost, the disk copy is still available.

You save your work in magnetic files, which store the data on a diskette or the hard disk. Over time, you may have hundreds or even thousands of files. Searching for a specific file among the thousands of file names that the File Manager displays could be very time consuming.

To make the job of finding files easier, hard disks are usually organized into *directories*. If you think of your hard disk as a filing cabinet, directories are like the drawers in the filing cabinet. In a filing cabinet, each drawer can hold a different category of documents. In a hard disk, each directory can hold a different category of files. The files in a directory can be programs or documents.

Within a filing-cabinet drawer, you can put hanging folders to further segment the drawer. Within a hard disk, you can segment a directory by putting *sub-directories* under it. Subdirectories also can hold files.

The process of organizing your hard disk is the same as organizing a filing cabinet. Using File Manager commands, you can create, name, and delete directories and subdirectories. (Some networks may prevent you from altering directory structures.) For example, you may want a WINWORD directory for word processing jobs. Within the WINWORD directory, you may want subdirectories with names such as BUDGETS, SCHEDULE, LETTERS, and REPORTS.

Starting the File Manager

To start the File Manager, you activate the Program Manager and open the Main group window.

The File Manager is located within the Main group window. Appropriately enough, the File Manager icon looks like a filing cabinet.

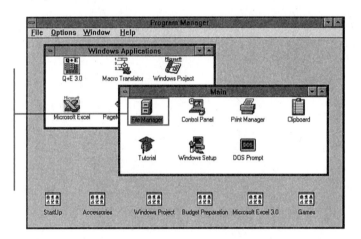

To start the File Manager after activating the Program Manager, activate the Main group window by clicking it or pressing Ctrl+Tab until it is selected. Open the File Manager by double-clicking its icon, or by pressing the arrow keys until the icon is selected and then pressing Enter.

Understanding the File Manager's Display

When you first start the File Manager, the directory window is divided into two parts. The *directory tree,* with the expanded structure of directories and subdirectories on drive C, occupies the left portion of the window. The *contents list* occupies the right portion of the window, showing the files in the selected directory.

Drive bar   Directory tree

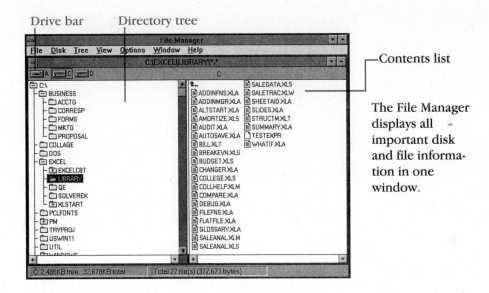

Contents list

The File Manager displays all important disk and file information in one window.

6

At the top of the directory window are icons that represent the available disk drives. Drives A and B are diskette drives; their icons look a little different than the icon for drive C, a hard disk drive (your own computer may have more or fewer drives). The title bar shows the directory path for the currently selected directory.

Notice the status bar at the bottom of the File Manager. At the right, the bar always displays the number and aggregate size of the files on the selected directory or subdirectory. When the directory tree portion of the window is active, the left portion of the bar shows the available storage on the active disk. When the contents list is active, this area shows the total size in bytes of the selected files. Scroll bars appear on the right and bottom sides of the directory tree and at the bottom of the contents list. If either segment contains more information than it can show at once, the scroll bar is shaded.

The directory tree contains miniature folder icons that represent directories and subdirectories, and the contents list shows files as icons that represent miniature documents. The first time you start the File Manager, a plus sign (+) in a directory or subdirectory icon indicates that additional subdirectories are inside the icon. A minus sign (–) in a subdirectory icon indicates that you can collapse the directory so that its directories do not show. An option in the Tree menu enables you to turn the plus and minus signs off and on. When the plus and minus signs are displayed, a folder icon without a plus or minus sign indicates that it contains no subdirectories. When a directory or subdirectory icon is expanded, you can see the subdirectories beneath it. Notice the vertical lines and indentations that show how directories and subdirectories are dependent.

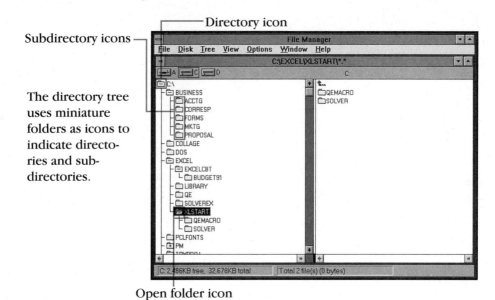

Subdirectory icons —

Directory icon

The directory tree uses miniature folders as icons to indicate directories and subdirectories.

Open folder icon

Open folder icons indicate that the directory's contents are shown in the contents list.

At any given time, only one area of the File Manager is active: the drive bar, the directory tree, or the contents list. The active area contains a selection with a dark background or with a dashed border, called the *selection cursor*. In the active area, you can use the arrow keys on the keyboard to move the selection. Press Tab to activate different areas.

The File Manager can display multiple windows at one time to show the file contents of any drive, directory, or subdirectory you select. Open multiple directory windows onto different disks and directories to make comparing disk contents or copying or deleting files easy.

Selecting and Opening Files and Directories

The File Manager follows the primary rule of all Windows programs: *Select, then do*. If you want to affect a file or directory in the File Manager, you must first find and select it. After you select a file, you can display information about it, open it, copy it, move it, or delete it. After you select a directory, you can find information about the directory contents, copy or move the directory, or open the directory to see the subdirectories or files it contains.

Selecting a New Disk Drive

Before you can work with files and directories, you must be in the correct disk drive. The disk drives available in your computer appear as icons above the directory tree. The current drive has an outline around it, and also has a dark background if the drive bar is active and the drive is selected. To change to a new drive with the mouse, click the drive icon you want to activate.

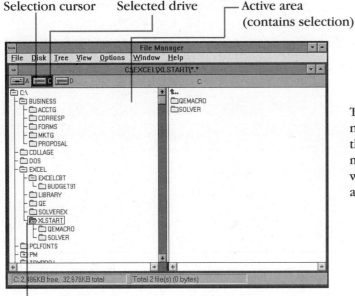

To change to a new drive with the keyboard, you must first notice which area is active.

Current directory

If the drive-icon bar is active, change to a new drive by pressing the left- or right-arrow key to move the selection cursor to a different drive; then press the space bar. The dark background moves behind the drive you selected. If the directory-tree area or contents-list area of the window is active, you can press Ctrl+*letter* to change to a different drive, where *letter* is the drive's letter.

119

Working with Networks

If your computer is connected to a local area network (LAN), you may have access to more than one hard disk drive. You can access those drives through Windows if you're logged on to a LAN. Each drive on the network shows up in the File Manager window as a disk icon different from the local-drive icons. When you select a network-drive icon, the path to that drive displays in the status bar at the bottom of the File Manager window. In a LAN environment your computer is referred to as a *workstation*.

Network drive icons

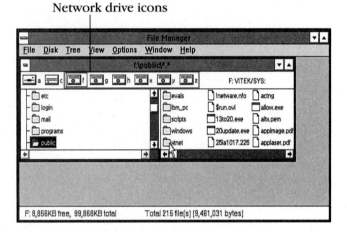

Drives on the network show up in the File Manager with a special network disk drive icon.

If you want to use network drives with Windows, you must log on to the network before you start Windows. See your network administrator for the procedure on how to log on to your network. When you connect your computer to a network, additional disk drives will be available. You can use these additional drives with Windows if you know the path name to the drive and the password.

Note: If you log on to the network before starting Windows in 386-enhanced mode, you may not be able to log off from the network while you are in Windows. To log off from the network, exit Windows and then type **LOGOUT**.

Note: If you want to use network drives with Windows, you must connect to the network before you start Windows. When you connect to the network and then start Windows, the Windows network commands will be available. If you start Windows without first connecting to the network, the network commands will be gray and therefore unavailable.

Note: If you connect a DOS program to a network while that program is running in Windows, disconnect from the network before quitting the program.

Expanding and Collapsing the Directory Structure

After you select a specific directory, you may want to see the subdirectories beneath it, or you may want to collapse the fully expanded directory structure so that you can see the directories at a higher level.

Collapsed directories do not show the subdirectories they contain.

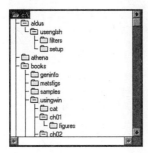

Expanded directories show the subdirectories located within them.

To expand or collapse a directory or subdirectory with the mouse, use one of the following mouse actions:

Action	Result
Double-click the plus (+) sign in a directory icon	Expands the directory one level.
Double-click the minus (–) sign in a directory icon	Collapses the directory.

Note: If the plus and minus signs don't appear, choose the Tree menu and select the Indicate Expandable Branches command.

To expand or collapse a directory or subdirectory with the keyboard, follow these steps:

1. Select the directory or subdirectory.

2. Press one of the following keys:

Key	Action
⌐-⌐	Collapses the selected directory.
⌐+⌐	Expands the selected directory one level.
⌐*⌐	Expands all subdirectories in the selected directory.
Ctrl + ⌐*⌐	Expands all subdirectories in the drive.
↵Enter	Collapses the selected expanded directory, or expands the selected collapsed directory.

To expand or collapse directories with the menu commands, follow these steps:

1. Select the directory or subdirectory.

2. Choose Tree and then one of these commands:

Command	Action
Expand One Level	Expands the selected directory to show all subdirectories at the next lower level.
Expand Branch	Expands the selected directory to show all lower subdirectories.
Expand All	Expands all subdirectories in the drive.
Collapse Branch	Collapses the lower-level subdirectories into the selected directory.

Selecting Directories

The directory window always displays in the File Manager window. It may be either in its own window or in an icon at the bottom of the File Manager window. The directory tree (in the left half of the File Manager) shows the hierarchical structure of the area of the disk you are currently examining.

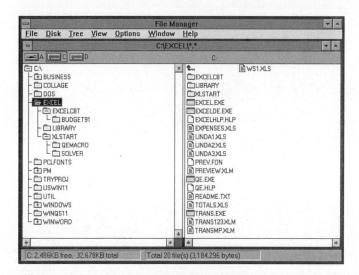

In this directory window, drive C contains an Excel directory containing three subdirectories: EXCELCBT, LIBRARY, and XLSTART. The EXCELCBT and XLSTART subdirectories contain additional subdirectories.

You can select only one directory at a time in a given directory window; however, you can open multiple directories so that each appears in its own directory window. Open more than one directory when you want to see the contents of multiple directories at one time. Also, copying files between directories is easier when you open a source-directory window and a destination-directory window.

To select a directory using the mouse, click the directory or subdirectory you want. If you cannot see the directory, use the vertical scroll bar in the directory tree to scroll it into sight before clicking. If you need files in a subdirectory, first open the directory above the desired subdirectory, as described later in this section.

To select a directory using the keyboard, follow these steps:

1. Press Tab⇥, if necessary, to activate the directory-tree area of the window.

2. If necessary, press Ctrl+*letter* to change to the drive containing the files you want.

3. Select a directory from the active drive by pressing one of the following keys or key combinations:

Key(s)	*Action*
↑ or ↓	Moves the selection to a directory or subdirectory above or below the currently selected directory.
→	Selects the first displayed subdirectory below the current directory.
←	Selects the directory one level above the current subdirectory.
Ctrl+↑	Selects the previous directory on the tree at the current indentation level.
Ctrl+↓	Selects the next directory on the tree at the current indentation level.
PgUp	Selects the directory at the top of the window.
PgDn	Selects the directory at the bottom of the window.
Home	Selects the root, or drive, directory.
End	Selects the last directory in the tree.
letter	Selects the next directory or subdirectory beginning with that letter.

Understanding File Icons

Each file within a directory window displays an icon that helps identify the type of file it is. These file shapes are given in the following list:

Icon	Type of File
	Open directory or subdirectory.
	Closed directory or subdirectory.
	Program or batch file with the extension EXE, COM, PIF, or BAT (choosing one of these files may start a program).
	Document file associated with a program (choosing one of these files starts the program that created the file).
	Other files.

6

Selecting Files

Files are listed on the right side of the directory window in the contents list. Before you can work on a file, you must select it. In some cases—when copying or deleting files, for example—you may want to select multiple files before giving a single command.

To select a single file with the mouse, click the file name. To select multiple adjacent files, click the first file, press and hold the Shift key, and click the last file. All files between the two files you clicked are selected.

In this example, eight files— totaling 82,783 bytes, as indicated on the status bar—are selected.

To select nonadjacent files, click the first file, and hold the Ctrl key as you click other files. If you want to retain current selections but deselect a file, press and hold Ctrl as you click the file you want to deselect.

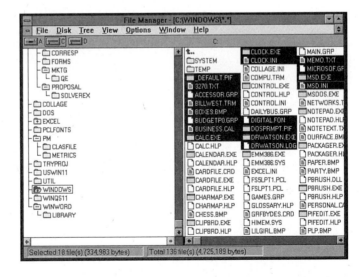

This window shows that 18 nonadjacent files are selected.

To select a single file with the keyboard, press the arrow keys to move the selection to the file name you want. If you want to select multiple adjacent files, move the selection to the first file, press and hold the Shift key, and press an arrow key.

To select nonadjacent files, select the first file, press Shift+F8, press an arrow key to move to the next file you want to select, and press the space bar. Move to the additional files you want to select and press the space bar. To deselect a file and retain other selections, move to the selected file and press the space bar. Press Shift+F8 to return to selecting individual files.

If you want to select all files with a given extension in a directory window, choose the File menu and select the Select Files command.

In the Select Files dialog box, you can type a specific extension and use DOS wild cards to select a particular group of files.

Note: To select all files in the window, choose the Select button while the Files box displays *.*. If you then want to deselect certain files, change the Files parameter and choose Deselect. Choose Close when you are done making your selections.

Controlling File Manager Windows and Displays

You will want to arrange your windows and files in a way that easily enables you to get your work done efficiently. Whether you are copying files between directories, making backup copies to a diskette, or deleting files, the display should provide easy access to your files. The following sections explain how to manipulate the appearance of the Windows display screen.

6

Opening and Selecting Directory Windows

You can have many directory windows that show the contents of individual directories. Each directory window can display a different directory—and even different disks.

Subdirectories   Path names

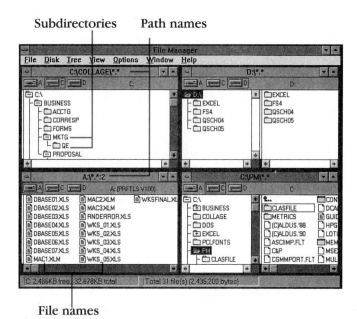

File names

Displaying multiple directory windows is a convenient way to move or copy files with the mouse.

6

To open a new directory window, choose the Window menu and select the New Window command. The new window will display the path name of the previously active window in the title bar, followed by a colon and the number *2,* which indicates that it is the second window associated with that particular directory. When you choose another directory, however, the path name in the new window changes.

Suppose that you have multiple directory windows open and want a specific window active. If you are using a mouse and can see the window you want, click a portion of that window to make it active. If you are using a keyboard, press Ctrl+Tab until the window you want is active, or select the Window menu and choose the name of the window you want from the menu.

Changing or Closing Directory Windows

Each directory window usually contains both a directory tree and a contents list; however, you can change this to another View option for any given window. For example, if you are doing intensive disk management, displaying multiple directory windows may make moving and copying easier. To save screen space, you could display one directory tree together with multiple contents lists, as follows:

1. With a single directory window open, choose the View menu and select the Tree Only command.

2. For each directory whose contents you want to see on-screen, open a new window. Select a directory for each window.

3. Select each window in turn and choose the View menu and select the Directory Only command. Leave one window in tree-only format and use it to sort through the directory structure quickly.

4. Choose the Window menu and select the Tile command if you want to see all the open directory windows at all times. If you have more than a few windows open, you might have to maximize the File Manager window to work effectively.

Directory windows are document windows, so you can use the mouse or Document Control menu to resize, move, or close each window. Activate the window you want to change by clicking it or by pressing Ctrl+Tab until its title bar is highlighted.

To close the active directory window using a shortcut key, press Ctrl + F4.

The directory tree and contents list exist side by side in the directory window. You can move the dividing line between the two sides (making one side wider and the other narrower) by positioning the mouse pointer over the left edge of the contents window so that the pointer turns into a two-sided arrow. Click and hold the left mouse button to display a *vertical split bar*. Drag the bar where you want the two sides to split, and release the mouse button. Alternatively, choose the View menu and select the Split command. Press the left- or right-arrow key to move the vertical split bar, and press Enter when the split is where you want it.

Arranging Directory Windows and Icons

You can arrange directory windows and icons in three ways. You can arrange them by manually positioning them, by cascading them to show all the window titles, or by placing them in tiles to show each window's contents.

6

129

To arrange directory windows in a cascade, choose the Window menu and select the Cascade command.

The active window becomes the top window in the cascade.

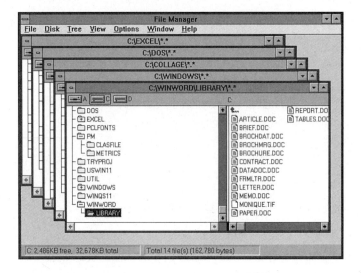

To arrange directory windows in tiles so that the screen is evenly divided by the windows, choose the Window menu and select the Tile command.

The active window becomes the window at the top left in the File Manager.

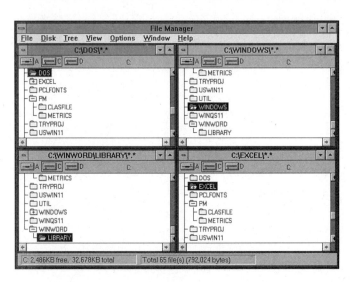

When windows are arranged by cascading or by tiling, you can still use the mouse or each directory window's Control menu to move a window manually. Chapter 3 describes how to move or size a window.

To reduce directory windows to icons inside the File Manager window, click the minimize button (the down arrow) at the right end of the window's title bar. (If a window is maximized, restore it to display the minimize button by clicking the restore icon, a two-pointed arrow.) Alternatively, press Alt+hyphen (-) and select the Minimize command.

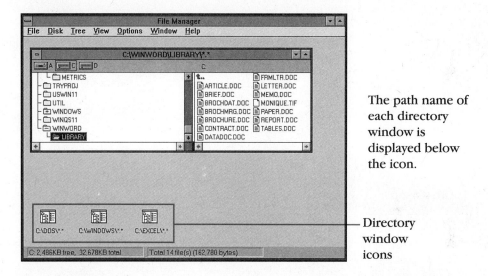

The path name of each directory window is displayed below the icon.

Directory window icons

6

You can maximize a directory icon by double-clicking it; or you can press Ctrl+Tab until you select it, and then press Enter.

Specifying File-Display Formats

You can specify what file information appears in the contents list. The two most common displays use View Name to show only the file names and extensions, and View All File Details to show all file information.

To display file information, follow these steps:

1. Activate the directory window you want to change.

2. Choose **V**iew and then select one of these options:

Command	Description
Name	Displays only names and directories.
All File Details	Displays the name, size, date and time last saved, and file attributes.

In this example, the contents list displays only file names.

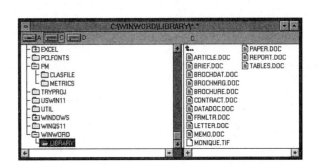

In this example, the contents list displays all file details: the name, size, date, and time that each file was last saved (attributes are displayed, but hidden by the right edge of the window).

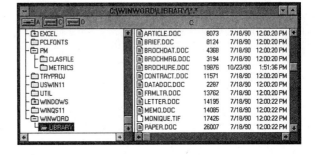

You also can view **P**artial Details, selecting the details you want to view; or you can view by File **T**ype, selecting only certain types of files to view.

Note: Some programs may not automatically update the information in the File Manager. As a result, you may activate the File Manager and not see a file you have just saved. Update the window manually with the **W**indow **R**efresh command.

Sorting the Display of Files and Directories

Finding files or directories can be easier when you reorganize the contents of a directory window. By default, the File Manager lists files alphabetically by name, but you can order the window contents alphabetically by file extension, by file size, or by the date the file was last saved.

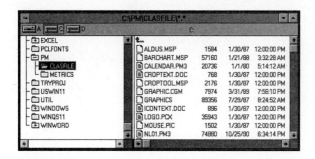

Sorting by name makes files easier to find.

6

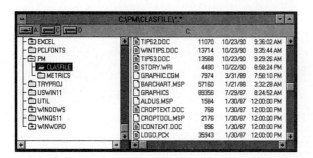

Sorting by date makes old files that can be deleted easier to find.

To sort a window's contents by name or file type, follow these steps:

1. Activate the directory window you want to sort.

2. Choose View and then select one of these options:

Command	Description
Sort by Name	Sorts the display alphabetically by file name.
Sort by Type	Sorts the display alphabetically by file extension and then by file name.
Sort by Size	Sorts by file size, from largest to smallest.
Sort by Date	Sorts by last date saved, from newest to oldest.

133

Note: You do not have to display the file date or size in the directory window to sort by those attributes. If you want to see the file's date and size in the directory window, choose the View menu and select All File Details or Partial Details.

Managing Files and Directories

Working without a hard disk can be difficult, but working *with* one can be confusing. Problems arise if people do not erase unnecessary files or if they do not make backup copies of files in case the hard disk fails.

This section shows how easily you can erase unwanted files, copy files to other disks, or move files between directories. You also learn how to make your own directories so that you can organize your disk to fit your work and data.

Understanding File Names and Wild Cards

File names and directory names have rules you must follow if you want to find your data again. If you do not name a file or directory correctly, you may not be able to find it later, or the name may not be accepted.

File names and directory names have three parts:

filename.ext

File name   File extension

Separator

The file name or directory name can contain from one to eight characters. The separator is always a period. The file extension can have as many as three characters. In most cases, Windows programs add their own file extensions to the file names you type. Therefore, you don't need to add a file extension when you are asked for the file name of a data document. If you do not type a file extension, do not type a period.

For file names and directory names, you can use any of the alphabetical and numerical characters. You also can use all the symbols across the top of your keyboard (! @ # $ % ^ & ( ) _ -) except the asterisk (*), plus sign (+), and equal sign (=). If you start a file name with a symbol, the name appears at the top of alphabetical lists of files (such as the list that appears in the Open dialog box)—this can be a good trick for naming files you use frequently and want to find quickly.

134

Note: Never use a space in a file name or directory name. Include a period only if you are using a file extension.

Searching for Files or Directories

Losing a file is frustrating and wastes time. With Windows, you can search disks or directories for file names similar to the file you have misplaced.

To search for a file by its name or part of its name, follow these steps:

1. Select the disk drive you want to search.

2. Select the directory (if you want to search a single directory).

   If you are not sure of the specific directory that contains a file, select the parent directory of all subdirectories that might contain the file.

3. Choose the File menu and select the Search command.

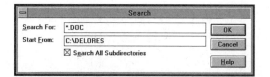

The Search dialog box appears.

4. In the Search For text box, type the name of the file for which you are searching. You can use a pattern of DOS wild cards in the file name.

5. To search all directories on the current disk, specify the root directory in the Start From text box. To search through all files on drive C, for example, type C:\ in the text box.

   By default, Windows searches all subdirectories beneath the directory you select. To search only the specified directory, turn off the Search All Subdirectories option.

6. Choose OK or press ⏎Enter.

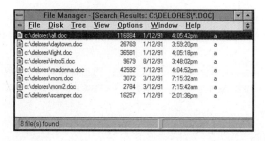

The Search Results window displays the paths and file names of all files that match the pattern for which you were looking.

135

When you use wild cards in a name pattern, remember that the * wild-card character finds any group of characters in the same or following positions. The ? wild-card character matches any single character in the same position as the ?. For example, use the pattern E*.XLS to search for all file names beginning with E and ending with the three-letter extension XLS. Use the pattern BDGT???.* to search for file names that start with BDGT and are followed by exactly three characters. Any file extension will match the *.

If you know the directory in which a file is located and the date or time at which the file was last saved, but don't know the file name, you can display the time and date of all the files in the directory window to help you locate the file. Choose the View menu and select the All File Details command to show the time and date on which files were last saved. This command also indicates file attributes at the right.

Copying Files or Directories

Copying files is an important part of keeping your work organized and secure. When organizing files, you may have to copy a file to make it accessible in two locations. A more important reason for copying files is security. The hard disk on which you store files is a mechanical device and has one of the highest failure rates among computer components. Should your hard disk fail, the cost of replacing the disk is insignificant compared to the cost of the hours you worked accumulating data on the disk. One way to prevent the loss of this data is to make a set of duplicate files.

If you ever have used DOS commands to copy files, you will find that copying files and directories is much easier with Windows and a mouse. All you do is drag the files you want to copy from one location in the directory window to another.

Follow these steps to copy files with a mouse:

1. Make sure that both the source and destination are visible.

   The *source* is the item you want to copy. It can be a file icon in the contents list; a directory icon from the contents list or the directory tree; a directory window; a directory icon; or a disk-drive icon.

   The *destination* can be a directory icon in the directory tree or the contents list. It also can be a directory icon at the bottom of the File Manager window, or a disk icon at the top of the File Manager window.

2. Activate the part of the screen containing the source file or directory. If you are copying an entire directory, you can activate either the directory tree or the contents list.

3. Select the directory, file (or files), or subdirectory (or subdirectories) you want to copy.

   In the directory tree, you can select only a single directory or subdirectory to copy. In the contents list, however, you can select multiple files or subdirectories to copy simultaneously. When you copy a directory or subdirectory, you copy all the files and subdirectories it contains.

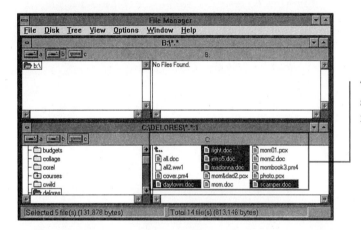

This example shows that several files are selected.

6

4. Drag the directory or the individual files to the destination. Press and hold Ctrl if the destination is on the same disk as the source files. (If you do not press and hold Ctrl, you *move* the files rather than copy them.)

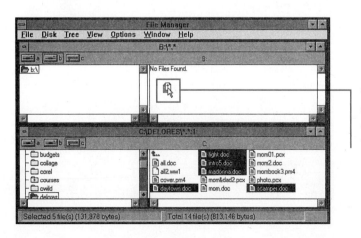

The selected files are dragged to the destination window.

5. When the file icon is over the destination, release the mouse button; release ⟨Ctrl⟩ if you were using it.

   If the destination has a file with the same name as the file you are copying, you are asked to confirm that the destination file can be replaced by the copy.

Note: Copy all the files from a directory by selecting all of them before you drag them to the new destination. To select all the files, click the first file, press and hold ⟨⇧Shift⟩, and click the last file. Alternatively, press ⟨Ctrl⟩+⟨/⟩.

To copy files with the keyboard, follow these steps:

1. Activate the window containing the files or directories you want to copy.

2. Select the files or directories you want to copy, using the techniques previously described in this chapter. To select a large number of files, use DOS wild cards in step 4, following.

3. Choose the File menu and select the Copy command.

The Copy dialog box appears with the selected file or files in the From text box.

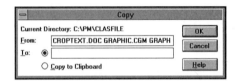

4. If you want to specify a group of files to copy, type a file-name pattern in the From text box. Use the DOS wild cards * and ? to specify groups of similar file names. To specify an entire directory, type the directory path, such as C:\BUDGET.

5. In the To text box, type the path name (drive and directory) of the destination location.

6. Choose OK or press ⟨↵Enter⟩.

   If the destination has a file with the same name as the file you are copying, you are asked to confirm that the destination file can be replaced by the copy.

You can copy a file to the Clipboard by choosing the Copy to Clipboard option in the Copy dialog box. Then you can embed the file in a document by opening the document and choosing the paste command. To learn more about linking and embedding, see Chapter 10, "Using Object Linking and Embedding."

Moving Files or Directories

You can move files just as easily as you can copy them. Moving files puts the files in a new location and removes the originals from the old location. You move files when you need to reorganize your disk. You can move files or directories to a new directory or disk. Moving a directory moves that directory's files and subdirectories.

To move files or directories with the mouse, follow these steps:

1. Make both the source and destination directory windows visible.

2. Select the files or directories you want to move.

3. Drag the file or directory to the destination if the destination is on the same disk. If the destination is on a different disk, press and hold Alt as you drag. (If you do not press and hold Alt, you *copy* the files rather than move them.)

4. Release the mouse button when the icon or file is over the destination.

5. If you are asked to confirm the move, consider whether you are copying or moving and how the files will change. Then choose Yes to complete the action, No to stop a single move, or Cancel to cancel all moves.

   The following table summarizes the mouse actions you take to move or copy files with the mouse.

Desired Action	Mouse Action
Copy to a different disk	Drag
Copy to the same disk	Ctrl + drag
Move to a different disk	Alt + drag
Move to the same disk	Drag

To move files or directories with the keyboard, follow these steps:

1. Activate the source and destination directory windows.

2. Select the files or directories you want to move.

3. Choose the File menu and select the Move command.

The Move dialog
box appears, with
the selected file
or files in the
From text box.

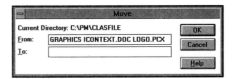

4. If you did not select files in step 2, type in the From text box the names of the files you want to move. Use DOS wild cards if you want to move multiple files with similar names.

5. In the To text box, type the destination path name, drive, and directory.

6. Choose OK or press ⏎Enter.

Printing Files

If a document is associated with a program, you can print the document from the File Manager (see the section "Associating Documents with a Program," further in this chapter). To print a file, select the file, choose the File menu, and select the Print command. When the Print dialog box appears, choose OK or press Enter. The file prints on the current default printer.

Creating New Directories

Creating new directories on your disk is like adding new drawers to a filing cabinet. Creating new directories is an excellent way to reorganize or restructure your disk for new categories. After you build directories and subdirectories, you can put existing files in them with the File Move and File Copy commands.

To make new directories, follow these steps:

1. Activate the directory tree area if necessary. (This step is not necessary if you want to put the new subdirectory under the currently selected directory.)

2. Select the directory under which you want a new subdirectory.

3. Choose the File menu and select the Create Directory command.

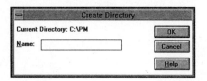

The Create
Directory dialog
box appears.

4. Type the name of the new directory in the Name text box. The name
   can be from one to eight characters long.

5. Choose OK or press ⏎Enter.

Adding new subdirectories is like growing new branches on a tree. New
subdirectories must sprout from existing directories or subdirectories. If you
want to create multiple layers of subdirectories, first create the directories or
subdirectories that precede the ones you want to add.

Renaming Files or Directories

Unless you do everything perfectly the first time, you will find times when you
want to rename a file or directory.

To rename a file or directory, follow these steps:

1. Select the file from a directory window.

2. Choose the File menu and select the Rename command.

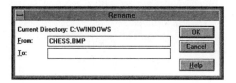

The Rename
dialog box
appears.

3. In the To text box, type the new file name.

4. Choose OK or press ⏎Enter.

Note: If you enter a file name that already exists, a warning message box
appears after you choose OK or press Enter. You can then type a unique file
name.

Deleting Files or Directories

Delete files or directories when you want to remove old work from your disk. Deleting files makes more storage space available on-disk. Deleting directories that don't contain any files makes very little difference in storage space, but it does unclutter your directory tree.

Unless you have prepared your hard disk with special software, you cannot recover files or directories after you delete them. Be very careful to select only the files or directories you want to delete. If you aren't sure about deleting files or directories, turn on the warning messages by choosing the Options Confirmation command and selecting the File Delete and Directory Delete boxes.

Note: Be careful that you do not accidentally select a directory when selecting files you want to delete. If you select a directory and choose File Delete, you delete all the files in the directory and the directory itself. Deleting entire directories can be convenient, but it also can be a real surprise if it is not what you wanted to do.

To delete files or subdirectories, follow these steps:

1. Activate the directory window containing the files you want to delete. Activate the directory tree area if you want to delete only directories.

2. Select the files or directories you want to delete; alternatively, you can use wild cards in step 4.

3. Choose the File menu and select the Delete command, or press Del.

The Delete dialog box appears.

4. If you have many files to delete, use DOS wild cards in the Delete text box.

For example, type *.* in the Delete text box to specify every file in the current directory.

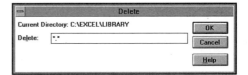

142

5. Choose OK or press ⏎Enter. If you are asked to confirm deletions, choose Yes after the Confirm File Delete dialog box appears, or choose Yes to All to confirm deletion of several files at once.

Displaying Warning Messages

During some File Manager operations, a warning message appears that asks you to confirm the action about to take place. For example, if you select a directory and choose File Delete, you are asked to confirm the deletion of each file and the removal of the directory. If you find the confirmation messages annoying, you can turn them off. Be aware, however, that these warning messages can prevent you from making mistakes; if you turn off the messages, you have no warning for potentially hazardous actions.

You turn off warning messages by first choosing the Options menu and then selecting the Confirmation command.

After the Confirmation dialog box appears, you can deselect the type of warning message you want to turn off.

Following is a list of the options in the Confirmation dialog box and the messages whose display they control:

Option	Action Confirmed by Message
File Delete	Each file being erased.
Directory Delete	Each directory being erased.
File Replace	One file being copied over another.
Mouse Action	Any mouse action involving moving or copying.
Disk Commands	Each disk being copied over or formatted.

As you gain more experience and confidence with your computer, you may want to turn off these messages. If you are a beginner or have difficulty accurately positioning the mouse, you may want to leave these messages on.

Using File Manager's Drag and Drop Feature

The File Manager's *drag and drop* feature enables you to print files, link or embed files, start programs, and create program item icons by using the mouse to drag File Manager icons or file names. You also drag and drop icons to copy and move files, as described in "Copying Files or Directories" and "Moving Files or Directories" in this chapter.

To use the drag and drop feature, you need to be able to see two things on-screen: the File Manager, displaying the file you want to drag; and the destination, displaying the icon, document, or window where you want to drag the file. Before you drag and drop File Manager icons, arrange windows on-screen so that you can see both, and so that when you click the File Manager to select the file you want to drag, the File Manager window doesn't hide the destination window. You should arrange windows side by side so that they don't overlap.

6

As you drag a file from the File Manager, a moving icon appears on-screen. Its appearance changes to reflect its status: as you are moving or copying the file, the icon appears as a blank page; if you cannot drop the file where the icon currently is located, the icon looks like a circle with a line through it; if you are printing, linking, or embedding the file, or if the file will start a program or create a program item icon, the icon appears as a page with a plus sign (+) inside it.

Note: Be careful. Because the moving icons for printing, linking, embedding, starting a program, and creating a program item icon all look the same, you must be sure that the icon is where you want it to be before you release the mouse button. If you want to print a file, for example, but accidentally drop the icon onto an open document that supports object linking and embedding, you will link or embed the file instead of printing it.

Printing with Drag and Drop

To use the the drag and drop feature to print a file, you must be able to see the file you want to print in the File Manager, and you must be able to see the Print Manager program icon or window on your desktop. If the Print Manager is not running, start it from the Program Manager.

You also must be sure that the document you want to print is associated with its program. To learn how to associate a document with its program, refer to "Associating Documents with a Program," further in this chapter.

To use the drag and drop feature to print a file, follow these steps:

1. Start the File Manager and locate the file you want to print.

2. Start the Print Manager.

3. In the File Manager, position the mouse pointer over the file you want to print. Click and hold the left mouse button, and drag the file onto the Print Manager window or icon.

   As you drag, the moving icon changes. When the icon appears as a page with a plus sign inside it, and you are sure the icon is on top of the Print Manager window or icon, release the mouse button.

If a message box appears, telling you that no association exists for the file or that the association data is incomplete, you must complete the association or use the program to print your file.

Linking and Embedding with Drag and Drop

One of the easiest ways to link or embed a file into a document is to drag the file name from the File Manager onto the open document. Using this method, embedding a file creates a package, which appears in the document as an icon. You can edit the package, or you can double-click the icon to start the program containing the embedded file. To learn more about linking and embedding and the Object Packager, refer to Chapter 10, "Using Object Linking and Embedding."

To use the drag and drop feature to embed a file, follow these steps:

1. Start the File Manager and locate the file you want to embed.

2. Start the program containing the document into which you want to embed a file, and open the document. Display the location in the document where you want to insert the embedded file.

3. In the File Manager, position the mouse pointer over the file you want to embed. Click and hold the left mouse button, and drag the file onto the document, positioning the icon where you want to embed the file.

   As you drag, the moving icon changes. When the icon appears as a page with a plus sign inside it, and you are sure that the icon is positioned where you want to embed the file, release the mouse button.

To use the drag and drop feature to *link* a file rather than embed it, follow the preceding steps, but hold Shift+Ctrl while you drag the file.

6

Starting a Program with Drag and Drop

If a document and its program are associated, you can open a document and start its program from the File Manager by dragging the document file name onto the program name. (To learn about associating a document and a program, see the section "Associating Documents with a Program," further in this chapter.) You need two windows in the File Manager: one displaying the document file you want to open; and another window displaying the program with which the document file is associated. An easy way to display these windows is to open a new window (choose the Window menu and select the New Window command) and then tile the two windows (choose the Window menu and select the Tile command). Then display the document file in one window and the program in the other window.

To use the drag and drop feature to start a program and a document, follow these steps:

1. Start the File Manager and locate the document file you want to open.

2. Open a second File Manager window, and display the program you want to start. The program must be associated with the document you want to open.

3. In the File Manager, position the mouse pointer over the document file you want to open. Click and hold the left mouse button, and drag the file onto the icon representing the program you want to start.

   As you drag, the moving icon changes. When the icon appears as a page with a plus sign inside it, and you are sure the moving icon is on top of the icon representing the program you want to start, release the mouse button.

Creating a Program Item Icon with Drag and Drop

You can quickly create a program item icon in the Program Manager by dragging a file from the File Manager onto the Program Manager. If you drag a program file, the program item icon represents only a program; if you drag a document file, the program item icon represents the document and its associated program.

To use the drag and drop feature to create a program item icon, follow these steps:

1. Start the File Manager and locate the file for which you want to create a program item icon in the Program Manager. The file can be a program or a document.

2. Display the Program Manager, and display the group window where you want to create the program item icon.

3. In the File Manager, position the mouse pointer over the file for which you want to create a program item icon. Click and hold the left mouse button, and drag the file into the group window in the Program Manager, positioning the moving icon where you want the program item icon to appear.

   As you drag, the moving icon changes. When the icon appears as a page with a plus sign inside it, and you are sure that the icon is inside the group window where you want your program item icon to appear, release the mouse button.

6

Managing Diskettes

The File Manager includes commands not only for copying files, but also for copying entire diskettes. You can copy one diskette to another—even if you have only a single disk drive. You also can use the File Manager to format new diskettes.

Copying Diskettes

Make duplicate copies of diskettes whenever you need to store diskette information off-site in a secure location or when you need a duplicate of original program diskettes. To duplicate a diskette, follow these steps:

1. Protect the original diskette by attaching a write-protect tab (5 1/4-inch diskettes) or sliding open the protect notch (3 1/2-inch diskettes).

2. Insert the original diskette (source diskette) into the source disk drive.

3. Insert the diskette to receive the copy (the destination diskette) into the second disk drive. If you don't have a second disk drive, don't be concerned.

4. Choose the Disk menu and select the Copy Disk command.

If you have only
one disk drive,
the Confirm Copy
Disk dialog box
appears, warning
you that all
information will
be lost from the
destination
diskette.

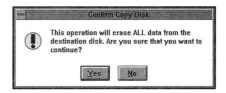

Select Yes or press ⏎Enter) in the Confirm Copy Disk dialog box. You
are prompted to switch the source diskette and destination diskette
in and out of the single drive. Windows prompts you to exchange
diskettes.

If you have two
disk drives, the
Copy Disk dialog
box appears.
Proceed with the
following steps.

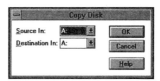

5. In the Source In list in the Copy Disk dialog box, select the drive letter
   for the source drive.

6. In the Destination In list in the Copy Disk dialog box, select the drive
   letter for the destination drive (even if it is the same as the source
   drive).

7. Choose OK or press ⏎Enter) in the Copy Disk dialog box.

To use the Copy Disk command, both of your diskettes must be identical. For
example, you cannot copy from a 3 1/2-inch diskette that holds 1.4M of data to
a 5 1/4-inch diskette that holds 1.2M of data. To duplicate a diskette, you
therefore use the same source and destination disk drive. File Manager
prompts you to switch diskettes when necessary. Labeling your diskettes
before you begin may help.

Note that copying diskettes always completely erases the destination diskette.
Before you use the Copy Disk command, make sure that you will not delete
important files from the destination diskette. The Copy Disk command
formats the destination diskette if it is not already formatted.

Formatting Diskettes

When you buy new diskettes for storing data and files, you cannot use them until you format them (some diskettes come already formatted). Formatting prepares diskettes for use by a specific type of computer. Formatting is like preparing a new, blank book for use by adding page numbers and making a blank table of contents. Part of the process of formatting is checking for bad areas on the diskette's magnetic surface. If any bad areas are found, they are identified so that data is not recorded there.

Note: If a diskette has data on it, formatting completely erases all existing data, which you cannot retrieve. Never format a program diskette.

To format a diskette, follow these steps:

1. Put the diskette you want to format in the disk drive.

2. Choose the **D**isk menu and select the **F**ormat Disk command.

The Format Disk dialog box appears.

3. In the **D**isk In list box, select the disk drive containing the diskette you want to format.

4. Select the appropriate diskette size in the **C**apacity list box.

5. If you want to assign a label to the diskette, type the label in the **L**abel text box.

6. Select **M**ake System Disk if you want to use the diskette to start your computer. Do not use this option unless it is needed, because the system files use storage space on the diskette that can otherwise be used for data.

7. Select **Q**uick Format to save time if you're reasonably sure that the diskette does not have bad areas.

8. Choose OK or press ⏎Enter. A message box warns you that formatting will erase all data on the diskette. If you're sure, choose **Y**es.

9. After this diskette is formatted, you are given the chance to format additional diskettes.

It's a good idea to format an entire box of diskettes at one time and put a paper label on each formatted diskette. This system notifies you that open boxes contain formatted diskettes; paper labels confirm that the diskettes are formatted.

Starting Programs and Documents

Using the Program Manager and group windows is the best way to start frequently used programs. As described in Chapter 5, "Grouping Programs and Documents," you can use the Program Manager to group together a frequently used program and an associated document to make them readily accessible.

On some occasions, however, the program you want to start may not be in a group window. When this happens, start the program directly from the File Manager. You can start any program from the File Manager.

Starting a Program

Starting a program from the File Manager is easy with the mouse: just open the directory window containing the program and double-click the name of the program.

Starting a program with the keyboard is almost as easy: open the directory window containing the program, select the program name, and press Enter. Alternatively, select the program, choose the File menu, and select the Open command.

Program file names end with EXE or COM. You may have to start some DOS programs by double-clicking a file with the extension BAT or PIF, as described in Chapter 20 "Running DOS Programs."

You can specify some document or data files so that they start a program. Choosing this associated document or data file starts the program and also loads the document or data, as discussed in the following section.

If a program is associated with a specific file extension, you can start a program by using the same starting procedures on a document file. Select the document file in the File Manager and press Enter, or choose the File menu and select the Open command.

You also can use the File Manager's drag and drop feature to start a document and its associated program. See the previous section in this chapter: "Using File Manager's Drag and Drop Feature."

Associating Documents with a Program

One of the convenient features of Windows is its capacity to start a program when you choose an *associated* document. An associated document is a document that runs with a particular program. When you choose an associated document, Windows finds the program that runs the document, starts the program, and then loads the document. Many Windows programs create associations for their own files by modifying the Windows WIN.INI file when the program is installed. In addition, you can add associations of your own to fit your programs and work habits.

6

Following are some programs and their common document file extensions:

Program	*Extensions*
Microsoft Excel	XLS, XLC, XLM
Microsoft Word for Windows	DOC, DOT
Aldus PageMaker	PM4
Lotus 1-2-3	WKS, WK1

To associate a document file with a specific program, follow these steps:

1. Activate the directory window containing the data file (document file) you want to associate with a program.

2. Select the name of the file you want associated. Windows associates document files to programs by checking the file extension of the document file.

3. Choose the File menu and select the Associate command. The Associate dialog box appears.

Some Windows programs automatically translate or convert data documents from other programs. Here, Lotus 1-2-3 files are being associated with the Microsoft Excel program located in C:\EXCEL.

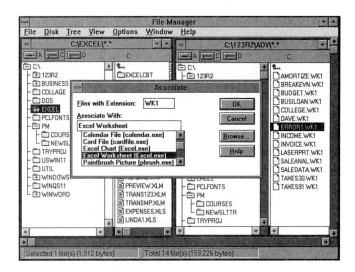

6

4. Scroll through the list box attached to the **Associate With** text box to find the name of the program you want to associate with files that have the extension shown in the **Files with Extension** box. Select the program name, if you find it. If you do not find the program name, proceed to the next step.

5. If you do not find the program name in the **Associate With** list, type the full path and file name of the program. If you're not sure of the correct directory path, you can search for it by choosing the **Browse** button.

6. Choose OK or press ⏎Enter.

Some DOS programs, such as WordPerfect, can use any file extension for their data documents. In such cases, you must associate each of the different file extensions you use with WordPerfect to the WordPerfect program.

Some DOS programs may not start directly from an associated file; some programs may start but not run as efficiently as they should. If this is true for the document files you are using, refer to Chapter 20 "Running DOS Programs," for information on creating a PIF.

Summary

The File Manager may help you sleep better at night. Having backup copies of your important document files stored in a location separate from your computer has a very calming effect.

The File Manager is also an excellent tool for organizing your hard disk. Use the File Manager to keep directories and files organized, just as you would organize a filing system. And don't let old and unused files overwhelm you. They waste space, slow down performance, and are hard to get rid of when you don't remember what they contain.

The following important points were covered in this chapter:

■ A directory window is divided into two parts: on the left side of the window is a directory tree showing the directory structure of your hard disk, and on the right side of the window is a contents list showing the files in the selected drive or directory.

■ You can open multiple directory windows to help you copy, move, or compare directory contents.

■ Using the mouse with the File Manager makes file management easy. Just click the files you want to copy, move, or delete. Then choose the appropriate command.

■ You can associate document files with programs so that choosing a document automatically starts the program and loads the document.

If you haven't learned about the Program Manager yet, return to Chapter 5, "Grouping Programs and Documents," and learn how the Program Manager can save you time starting programs and opening documents you use frequently.

To learn how to customize Windows to use the desktop background and colors you want, to add new printers, and to change mouse speed, move to the next chapter, "Customizing Your Work Area."

If you want to begin using Windows with the Windows and DOS programs you have used in the past, turn to Chapter 19, "Integrating Multiple Programs," and to Chapter 20, "Running DOS Programs."

6

Customizing
Your
Work Area

With the Control Panel, you can customize Windows in many ways to suit your needs. You can change the appearance of your desktop and windows by changing the windows colors or adding a pattern or picture to the desktop background. You can add a screen saver that replaces your screen with a different image when you're not using it. You can reset the date or time, or choose a different format for the date or the time.

You can change two aspects of the keyboard: how long you must hold down a key before it repeats, and how fast it repeats when you hold down a key. You can reverse your mouse buttons to make the mouse easier to use if you're left-handed. You can add and configure ports and drivers for printers and multimedia equipment. You can turn the sound on or off.

Key Terms in This Chapter

Color scheme	A predefined set of colors for Windows backgrounds, title bars, edges, and other elements.
Wallpaper	The bit-mapped (BMP) drawing used as a backdrop behind windows on the desktop.
Screen saver	A program that replaces your screen image with a moving pattern when you haven't used your computer within a specified time period—thus helping to prevent an image from "burning into" your computer screen.
Driver	The software that enables Windows to use special features in your printer or other device.
Printer port	A physical connection point (LPT1, LPT2, LPT1.DOS, or LPT2.DOS) where most printers are connected.
Communication port	A physical connection point (COM1 or COM2) where modems (telephone connections) and some printers are connected.

Operating the Control Panel

The Control Panel is a program item icon within the Main group window of the Program Manager. The tools contained in the Control Panel enable you to customize many features in Windows.

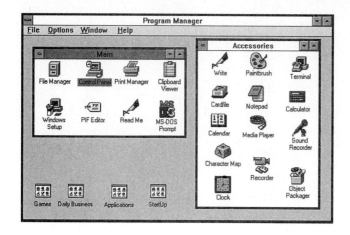

To open the
Control Panel,
you first open the
Program Manager
and then activate
the Main group
window.

You then double-click the Control Panel icon, or select it with the arrow keys
and press Enter.

Each icon within
the Control Panel
window repre-
sents a program
you can use to
customize a
Windows feature.

The 386 Enhanced icon is displayed only when you are running in 386-
enhanced mode. You also will see a Network icon if you are connected to a
network, and a MIDI Mapper icon if your computer is equipped for multimedia.

Table 7.1 lists the Control Panel's programs and describes their purposes.

Table 7.1
Control Panel Tools

Tool	Description
Color	Changes the colors in the desktop and parts of windows.
Fonts	Adds or removes printer fonts, screen fonts, and TrueType fonts.
Ports	Defines your serial communication ports.
Mouse	Adjusts mouse speed and left or right button control; sets mouse trails.
Desktop	Changes the patterns or pictures of the desktop background.
Keyboard	Changes the keyboard's rate of repeating.
Printers	Adds or removes printers, configures printers, and sets the default printer.
International	Changes displays for different languages, dates, times, and currencies.
Date/Time	Resets the computer's date and time.
386 Enhanced	Indicates how programs share the power when Windows is in 386-enhanced mode. (This icon appears only when you are running in 386-enhanced mode.)
Drivers	Installs and configures drivers for peripherals such as sound boards and pen tablets.
Sound	Turns the warning beep on or off; assigns sounds to events.

You start one of these customizing programs by double-clicking its icon, or by pressing the arrow keys to select the icon and then pressing Enter. As an alternative, you can start a Control Panel program by choosing the Settings menu and selecting the program you want to start from the list that appears.

This chapter discusses all the tools listed in table 6.1 except Fonts and 386 Enhanced. The Fonts program is explained in Chapter 9, "Managing Fonts and TrueType." The 386 Enhanced program is discussed in Chapter 20, "Running DOS Programs."

158

Customizing Windows with Color

You can customize the color schemes that define colors for window elements. The colors you use can make working with Windows programs more enjoyable than working with monochrome DOS programs.

Using Existing Color Schemes

Windows comes with a list of predefined color schemes that determine the colors of your windows, desktop, and screen elements. You can use them or create your own. To select from one of the predefined color schemes, follow these steps:

1. Choose the Color icon from the Control Panel.
2. Click the down arrow at the right side of the Color Schemes drop-down list box.
3. Select a named color scheme from the list.

7

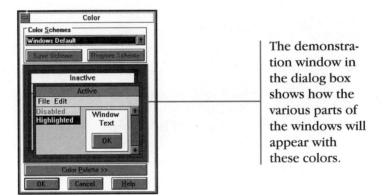

The demonstration window in the dialog box shows how the various parts of the windows will appear with these colors.

4. Select a different color scheme, and choose OK or press ⏎Enter. Choose Cancel to retain the existing color scheme.

Creating New Color Schemes

You can apply your own colors to different parts of the windows. To choose colors, follow these steps:

159

1. Open the Control Panel and choose the Color icon.

2. Select the Color Schemes list and then select the color scheme that most closely matches the colors you want.

3. Choose the Color Palette button.

The right side of the Color dialog box expands to show the palette of Basic Colors.

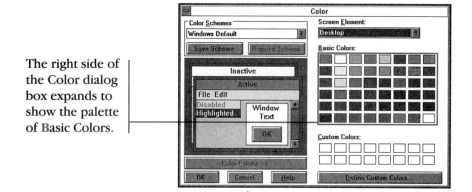

7

4. Click the part of the demonstration window that you want to change, or select from the Screen Element drop-down list the part of the window that you want to change.

5. Click the color you want from the Basic Colors palette. Or press Tab⇥ to move to the Basic Colors palette, press the appropriate arrow key to move to the color you want, and then press space bar to select the color. The selected color appears with a dark border around it, and the demonstration window changes to the new color you selected.

6. Repeat steps 4 and 5 until the demonstration window shows the colors you want in your programs.

7. If you want to save the color scheme, choose the Save Scheme button and type a color scheme name, which will appear in the Color Schemes box. If you do not save your custom color scheme, you cannot return to that color scheme if you change schemes later. Choose Cancel if you do not want to use the color schemes you created.

If Windows seems a little sluggish when it "redraws" your screen, try using only solid colors to speed up the screen redraw rate. Using the same color for the active and inactive borders also can save screen redraw time.

Note: Windows programs use, as standards, a solid title bar for an active window and a shaded title bar for an inactive program.

To remove a color scheme, select it from the Color Schemes drop-down list box, choose the Remove Scheme button, and then choose the Yes button for confirmation.

Blending Your Own Colors

If you are feeling artistic, you can create your own palette of colors to use instead of (or in addition to) the basic colors offered. You can store as many as 16 custom-blended colors in the Custom Colors palette. After storing them there, you can use the color schemes to color window elements, just as you would use the Basic Colors palette. You can define colors in one of two ways: by pointing at the color you want and clicking the mouse button; or by specifying the quantities of hue and light that make up the color. Using either technique, you can produce a rainbow of colors.

To blend your own colors, follow these steps:

1. Open the Control Panel and choose the Color icon.

2. Choose the Color Palette button to expand the Color dialog box.

3. Click the Custom Colors box in which you want to store your custom color. Or press Alt + C, use the arrow keys to move to the box in which you want to store your custom color, and then press **space bar**. The selected box has a dark border around it.

4. Choose the Define Custom Colors button.

Color Refiner box   Color Refiner cursor

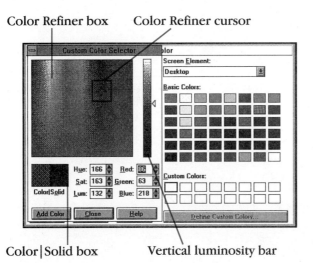

The Custom Color Selector window is displayed on top of the Color dialog box.

Color|Solid box   Vertical luminosity bar

7

161

You can blend your own colors in this window, or select a blended color from the Color Refiner box, and add them to the Custom Colors palette in the Color dialog box.

5. Choose the color you want from the Custom Color Selector window by clicking that color in the Color Refiner box, or by dragging the Color Refiner cursor to the color you want. Adjust the luminosity (brightness) for that color by dragging the arrowhead up or down along the side of the vertical luminosity bar.

   To blend a color with the keyboard, select the **Red**, **Green**, or **Blue** box and adjust its value by typing a new number. Then select **Hue**, **Sat** (Saturation), or **Lum** (Luminosity) and adjust its value by typing a new number. The Color|Solid box shows how the color will appear in a large area.

6. If you want a solid color rather than a blended color, select **Solid** by double-clicking the solid side of the Color|Solid box or by pressing [Alt]+[O].

7. Choose the **Add** Color button to add the color to the box you selected in the Custom Colors palette.

8. Return to step 5 if you want to add more colors to the palette; otherwise, choose the **Close** button to close the Custom Color Selector window.

Use the **Custom** Colors palette to select new colors for window elements in the same way that you choose them with the **Basic** Colors palette.

Customizing the Desktop

 In addition to changing the colors of your windows, you can change the pattern or picture of the desktop behind the windows.

The desktop behind windows and icons can have a color, selected from the Color dialog box; a pattern, selected from the Desktop dialog box; or a picture, selected also from the Desktop dialog box. A picture that covers the desktop is known as *wallpaper*. (Even when wallpaper is on the desktop, the desktop color and pattern affect its appearance.)

Customizing the Background Pattern

Your desktop—the part of your screen outside all windows—doesn't have to be a solid color or shade. Instead, you can decorate it with a pattern. Windows comes with predefined patterns you can select, or you can create your own. The color of the pattern is the same as the color for window text (usually black), which you define in the Color dialog box.

To choose an existing desktop pattern, follow these steps:

1. Choose the Desktop icon from the Control Panel.

The Desktop dialog box appears.

2. Select the Pattern Name drop-down list and then select a pattern from the list.

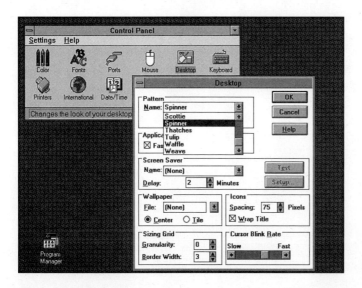

Many predefined background patterns are available, such as the Spinner pattern shown here.

3. Choose OK or press ⏎Enter to add the pattern to the desktop.

You must use a mouse to edit or create new patterns. To edit an existing pattern or create a new pattern, follow these steps:

1. Choose the Desktop icon.

2. Choose the Edit Pattern button.

The Desktop-Edit Pattern dialog box appears.

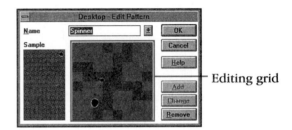

Editing grid

3. Select the Name drop-down list box and then select a pattern name from the list (to modify an existing pattern) or type a new name (to create a new pattern).

4. In the editing grid, click where you want to reverse a dot in the pattern. Watch the Sample box to see the overall effect.

5. Continue to click in the editing grid until you are satisfied with the pattern.

6. If you started with a predefined pattern that you want to change, choose the Change button. Or if you created a new pattern and typed its name in step 3, choose the Add button to save that pattern.

   To remove an unwanted pattern from the list, select the pattern from the list and choose the Remove button. Confirm the deletion by choosing the Yes button that appears. The Remove button is available only immediately after you select a pattern name.

7. Choose OK or press ⏎Enter to return to the Desktop dialog box. Choose OK or press ⏎Enter again to close the Desktop dialog box.

Displaying Graphics as a Desktop Background

You can customize the desktop so that it displays a picture or graphic. For the desktop wallpaper, you can use the drawings that come with Windows, create your own drawings with Windows Paintbrush, or scan photographs with a scanner.

Wallpaper uses files stored in bit-map format, with a BMP extension. To use these files as wallpaper, you must store them in the Windows directory. You can edit existing BMP files or create new ones with Windows Paintbrush. Save in the Windows directory the BMP file that you want to use as wallpaper.

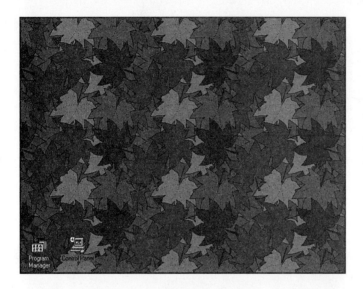

The LEAVES.BMP file produces a colorful desktop background.

7

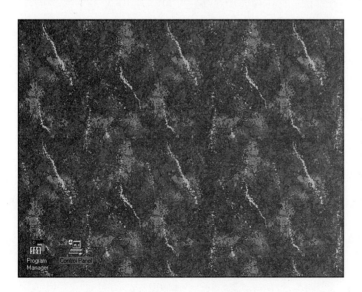

The MARBLE.BMP file offers another desktop background.

Note: Using wallpaper for a desktop background takes up more memory than a plain background. If your computer is low on memory, do not use a wallpaper desktop.

To display an existing BMP file as the desktop background, follow these steps:

1. Choose the Desktop icon from the Control Panel.
2. Select the Wallpaper File drop-down list box and then select a BMP file from the list.
3. Select Center to center the image in the desktop or Tile to fill the desktop with the image. If you center the image, the surrounding desktop displays the selected pattern. Tile uses multiple images to fill the background.
4. Choose OK or press ⏎Enter.

If you have selected a pattern and wallpaper, the pattern appears behind the names of program icons. If the pattern makes the names hard to read, select None from the Pattern Name list.

7

Using the Screen Saver

The Screen Saver replaces your desktop with a picture or patterns when you don't use your computer for a specified period of time, helping to prevent a static screen image from "burning into" your monitor. Pressing any key or using the mouse restores the desktop to the screen. Several screen saver images are included with Windows 3.1, which you specify in the Desktop program.

To use a screen saver, follow these steps:

1. Choose the Desktop icon from the Control Panel.
2. Select the desired screen saver from the Screen Saver Name list.
3. Select the Screen Saver Delay box and specify the Delay time—the number of minutes that pass before the screen saver activates—by entering a number or clicking the up or down arrow to increase or decrease the number.
4. Select the Setup button to specify other parameters for the selected screen saver.

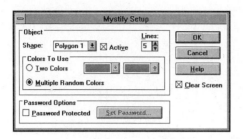

Each screen saver, such as Mystify, has different parameters that you can set up, but all have password protection. (Blank Screen has no setup parameters.)

5. Choose OK or press ↵Enter) to save the Setup parameters.

6. Select Test to see how the screen saver works.

To disable the screen saver, type **0** as the Delay time or set the Screen Saver Name to None.

Some screen savers have a password option that you can enable. When enabled, you must correctly enter the password before the normal desktop is restored to the screen.

To set the password for the screen saver, follow these steps:

1. From the Desktop dialog box, select a screen saver name and then select Setup.

2. Select the Password Protected check box, or press Alt)+P) and then **space bar.** You also can press Tab⁺) to move to the Password Protected check box, and then press **space bar.**

3. Choose Set Password.

The Change Password dialog box appears.

4. If a password already exists, type it in the **O**ld Password text box. An asterisk (*) appears for each character you type.

5. Enter the **N**ew Password and then **R**etype New Password. Both must match and can be up to 20 characters, including spaces. Passwords are not case-sensitive.

6. Select OK; if the passwords match, you are returned to the screen saver's Setup dialog box.

After the screen saver activates, you must type the correct password to return to your screen; otherwise, an error dialog box is displayed. Make sure that you don't forget the password!

If you are switching to a new screen saver and your old screen saver had a password, you must enter the old screen saver's password before you can enter a new password.

Switching Quickly Between Programs

When you're running several programs at the same time, called *multitasking*, you want to be able to switch between them as quickly as possible. The Desktop dialog box gives you the option to turn on a "fast switching" option. With this option turned on, you can hold down the Alt key and repeatedly press the Tab key to cycle through currently running programs. While you're holding down the Alt key, Windows displays only the program names—not entire screens—which is how it saves time. When you release the Alt key, the program screen appears. (You can still press Alt+Tab to switch between running programs with the "fast switching" option turned off, but it's slower.)

To turn on fast switching, follow these steps:

1. Choose the Desktop icon from the Control Panel.

2. From the Desktop dialog box, select the Fast "Alt+Tab" Switching option.

3. Choose OK or press ⏎Enter.

You can press Alt+Esc to return to your original program.

Adjusting the Insertion Point's Blink Rate

If the insertion point blinks at an annoying rate, you can change it by choosing the Desktop icon and selecting the Cursor Blink **R**ate box. Drag the box in the scroll bar or press the left- or right-arrow keys to adjust the rate. Dragging or clicking left slows the blink rate; dragging or clicking right speeds the blink rate. Watch the sample insertion point for the blink rate you prefer.

Resetting the Date and Time

 Choose the Date/Time icon from the Control Panel to reset the date or time currently set in your computer; for example, you may need to use this tool when daylight savings time comes or goes. Many programs use the Date/Time information when they automatically add the date or time to a file.

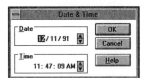

When you choose the Date/Time icon, the Date & Time dialog box appears.

Select either the Date or the Time option. Press Tab to cycle through the month, date, and year values in the Date box, and through the hour, minute, and second values in the Time box. Click the up or down arrows to scroll rapidly to the date or time you want. Alternatively, with the keyboard, press Tab to move to the Date or Time box, and then type the new number. Choose OK or press Enter to reset the date and time.

You can change the format for the date and time using the International program. See the later section "Customizing International, Date, Time, and Number Settings."

Changing Keyboard Speed

 You can change the rate at which characters repeat when you hold down a key. To change the rate, choose the Keyboard icon from the Control Panel.

7

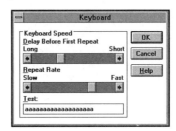

When you choose
the Keyboard
icon, the Key-
board dialog
box appears.

To change the length of the delay before a key repeats when you hold it down, select Delay Before First Repeat scroll bar and click the left or right arrows, or press the left- or right-arrow key to change the delay factor. Move left to increase the delay; move right to shorten the delay. A long delay means you have to hold down a key a long time before it repeats.

To change the rate at which a key repeats as you hold it down, select the Repeat Rate scroll bar and click the left or right arrows or press the left- or right-arrow key. Move left for a slower repeat rate; move right for a faster repeat rate.

Test the repeat delay and repeat rate by selecting the Test box and holding down a character key.

Changing the Mouse

To switch the mouse buttons or to speed up mouse reaction times, choose the Mouse icon.

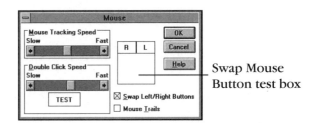

The Mouse dialog
box appears.

Swap Mouse
Button test box

To change the speed at which the pointer moves, select the Mouse Tracking Speed scroll bar. Then click the left or right arrows or press the left- or right-arrow key to change the pointer's speed. Move left for a slower mouse; right for a faster mouse.

If you want a faster or slower double-click response rate, select the Double Click Speed scroll bar. Click the left or right arrows or press the left- or right-arrow key to change the response.

Double-click the TEST box to test the new rate (its colors reverse when you double-click successfully).

If you are left-handed, you may want to select the Swap Left/Right Buttons check box to switch the mouse buttons. If you swap the left and right buttons, you always should click the right mouse button instead of the left mouse button. For example, you must press the right mouse button to deselect the Swap Left/Right Buttons option.

The L and R in the Swap Mouse Button test box change places when you select the Swap Left/Right Buttons option. Position the mouse pointer inside the test box and click the left and right mouse buttons to highlight the L and R boxes; in this way, you can test the mouse buttons.

7

Select the Mouse Trails check box to leave a trail of arrows when you move the mouse. This feature is especially handy for laptop and notebook computer displays, which sometimes redraw the screen too slowly to track a moving mouse pointer.

Turning Sound On or Off

When you are tired of listening to your computer announce your mistakes with a beep, or when you need to hide the fact that you're playing a game, you can turn off the computer's beep. To turn off the beep, choose the Sound icon, deselect the Enable System Sounds check box, and choose OK or press Enter. This action disables all beeping for all programs used in Windows.

If your computer is equipped with a sound board (as are all multimedia PCs), you also can assign sounds to various computer events, such as pressing the asterisk key. (These options are grayed if you don't have a sound board.)

To assign sounds to events, follow these steps:

1. Choose the Sound icon from the Control Panel.

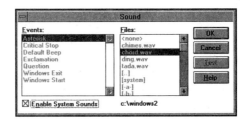

The Sound dialog
box appears.

2. From the Events list, select the event to which you want to assign sound.

3. From the Files list, select the sound you want to assign to the event you selected.

4. Choose Test to hear a sample of your sound.

5. Choose OK or press ↵Enter.

7

Customizing International, Date, Time, and Number Settings

 Most Windows programs can switch between different international character sets, time and date displays, and numeric formatting. Use the International icon in the Control Panel to choose these settings.

The International dialog box changes date, time, currency, and numeric formats for different languages and countries—including English. Use this program to change time, date, and numeric formats, even if you're not changing the language.

Make sure that you select both the correct language and the correct country.

To set up Windows for one of the predefined country formats, languages, and measurement systems, follow these steps:

1. Choose the International icon from the Control Panel.

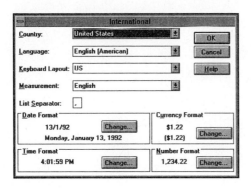

The International dialog box appears.

2. Select the Country drop-down list box and select a country from the list.

3. Select the Language drop-down list box and select the language you want to use. This selection can affect sorting in a program.

4. Select the Keyboard Layout drop-down list box and select the international keyboard style your keyboard uses. This selection enables you to use keyboard characters specific to your language.

5. Select the Measurement drop-down list box and select either English or Metric.

6. Select the List Separator text box and type the character you want to use to separate lists. This selection is useful in programs such as Microsoft Excel in which you might want to separate a list of arguments used in math functions.

7. Choose OK or press ↵Enter.

When you choose a different country and language, the sample formats change in the Date Format, Currency Format, Time Format, and Number Format boxes.

You can change the format for display of dates, times, currencies, and numbers. For example, you can change the order that the month, date, and year appear in a date. These formats apply wherever dates, times, currencies, and numbers are displayed or formatted automatically. Word for Windows, for example, can automatically display a date and time in a page header or footer; Microsoft Excel can automatically format numbers.

To change the number format, follow these steps:

1. Choose the International icon from the Control Panel.

2. Select the Number Format box by clicking its Change button or by pressing Alt + N.

The International-
Number Format
dialog box
appears.

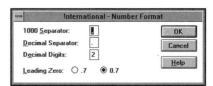

3. Select the formatting options you want:

Option	Description
1000 Separator	Changes the character separating thousands.
Decimal Separator	Changes the character separating decimal and whole numbers.
Decimal Digits	Changes the number of decimal digits displayed.
Leading zero	Specifies whether a leading zero displays in front of decimal numbers.

4. Choose OK or press ↵Enter.

Change the currency format in the same way you changed the number format. Select the Currency Format option, or simply click its Change button.

The International-
Currency Format
dialog box
appears.

Then select options from the drop-down list boxes or type your entries. The options you can select are as follows:

Option	Description
Symbol Placement	Selects from a drop-down list the placement and spacing of the currency symbol.
Negative	Selects how you want negative currencies to appear.
Symbol	Specifies the currency symbol. (You may have to select a different keyboard to type the character you want.)
Decimal Digits	Specifies the number of decimal digits you want.

When you change date and time formats, you change how dates and times display in the Windows accessories and in the defaults in most Windows programs. In most cases, choosing the country changes the date and time to that country's standard. If you want to make specific changes, however, choose the Date Format or Time Format option from the International dialog box and select from the lists presented.

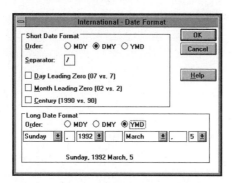

When you choose the Date Format option or click its Change button, the International-Date Format dialog box appears.

Notice that the formatting group at the top of the dialog box is for short dates, such as 5/22/92, and the bottom formatting group is for long dates, such as May 22, 1992. With many Windows programs, you can format dates so that they spell out the full month or day. The date format options are listed in table 7.2.

175

Table 7.2
Date Format Options

Short Date Option	Description
Order	Changes the order in which month (M), day (D), and year (Y) display.
Separator	Changes the character separating the month, day, and year (for example, the / in 5/22/92).
Day Leading Zero	Changes how day digits display (for example, 5/1/92 or 5/01/92).
Month Leading	Changes how month digits display (for example, 5/1/92 or 05/1/92).
Century	Changes how years display (for example, 1992 or 92).

Long Date Option	Description
Order	Changes the order in which month (M), day (D), and year (Y) display.
Day of the week	Changes between full day name or abbreviated name.
Separator	Separates day of the week from the month (usually a comma).
Month	Changes from full month name, abbreviation, or numeric (with or without leading zeros).
Separator	Separates month from day of the month (usually blank).
Day of the month	Changes between numeric day formats (with or without leading zeros).
Separator	Separates day of the month from the year (usually a comma).
Year	Changes between numeric year formats (the last two or all four year digits).

7

Note: When you change the long date format, notice the sample date at the bottom of the dialog box. (No sample date appears for short date formats.)

Be careful not to miss the Separator text boxes. These boxes contain the character you want to appear between segments of long dates. Type the character you prefer to use (usually a period, a slash, or a comma).

The long date format boxes are dynamic; they change order as you select different MDY orders. If you use a keyboard, move between the boxes by pressing Tab. Display a drop-down list in the selected box by pressing Alt+down arrow.

When you choose the Time Format option or click its Change button, the International-Time Format dialog box appears.

7

Select new time formats the same way you selected date formats. The time format options are listed as follows:

Option	Description
12 hour 00:00–11:59	Displays times from a 12-hour clock.
12 hour text box	Specifies the 12-hour time format you want (for example, am and pm or AM and PM).
24 hour 12:00–23:59	Displays times from a 24-hour clock.
24 hour text box	If you select the 24-hour format, use this text box to specify a time zone abbreviation (like EST for Eastern Standard Time).
Separator	Specifies the character separating time segments.
Leading Zero	Selects leading zeros for times.

After selecting Number Format, Currency Format, Date Format, or Time Format options, choose OK or press Enter to accept your changes and return to the International dialog box. Choose OK or press Enter to confirm your changes to the International dialog box, or choose Cancel to discard your changes.

Adding and Setting Up Printers

 With the Control Panel, you can add printers that were not initially installed with Windows. To do this, you probably will need your original Windows installation diskettes or the diskette from your printer's manufacturer that contains the Windows printer driver for your printer. (A *printer driver* tells Windows how to control your printer and use the printer's features.)

To install a new printer, follow the procedures in the next sections, in the order in which the procedures appear. The basic steps to install a new printer, detailed in the next sections, are:

1. Add the printer driver files to the hard disk.
2. Assign a port to the printer.
3. Change the timeout settings.
4. Select printer settings for layout and features.
5. Make the printer the default printer.
6. Specify any network connections, if needed.

Before you install a new printer, be sure to plug in the printer and connect it to your computer with a printer cable. Most printers use a parallel connection on the computer port called LPT1, but check your printer's documentation to make sure that you use the correct cable and port.

In many printer dialog boxes, the Cancel and Close buttons are interchangeable. You will see a Close button when you have made a change in the dialog box; you will see a Cancel button when you have not made a change.

Installing a New Printer

To install a new printer, follow these steps:

1. Choose the Printers icon.

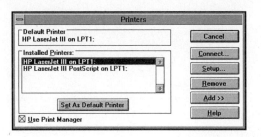

The Printers
dialog box
appears.

2. Choose the Add button.

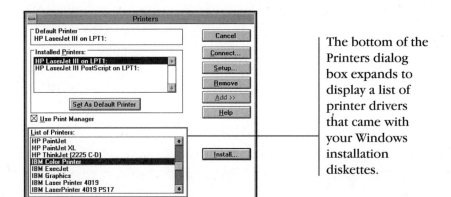

The bottom of the
Printers dialog
box expands to
display a list of
printer drivers
that came with
your Windows
installation
diskettes.

7

The printers listed in the List of Printers list box are those with which all Windows programs work.

3. Select the printer you want to install from the List of Printers list box.

If your printer's model is not listed, select an earlier model from the manufacturer's same family of printers. If you have a diskette from your printer's manufacturer containing the Windows driver for your printer, select Install Unlisted or Updated Printer (which appears out of alphabetical order at the top of the list).

4. Choose the Install button.

If you are installing a new driver you have not used before or if you are updating an existing driver, Windows displays the Install Printer dialog box, prompting you to insert into drive A the diskette containing the printer driver.

A message at the top of the box specifies which diskette to insert.

5. Insert the diskette requested.

   This diskette is either one of your initial installation diskettes or a manufacturer's diskette with a new printer driver. If the printer driver files are located on another disk or directory, change the path name and choose OK or press ⏎Enter. (For help locating the correct path, choose Browse, locate the driver file, and then choose OK or press ⏎Enter.)

6. If Windows needs additional screen fonts for this printer, you are prompted to insert the diskette containing the fonts. Insert the diskette requested and choose OK or press ⏎Enter.

   Windows adds the printer driver to the Installed Printers list and connects the driver to the LPT1 port.

   Proceed to the following sections to continue the installation and configuration.

Note: If you don't have a printer driver for your printer, call Microsoft or the printer's manufacturer to see whether one has been written, or use a printer driver for an earlier model of the same printer. Another alternative is to select the Generic/Text Only printer from the List of Printers list box. This selection enables most printers to print, but it does not use any enhanced features, such as graphics, fonts, styles, or sizes.

Connecting and Setting Up the Printer

After you add your printer to the Installed Printers list, you need to connect the printer to a printer port. (By default, Windows connects all new printers to LPT1; if this port is correct, you can bypass this step.) After you tell Windows which port the printer is connected to, you can set up the printer for special features, such as font cartridges, paper size, bins, and printing orientation.

180

To configure the printer for a port, follow these steps:

1. Choose the Printers icon from the Control Panel, unless the Printers dialog box is already open.

2. From the Installed Printers list box, select the printer you want to configure.

3. Choose the Connect button.

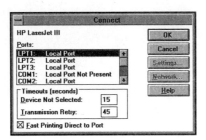

The Connect dialog box appears.

4. Select from the Ports list box the hardware port (the connection for the printer cable) to which the printer you selected is connected. (Most printers are connected to LPT1. If you are not sure, experiment with other ports or call your dealer or PC administrator.)

   Note: If you have a parallel printer connected to LPT1 or LPT2, but the printer does not work when you select either port from the Ports list, select instead LPT1.DOS or LPT2.DOS from the Ports list.

5. Select Timeout settings as defined by your printer manual or the README.TXT file for your printer. Read the file with Notepad. If no information is available for your printer, leave these settings as they are.

6. Choose OK or press ⏎Enter to save the Connect settings.

   Now that you have connected the printer, set it up for the special features available for that printer.

7. Choose the Setup button to display your printer's printer-setup dialog box.

   Note: You can change the printer setup at a later time while you are in a Windows program by using the program's File Print Setup command.

Because each
printer has
different capabili-
ties, each printer-
setup dialog box
may be different.
This example
shows the printer-
setup dialog box
for the HP
LaserJet III
printer family.

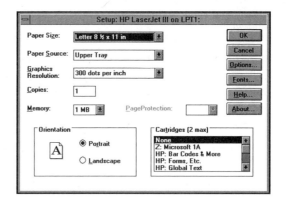

Typically the printer-setup dialog box asks you to specify the paper
size and source, the number of copies you want to print, and the page
orientation (*portrait* for vertical printing; *landscape* for horizontal
printing). Depending on the printer, you have other options as well.
For example, you must select the font cartridges you plan to use with
your HP LaserJet III printer.

Note: If your printer accepts two font cartridges, you can select both
cartridges from the Cartridges list: click one cartridge, scroll to the
second one, and hold down the Shift key as you click the second
cartridge.

8. Select the printer options you use most frequently, and then choose
   OK or press ⏎Enter. You return to the Printers dialog box.

9. To leave the printer inactive, choose the Close button. To use the
   printer when you return to Windows, follow
   the next procedure.

Selecting the Default Printer

Windows can have multiple printers connected to the same port, but only one
printer can be the default printer. You can set the default printer with these
steps:

1. Choose the Printers icon if the Printers dialog box is not already
   displayed.

2. From the Installed Printers list, select the printer you want to use as
   the default printer.

7

3. Choose Set as Default Printer.

4. Choose the Close button.

Note: You can have two different printers installed on the same port, but only one printer is the default printer. You can use your Windows program's File Print Setup command to select the printer to be used by that program.

Connecting to and Disconnecting from a Network Printer

If you are connected to a network printer, you can print from Windows to that printer. To connect to a network printer, follow these steps:

1. Choose the Printers icon if the Printers dialog box is not already displayed.

2. Choose the Connect button.

3. Choose the Network button. This button is gray if you are not connected to a network printer.

4. Select the printer port from the Port drop-down list box in the Printers-Network Connections dialog box.

5. In the Path text box, type the path to the printer, or choose the Browse button to look for printers. Select a printer from the Resources box and then choose OK or press ↵Enter.

6. Type a password, if requested.

7. Choose Connect to link with the network printer.

Some networks do not allow browsing; in that case, the Browse button is gray.

To disconnect from the network printer, follow this same procedure, selecting the printer from the Printers-Network Connections dialog box and choosing the Disconnect button.

Removing a Printer

Removing a printer saves only a small amount of disk space, but unclutters the printer selection and setup dialog boxes. To remove a printer, choose the Printers icon from the Control Panel. When the Printers dialog box appears, select the printer from the Installed Printers list and choose the Remove button. You are then asked to confirm that you want to remove the printer driver.

7

Turning Print Manager On or Off

If you do not want to use the Print Manager, you can print only one document at a time, and you cannot print in the background; however, printing may be faster. The Print Manager is usually turned off for printing to a network printer. If your printer has limited memory and you have trouble printing graphics or other large files, try turning off the Print Manager. To turn off the Print Manager, choose the Printers icon from the Control Panel and deselect the Use Print Manager check box.

To learn more about the Print Manager, refer to Chapter 8.

Installing Drivers

 Computers with sound boards, CD players, and video capability need special drivers to operate this special equipment. The process of installing and configuring these drivers is similar to the process of installing a printer, but it's simpler. To learn more about multimedia drivers, see Chapter 18.

To install multimedia and speaker drivers, follow these steps:

1. Choose the Drivers icon in the Control Panel window. The Drivers dialog box appears.

2. Choose the Add button.

The Add dialog box appears, listing all available drivers.

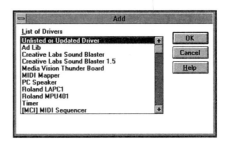

3. From the List of Drivers box, select the driver you want to add. A dialog box appears, prompting you to insert in drive A the disk containing the driver. A message explains exactly which disk to insert.

4. Insert into drive A the disk containing the driver, or choose Browse to locate the driver on another disk or in another directory on your hard disk.

5. Choose OK or press ⏎Enter. When the installation is complete, you return to the Add dialog box.

6. Choose Setup and select settings for your driver (make sure that they don't conflict with settings for other devices on your system).

7. Choose OK or press ⏎Enter. To use your driver right away, choose the Restart Now button.

Setting Up Communication Ports and Printer Ports

Serial ports are hardware connections (in a computer) to which you connect a few types of printers, all modems, and various other peripherals, such as scanners. Serial ports are called COM1, COM2, COM3, and COM4. If you do not have a serial printer, modem, or another serial device, you do not need to set up these ports.

To set up a serial port, follow these steps:

1. Choose the Ports icon from the Control Panel. The Ports dialog box appears.

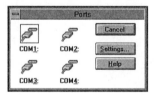

Windows has up to four communication ports for modems or serial printers.

2. Select the serial (COM) port that you want to set up.

3. Choose the Settings button.

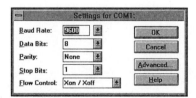

The Settings dialog box for the selected port appears.

7

4. Select the COM settings you need for your modem, serial printer, or other serial device. See your modem or printer manual or contact your modem or printer manufacturer or dealer for these settings:

Setting	Description
Baud Rate	Determines the speed at which information is sent.
Data Bits	Determines the amount of information sent.
Parity	Determines the type of error checking.
Stop Bits	Determines how data packets are marked.
Flow Control	Determines how the computer and the device signal each other.

Summary

This chapter showed you some of the ways you can customize Windows and Windows programs so that your work is more enjoyable and more productive. You learned how to change colors and desktop backgrounds to personalize your screens. You learned how to add printers and set them up so that you can best use their features. And you learned how to switch mouse buttons and adjust your mouse and keyboard sensitivity.

The following important points were covered in this chapter:

- You can customize the appearance of Windows and some operating characteristics to fit your work style.

- You customize the color, pattern, or graphics background of your windows with the Color and Desktop tools from the Control Panel. You also can add a screen saver.

- You adjust your mouse and keyboard operation with the Mouse and Keyboard tools from the Control Panel.

- The Printers tool enables you to install, configure, and set up new printers. You use the Ports tool to configure the port of printers or modems connected to a COM port. You can use the Print Setup command from the File menu to change the printer setup within Windows programs.

186

You now are ready to learn about some of the free programs included with Windows, which are described in Chapters 11 through 14. If you work with DOS programs, read Chapter 20, "Running DOS Programs," for a detailed discussion of how to customize Windows to handle your DOS programs better.

7

Controlling the Printer

Windows programs share more than a common graphical interface. They share printing resources also. Windows' Print Manager manages printing for all Windows programs, transferring information and instructions to your printer while you continue working.

In this chapter, you learn how to determine which print jobs are waiting in the printing queue and how to pause, remove, or change the order of print jobs.

Note: The Print Manager works only with programs designed for Windows. DOS programs running in Windows do not use the Print Manager. A DOS program prints just as though it were not in Windows. DOS programs cannot share the common printer drivers used by Windows programs. You therefore must complete the printer installation and setup required for each DOS program.

Understanding how Windows manages printing

Controlling print jobs

Changing printer or program performance

Printing on a network

Understanding How Windows Manages Printing

When you issue a print command in a Windows program, the Print Manager springs into action to complete two tasks. First, Windows sends your file to the Print Manager, where files to be printed are lined up (or *queued*) for printing. Second, the Print Manager routes the files, in the order received, to your printer.

8

If your program is in a window that enables you to see program icons at the bottom of the screen, the Print Manager icon appears whenever a Windows program sends a print job to the printer.

In this example, the Print Manager icon appears at the bottom of the screen.

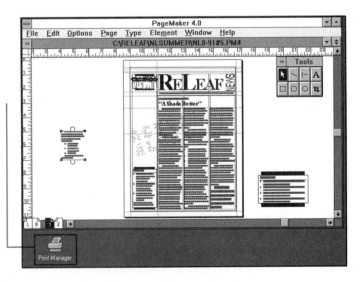

190

For an important reason, Windows gives the Print Manager control over your printing, instead of letting your program control printing (as happens with DOS programs). You can continue working in your Windows program while the Print Manager handles your print job from the program you're using or from another Windows program.

Despite the Print Manager's advantages, you may not always want to use it. For example, a network printer sometimes prints faster with the Print Manager turned off, and printing large files to printers with limited memory sometimes causes problems you can solve by turning off the Print Manager.

To turn the Print Manager off or on, follow these steps:

1. In the Main window, choose the Control Panel.

2. Choose Printers. The Printers dialog box appears.

3. If the Use Print Manager option is selected—if it has an X in the box beside it—the Print Manager is turned on. Turn it off by selecting the option so that no X appears in the box. Turn it on by selecting Use Print Manager so that an X appears in the box.

4. Choose Close.

With the Print Manager turned off, you print in the usual way from your program.

8

Controlling Print Jobs

The Print Manager is located in the Main group window of the Program Manager. When you print from a Windows program, the Print Manager automatically starts, appearing as an icon at the bottom of the desktop.

If you want to restore the Print Manager icon to a window so that you can view or control your print jobs, double-click the icon. Alternatively, press Ctrl+Tab until the Print Manager program icon is active, and then press Enter.

Viewing the Order of Print Jobs

The Print Manager window shows the status of your print queue. You can see which printer or printers are active, which printer is printing, which file is being printed, what other files are queued for printing, and optionally, the file's size and the time and date you sent the file to the printer.

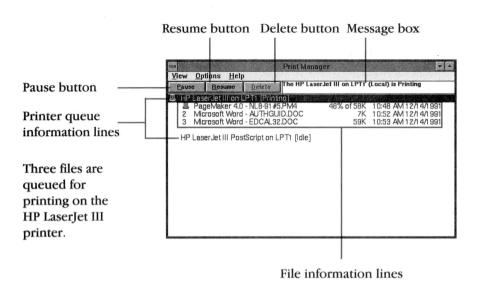

Resume button   Delete button Message box

Pause button

Printer queue
information lines

Three files are
queued for
printing on the
HP LaserJet III
printer.

File information lines

Table 8.1 describes the items in the Print Manager window.

8

Table 8.1
The Print Manager Window

Item	Description
Pause button	Temporarily stops a printer from printing.
Resume button	Restarts printing after pausing.
Delete button	Removes a file from the print queue.
Message box	Provides information about the print job.
Printer queue information lines	Tells you the printer name, printer port, and printer status. (If you have more than one printer connected to your computer, a printer queue information line appears for each printer.)
File information lines	Shows you the file's position in the queue, the title of the print job, and optionally, the file size (as well as the percentage of the file that has printed already) and the time and date you sent the file to the printer. When a print job is complete, its file information line disappears.

Changing the Print Order

The number at the left of each file information line tells you the order in which the files will print. You can change the order if you need to rush a job.

To change the print order with the mouse, drag the file information line up or down to reposition it in the Print Manager window. For example, to move up file 3 so that it prints next, drag its file information line above the file information line for file 2, and then release it.

To change the print order with the keyboard, follow these steps:

1. Press ↑ or ↓ to select the file line you want to reorder.
2. Press and hold Ctrl.
3. Press ↑ or ↓ to move the file to its new position in the queue.
4. Release Ctrl and the arrow key.

Pausing or Resuming Printing

You may want to pause the Print Manager temporarily to fix a printer problem or to give more computer power to a program you are operating. When the printer or file is paused, you see the message [Paused] at the end of the printer queue information line, and you see a hand icon at the beginning of the line.

To pause printing, follow these steps:

1. Select the printer queue information line for the printer or file you want to pause.
2. Choose the Pause button or press Alt+P.

To resume printing after you have paused, follow these steps:

1. Select the printer queue information line for the printer you paused.
2. Choose the Resume button or press Alt+R.

When you resume printing, a printer icon appears at the left end of the printer information line.

Deleting a Print Job

If you want to cancel a specific print job, you can delete a file information line from the print queue. If you want to cancel all printing, exit the Print Manager.

To delete a print job from the print queue, follow these steps:

1. Select the file information line of the job you want to delete.

2. Choose the Delete button or press Alt + D.

A Print Manager
dialog box
appears, asking
you to confirm
the deletion.

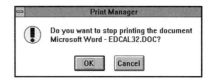

3. Choose OK or press ↵Enter to confirm that you want to delete the print job. Or choose Cancel or press Esc to cancel the deletion request.

To cancel all printing, follow these steps:

1. Choose the View menu and select the Exit command.

Another Print
Manager dialog
box appears,
asking for confir-
mation.

2. Choose OK or press ↵Enter to confirm that you want to exit Print Manager and cancel all print jobs. Choose Cancel or press Esc to cancel the request.

Note: If you delete a file that currently is being printed, especially if the file contains graphics, you may need to reset your printer to clear its print buffer. Reset the printer by turning it off and then back on (or by selecting the Reset option, if your printer has one). Laser printers often need to be reset after you delete a print job.

Changing Printer or Program Performance

When the Print Manager prints while programs are running, your computer must divide its processing power between the Print Manager and the programs. You can choose which—the Print Manager or your programs—has greater priority and, therefore, gets a greater share of computer power. If you

8

give the Print Manager *high* priority, jobs print faster, but your programs may slow down. If you give the Print Manager *low* priority, jobs print slower, but your programs operate faster. If you give the Print Manager *medium* priority (which is Windows' default choice), your computer shares its computing power equally between the Print Manager and other programs.

To change the printer priority, follow these steps:

1. Choose the Options menu.

2. Select one of the following options:

Option	Description
Low Priority	Prints slower but increases program speed.
Medium Priority	Splits computer power evenly.
High Priority	Prints faster but decreases program speed.

A check mark appears to the left of the printer priority option you select from the Options menu.

The Options menu is shown here with Medium Priority selected.

The selection remains in effect—for all printing—until you change it again.

Note: If you want to devote all of your computer's power to the program you are using, save your printing until you are finished working. Open each file you want to print, and print it. The files "queue up" in the Print Manager and print, one after the other.

Displaying Print Manager Alert Messages

Occasionally, the printer needs your attention. For example, the printer may run out of paper. You can control whether the Print Manager *always* alerts you, whether the Print Manager icon *flashes* to alert you, or whether the Print Manager icon does nothing when your printer needs attention.

To specify how the Print Manager handles alert messages, follow these steps:

1. Choose the Options menu.

2. Select one of the following options:

Option	Description
Alert Always	Always alerts you with a message box.
Flash if Inactive	Beeps and flashes when the Print Manager is inactive.
Ignore if Inactive	Ignores the alert message if the Print Manager is inactive.

If you choose the Flash if Inactive option, the Print Manager icon flashes when a problem arises. To see what the problem is, restore the Print Manager icon to a window.

Note: If you choose the Ignore if Inactive option, you may miss an important message.

Displaying File Size and Print Time and Date

You have the option to display each file's size and the time and date you sent the file to the printer. To display this information, follow these steps:

1. Choose the View command.

2. Select one of the following options:

Option	Description
Time/Date Sent	Displays the time and date.
Print File Size	Displays the size of the file.

Percent printed   File size

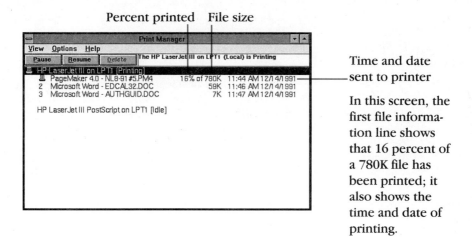

Time and date sent to printer

In this screen, the first file informa-tion line shows that 16 percent of a 780K file has been printed; it also shows the time and date of printing.

The percentage of the file printed appears to the left of the file size, letting you know how close to completion a print job is.

Closing the Print Manager Window

Usually when you print, the Print Manager appears as an icon at the bottom of the screen. When all print jobs are finished, the Print Manager shuts itself down. If the Print Manager is in a window, however, you must manually exit the Print Manager to close it when it is finished printing.

Note: If you exit the Print Manager while print jobs remain, they are canceled. To reduce the Print Manager window to an icon without losing print jobs, minimize the window by clicking the down arrow at the top right corner of the window. Alternatively, press Alt and then the space bar to display the Program Control menu, and then select the Minimize command. When the window is minimized to an icon, the Print Manager automatically shuts itself down when printing is completed.

To exit the Print Manager so that it disappears from the screen, choose the View menu and select the Exit command.

197

Running the Print Manager from the Program Manager

The Print Manager program automatically starts when you print a file (unless the Print Manager is turned off). It appears as an icon at the bottom of the desktop, and you can open that icon into the Print Manager window.

You also can start the Print Manager window directly from the Program Manager, when you're not printing files. For example, you may want to start the Print Manager so that you can install a new printer or connect to a network printer. When you start the Print Manager from the Program Manager, you will see printer information lines for all the printers connected to your PC, but you will not see any file information lines, because no files are printing.

To start the Print Manager from the Program Manager, follow these steps:

1. In the Program Manager, activate the Main window.

The Print Manager icon is among the Main icons.

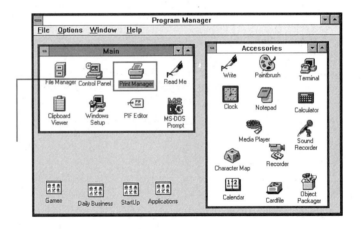

2. Double-click the Print Manager icon, or press the arrow keys to select the Print Manager icon and then press ⏎Enter.

Adding Printers from the Print Manager

You can use the Print Manager to add, configure, and remove a printer on your system—just as you can use the Printers program in the Control Panel.

To use the Print Manager to add, configure, or remove a printer, follow these steps:

1. Choose Print Manager from the Main window.
2. Choose the Options menu, and select the Printer Setup command. The Printers dialog box appears.
3. To add a printer, choose Add.

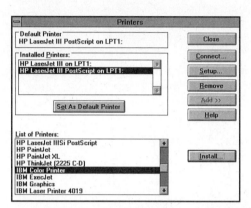

The Printers dialog box expands to show a list of available printers.

Select the printer you want to add, and then choose Install. Follow instructions for inserting the diskette containing the driver for the printer you want to install, and choose OK.

4. Select your newly installed printer from the Installed Printers list, and choose Connect to link your printer to a port or to a network. Choose OK when you're finished.
5. With your printer still selected in the Installed Printers list, choose Setup to change the paper size and orientation. Choose OK when you're finished.
6. If you want to use your printer as the default printer, while it is still selected choose the Set As Default Printer button.
7. Choose the Close button.

If you want to remove a printer, select it in the Installed Printers list and choose Remove.

For details about installing printers, refer to the section "Adding and Setting Up Printers" in Chapter 7.

8

Printing on a Network

If you share a printer with other people on a local area network, printing is a little different from the previous procedures. You have additional Print Manager options, such as viewing the print queue for the entire network and updating the network queue status. You also have the option of bypassing the Print Manager altogether, which is a faster way to print when on a network.

Connecting to a Network Printer

If a network is installed in Windows on your computer, you can print on a network printer. First, though, you must be sure that you are connected to the network printer you want to use. You can do this while you are installing a printer or by using the Print Manager window.

To connect to a network printer from the Print Manager window, follow these steps:

1. Choose the Print Manager from the Main group. The Print Manager dialog box appears.

2. Choose the Options menu and select the Network Connections command.

The Network-Printer Connections dialog box appears, listing the network printers to which you already are connected.

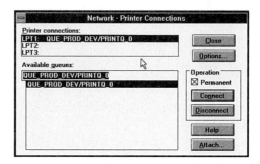

3. Select a printer port from the Printer connections box.

4. Type the name of the network printer queue you want to use in the Available queues text box, or select it from the list of printer queues below the text box.

A network printer may already be connected to the port you want to use. Disconnect it before connecting a new printer (see "Disconnecting from a Network Printer," further in this chapter).

5. Select the Permanent check box in the Operation group to indicate that the connection is permanent.

6. Choose Connect.

7. Choose Close.

Viewing Network Print Jobs

When you print to a network printer, the Print Manager lists the files you have sent to the printer. By choosing the Selected Net Queue command, however, you can see all the files that everyone on the network has sent to the same printer. Seeing this list gives you an idea of how long it will be before the printer gets to your job.

To view a network print queue, follow these steps:

1. Print your file and open the Print Manager window.

2. Select the printer information line for the network printer.

3. Choose the View menu and select the Selected Net Queue command. The Print Manager displays a list of all files queued for the printer.

4. Select Close to close the dialog box.

Viewing Other Printer Queues on a Network

If you have access to a number of printers on a network, you can view queues for any of the printers before you decide which one to use. To view network queues for printers other than the default network queue, follow these steps:

1. Open the Print Manager window.

2. Choose the View menu and select the Other Net Queue command. The Other Net Queue dialog box appears.

3. In the Network Queue box, type the network path name for the network queue you want to view.

4. Choose the View button.

5. Type the name of another queue or choose the Close button.

8

Updating Network Queue Status

The Print Manager, by default, tracks and periodically updates the status of a network queue. If you prefer, you can turn off network queue updating so that you can manually update the status.

To turn off the automatic network status updating, follow these steps:

1. Open the Print Manager window.

2. Choose the Options menu and select the Network Settings command.

The Network Options dialog box appears.

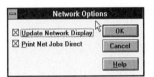

3. Deselect the Update Network Display check box so that no X appears inside it.

4. Choose OK or press ↵Enter.

To update the network queue status manually, choose the View menu and select the Refresh command.

Printing Directly to a Network

In most cases, printing is faster when you bypass the Print Manager and print files directly on a network. Printing on the network is therefore the Print Manager's default choice. Because networks differ, however, experiment with printing times on your own network to find out whether printing directly to the network printer is faster than using the Print Manager.

To print directly to a network printer, follow these steps:

1. Open the Print Manager window.

2. Choose the Options menu and select the Network Settings command.

3. Select the Print Net Jobs Direct check box so that an X appears in it.

4. Choose OK or press ↵Enter.

Note: When you are printing directly to a network printer or a network print spooler, no Print Manager icon appears at the bottom of the Windows desktop.

Disconnecting from a Network Printer

If you're finished using a network printer, you can disconnect from it. Disconnect when you need to connect a different network printer to the same port.

To disconnect from a network printer, follow these steps:

1. Open the Print Manager window.
2. Choose the Options menu and select the Network Connections command.

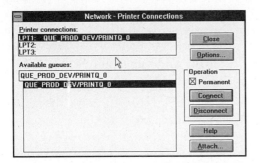

The Network - Printers Connections dialog box appears.

3. In the Printer connections list box, select the printer you want to disconnect.
4. Choose Disconnect.
5. Choose Close.

Summary

In this chapter, you learned how the Print Manager manages printers and print jobs while you continue working in other Windows programs. With the Print Manager, you can control the order in which jobs print, pause a printer, and delete specific print jobs. You can even determine how much computer power to devote to printing and to the programs you are running.

As long as you operate with the Print Manager on, you can use it to control printing from Windows programs. This chapter covered the following important points:

■ You view the order of print jobs by choosing the Print Manager icon at the bottom of the desktop. The order in which documents print is shown by the number on the left end of each file information line.

■ You pause or resume printing from a specific printer by selecting the printer queue information line for the printer you want to pause or resume, and then choosing the Pause or Resume button.

■ You delete a print job by selecting the file information line for the job you want to delete, and then choosing the Delete button.

■ You can use the Print Manager to install new printers and change the default printer.

Now that you are familiar with the Print Manager, you should become familiar with your own Windows programs or the free programs that come with Windows, such as Windows Write, discussed in Chapter 11, or Windows Paintbrush, covered in Chapter 12. Experiment with printing multiple documents from various programs and see how the Print Manager can make your work easier.

8

Managing Fonts and TrueType

Gone are the days of limited font selections—when the one or two fonts that came with your printer were all you had. Fortunately, the days of complex solutions to the problem of limited font selections also are gone. TrueType brings you easily accessible built-in scalable fonts you can use with any kind of printer or computer. Although Windows comes equipped with only a few TrueType fonts, you can easily add more fonts to your system.

You aren't limited to using only TrueType fonts with Windows, however. If you have already invested in downloadable fonts, you can still use them. If you want to use the fonts built into your printer, you can easily turn off TrueType.

Using TrueType

Advantages of scalable fonts

Choosing the right font

Adding new fonts

Key Terms in This Chapter

Font	A style of type. Each font style has a unique appearance. Fonts are usually grouped into typeface *families*. The Times New Roman family, for example, includes the fonts Times New Roman, Times New Roman bold, Times New Roman italic, and Times New Roman bold italic.
TrueType	A font management technology that provides scalable font outlines that adapt to both screen and printer, and that you can use on any computer or printer.
Scalable font	Fonts defined by an outline you can scale to any size. These fonts usually take up less disk space than bit-mapped fonts.
Bit-mapped font	Screen or printer fonts stored as *bit maps*—"bits" that are "mapped" to the screen or printer. Each font in each size requires a separate bit-mapped image in your computer.

Understanding Fonts

9

A *font* is a style of type. It's the way the letters and numbers look—whether they have straight lines of uniform thickness, or thick and thin lines and strokes extending from the ends of each line; whether they are wide and rounded, or thin and condensed; whether they have an old-fashioned appearance, or look contemporary. Type design has been an art form for hundreds of years, and hundreds—if not thousands—of fonts are available.

Despite the many font styles in existence, only a few basic categories of font styles exist: serif, sans serif, script, symbol, and decorative fonts are the most common. *Serif* fonts are characterized by thick and thin lines and by strokes (called *serifs*) at the ends of characters. Most books, magazines, and newspapers use serif fonts. *Sans serif* fonts have lines of uniform thickness and have no strokes (serifs). Designers frequently use sans serif fonts for display type, such as signs and headlines. *Script* fonts look like handwriting; *symbol* fonts replace characters with mathematical or "dingbat" symbols; and *decorative* fonts each have a specialized appearance.

Times Roman is one of the most commonly used serif fonts.

Helvetica is a popular sans serif font.

Each font consists of a standard set of letters, symbols, and numbers. Most fonts come in four styles: regular, bold, italic, and bold italic.

Fonts are measured in *points*, and 72 points equal one inch. A typical font size for a newspaper might be 9 or 10 points. Books frequently are printed in 10- or 11-point fonts. Subheadings are larger: 12, 14, or even 18 points. Titles usually range from 18 points to 36 points. Important front-page headlines in a newspaper may measure more than 100 points.

Fonts on most computers today are *proportional* rather than *monospaced;* that is, each character's width is proportional to the character's shape. Monospaced characters, on the other hand, are all the same width.

Fonts do much more than simply deliver words to a reader. They make your text easier or harder to read; they determine how much text fits on a page; they create a mood; they set a tone. Don't use fonts carelessly. Pick the font best suited to the job at hand.

9

Understanding How Computers Use Fonts

With so many fonts available, it may be comforting to know that most computers have access to only a select group of fonts. It greatly simplifies the job of selecting the right font for the task. (You can always add more fonts to your system as you grow more discriminating about the fonts you use.)

Computers gain access to fonts in several ways. Some fonts, such as Windows' TrueType fonts, are built into the operating system. Fonts also can be built into the printer, as they are in many PostScript printers and some HP LaserJet models. You can add fonts to the printer with a *cartridge*, and you can add *soft fonts,* or *downloadable fonts,* to the computer hard disk. When adding fonts to the hard disk, you usually must download the fonts to the printer before you can use them.

The fonts you have in your computer or on your printer are stored in one of two ways. They are either *bit-mapped* representations or *scalable* outlines.

This example shows a bit-mapped charac-ter. Bit-mapped fonts store a unique bit-mapped (or graphic) image for each font, each font style, and each font size.

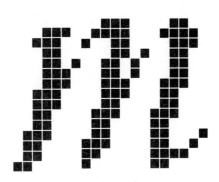

When you want to print a 10-point Helvetica bold uppercase *E*, your computer searches for just that picture. Bit-mapped fonts can quickly consume a great deal of storage space on your computer or in your printer, or both. Many downloadable and cartridge fonts use bit-map technology.

This example shows a scalable character. Unlike bit-mapped fonts, scalable fonts store an outline of each character in a font and then scale the outline to size when needed.

When you want to print a 10-point Helvetica bold *E*, your computer searches for the outline representing a bold, uppercase, Helvetica *E* and scales it to 10 points. The computer stores only one outline rather than a separate bit-mapped image for each size. As a result, scalable fonts consume much less disk storage space than bit-mapped fonts. PostScript fonts, TrueType fonts, and fonts built into the HP LaserJet III are scalable fonts.

No matter how you store fonts on your system, each font has to fulfill two roles: it has to appear on your screen, and it has to print on your printer. With the introduction of TrueType, a single font outline fulfills both roles. Most non-TrueType fonts, however, include two versions—*printer fonts* and *screen fonts*—because your screen has a much different resolution than your printer.

TrueType fonts, then, have two space-saving advantages over other fonts: they are scalable, so you need to store only one picture of each character (rather than one for each character in each size); and they are *device independent*, so only one version of the font must reside in your system (rather than one version for the screen and another for the printer).

Understanding Printer Fonts

With Windows, you can use three types of printer fonts—resident, cartridge, and soft—depending on how the fonts are stored.

Resident fonts are fonts built into the printer. For example, many PostScript printers come with a standard set of thirteen built-in scalable typeface families. (PostScript is a page description language.) Each typeface family contains many fonts, such as Times Roman, Times Roman italic, Times Roman bold, and so on. Hewlett-Packard LaserJet printers also come with built-in fonts; the number of built-in fonts depends upon the printer model. Resident fonts are preferable to cartridge or soft fonts because built-in fonts print faster and do not take up processing power or computer memory.

Cartridge fonts come in hardware modules that you plug into a printer. They act as resident fonts. Each cartridge contains one or more sets of fonts. You usually use cartridges with HP-compatible laser printers. During printer installation or setup, you must select from a list the cartridges available to the printer, which lets Windows know which additional fonts are available.

9

Soft fonts are fonts generated by a software program and stored on your computer's hard disk or on the network. When you need to use a font, Windows sends (downloads) the font information to the printer. The printer stores the font information in memory and composes a page. After you download a font, it stays in the printer. Soft fonts take up hard disk storage and slow down printing time. You must use the Windows Control Panel to install the soft fonts in Windows.

Printer fonts can be bit-mapped fonts or scalable fonts. PostScript printers and HP LaserJet III printers contain scalable fonts, while dot-matrix printers contain bit-mapped fonts. Some printer font cartridges contain scalable fonts, while others contain bit-mapped fonts. Soft fonts are usually bit-mapped fonts, unless they are scalable PostScript fonts.

Understanding Screen Fonts

Without TrueType, your computer needs not only printer fonts but also a separate set of fonts for displaying text on-screen. Printer fonts usually do not display satisfactory results on-screen, because printers generally print at a much different resolution than screens display. Most fonts, whether they are cartridge, soft, or printer-resident, include a set of screen fonts and a set of printer fonts.

Unless you use a type management program like Adobe Type Manager or TrueType, screen fonts are not scalable. (Adobe Type Manager and TrueType scale screen fonts the same way they scale printer fonts.) If your screen fonts are not scalable, they probably are stored in a limited number of sizes to conserve disk space. You can display your text in a size for which you don't have a screen font, but Windows substitutes a different screen font that it does have in that size. The text you see on-screen may look slightly different from the printed text, but line endings are the same on-screen as in the printed document.

With Windows, you can use three types of screen fonts: system, screen soft, and type management fonts.

Windows' *system fonts* are generic serif, sans serif, and symbol fonts that are designed to match printer fonts. Windows uses system fonts in its dialog boxes, title bars, and so on, and as screen fonts to represent printer-resident or cartridge fonts. Because a slight difference may exist between a generic screen font that comes with Windows and a specific printer font, you may see a difference between a font's screen appearance and the printed result. If no equivalent font is available in the printer, Windows uses a system font when printing.

A special form of *screen soft font* matches a printer font as closely as possible. These fonts are stored in software files and are available with soft fonts designed for downloading to the printer. Because these screen fonts are designed to match a specific printer soft font, the on-screen display closely matches the printed result. Screen soft fonts are usually added to your computer when you install printer soft fonts. Most often, they are bit maps. Screen fonts end with the extension FON.

Type management programs are designed to generate screen and printer fonts simultaneously. Unlike soft fonts, which are bit mapped, these fonts are scalable, reducing the disk storage devoted to bit-mapped soft fonts and ensuring that screen displays are nearly an exact match to printed results. Using type management programs to print pages is slower than using other forms of fonts. TrueType and the Adobe Type Manager are type management programs.

210

Screen fonts are bit-mapped fonts unless they are generated from scalable outlines by a type management program such as Adobe Type Manager or TrueType.

Using TrueType Fonts

Windows comes with TrueType font technology built in, along with 14 TrueType fonts in five families. These scalable fonts are automatically installed in Windows and are ready for you to use immediately.

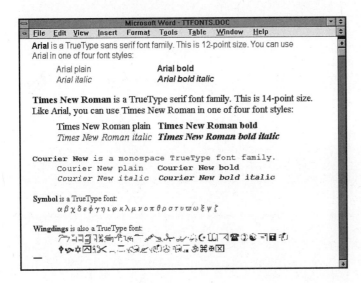

The five TrueType font families that come with Windows are Arial, Times New Roman, Courier New, Symbol, and Wingdings. Each family comes in plain, bold, italic, and bold italic fonts.

9

The Symbol and Wingding fonts are single-font families. Times New Roman, a serif font, is quite similar to the popular Times Roman font. Arial, a sans serif font, is similar to Helvetica. Courier New, a monospaced font, is similar to the traditional Courier typewriter font.

TrueType offers several advantages over other alternatives for producing fonts on your screen and printer.

First, it is a scalable font, so you have to store only a single version of each font on your computer. A single outline can produce a font of any size. In contrast, bit-mapped fonts store a different picture for each font in each size and either consume massive amounts of storage or severely limit the sizes you have available.

Second, TrueType fonts adapt to both your screen and your printer. A single outline suffices for both and produces equally high quality on both screen and printer. Most other fonts, on the other hand, require separate screen and printer fonts. To save disk space, most fonts come in only limited screen sizes, rendering blocky representations of a size you request that isn't stored as a screen font.

Third, TrueType fonts print on any printer that Windows supports, whether it's a laser printer or a dot-matrix printer. Most other fonts are printer specific, forcing you to use a single printer. If you do switch printers, you can switch to a different set of fonts, resulting in different line breaks and page breaks (in other words, without TrueType, switching printers means your document may be reformatted).

A fourth advantage TrueType has over many downloadable fonts is that TrueType fonts are automatically available to all Windows programs, whereas many downloadable fonts must be installed for each program with which you want to use them.

Finally, TrueType screen and printer fonts match closely. In contrast, other types of fonts may look different on-screen than they do when printed. That's because if there is no specific screen font to match a printer font, Windows substitutes one of its own screen fonts. For example, if you pick the Bookman printer font but do not have the Bookman screen font, Windows substitutes its generic serif screen font (if you're not using TrueType) or Times New Roman (if you are using TrueType). Neither of these condensed screen fonts matches Bookman, which is a wide, open font. At worst, you can end up with incorrect line and page breaks or, at best, mismatched line lengths. TrueType solves the problem of mismatched screen and printer fonts by drawing both fonts from the same outline. (Another solution to the problem exists: for many printer fonts, you can add specific bit-mapped screen fonts to your hard disk; these bit-map files, however, can consume a great deal of disk space.)

Because of its benefits, TrueType is a Windows default: when you start using Windows, it's on. You can turn it off, however, if you want to use other fonts you have in your system or your printer.

Turning TrueType On and Off

By default, TrueType is on in Windows, but TrueType fonts consume memory on your computer and may be slower to display and print than other fonts. If your computer has limited memory or runs slowly, you may want to turn off

9

212

TrueType. With TrueType turned off, you have access to any other fonts installed in your computer or on your printer. You can turn TrueType back on for printing, if necessary.

If you want to use TrueType fonts exclusively, you can turn off all other fonts so that they do not appear in font lists in your programs.

To turn TrueType off or on, or to turn other fonts off or on, follow these steps:

1. Display the Windows Program Manager and open the Main Window.

2. Choose the Control Panel.

   Double-click the Control Panel icon, or press arrow keys to select the Control Panel icon and press ↵Enter.

The Control Panel window appears, containing the Fonts icon.

3. Choose the Fonts icon.

   Double-click the Fonts icon, or press arrow keys to select the Fonts icon and press ↵Enter.

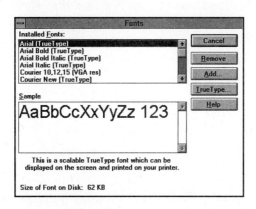

The Fonts window appears. Currently installed fonts are listed in the Installed Fonts list box.

4. Choose the TrueType button.

The TrueType
dialog box
appears.

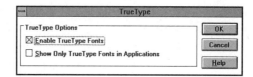

5. To turn off TrueType, deselect the Enable TrueType Fonts option so that no X appears in the check box.

   To display only TrueType fonts in your programs, select the Show Only TrueType Fonts in Applications option. (This option is not available if you have deselected the Enable TrueType Fonts option.)

6. Choose OK or press ⏎Enter.

   If you turn off TrueType, a dialog box advises you that you must restart Windows for your change to take effect.

7. To restart Windows, choose the Restart Now button.

Adding New Fonts

You can easily add fonts to your system, whether they are TrueType fonts or another type of font.

To install TrueType fonts, you can use the Fonts program you see in the Windows Control Panel. To install downloadable or cartridge fonts, you may need to use special installation software that comes with the fonts (but first try using the Fonts program). Printer-resident fonts are usually installed automatically when you install a printer.

Before you add a new font, be sure that you have the font diskettes available. You will need them during the installation process.

To use the Fonts program to add a new font to your system, follow these steps:

1. Display the Windows Program Manager, and open the Main window.

2. Choose the Control Panel.

3. Choose the Fonts icon.

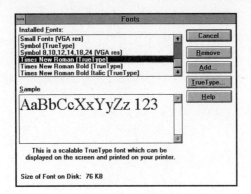

The Fonts window appears. Currently installed fonts are listed in the Installed Fonts list box.

4. Choose the Add button.

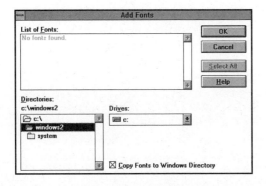

The Add Fonts dialog box appears.

5. In the Drives list, select the drive containing the font you want to add.

6. In the Directories list, select the directory containing the font you want to add.

   The fonts in the directory and drive you selected appear in the List of Fonts box.

7. In the List of Fonts box, select the font or fonts you want to add.

   If you want to add all the fonts, choose the Select All button.

8. If you don't want to add the fonts to your system, but instead want to use them from the drive and directory where they're currently located, deselect the Copy Fonts to Windows Directory so that no X appears in the check box.

   Use this option if you want to use the fonts only occasionally and don't want to use up disk space by storing them permanently.

9

215

9. Choose OK or press ⏎Enter to add the font to your system.

10. Choose Close to close the Fonts window.

If you are adding fonts by installing a new font cartridge, you must set up your printer so that it recognizes the new cartridge (refer to the section "Adding and Setting Up Printers" in Chapter 7). If the fonts are built into the print driver, you do nothing more; however, if you don't have access to the fonts after you have installed the printer and set up the cartridge, you must install the fonts. Use the Fonts program or check the font documentation to see whether you must use a special font installation program. Note that using the Fonts program installs both the screen fonts and printer fonts at the same time.

If you are adding Adobe PostScript fonts, use Adobe Type Manager to install them. Refer to your documentation to learn how.

Using Fonts in Windows Programs

After you install them, fonts become available for you to use in all your Windows programs. Because you may have several types of fonts installed in Windows, special icons identify each font. By looking at these icons—which appear to the left of the font names in font list boxes—you can tell whether a font is a TrueType font, a printer font, or a Windows system font.

9

In this Word for Windows font list, a TT icon appears to the left of TrueType fonts; printer fonts display a printer icon.

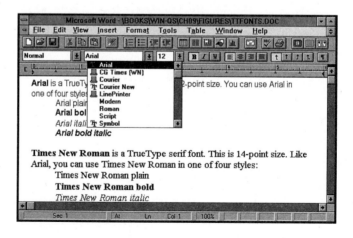

Removing Old Fonts

If you no longer need a font, you can remove it from Windows. Removing fonts can save memory on a computer with limited memory and can be useful when you're running memory-hungry programs. If you also remove the disk file, you can save even more disk space (but you have to go through the installation process if you ever want to use the font again).

To remove a font, follow these steps:

1. Display the Windows Program Manager, and open the Main window.
2. Choose the Control Panel.
3. Choose the Fonts icon.
4. In the Installed Fonts list box, select the font you want to remove.

   Note: Do not remove the MS Sans Serif font, which is used in Windows dialog boxes.

5. Choose the Remove button.

   A dialog box prompts you to confirm that you want to remove the font. If you also want to remove the font files from your disk, select the Delete Font File From Disk check box.

   Note: *Do not* delete font files from the disk if you deselected the Copy Fonts To Windows System Directory option when you installed your fonts (in other words, if you were using fonts from their original diskettes rather than copying them to Windows). Doing so deletes the font files from your original font diskette, and you will not be able to reinstall the fonts.

6. Choose Yes. To remove several fonts at once, choose Yes to All.

   You return to the Fonts dialog box.

7. Choose Close.

Summary

Windows comes equipped with ready-to-use TrueType fonts—scalable fonts that adapt identically to both your screen and your printer. TrueType fonts offer many advantages over other types of fonts.

Windows also enables you to use soft (downloadable) fonts, printer-resident fonts, and cartridge fonts. If the fonts that come with Windows and your printer don't give you enough variety, you can purchase additional fonts and install them easily.

You learned these important points in this chapter:

- TrueType fonts are scalable, from very small sizes to very large sizes.
- TrueType fonts are identical on the screen and printer.
- TrueType fonts consume less disk space than bit-mapped fonts.
- You can print TrueType fonts on any printer installed in Windows.
- You easily can install new fonts and remove fonts you no longer need.

In the next chapter, you learn about object linking and embedding, a technology that enables you to create compound documents. With object embedding, you can start a program from within another program. With object linking, you can update the contents of a file by changing the data in another file.

9

Using Object Linking and Embedding

10

One of the unique advantages of Windows programs is their capability to exchange and link information easily with other Windows programs. This technology is called *object linking and embedding*, or OLE. If you are accustomed to working with a single program, the value of linking or embedding data is not always immediately apparent. After you begin to link and embed data, however, you will see how much it can improve your communication. For example, the following list describes examples of how linking and embedding can work with various programs:

- You can link a mailing list in a Windows database or worksheet to a mail merge data document in a Windows word processing program.

- You can create sales projections, financial analyses, inventory reports, and investment analyses with Microsoft Excel or Lotus 1-2-3 for Windows, and link or embed them into Windows word processing documents.

- You can maintain client reminder letters and callbacks by linking PackRat, a personal information manager, to Word for Windows through the WordBASIC macros that come with PackRat.

- You can embed into Word for Windows or Ami Pro drawings or schematics that you can update using Microsoft Draw from within the word processing program.

Transferring data with copy and paste

Linking data between programs

Embedding data into a document

Viewing data in the Clipboard

Managing links

• You can link Microsoft Excel to a Windows database or SQL Server to monitor and analyze inventory.

Key Terms in This Chapter

Applets	Small programs that run within larger programs to enhance or add features to the large program.
Client	A document or program receiving linked or embedded data.
Data	Text, worksheet, database, or graphics information.
Embed	To store data from the server document within a client document.
Link	A reference from within a client document to data in a server document. The link transfers data from the server document to a client document.
Object	Information created by one program and stored within another.
Object linking and embedding	The capability of certain Windows programs to transfer or store data from the server document to a client document.
Packages	An icon (pictorial) representation of data stored within a client document.
Server	A document or program supplying linked or embedded data.

You can link your documents to databases, worksheets, or graphics programs.

10

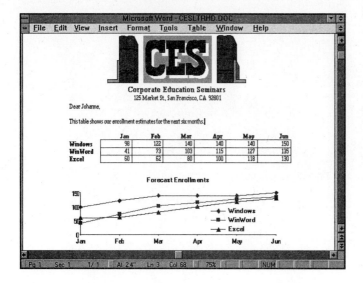

This letter is linked to a Microsoft Excel worksheet and chart; the corporate logo is an embedded WordArt object.

For more information on using programs together, see Chapter 19, "Integrating Multiple Programs."

Throughout this chapter are references to the *server* and *client.* The server is the file or program supplying data. The client is the file or program receiving information. Some programs are both a server and a client; others are one but not the other. For example, Microsoft Write and Cardfile are clients—they only receive information. Windows Paintbrush, however, is a server; it only supplies information.

Copying, linking, or embedding data between Windows programs may require the same or similar commands, and the results may appear the same on-screen or in the document; however, copying, linking, and embedding fit different situations and have different advantages and disadvantages. Table 10.1 describes each of these methods of data transfer: the situations in which you should use each method, and each method's advantages and disadvantages.

Table 10.1
Methods of Transferring Data

Method	Description
Copying	Use this method when you do not want to update data. To update this data, you must replace it.

continues

221

Table 10.1 Continued

Method	Description
	Advantages
	• Data is not changed when you update other parts of the document.
	• Less memory and storage is required to use or save the document.
	Disadvantages
	• Pictures may print at a lower resolution if you copy them as bit-mapped images.
	• Updating data requires recopying the original data and repasting it into the client document.
Linking	Use this method when you want to update the server document and have the changes automatically cascade into multiple client documents.
	Advantages
	• Less memory is required than for an embedded object.
	• Updates many client documents by changing one server document.
	• Older Windows programs incapable of embedding objects can still link data.
	Disadvantages
	• Links between the server and the client may be broken if you change or delete the server file name or path name.
	• Automatically updated links may slow down Windows operation.
	• You must save server data and maintain its name and path name.
Embedding	Use this method when you have only a few client documents that may need updating, and you want

10

to include the server data (an embedded object) as part of the document.

Advantages

- Client document and server data are stored as a single file so that you do not have to maintain links, path names, and server files.

- You do not have to keep the server data, because it is saved as part of the client document.

- You can stay within the server document and use the client program to update the embedded object.

Disadvantages

- Documents containing embedded objects are larger than other documents because they contain both client and server data.

- Updating an embedded graphic may result in a file with lower printer resolution than the original.

- You must update each client document individually.

For information about linking and embedding with Windows accessories, refer to the following chapters: Chapter 11, "Using Windows Write"; Chapter 12, "Using Windows Paintbrush"; Chapter 14, "Using Desktop Accessories"; and Chapter 18, "Using Multimedia."

10

Transferring Data with Copy and Paste

The simplest method of transferring small amounts of data or graphics from one program to another is by copying and pasting, the same method you use to move text or graphics within a document. If you are not familiar with copying and pasting between programs, you should review Chapter 4, "Editing, Copying, and Moving in Windows."

Linking Data between Programs

You also can transfer data between Windows programs by *linking* documents together. Links create a reference to data in another program or to a different document in the same program. The data remains stored in the server document, and a copy is sent through the link to the client document.

Creating a Link

Creating a link between Windows programs that are capable of linking is as easy as copying and pasting. When you use the paste command to create a link, you have the option of making a link that updates automatically or a link that requires manual updates. The command to paste a link may vary between programs. If your server program does not have linking capabilities, it will not have an Edit Paste Link command, nor will it have an Edit Paste Special command with a following Paste Link button.

To create a link, follow these steps:

1. Open both Windows programs and their documents. Activate the server document.

2. Save the server document under a file name you want the server to have during all future transactions. (You must save the server document to create the link with the correct file name.)

3. Select the text, range of cells, graphic, or database records you want to link.

4. Choose the Edit menu and select the Copy command.

5. Activate the client document. Move the insertion point to the place where you want the link.

6. Choose the Edit menu and select the Paste Link command. (If you have a Paste Link command, you do not need to continue.)

   Alternatively, choose the Edit menu and select the Paste Special command.

The Paste Special dialog box displays the server of the link and presents a list of different forms in which you can paste linked data.

7. From the Data Type list, select the form in which you want your linked data. These link types are described in the ensuing table. Note that some data types may not be available as a pasted link.

8. Choose the Paste Link button.

Pasted links automatically update to reflect a change in the server data. Later in this chapter, the "Managing Links" section describes how to create a link that updates only when manually requested and how to change a link from automatic to manual.

When you create a link in the client document, you may be able to display the data from the server in different forms, depending on the server program. The following table describes some of the data types:

Data Type	Type of Link Created
Object	Data is a self-contained embedded object. No link is maintained with the server worksheet or chart. Refer to the following section for more information.
Formatted Text (RTF)	Text transfers with formats. Worksheets appear formatted in tables. You can edit or reformat data. If you choose Paste Link, a LINK field is inserted that links to the server document. If you choose Paste, the data appears as unlinked text.
Unformatted Text	Text is unformatted. Worksheets appear as unformatted text with cells separated by tabs.
Picture	Pictures, text, database tables, or worksheet ranges appear as a picture. You can format them as pictures, but you cannot edit text. Unlinking changes them to Microsoft Draw objects.
Bitmap	Pictures, text, or worksheet ranges appear as bit-mapped images at screen resolution. You can format them as pictures, but you cannot edit the text.

10

Passing Linked Documents to Other Computer Users

If you break a link, you change the linked word processing and worksheet information into text, as though the text were typed in the client document. Graphics become pictures or bit-mapped images. If you break the link, you do not have to include a copy of the server file with the client document; however, breaking the link also means that the person receiving the data cannot update it.

To break a link, follow these steps:

1. Select the linked data.

2. Choose the Edit menu and select the Links command.

The Links dialog box enables you to freeze linked data by breaking the link.

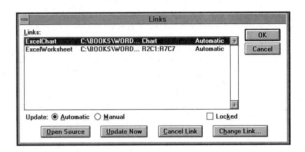

3. If you did not select the links you want to break in step 1, select the links from the Links list.

4. Choose the Cancel Link button. If a dialog box prompts you to confirm that you want to cancel the link, choose Yes.

If you want to remove linked data rather than break the link, select the linked data and press the Del key.

Updating Linked Data

If your link is automatic, the linked data in the client document automatically updates when you make a change to the data in the server document. If your link is manual, however, you must tell the client program to update the link.

To update linked data, follow these steps:

1. Select the linked data.

2. Choose the Edit menu and select the Links command.

10

3. If you did not select the linked data in step 1, select the links from the Links list.

4. Choose the Update Now button.

If a link is set to update manually, it will not update when you edit it. To see the update, you must use the Update Now button.

Some programs have a shortcut for updating manual links. In Word for Windows, for example, you select the linked data and press the F9 key to update the link.

Embedding Data into a Document

Another method of inserting data from one program into another is *embedding*, which enables a server document to store its data directly within a client program's document. For example, you can store a picture from Windows Paintbrush within a Windows Write letter, or store a budget and chart from Microsoft Excel within a Word for Windows document. Not only can you see the budget table and chart, but the actual worksheet and chart data are stored in the client document so that you can make changes or review the originals.

Two basic types of object linking and embedding (OLE) server programs exist. Windows Paintbrush is one type—a stand-alone program you can use as an OLE server program or as you use any other program. You can embed a Paintbrush object in a client document by copying and pasting it or by inserting it. The other type of OLE server program is called an *applet*—a miniature program you operate only from within a client program. The word processing program Word for Windows, for example, comes with several free applets, including Microsoft Draw, a drawing applet, and MS WordArt, an applet you can use to create logos.

Embedding data does away with the need to include server data files whenever you send someone a document that contains links. Embedded data is stored within the client document, not as a separate file. This method, however, creates large files.

Creating an Embedded Object

You can create embedded objects in two ways. You can copy data from the server program and embed that data into a client document as an object. Use this technique when you want to embed an object you created using a stand-alone OLE server program such as Paintbrush. The other way to create an

10

227

embedded object is to start the server program from within a client document, create the object, and then insert it into the client document. Use this technique whenever you are using an OLE applet.

To insert an embedded object using any OLE server or applet, follow these steps:

1. Move the insertion point to the place where you want to insert the embedded object.

2. Depending on your program, choose the Edit menu and select the Insert Object command, or choose the Insert menu and select the Object command.

The Object dialog box appears, showing the types of objects you can embed.

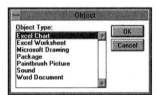

3. From the Object Type list, select the type of object you want to insert, and then choose OK or press ⏎Enter.

4. In the server program, create the data you want.

    You can create the server data from scratch, or you can copy an existing file into the server document.

5. Use one of the following techniques to embed the server data, as appropriate to the program creating the object:

    • Choose the File menu and select the Exit and Return command. When a dialog box prompts you to save your changes, choose Yes.

    • Close the document window containing the object.

    • Choose the File menu and select the Update command.

For a program to appear in the Object Type list, the program must be registered with Windows and must be capable of producing embedded objects. Programs capable of object linking and embedding are registered when you install them in Windows.

To embed an object you created using a stand-alone OLE server program such as Microsoft Excel, follow these steps:

1. Start the server program and create the object or open the file that contains the object.

2. Select the object, and then choose the Edit menu and select the Copy command.

3. Activate the client program and position the insertion point where you want to embed the object in the document.

4. Choose the Edit menu and select the Paste Special command.

The Paste Special dialog box lists the objects you can paste.

5. Select the item labeled *object* of the server program (for example, Excel Worksheet Object) from the Data Type list.

6. Choose the Paste button.

Some programs, such as Windows Paintbrush and Windows Write, enable you to embed an object by copying and pasting it. To embed a picture from Paintbrush into a letter in Write, for example, select and copy the picture in Paintbrush, switch to Write, and paste in the picture. The picture is automatically embedded.

Editing Embedded Objects

You edit an embedded object by starting the server program from within the client document. To edit an embedded object with a mouse, double-click the object. To edit an embedded object with the keyboard, select the object, choose the Edit menu, and then select the Object command of the server program. If the object you select is an Excel worksheet, for example, choose the Edit menu and select the Excel Worksheet Object command. If the OLE server program you used to create the embedded object is already running, it activates. If the program is not already running, it starts.

When the server program starts, it also opens the file that contains the embedded object, enabling you to make changes. Make your changes, and then update the client document. Note that if you do not update the client document, you lose your changes.

To update the object and exit the server program, use whichever of the following commands is appropriate:

10

- Choose the File menu and select the Exit and Return command to close the program and update the object.
- Close the document window containing the object to close the object and keep the program open. You are prompted to specify whether you want to update the object.
- Choose the File menu and select the Update command to update the embedded object and keep the program and object open.

Note: After you edit an embedded object and update the client document, make sure that you save the client document.

Embedding Data as Packages

In addition to linking or embedding data, you can enclose data as a *package* and embed into your client document an icon that represents that data. The icon, a small picture, can represent part of a document or an entire document. The advantage to embedding packages in your client document is that a package conserves space—a package appears as an icon, but an object appears in its entirety. Only programs that support object linking and embedding can support embedded packages.

10

This document contains packaged data. Embedded packages can contain all or part of a file, sound, or animation.

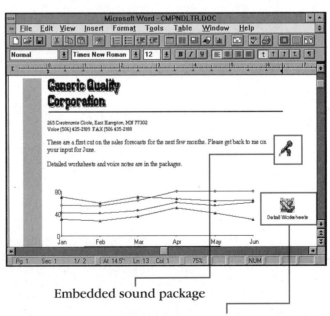

Embedded sound package

Embedded worksheet package

Activating an embedded package presents the data that the package contains. Embedded packages can be text, worksheets, graphics, sound, voice, or animation. Package icons can even have labels, and you can create custom icons.

You may want to embed a package when:

- A previous report is referred to in a memo and you want to package that report with the memo, but you don't want to burden the reader with a large number of pages. As a package, the report is opened only if the reader double-clicks the icon.

- A new product proposal needs detail, but you don't want it to get in the way of your short and concise report. You package the worksheets, charts, and notes and embed them in the proposal.

- A variance report needs an explanation of each sales item that is off the forecast. To keep the report manageable, package a note on each variance and put the icon containing that note next to each variance.

Different Windows programs work differently with packages, depending on the date when they were written. The following procedures describe different methods of creating object packages and embedding them as icons in a document. In many instances, you use the Object Packager, a Windows accessory program, to package data you want to embed.

The remainder of this section describes several ways to package objects using the Object Packager, which appears on-screen as a two-sided window.

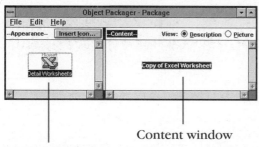

You can use the Object Packager to embed icons that represent data in a client document.

10

Content window

Appearance window

The left side of the Object Packager is the *Appearance window,* which displays the icon that will represent the data. The right side of the Object Packager is the *Content window,* which shows a picture of the object or the object's name, such as a file name. If you select View Description, the object's name appears in the Content window; if you select View Picture, a picture of the object appears.

Packaging Entire Files

You can package and embed files using the Object Packager or the File Manager. The File Manager method is easy and enables you to link a package to the server document, but the Object Packager enables you to change the icon and add a custom label.

When you package an entire file, displaying or playing the package starts the program you used to create the packaged object and opens the file containing that object. If the object is a sound or video object, you must use the program's commands to play it.

Packaging a File with the Object Packager

If you want to include the entire contents of a file or document in the package, follow these steps:

1. Choose the Object Packager from the Accessories program window.
2. Select the Content window by clicking it or by pressing (Tab⇥) until Content is highlighted.
3. Choose the File menu and select the Import command.
4. Select the file you want to package and choose OK.

The package and its description appear in the Object Packager.

To embed the package into a document that has object linking and embedding ability, follow these steps:

1. With the Object Packager still active, activate the Appearance window by clicking it or by pressing (Tab⇥) until Appearance is highlighted.
2. Choose the Edit menu and select the Copy Package command.
3. Activate the client program and open the document. Move the insertion point to the place where you want the package icon to appear.
4. Choose the Edit menu and select the Paste command.

The package appears in the document as the icon you saw in the Object Packager.

Packaging Files with the File Manager

To use the mouse to package a file with the File Manager, follow these steps:

1. Activate the File Manager and scroll through the files until the file you want to package is visible.

10

2. Activate the program to receive the package. Move the insertion point to the place where you want the package.

3. Arrange both windows so that you can see the file name and the client document.

4. To create an embedded package, drag the file name from the File Manager onto the client document and release it. To create a linked package, hold down ⌈⇧Shift⌉+⌈Ctrl⌉ as you drag the file name from the File Manager onto the client document, and then release it.

To use the keyboard to package a file with the File Manager, follow these steps:

1. Activate the File Manager and select the file name you want to package.

2. Choose the File menu and select the Copy command.

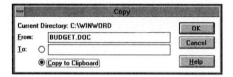

The Copy dialog box appears, enabling you to copy a file to the Clipboard.

3. Select the Copy To Clipboard option, and choose OK or press ⌈↵Enter⌉.

4. Activate the program and open the document to receive the package. Move the insertion point where you want the package.

5. To embed a package, choose the Edit menu and select the Paste command. To create a linked package, choose the Edit menu and select the Paste Link command.

Packaging Part of a Document

If you want to package only part of a document, use the Object Packager as an intermediary to hold the data as it is being packaged. When you package only part of a document, playing a sound or video object plays the sound or video without starting the program you used to create the object.

To package part of a document, follow these steps:

1. Open the document containing the data. Save the document if you want to create a linked package.

2. Select the data or graphic you want to package.

233

3. Choose the Edit menu and select the Copy command.

4. Activate the Object Packager and select the Content window (if it is not already selected) by clicking it or by pressing ⌜Tab⇄⌟ until Content is highlighted.

5. Choose the Edit menu and select the Paste command to create an embedded package, or choose the Edit menu and select the Paste Link command to create a linked package.

6. Choose the Edit menu and select the Copy Package command.

Now that the package is in the Clipboard, you can paste it into the client document by following these steps:

1. Activate the client program and open the client document.

2. Move the insertion point to the place where you want the package.

3. Choose the Edit menu and select the Paste command.

Displaying or Playing Package Contents

A package can contain any form of Windows data. The procedure for displaying or playing the contents of a package varies: you display graphics or text objects in the programs you used to create them; you open a sound or video object in the program you used to create it; or you simply play the sound or video. You can double-click the package to display or play the package contents (sound and video objects behave somewhat differently than graphics or text objects; for details, refer to Chapter 18, "Using Multimedia"). As an alternative, you can display or play the package using a command, which varies between programs. In Windows Write, for example, you can display or play a packaged object by choosing the Edit menu, selecting the Package Object command, and then selecting Activate Contents from the submenu that appears.

Selecting an Icon for Your Package

Normally when you paste or import data into the Object Packager, the icon that appears in the Appearance window is the icon related to the data's document. You can change that icon. To change an icon while it is in the Object Packager, follow these steps:

1. Select the Appearance window.

2. Choose the Insert Icon button.

10

The Insert Icon dialog box appears, displaying the current icon related to the data you are packaging.

3. Choose the Browse button.

4. From the Browse dialog box that appears (similar to an Open dialog box), select the name of a file containing icons, and then choose OK.

If you do not have a file containing a library of icons, select the PROGMAN.EXE file from the WINDOWS directory. It contains many files that you can use with Windows and DOS programs.

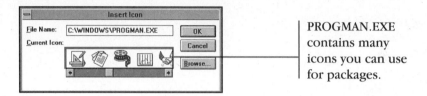

PROGMAN.EXE
contains many
icons you can use
for packages.

5. Select an icon from the Current Icon list shown in the Insert Icon dialog box. Then choose OK or press ↵Enter.

Editing a Package Label

Each package has a label. If you package a document, the label is the file name; if you packaged part of a file, the label is the object type. You can create your own label name.

To change a label while it is in the Object Packager, choose the Edit menu and select the Label command. In the Label dialog box that appears, enter a new name and choose OK. To change a label for a package in your program, refer to the following section.

Editing a Package from within Your Program

You can change anything about a package from within the program containing the package. To edit a package from within the program, start the Object Packager from your program. Although the commands for starting the Packager vary from program to program, the basic procedure is to select the package icon and choose an edit command. In Write, for example, choose the Edit menu, select the Package Object command, and then select Edit Package from the submenu that appears. After Object Packager appears, you can

10

choose any command necessary to edit the package. You can, for example, change the label or change the server file. When you finish editing the package, choose the File menu and select the Update command, and then close the Packager. Alternatively, close the Packager and choose Yes when a dialog box prompts you to update the package.

Sizing and Moving Package Icons in Your Program

Within some programs, such as Windows Write, you can size and move a package icon the same way you size or move graphics objects. For information on how to size and move a package icon in Write, refer to Chapter 11, "Using Windows Write."

Viewing Data in the Clipboard

If you need to see the information currently in the Clipboard, open the Clipboard Viewer program located in the Main program window. The Clipboard Viewer displays the contents of the Clipboard. From within the Clipboard Viewer, you can see the contents or a description of the Clipboard's contents.

Managing Links

Keeping track of the many links included in a complex document can be difficult, but the Edit Links command makes the job considerably easier. When you choose the Edit menu and select Links, the Links dialog box displays a list of each link in the document, its type, and whether it updates manually or automatically. You can use the buttons and check boxes to update linked data, lock links to prevent changes, cancel links, and change the file names or directories in which the linked data is stored.

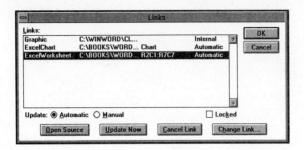

The Links dialog box simplifies managing multiple links in a document.

Before you can edit a link, you must select it. To select a link, click the link or select the Links list and press the up- or down-arrow key to select a link. To select multiple adjacent links in the Links dialog box, click the first link and then Shift+click the last link. To select or deselect multiple nonadjacent links, hold down the Ctrl key as you click the links.

Updating Links

To update individual links in a document so that the destination file is refreshed with new information, select the linked data and choose the Edit Links command. After the Links dialog box appears, select the links you want to update and choose the Update Now button.

When you want to update all the links in an entire document, select the entire document or select all the links in the Link dialog box, and choose the Update Now button.

Controlling Manual versus Automatic Updates

Some programs enable you to specify whether a link should automatically update itself or whether it should be updated only under manual control. If you paste a link, the link updates itself automatically; however, you may want your linked data to update only when you request it. Manually controlled updates can improve Windows performance, and enable you to control how frequently an update occurs.

To change an automatically updated link to a manual link, follow these steps:

1. Select the linked data or graphic.
2. Choose the Edit menu and select the Links command. The Links dialog box appears.

10

237

3. Select the Update option that specifies how you want the link updated.

- Select Manual if you want to update the link when you specify.

- Select Automatic if you want to update the link every time the server data changes.

4. Choose OK or press ⏎Enter.

To update a manual link, use the procedure described in the preceding section titled, "Updating Links."

Unlinking Inserted Files or Pictures

When you want to unlink the server document and change the linked data to normal text or a graphic, select the linked data. Then choose the Edit menu and select the Links command. Choose the Cancel Links button. A dialog box appears, prompting you to confirm that you want to cancel the link. Choose Yes to cancel the link.

Editing Links When Server File Names or Locations Change

If a server document's location, file name, or the linked range within the document changes, you need to change the link so that the server data can be found.

To update a link that does not work, follow these steps:

1. Choose the Edit menu and select the Links command.

2. Select the link you need to edit, and then choose the Change Link button to display the Change Link dialog box.

Use the Change Link dialog box when a linked file's name or directory changes.

```
┌─────────────────────────────────────────┐
│ ═  │        Change Link                  │
│ ┌──────────────────────────┐ ┌────────┐ │
│ Application:                 │   OK     │ │
│ ExcelWorksheet               └────────┘ │
│ File Name:                   ┌────────┐ │
│ C:\MARKETNG\SALES.XLS        │ Cancel │ │
│ Item:                        └────────┘ │
│ FORECAST                                │
└─────────────────────────────────────────┘
```

3. Edit the Application, File Name, or Item text boxes.

Ensure that the program, path and file name, and range name are correct for the new server document. The Item is the range name or bookmark that describes the linked data within the document.

238

Locking a Link To Prevent Accidental Changes

You may want to prevent accidental updating of a link, yet be able to update it at your discretion. You can prevent accidental changes by locking the link, and you can unlock it when you are ready to update the link. To lock or unlock a link, select the linked data and choose the Edit Links command. Select the link you want to lock or unlock, and then select or clear the Locked check box.

Summary

This chapter discussed the techniques you need to create compound documents—documents created from many different programs and collected together. Word for Windows and the Windows programs with which it can exchange data create the most powerful document-building system available.

In this chapter, you learned the following important points:

■ Object linking and embedding, or OLE, enables you to link data between documents (or between programs) or to embed an object created in one program within a document created in another program.

■ Object linking and embedding requires two programs: a server program, which you use to create the linked data or the embedded object, and a client program, in which you link data or embed an object.

■ To take advantage of object linking and embedding, your programs must support OLE. Some programs (such as Word for Windows) can function as a client and as a server. Other programs, such as Windows Write, function only as clients. Still other programs, such as Windows Paintbrush, function only as server programs.

■ You can embed an object in a client document without ever leaving the client document. After you embed an object in your client document, you can double-click the object to activate the program you used to create the object. Thus, you also can edit the embedded object without leaving the client document.

■ Using the Object Packager—a Windows accessory program—you can embed data as a *package*. An embedded package appears as an icon in the client document.

■ You can double-click a package icon to display or play its contents. If your computer is equipped for multimedia, you can double-click a sound package to play a tune.

10

■ You can edit a link in your document, specifying that it update automatically or manually, or changing the server file.

Remember that to use Windows' object linking and embedding (OLE) technology, your programs must support OLE. The Windows accessory programs described in the following two chapters, Chapter 11, "Using Windows Write," and Chapter 12, "Using Windows Paintbrush," both support object linking and embedding. To learn about using object linking and embedding with sound, video, and CD-ROM devices, refer to Chapter 18, "Using Multimedia."

For more information on using programs together, refer to Chapters 4 and 20. To integrate Windows programs so that they can share data, refer to Chapter 19.

10

Using Windows Write

11

Windows Write is a word processing program that's simple to use but powerful enough to help you get your work done quickly. The two main benefits to using any word processing program are that you can edit your work on the computer screen and save your work as a file for use later. But Windows Write goes much further than that.

With Write, you can enhance typed text by making it bold, italic, a larger size, or a different *type style* (font). You can add automatic headers and footers to your pages, including automatic page numbers. You can control the line spacing and change how the text is aligned with the margins of the pages—whether text is centered, aligned to the left or right, or *justified* (with both margins even). You can move text from one place in a document to another, and you can search for specific words—and even replace them. You can do all these tasks efficiently, using the Windows Write pull-down menus and dialog boxes. And you don't have to memorize commands.

11

Key Terms in This Chapter

Word processing program	A program that enables you to work with words to create such documents as memos, letters, and reports.
Document	The text you create in a word processing program.
File	A magnetic copy of your document after you name it and save it on the computer.
Margins	The space between the working area on your page and the edges of the paper.
Select	To highlight text so that you can make changes to it.
Format	To change the appearance of selected text, such as making it bold or aligning it at the center of the page.
Cut and paste	The process of moving text from one area of a document to another area, to another document, or to another program.
Clipboard	The temporary file that stores text you have cut or copied. (Because the Clipboard is shared by all Windows programs, you can cut or copy, and then paste between programs.)

Learning Windows Write has another advantage. When you become proficient with it, you can easily make the switch to a word processing program that has even more power, such as Word for Windows. Many of the commands and shortcuts you learn to use in Write are similar (or the same) in Word for Windows, and you can use all your Write files in Word for Windows.

Starting Windows Write

To start Write, you first must start Windows. (Refer to Chapter 2, "Getting Started," if you need help starting Windows.) When you first start Windows, a window called the Program Manager appears on-screen. The Program Manager contains the following program groups: Main, Accessories, StartUp, and

242

Games. Another program group, Applications, appears if you asked Windows to create this group when you installed Windows. (Because you can create your own program groups, you may see additional groups on-screen.) The program groups may appear as *icons* (pictures) or as open windows.

You can open a program group icon, such as Accessories, into a window by double-clicking the icon. When the program group is open as a window, you can see the programs it contains. Windows Write is a Windows accessory program located in the Accessories program group.

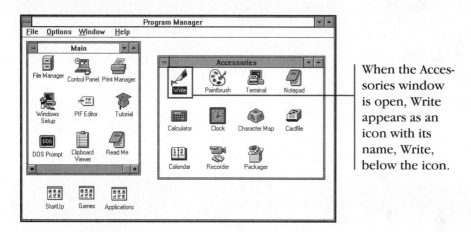

When the Accessories window is open, Write appears as an icon with its name, Write, below the icon.

To start the Write program, double-click its icon. Alternatively, if you are using the keyboard, press Ctrl+Tab until you select the Accessories window, use the arrow keys to select the Write icon, and then press Enter to start the program. This procedure is the same for starting any Windows program.

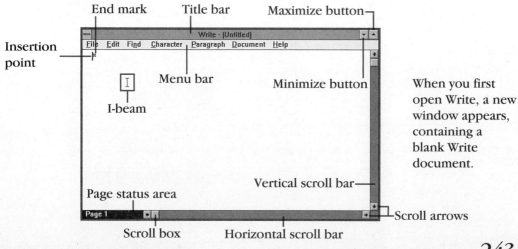

When you first open Write, a new window appears, containing a blank Write document.

243

11

Some parts of the window are like those in other windows. A title bar across the top displays the name of the program and the name of the document (untitled until you name it). A menu bar is below the title bar, and scroll bars are on the right and bottom sides of the window.

Besides these familiar window parts, Write has some unique features: an *insertion point* where characters appear as you type, an *end mark* that shows the end of your typing, and a *page status area* at the bottom left corner of the window. Also on-screen is a *pointer* that moves around as you move the mouse. The pointer may appear as an arrow (over a menu name or scroll bar) or as an I-beam (in the typing area of the screen).

Typing Text in a New Document

When you start Write, you open a new Write document. You are then ready to start typing. Like all word processing programs, Write offers word wrap, a feature that enables you to type to the right margin and just keep typing. As you type, the text automatically wraps to the next line. When you get to the end of a paragraph, press Enter. (Press Enter twice to leave a blank line between paragraphs.)

Note: Be sure that you don't press Enter until you reach the end of a paragraph.

Each character you type appears at the blinking insertion point, pushing the insertion point one character to the right.

Notice that the end mark stays ahead of the insertion point.

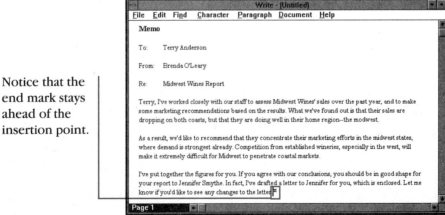

11

If your computer screen is not wide enough to show the full document width, the typing area may be wider than the screen. In that case, the screen scrolls left and right as you type, attempting to show you each word typed. If you find the scrolling annoying, refer to the section "Setting Margins and Tabs," further in this chapter, for details on making your margins wider (so that the typing area is narrower).

If you make a mistake as you type, you can erase it by pressing the Backspace key, which erases the character to the left of the insertion point. You learn many other ways to edit text in subsequent sections of this chapter.

Saving and Opening a Document

Until you save a document, it's like a song on the radio. If the radio goes off, you lose the song. A saved file, however, is like a song on a CD. Even if the electricity goes off, you still have the song, because it was recorded on the CD. Therefore, to make sure that you do not lose a document, save it every 15 minutes or so. Saving the document "records" it on-disk. After you save a document, you can open it again at a later time to edit or print it.

Saving a Document

Until you save the document, it has no name; it is called *Untitled*. The first time you save the document, you give it a name. From then on, the document has a name, which appears in the title bar at the top of the Write window. Your file name can contain up to eight letters or numbers; Write automatically assigns the three-letter extension WRI to each file name.

When you save a document, you save it as a computer file.

You therefore use the File menu to choose the command to save your file.

11

To save and name the file, follow these steps:

1. Choose the File menu and select the Save As command. The Save As dialog box appears.

2. From the Directories list, select a directory if you want to save the file in a directory other than the current one, which is shown above the Directories list.

3. From the Drives list, select a drive if you want to save your file to a drive other than the current drive.

4. In the File Name text box, type a file name for the document. A file name can have as many as eight letters or numbers.

In this example, the file name MEMO is in the File Name text box.

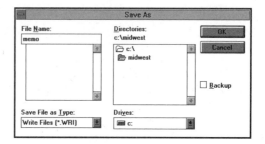

5. If you want to save your file in a format other than the Write format (to use the file in another program), select the format you want from the Save File as Type list.

6. Choose OK or press ↵Enter.

You may notice an additional check box in the Save As dialog box. Select Backup to make an automatic *backup* (an extra copy) of the file. Write saves the backup file under the name you specify in the File Name text box, but gives it the extension BKP instead of WRI.

Now that the document has a file name, you have two options the next time you want to save the file. If you want to keep only one copy of the file on-disk, choose the File menu and select the Save command (instead of Save As). The Save command saves the new version of the file on top of the previous version, thus replacing it. The second option is to select the Save As command and give the file a new name. By creating a new file, you preserve the previous version of the file.

246

Opening a Saved Document

11

Often you will want to edit a document you created earlier. You must first use the **O**pen command to retrieve the document you saved earlier.

Notice that when you open an existing file, the one you're currently working on closes. If you have made changes to the current document since you last saved, Write asks whether you want to save your changes. Choose **Y**es, **N**o, or Cancel.

To retrieve an existing file, follow these steps:

1. Choose the **F**ile menu and select the **O**pen command.

Write gives you a chance to save your current document before opening another document.

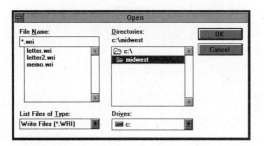

When you select the **O**pen command, the Open dialog box appears.

2. From the **D**irectories list, select the directory containing the file you want to open, if the directory is different from the current one (which is shown above the **D**irectories list).

3. From the **D**rives list, select the drive containing the file you want to open, if the drive is different from the current drive.

4. From the List Files of Type list, select the file format of the file you want to open, if it is not a Write file.

5. In the File **N**ame list, select the file you want to open, or type the name of the file you want to open in the File **N**ame text box.

6. Choose OK or press ⏎Enter.

247

11 Moving Around in a Document

Because one of the biggest advantages of a word processing program is its capability to edit text, you need to know how to move around on-screen to locate the text you want to edit. You can move around in many ways, including using the arrow keys, using the mouse, and using special keys (such as PgUp and PgDn). You are not restricted to one method of moving around in a document; people who use a mouse often use keyboard shortcuts as well.

You can move the insertion point anywhere within the document's text. You cannot, however, move the insertion point beyond the end mark.

Moving Around with the Keyboard

One of the simplest ways to move around on-screen is to use the arrow keys to move the insertion point. You can press the up-arrow key to move up one line, the down-arrow key to move down one line, or the left- or right-arrow key to move respectively left or right one character. By holding down any of the arrow keys, you can move many lines or characters at once.

To move the insertion point a little faster, use the movement keys on your keyboard. The PgUp key moves the insertion point up one screen, and the PgDn key moves the insertion point down one screen. The Home key moves the insertion point to the beginning of the line, and the End key moves the insertion point to the end of the line.

Using the Ctrl key in combination with other keys extends their movement. For example, if you hold down Ctrl while you press the left- or right-arrow key, the insertion point moves one word at a time. Ctrl+Home or Ctrl+End moves the insertion point to the beginning or end of the document. Ctrl+PgUp or Ctrl+PgDn moves the insertion point to the top or bottom of the current window.

You can use one final key, the number 5 on the numeric keypad, to move the insertion point. (If Num Lock is on, turn it off by pressing the Num Lock key.) Press 5+left arrow or 5+right arrow to move respectively left or right by one sentence. Press 5+up arrow or 5+down arrow to move respectively to the preceding or next paragraph. Press 5+PgUp or 5+PgDn to move respectively to the preceding or next page break (the document must have page breaks). Alternatively, choose the Find menu, select the Go To Page command, type the number of the page you want to go to, and press Enter.

Table 11.1 summarizes the keystrokes you can use to move the insertion point. Remember that you use the numeric keypad for the 5 key; first make sure that Num Lock is turned off.

Table 11.1
Keystrokes for Moving the Insertion Point

Keystroke(s)	Movement
← or →	Single character, left or right
↑ or ↓	Single line, up or down
Ctrl + → or Ctrl + ←	Next or preceding word
Home	Beginning of the line
End	End of the line
5 + → or 5 + ←	Next or preceding sentence
5 + ↓ or 5 + ↑	Next or preceding paragraph
Ctrl + PgUp or Ctrl + PgDn	Top or bottom of the window
PgUp or PgDn	One screen, up or down
Ctrl + Home	Beginning of document
Ctrl + End	End of document
5 + PgDn or 5 + PgUp	Next or previous page (the document must include page breaks)

Note: For continuous movement, hold any of the keys or key combinations listed in this table.

Moving Around with the Mouse

As you move the mouse, a pointer moves correspondingly on-screen. The pointer generally has two different shapes: an I-beam and an arrow. In the typing area of the screen, the pointer becomes an I-beam; near a menu, a scroll bar, the title bar, the left margin, or a dialog box, it becomes an arrow. (The pointer has a third shape, a double-headed arrow, which appears when you move the pointer over a window border.)

11

The I-beam serves a special function: it moves the insertion point to a new location on-screen. Suppose, for example, that you have just finished typing a three-paragraph letter, and you want to edit a word in the first paragraph. Use the mouse to position the I-beam to the right of the word, and then click the mouse button. The insertion point moves to the I-beam's position. Remember that the I-beam is different from the insertion point: you use the I-beam to move the insertion point (or to select text, as you learn later in this chapter); the insertion point is where your edits appear.

You can use the mouse also to scroll the screen. Suppose that your letter is instead two pages long, and you want to move from the second page back to the first page. Use the mouse to point to the vertical scroll bar, and click the up arrow at the top of the scroll bar. You scroll upward, toward the beginning of the document. To move down, you can point to the down arrow and click. To move left or right, you can click the left or right arrow at either end of the horizontal scroll bar. (If you click and hold the scroll arrows, you scroll continuously.) You also can drag a scroll box—which represents your position in the document—in either direction. Alternatively, you can click in the shaded area on either side of the scroll box to move the scroll box in that direction one screen at a time (for example, click in the vertical scroll bar above the scroll box to move up one screen).

Scrolling isn't quite the same as moving. When you scroll, you display a different part of the document, but the insertion point remains where it was. You often will use the scroll bars together with the I-beam, first scrolling to display the text where you want to move and then clicking the I-beam to move the insertion point there.

Editing a Document

With Write, you easily can edit or revise your documents. Editing includes such changes as correcting spelling errors, rewording sentences, and reorganizing paragraphs.

Inserting and Deleting Characters

The simplest way to edit text is to delete and insert characters. Start by moving the insertion point to the location in which you want to delete or insert text. Press the Backspace key to erase the character to the left of the insertion point (if you hold down Backspace, you will erase a string of characters). Then type

11

the new text. As you type, the new text is inserted to the left of the insertion point, and the text to the right moves farther right to make room for the new text.

Selecting Text

More complicated editing requires that you begin by selecting the text you want to edit. To select simply means to highlight text, identifying it as the text you want to affect when you press a key or choose an editing command. If you want to erase a sentence from a letter, first select the sentence, and then press the Backspace key or the Del key.

┌Selection bar   ┌Selected text

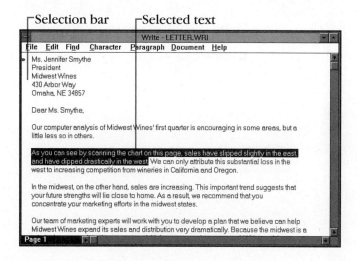

Selected text is highlighted, ready to be edited.

You can select text in several ways, using the keyboard or the mouse.

To select text with the keyboard, follow these steps:

1. Move the insertion point to the place where you want to begin selecting text.
2. Press and hold down ⇧Shift.
3. Press any arrow key to move the insertion point across the text you want to select. (The text is selected because you are holding down ⇧Shift.)
4. Release both keys.

11

You aren't limited to using just the arrow keys to select text. You can use the Shift key in combination with any of the other keys that moves the insertion point. For example, to select one word at a time, hold down the Shift and Ctrl keys and then press the left- or right-arrow key.

One way to select text with the mouse is to follow these steps:

1. Move the I-beam to one side of the text you want to select.
2. Hold down the left mouse button.
3. Drag the I-beam over the text you want to select (you can drag in any direction).
4. Release the mouse button.

If you need to select more than one full screen of text, continue holding down the mouse button while you drag the I-beam to the edge of the screen. The screen scrolls automatically when the I-beam touches the edge of the screen.

Several shortcuts are available for selecting text with the mouse. You can, for example, double-click a word to select it. Or you can move the I-beam into the left margin of the document, until the I-beam becomes an arrow that points toward the text. This area to the left of the left margin is called the *selection bar*; you can use it to select large areas of text. Table 11.2 shows a number of techniques for selecting text with the mouse.

Deselecting Text

When you finish editing the selected text, you may want to deselect it. With the keyboard, press any arrow key to deselect text. With the mouse, click the I-beam anywhere in your document to deselect the current selection.

Replacing Text

One way to replace text is to delete it and type new text. A second method can save you a step: select the text you want to replace, and then type the new text. The new text replaces the old.

Undoing an Edit

Because no one is perfect and people sometimes change their minds, many programs—including Write—come equipped with an "oops" command. More accurately, it's called the Undo command, and it undoes your most recent

11

edit. For example, if you delete a paragraph and then realize that you deleted the wrong one, you can undo the deletion. You can even undo an undo.

Table 11.2
Techniques for Selecting Text with the Mouse

Selection	Technique
One word	Double-click the word.
Several words	Double-click the first word and drag to the end of the last word.
Any amount of text	Drag from the beginning to the end of the text.
Text between two distant points	Move the insertion point to the beginning point, click, move to the second point, press and hold down ⇧Shift, and click the second point.
One line	Click in the selection bar (white space) to the left of the line.
Several lines	Click and drag up or down in the selection bar.
Paragraph	Double-click in the selection bar to the left of the paragraph.
Entire document	Press Ctrl and click in the selection bar.

To undo an edit, follow these steps:

1. Choose the Edit menu.
2. Select the Undo command.

```
Edit
Undo Formatting   Ctrl+Z

Cut               Ctrl+X
Copy              Ctrl+C
Paste             Ctrl+V
Paste Special...
Paste Link

Links...
Object
Insert Object...

Move Picture
Size Picture
```

The "undo" command may appear as Undo, Undo Typing, Undo Editing, or Undo Formatting, depending on your last action.

253

11

A quick way to undo an edit is to use the Undo command's shortcut: press Ctrl+Z.

Copying and Moving Text

One of Windows' most important features, the Clipboard, is shared by Write. The Clipboard is a temporary holding file that stores text you have selected and then cut or copied with the Cut or Copy command in the Edit menu. To retrieve text from the Clipboard, you use the Paste command from the Edit menu. You can use these commands to move text (by first cutting and then pasting it) or to duplicate text (by first copying and then pasting it).

To copy text, follow these steps:

1. Select the text you want to copy.

2. Choose the Edit menu and select the Copy command.

The Copy command's shortcut key combination is Ctrl+C.

A copy of the selected text is stored in the Clipboard.

3. Move the insertion point to the place where you want to put the copied text.

4. Choose the Edit menu and select the Paste command.

The Paste command's shortcut key combination is Ctrl+V.

11

Text stays in the Clipboard until you replace it with different text or turn off your computer. You can paste the contents of the Clipboard as many times as you want, duplicating the original text indefinitely.

To move text, follow these steps:

1. Select the text you want to move.
2. Choose the Edit menu and select the Cut command.

The Cut command's shortcut key combination is Ctrl + X.

The text is moved into the Clipboard (and removed from the document).

3. Move the insertion point to the place where you want to move the text.
4. Choose the Edit menu and select the Paste command.

Finding and Replacing Text

In a long document, finding a single word may be difficult. And if your document contains many occurrences of a word or phrase that you must change, making the changes one by one can be tedious. Write can help you with both tasks through the Find and Replace commands in the Find menu.

Finding Text

When you ask Write to find text, the program searches through the document from the insertion point forward, selecting the first occurrence of the text.

To find text, follow these steps:

1. Choose the Find menu and select the Find command.

255

11

The **F**ind com-
mand is selected
from the Find
menu.

When you choose Find, the Find dialog box appears.

2. In the Find What box, type the text you want to find.

In this example,
Write will look for
occurrences of
the complete
word *west*.

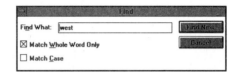

3. Choose Find Next. Write finds and selects the text, leaving the Find
   dialog box open.

   If the Find dialog box hides the selected text in your document, you
   can move the Find dialog box. With the mouse, click the dialog box's
   title bar and drag it to a new location. With the keyboard, press
   Alt +space bar, choose Move, press the arrow keys to move the
   dialog box, and then press ↵Enter to confirm its new location.

4. Press Esc or choose Cancel to close the Find dialog box, or choose
   Find Next again to find the next occurrence of the text.

The Find dialog box contains two check boxes: Match Whole Word Only and
Match Case. Select Match Whole Word Only to find your text only if it is a
whole word—for example, *is* but not *this*, *issue*, or *isn't*. Select Match Case if
you want to find exact upper- or lowercase matches of your text—for example,
Computer but not *computer*.

To search again for the same text, choose the Find menu and select the Repeat
Last Find command. You also can press F3 to repeat the last find.

After Write finds and selects text, you can edit that text without closing the
Find dialog box. Click the Write window or press Alt+F6 to activate the
document window. After you edit the text, click the Find dialog box or press
Alt+F6 to switch back to the dialog box.

Replacing Text

The Replace command is handy when you need to change text throughout
your document. This command helps you find every occurrence of the text

11

you want to change, and then replace it. By using the Replace command, you can be sure that you won't miss any occurrences. Like Find, Replace searches for and changes text from the insertion point forward in the document.

To replace text, follow these steps:

1. Choose the Find menu and select the Replace command.

The Replace command is selected from the Find menu.

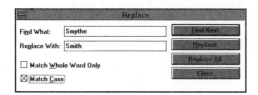

When you select the Replace command, the Replace dialog box appears.

2. In the Find What box, type the text you want to change.

3. Type the replacement text in the Replace With box.

4. Choose Find Next. Write selects the next occurrence of the text you typed in the Find What box.

5. Choose the Replace button to change the selected text and find the next occurrence of the text you want to change.

   Or choose Replace All to change all occurrences of the text.

   Or choose Find Next to find the next occurrence of the text without changing the current occurrence.

6. Press Esc or choose Close to close the Replace dialog box.

The Replace dialog box contains two check boxes: Match Whole Word Only and Match Case. Select Match Whole Word Only to replace your text only if it is a whole word—for example, *vision* but not *television*. Select Match Case if you want to replace exact upper- or lowercase matches of your text—for example, *City* but not *city*.

To replace text in just part of your document, select that part of the document before you choose the Replace command. The Replace All button changes to Replace Selection.

257

11

Note: If you mistakenly replace all occurrences of the text in your document, you can undo the replacement by choosing the Edit menu and selecting the Undo command. Be careful when you use Replace All, though; Undo is available only immediately after you perform the replacement.

Enhancing the Text

Enhanced text not only makes a document look better by adding variety to your pages, but also helps make the document more organized, and thus more readable, by adding emphasis to important words or headings. Write includes many tools for enhancing characters, including bold and italic, various font styles, and numerous font sizes. All text-enhancement commands are located in the Character menu.

A check mark indicates each currently selected text-enhancement command in the Character menu.

To enhance existing text, you must first select it. (If you don't remember how to select text, refer to "Editing a Document," a previous section in this chapter.) You can enhance text as you type by first choosing the enhancement, then typing the text, and finally choosing the enhancement a second time to turn it off.

Emphasizing Characters

Bold text stands out and is excellent for adding emphasis to headlines, subheadings, or other important text. Italic text adds more subtle emphasis and is also useful for identifying titles and names within a document. Underlining, a holdover from the days of the typewriter, is less useful but may be appropriate for headings in tables or for dividing sections of text. Superscript and subscript characters are raised or lowered, respectively, from the rest of the text and are used for footnotes or scientific notations.

11

To emphasize characters, follow these steps:

1. Select the text you want to emphasize, or move the insertion point to the place where you want the enhanced text to start.

2. Choose the Character menu.

3. Select the emphasis command you want to apply to the selected text:

   Bold

   Italic

   Underline

   Superscript

   Subscript

The Character menu lists shortcut key combinations for three commands. To use these shortcuts, select the text and press the shortcut key combination. To make a word bold, for example, select the word and then press Ctrl+B. You can apply several styles of emphasis to the same text. For instance, to make text both bold and italic, select the text, select the Bold command, and then, without deselecting the text, select the Italic command.

To return text to its normal appearance, follow these steps:

1. Select the text you want to return to normal.

2. Choose the Character menu.

3. Select the Regular command to remove all character enhancements, or press F5.

   Or select the single enhancement you want to remove (for example, select Bold to remove the bold formatting from bold text). If you use this technique, be sure that you have selected only the text from which you want to remove bold formatting; if you select text that is not already bold, you will *apply* the formatting rather than remove it.

Reducing and Enlarging Characters

A quick way to make text larger or smaller is to use the commands in the Character menu. Each time you choose the Reduce Font or Enlarge Font command, the text changes to the next standard font size. (Typically, standard font sizes are 10, 12, 14, 18, 24, and 36.) If you select 10-point type and select the Enlarge Font command, for example, the text enlarges to 12 points (rather than 11).

11

To reduce or enlarge characters, follow these steps:

1. Select the text you want to reduce or enlarge, or move the insertion point where you want the reduced or enlarged text to begin.

2. Choose the Character menu.

3. To reduce text, select the Reduce Font command; to enlarge text, select the Enlarge Font command.

You also can use the Font dialog box to change the size of characters, as explained in the following section.

Changing the Font

A font is a style of type, or a *typeface.* The font used in a newspaper is different from that of a road sign—a font that works well for a newspaper or book usually is not suitable for a large sign or poster. Write enables you to change your text to any font you have available in your computer or printer. Font sizes are measured in points, where 72 points equal one inch. Newspaper text may be 9 or 10 points in size, and headlines may be 18 to 36 points (72 if they are really important). A road sign, of course, is printed in a much larger font size.

Windows supplies several of the fonts available to you. These fonts are TrueType fonts, which look crisp on-screen and print with high quality on any printer that Windows supports. Other fonts may also be available for you to use. (To learn more about fonts, see Chapter 9, "Managing Fonts and TrueType.")

The Character menu provides two ways to change fonts. One way is to use the Fonts command to display the Font dialog box, in which you can change not only the font but also the font size and style. The fonts, styles, and sizes that appear in the Font dialog box depend on the fonts you have available on your computer or in your printer. The other way you can change fonts is to select one of the three fonts listed in the Character menu. These three fonts may change from time to time; they are simply the three fonts you have selected most recently.

In Write, you have two ways to change your fonts using the Character menu. You can select commands such as Bold, Italic, Reduce Font, and Enlarge Font from the menu, or you can choose the Fonts command to display the Font dialog box. In the Font dialog box, you can change the font, the font style (such as bold or italic), and the font size. A sample box shows you what the font looks like; a message below the sample box describes the status of the font on-screen and when printed.

260

11

To change fonts, font style, and font size, follow these steps:

1. Select the text you want to change.
2. Choose the Character menu and select the Fonts command.

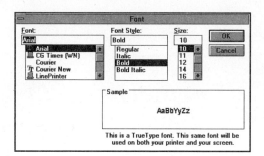

The Font dialog box appears.

3. Select the font you want from the Font list box (scroll the list if necessary). The selected font appears in the Font text box.

   An icon to the left of each font indicates the font type. A TT icon indicates a TrueType font; a printer icon indicates a printer font; no icon indicates a system font.

4. From the Font Style list, select the font style you want.
5. From the Size list box, select the point size you want, or type the size you want in the Size box.
6. Choose OK or press [↵Enter].

The Sample box in the Font dialog box shows you how the font will look in your document.

Changing Alignment, Spacing, and Indents

The changes you make to the appearance of a document are called *formatting*. Write provides three levels of formatting. In a previous section, "Enhancing the Text," you learned how to format text at the character level, using the Character menu. Character-level formatting applies to blocks of text as small as one character. In this section, you learn how to format text at the paragraph level, using the Paragraph menu. Paragraph-level formatting applies to entire paragraphs—and remember, a paragraph is any block of text that ends when you press the Enter key. In the next section, you learn about document-level formatting, which applies to an entire document.

11

You can format paragraphs in two ways: with the Paragraph menu or with the ruler. The ruler has icons that illustrate the type of formatting you are selecting; for example, the icon for centered text looks like several lines of centered text. To use the ruler, you must first display it.

To display the ruler, follow these steps:

1. Choose the Document menu.

2. Select the Ruler On command.

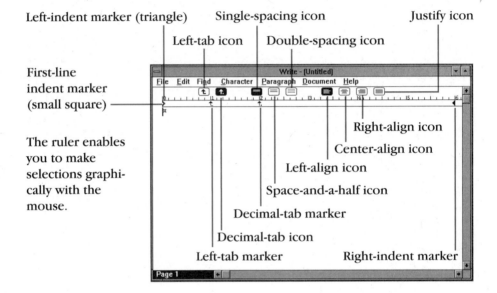

Left-indent marker (triangle) Single-spacing icon Justify icon

Left-tab icon Double-spacing icon

First-line
indent marker
(small square)

Right-align icon

Center-align icon

The ruler enables
you to make
selections graphically with the
mouse.

Left-align icon

Space-and-a-half icon

Decimal-tab marker

Decimal-tab icon

Left-tab marker Right-indent marker

When the ruler is displayed, the Ruler On command in the Document menu changes to Ruler Off. Choose the Document menu and select Ruler Off to hide the ruler.

Changing Paragraph Alignment

You can align paragraphs of text at the left margin, the right margin, or both margins (justified), or you can center paragraphs between margins.

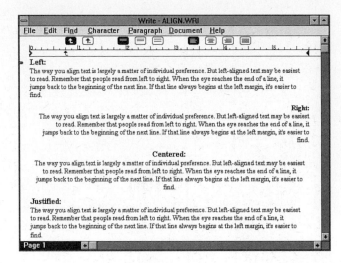

By default, Write's paragraphs are aligned at the left, but you can easily change the alignment for any paragraph you select.

To change paragraph alignment, follow these steps:

1. Select the paragraph or paragraphs you want to affect.

2. Choose the Paragraph menu.

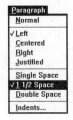

The Paragraph menu offers several alignment and spacing commands.

3. Select one of the alignment commands:

   Left

   Centered

   Right

   Justified

A check mark indicates the current paragraph alignment selection in the Paragraph menu.

11

To change paragraph alignment with the ruler, follow these steps:

1. Select the paragraph or paragraphs you want to affect.
2. Click the alignment icon for the alignment you want.

Changing Line Spacing

You can single-space (no extra spacing between lines) or double-space (one full line of space between lines) paragraphs. You also can separate paragraph lines by a space and a half.

To change line spacing, follow these steps:

1. Select the paragraph or paragraphs for which you want to change the line spacing.
2. Choose the Paragraph menu.
3. Select one of the line-spacing commands:

   Single Space

   1 1/2 Space

   Double Space

To change line spacing with the ruler, follow these steps:

1. Select the paragraph or paragraphs for which you want to change the line spacing.
2. Click the line-spacing icon for the spacing you want.

Changing Indents

Indenting means moving text in from the margin. You can indent only the first line of a paragraph, or you can indent either the left or the right edge of a paragraph (or both edges). If you want all your paragraphs to have a first-line indent, set the first-line indent before you start typing. Every time you press the Enter key, the indent carries over to the next paragraph.

To indent a paragraph, follow these steps:

1. Select the paragraph or paragraphs you want to indent.
2. Choose the Paragraph menu and select the Indents command.

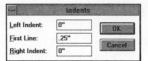

The Indents
dialog box
appears.

11

3. Type an indent distance (in decimal numbers) in the **Left** Indent, **First**
   Line, or **Right** Indent text box. To indent the first line of the selected
   paragraphs by 1/4 inch, for example, type **.25** in the **First** Line text box.

4. Choose OK or press ⏎Enter.

Setting indents with the ruler—especially first-line indents—requires good
eye-hand coordination. The ruler contains three indent markers. The black
triangle on the left side of the ruler is the left-indent marker. The first-line
indent marker is a small black square. (When the first-line indent marker is on
top of the left-indent marker, the first-line indent marker appears as a small
white square.) The black triangle on the right side of the ruler represents the
right indent. To set an indent, drag an indent marker to a new position on the
ruler.

First-line indent marker

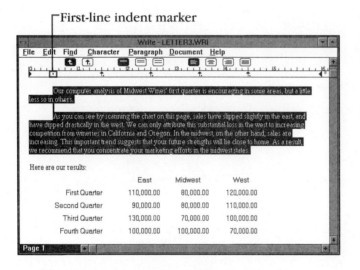

Dragging the
first-line indent
marker to the
half-inch mark on
the ruler indents
the first line of
selected para-
graphs.

To indent a paragraph with the ruler, follow these steps:

1. Select the paragraph or paragraphs you want to indent.

2. Drag the indent marker to a new position on the ruler.

11

Removing Paragraph Formatting

You can always change the alignment, line spacing, or indents for any selected paragraph. But if you want to remove all formatting at once and revert to Write's default of left-aligned, single-spaced paragraphs with no indents, select the paragraph or paragraphs you want to affect, choose the Paragraph menu, and select the Normal command.

Setting Margins and Tabs

In Write, margin and tab settings apply to an entire document. Write starts out with default settings: tabs every half inch, left and right margins of one and one-quarter inches, and top and bottom margins of one inch. You can use the Document menu to change margins and tabs, and you can use the ruler to change tabs.

To change the paper size or orientation, you must use the Print Setup dialog box. For a detailed discussion, refer to the section "Printing a Document," further in this chapter.

Setting Margins

To change a document's margins, follow these steps:

1. Choose the Document menu and select the Page Layout command.

The Page Layout dialog box appears.

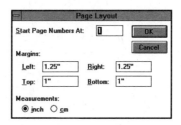

2. Type a margin distance (in decimal numbers) in the Left, Top, Right, and Bottom Margins boxes. To create a 2 1/2-inch top margin, for example, type 2.5 in the Top text box.
3. Choose OK or press ⏎Enter.

You can make two additional changes in the Page Layout dialog box. If you prefer working with centimeters rather than inches, choose the cm Measurements button. The ruler and dialog boxes will then show centimeters. In the Start Page Numbers At box, you can change the starting number for automatic page numbers. Automatic page numbering starts with that number. Automatic page numbers are more fully explained in "Adding Headers and Footers," further in this chapter.

Setting Tabs

In all word processing programs, using tabs is a two-part process: setting the tab stops and pressing the Tab key. When you press the Tab key in a document window, the insertion point moves to the next tab stop. In Write, you set the tab stops with either the Tabs dialog box or the ruler. Two types of tab stops are available: left and decimal. Left tabs align text on the left side of the tab stop, and decimal tabs align text on a period (useful for decimal numbers). When you set tab stops in Write, they apply to the entire document (whereas in most word processing programs, you also can set tab stops for selected text).

In the Tabs dialog box, you must type the location for each tab stop, measured in decimal inches from the left margin. For example, if you want tab stops every quarter inch, you must set tabs at 0.25, 0.5, 0.75, and so on.

If you change existing tab stops, any text in your document that uses those tab stops also changes. For example, if you use tab stops to set up a table and then you move the tab stops, the columns in the table move to align with the new tab stops.

To use the Tabs dialog box to set tabs in a document, follow these steps:

1. Choose the Document menu and select the Tabs command.

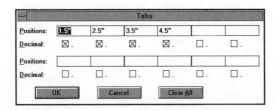 The Tabs dialog box appears.

2. In the Positions boxes, type the positions where you want tab stops, measured in decimal inches from the left margin. Press Tab⇅ to move between the Positions boxes and the Decimal boxes below them.

267

11

3. If you want a tab to be a decimal tab, select the Decimal box below the appropriate Positions box so that an X appears inside the Decimal box.

4. Choose OK or press ⏎Enter.

If you want to clear all the existing tab stops so that you can start over, choose Clear All in the Tabs dialog box. To change individual tab stops, select the existing tab stop positions and type new positions.

To use the ruler to add or change tabs, follow these steps:

1. Select either the Left-tab icon or the Decimal-tab icon on the ruler.

2. Click the ruler where you want the tab stop to appear. (Click the white area below the numbers.)

You can move tab stops on the ruler by dragging them left or right. You can remove tab stops from the ruler by dragging them down off the ruler.

Adding Headers and Footers

Headers and footers are strings of text that appear at the top or bottom of each page of a document (although you can exclude them from the first page if you prefer). Headers and footers don't appear on the computer screen—you see them when they print. One handy feature of headers and footers is that they can include automatic page numbers.

To create a header or footer, follow these steps:

1. Choose the Document menu and select the Header or the Footer command. The Page Header or Page Footer dialog box appears, and your document disappears.

11

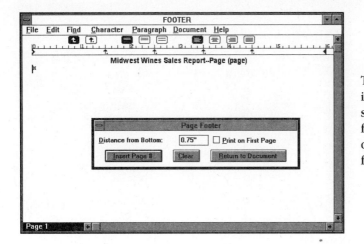

The document is replaced by a special window for typing the text of your header or footer.

2. Type the text of the header or footer, formatting it any way you want. Move between the dialog box and the header or footer window by clicking the location or by pressing [Alt]+[F6].

3. In the **D**istance from Bottom box or the **D**istance from Top box, type (in decimal numbers) the distance at which you want the header or footer to appear from the edge of the page. This distance should be less than the width of the top or bottom margin, so that the header or footer does not overlap your text.

4. Select the **P**rint on First Page option if you want the header or footer to appear on page 1 of the document. Do not select this option if you want to exclude the header or footer from the first page.

5. Choose Insert Page # to include automatic page numbering at the current location of the insertion point. In a header or footer, an automatic page number appears as (page) on-screen; the correct page number appears on the printed page.

6. Choose **R**eturn to Document to accept the header or footer.

To change the starting page number, choose the **D**ocument menu and select the **P**age Layout command. When the Page Layout dialog box appears, type the starting page number in the **S**tart Page Numbers At box. You might want to change the starting page number, for example, if your document is the second chapter of a multichapter report and you want sequential page numbering throughout the report.

If you are rewording an old header or footer, you can clear out the old before you start the new by choosing **C**lear in the Page Footer or Page Header dialog box.

11

Inserting Page Breaks

When you print, Write inserts automatic page breaks in a document, based on the size of the type, the width of the margins, the line spacing, and so on. If you want to preview the page breaks before you print, you can repaginate the document. If you want page breaks to appear in specific places, you must insert them manually.

To repaginate a document, follow these steps:

1. Choose the File menu and select the Repaginate command. The Repaginate Document dialog box appears.

2. Select the Confirm Page Breaks option if you want to confirm each page break or to move suggested page breaks.

3. Choose OK or press ⏎Enter. The Repaginating Document dialog box appears. Suggested page breaks appear as double arrows in the left margin.

4. Choose Up or Down to move the suggested page breaks up or down. You can move down a page break only if you moved it up earlier.

5. Choose Confirm.

You can insert manual page breaks without using the Repaginate command. Position the insertion point where you want to begin a new page, and press Ctrl+Enter. You can remove a manual page break by positioning the insertion point at the left end of the line below that page break and pressing Backspace.

In your document, an automatic page break appears as a double arrow in the left margin; a manual or confirmed page break appears as a heavy dotted line.

Adding Pictures or Graphics

You may think that you don't want to put pictures or graphics in your Write documents, but you may change your mind when you find out how much fun Paintbrush—another Windows accessory program—is to use, or how helpful a chart from the spreadsheet program Microsoft Excel can be.

To get a picture or graphic into Write, you can use one of three techniques. You can use the Clipboard to copy the picture from the program you used to create it, and then paste the picture into Write. A second technique is to embed a picture in your document. You can edit an embedded picture from within Write. The third technique is to link a picture when you paste it into your Write document. A linked picture in Write automatically updates when you change the original picture.

Copying Pictures into Write

To copy a picture into Write from another program, such as Microsoft Excel, you must run both programs. Use commands in the Edit menu of both programs to copy the picture into your Write document.

To copy a picture into Write, follow these steps:

1. Open the graphics program containing the picture you want to copy into your Write document.
2. Select the picture.
3. Choose the Edit menu and select the Copy command to copy the picture.
4. Close or Minimize the graphics program.
5. Open or activate the Write file.
6. Position the insertion point where you want the picture.
7. Choose the Edit menu and select the Paste command.

If the program from which you copy the picture supports object linking and embedding (as does Windows Paintbrush), pasting the picture into Write automatically embeds the picture in your document. You can edit an embedded picture from within Write; see the section "Editing Linked and Embedded Pictures," further in this chapter.

If you do not want to embed a picture you copy from a program that supports object linking and embedding (OLE), copy the picture as usual, choose Write's Edit menu, but select the Paste Special command rather than Paste. The Paste Special dialog box appears. From the Data Type list, select Bitmap or Picture, and then choose Paste.

Embedding a Picture in Write

To embed a picture, you can open a graphics program such as Windows Paintbrush from within your Write document. You can then use the graphics program to create a picture. When you update the file or exit the graphics program, the picture is added to your Write document. You can edit the picture from within Write.

11

To embed a picture in a Write file, follow these steps:

1. Position the insertion point where you want the picture to appear in your Write document.

2. Choose the Edit menu and select the Insert Object command. The Insert Object dialog box appears.

The Insert Object dialog box lists the graphics programs you can use to embed a picture.

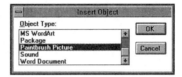

3. Select the graphics program you want to use to create an embedded picture. For example, select Paintbrush Picture.

4. Choose OK or press `↵Enter`. Paintbrush opens.

Paintbrush opens over your Write document.

5. Create a picture in Paintbrush.

6. When you're finished with your picture, choose the File Update command to include a copy of the picture in your Write document.

7. From the Paintbrush window, choose the File menu and select the Exit & Return command.

272

Linking Pictures

When you link a picture to a Write document, any time you change the original picture, the linked version in your Write document changes. Not all programs support linking; for example, Microsoft Excel supports linking, but Paintbrush does not.

To link a picture to a Write file, follow these steps:

1. Position the insertion point in your Write document where you want the linked picture to appear.

2. Open the program containing the picture you want to link. For example, open Microsoft Excel to link a chart into your Write document.

3. Open the file containing the picture you want to link, or create and save a new picture.

4. Select the picture.

5. Choose the Edit menu and select the Copy command.

6. Switch back to your Write document (Alt + Tab⇕ switches you between running programs).

7. Choose the Edit menu and select the Paste Link command.

8. Choose the File menu and select the Save or Save As command to save the Write file.

Editing Linked and Embedded Pictures

From within Write, you can edit pictures that are embedded from Windows Paintbrush or that are linked from another program such as Microsoft Excel. Editing the picture causes the graphics program to open, with the picture displayed in its window.

Commands can vary from program to program. Paintbrush, which supports embedding but not linking, has a File Update command for updating embedded pictures. Microsoft Excel, which supports both embedding and linking, does not have a File Update command, but does update pictures when you save the edited worksheet or chart. The following steps include commands that work with Paintbrush; you may need to scan menus to find an equivalent command in your program.

To use the mouse to edit an embedded drawing, follow these steps:

1. Double-click the drawing to open the graphics program and display the picture.
2. Edit the picture.
3. Choose the File menu and select the Update command.
4. Choose the File menu and select the Exit & Return command.

To use the keyboard to edit an embedded drawing, follow these steps:

1. Position the insertion point above the picture you want to edit.
2. Press ⬇ to select the picture.
3. Choose the Edit menu and select the Edit (program name) Object command. The graphics program opens, with the picture in its drawing window.
4. Edit the picture.
5. Choose the File menu and select the Update command to update the picture in Write.
6. Choose the File menu and select the Exit & Return command.

You can edit a linked picture in Write the same way that you edit an embedded drawing.

To use the mouse to edit a linked drawing, follow these steps:

1. Double-click the drawing to open the program used to create the picture. The picture is displayed.
2. Edit the picture.
3. Choose the File menu and select the Save command. The picture in your Write document is automatically updated.
4. Choose the File menu and select the Exit command.

To use the keyboard to edit a linked drawing:

1. In Write, select the picture you want to edit.
2. Choose the Edit menu and select the Edit (program name) Object command.
3. The program you used to create the picture appears on-screen. The picture is in the drawing window.
4. Edit the picture.
5. Choose the File menu and select the Save command. The picture in your Write document updates to reflect the changes you made.
6. Choose the File menu and select the Exit command.

Moving and Sizing Pictures

You can use special Write commands to move a picture or change its size. But first you must select the picture: select it just as though it were text, or point to the picture and click the mouse button.

To move a picture, follow these steps:

1. Select the picture.
2. Choose the Edit menu and select the Move Picture command.

   A dotted line outlines the picture, and a double-square icon appears inside the outline.
3. Move the outline left or right by dragging the mouse to the left or right, or by pressing ⟵ or ⟶.
4. Drop the picture into its new location by clicking the mouse button or pressing ↵Enter.

To change the size of a picture, follow these steps:

1. Select the picture.
2. Choose the Edit menu and select the Size Picture command.

   A dotted line outlines the picture, and a double-square icon appears inside the outline—just as for moving a picture.
3. Move the double-square icon to the outline's edge or corner that you want to move. To move the icon, drag the mouse or press the arrow key that points to the edge you want to move. (You press the arrow key only once.)
4. Size the picture by moving the edge or corner to a new position. To move the edge or corner, drag the mouse or press the arrow key. For example, if you want to move the edge or corner to the left, either drag the mouse to the left or press ⟵.
5. Accept the new size by clicking the mouse button or pressing ↵Enter.

Printing a Document

To print a document, you must give Write a few details about your printer, the orientation of the paper, the source of the paper, and so forth. Then you must specify how many copies you want and which pages of your document you want to print. If you do not intend to change any of these print settings, all you have to do is print.

275

11

To change print settings and print a document, follow these steps:

1. Choose the File menu and select the Print command.

The Print dialog
box appears.

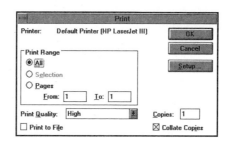

2. Select the Print Range All button to print all the pages.

    Or select Print Range Selection to print only the selected text.

    Or select the Print Range Pages From and To text boxes and type a range of pages to print. (To print pages 1 through 3, for example, type 1 in the From box and 3 in the To box.)

3. In the Copies box, type the number of copies you want to print.

4. If you want to change printer settings, choose Setup.

The Print Setup
dialog box
appears.

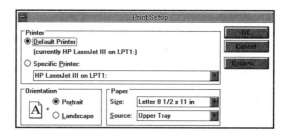

5. To change to a different printer, select the printer you want from the Printer group. You can select either the Default Printer or another printer from the Specific Printer list, which lists all the printers installed in Windows.

6. Change the paper orientation by selecting Portrait (vertical) or Landscape (horizontal).

7. Choose OK or press ↵Enter to close the Print Setup dialog box and return to the Print dialog box.

8. Choose OK or press ↵Enter to print your document.

The Print and Print Setup dialog boxes include additional options besides those described in the steps. In the Print dialog box, you can select the print resolution you want from the Print Quality list (printing at a lower quality improves speed). You can select the Print to File option to print to a file rather than to the printer. You can select the Collate Copies option to collate multiple copies of your document (if your printer supports collating).

In the Print Setup dialog box, you can select a different paper size from the Size list, or a different paper source from the Source list.

Quitting Write

After you create, save, and print your document, you probably are ready to call it a day (and with a little luck, it's quitting time, too). This step is the easiest part of all.

To quit Write, follow these simple steps:

1. Choose the File menu.
2. Select the Exit command.

If you have made changes to your document since you last saved it, Write prompts you to save them.

Summary

Write is a simple but powerful word processing program you can use to do much of your work. Although Write contains all of the most important word processing features, it lacks some advanced tools, such as a spelling checker, automatic tables of contents, and footnoting. If you find your needs expanding, you can easily move to a more powerful program like Word for Windows. Many of Write's commands are the same as those in Word for Windows, and your existing Write files are compatible with Word for Windows files.

Important features in Write include the capability to format text (for example, with bold and italic), to cut and paste, and to find and replace text. Like all Windows programs, Write works well with other Windows programs, using the Clipboard to transfer selections, such as pictures and graphics, between programs.

11

Some of Write's most important concepts and procedures are the following:

- Write shows you on-screen how the document will appear when printed, except for headers and footers.

- Turning on the ruler enables you to use the mouse to format a document quickly and easily.

- Write accepts graphics, pictures, and charts pasted from the Clipboard using Edit Paste.

- Write files, the ruler, shortcut keys, and some commands are compatible with the more powerful Word for Windows word processing program.

The next chapter, "Using Windows Paintbrush," teaches you how to use the simple graphics program included in the Windows package among the accessories. You can use Paintbrush to illustrate your work or to create computer drawings just for fun.

Using Windows Paintbrush

Y ou may wonder why you would ever need a program like Windows Paintbrush. You may think that you're not the artistic type, and what's more, you may think that you don't have time for Paintbrush because you have real work to do. What does drawing pictures have to do with work?

Plenty. Think about a long report filled with statistical facts and a lot of numbers—but no illustrations. How many people would want to read such a report? But imagine the same report spiced up with a few well-placed charts and graphs. Those illustrations would not only make the report more inviting to readers, but also would help clarify many points that might otherwise seem abstract.

Windows Paintbrush is a simple program you can use to create all kinds of illustrations—from free-form drawings to precise charts and graphs. You can copy the illustrations into many other Windows accessory programs, such as Write, Cardfile, or Notepad. Or you can use the illustrations in Windows programs such as Word for Windows, a powerful word processing program; Page-Maker, a desktop publishing program; or PowerPoint, a slide-show presentation program.

Using the toolbox, line-width box, and palette

Drawing lines and shapes

Using the painting tools

Adding text

Editing a drawing

Printing a drawing

Saving a drawing

Embedding and linking drawings

12

Key Terms in This Chapter

Draw	To draw a line, box, circle, or polygon in Paintbrush.
Paint	To paint a free-form line or shape in Paintbrush.
Toolbox	The box, on the left of the Paintbrush screen, that contains all the drawing and painting tools.
Line-width box	The box, at the bottom left of the Paintbrush screen, from which you can select the width for lines, for the borders of shapes, and for some tools.
Palette	The palette of colors (if you have a color monitor) or shades (if you have a monochrome monitor) you can use in your Paintbrush drawings.
Zoom in or out	To enlarge a drawing so that you can edit it dot by dot, or to reduce the drawing so that you can see the whole page.
Font	An alphabet of letters in a particular style.

Paintbrush is a simple program, but at the same time, it's powerful enough to illustrate your reports, presentations, newsletters, instruction manuals, or training guides—whatever you create on your computer.

Paintbrush is a powerful illustration tool that is both useful and fun.

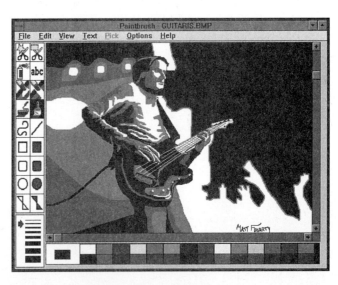

Starting Windows Paintbrush

12

To start Paintbrush, you must first start Windows (refer to Chapter 2, "Getting Started," if you need help starting Windows). When you first start Windows, a window called the Program Manager appears on-screen. The Program Manager contains at least four program groups: Main, Accessories, StartUp, and Games. A group called Applications also is among the program groups if you requested that it be created when you installed Windows. (Because you can create your own program groups, you may see more than four or five groups on-screen.) The program groups appear as *icons* (pictures) or as open windows.

You can open a program group icon, such as Accessories, into a window by double-clicking the icon, or by pressing Ctrl+Tab until the Accessories icon is selected and then pressing Enter. When the Accessories program group is open as a window, you can see the programs it contains. Windows Paintbrush is a Windows accessory program located in the Accessories program group.

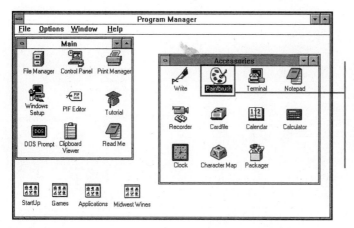

When the Accessories window is open, Paintbrush appears as an icon with its name, Paintbrush, below the icon.

To start the Paintbrush program, double-click the Paintbrush icon; alternatively, with the Accessories window selected, press an arrow key until you select the Paintbrush icon, and then press Enter. (This procedure is the same one you use to start any Windows program.)

12

When you first open Paintbrush, a new window appears, containing a blank Paintbrush document.

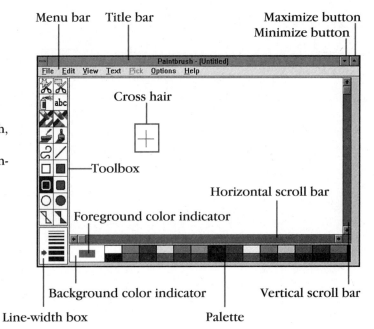

Menu bar   Title bar   Maximize button
Minimize button

Cross hair

Toolbox

Horizontal scroll bar

Foreground color indicator

Background color indicator   Vertical scroll bar

Line-width box   Palette

Some parts of the window are like those in other windows. A title bar across the top tells you the name of the program and the name of the document (untitled until you name it). A menu bar is below the title bar, and scroll bars are located on the right and bottom sides of the window.

Besides these familiar window parts, Paintbrush has several unique features. A *toolbox* appears on the left side of the screen, containing the tools you use to create a Paintbrush drawing or painting. At the bottom left corner is a *line-width box*, which you use to select the width of lines. A *palette* at the bottom of the screen contains the colors or shades you use to fill shapes. *Foreground* and *background color indicators* show you which colors are selected from the palette.

Also on-screen is a pointer that correspondingly moves as you move the mouse. The pointer may appear as a cross hair (when you select a drawing tool), as a special tool (when you select an eraser tool or a painting tool), as an arrow (when you move the pointer over a menu name or scroll bar), or as an I-beam (when you type text).

Understanding How Paintbrush Works

12

Before you plunge into using Paintbrush, you should understand how the program works.

The middle, blank area of the screen is the drawing area, where you create your Paintbrush masterpiece. To draw or paint, you must first select a tool by pointing to its icon in the toolbox and clicking the mouse button. For example, if you want to draw a straight line, you select the Line tool. After you select a tool, move the pointer into the drawing area, where the pointer becomes a cross hair or another drawing (or painting) icon.

Though the procedure varies from tool to tool, you generally draw or paint by holding down the mouse button, dragging the mouse, and then releasing the mouse button. To draw a line, for instance, you position the cross hair where you want the line to begin, hold down the mouse button, drag the cross hair to where you want the line to end, and release the mouse button.

The line-width box and the palette function as accessories to the tools. For instance, when you draw a line, it appears in a certain width. You determine that width by selecting a line from the line-width box. Similarly, when you draw a filled shape, its fill pattern is determined by the color or shading choices you make in the palette.

You can make additional refinements to a drawing by selecting commands from the Paintbrush menus. For example, you can select a type style or size for any text you add to the drawing. You also can tilt, flip, or shrink objects in the drawing.

Using the Keyboard with Paintbrush

Paintbrush is easiest to use if you have a mouse, but if you don't, you can still use the program. In this chapter, the instructions assume that you have a mouse; if you're using the keyboard, use the following keystrokes in place of the equivalent mouse actions.

12

Mouse Action	Keyboard Equivalent
Click left mouse button	Ins
Click right mouse button	Del
Double-click left mouse button	F9 + Ins
Double-click right mouse button	F9 + Del
Drag the insertion point	Ins + arrow keys

You also can move around the Paintbrush screen using the keyboard. You may find that some of these techniques work as shortcuts, even if you have a mouse:

Keystroke(s)	Action
Tab⇄	Move among drawing area, toolbox, line-width box, and palette
← → ↑ ↓	Move through drawing area, toolbox, line-width box, and palette in direction of arrow
Home	Move to top of drawing area
End	Move to bottom of drawing area
PgUp	Move up one screen
PgDn	Move down one screen
⇧Shift + ↑	Move screen up one line
⇧Shift + ↓	Move screen down one line
⇧Shift + Home	Move to left side of drawing area
⇧Shift + End	Move to right side of drawing area
⇧Shift + PgUp	Move left one screen
⇧Shift + PgDn	Move right one screen
⇧Shift + ←	Move screen left one space
⇧Shift + →	Move screen right one space

Using the Paintbrush Menus

As in all Windows programs, Paintbrush's first two menus are File and Edit.

12

The File menu contains commands for saving your drawing to a computer file, for opening a new file, and for printing.

The Edit menu contains commands for cutting, copying, and pasting.

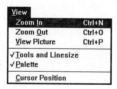

The third menu, View, contains commands for zooming in for a close look at a drawing and then zooming back out.

The View menu also enables you to hide the toolbox, line-width box, and palette so that you can make the drawing area larger.

You use the next menu—Text—to control the appearance of text in your drawing. You can change the font, style, and size of text.

12

The Pick menu is quite unique. You can use it only after you select an object with one of the two cutout tools, Scissors or Pick (which both look like scissors).

With the Pick menu, you can flip, invert, tilt, or resize the selected object.

The Options menu enables you to change the size of the drawing area, change your colors, change the brush shapes, or remove formatting.

Like any Windows Help menu, the Paintbrush Help menu is handy when you can't remember a definition or procedure.

Using the Paintbrush Toolbox

The toolbox is the heart of Paintbrush, containing all the tools you need to create the lines and shapes that make up a drawing.

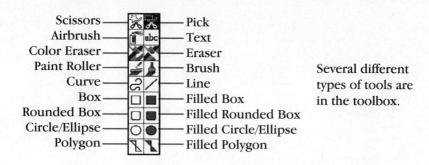

Scissors — Pick
Airbrush — Text
Color Eraser — Eraser
Paint Roller — Brush
Curve — Line
Box — Filled Box
Rounded Box — Filled Rounded Box
Circle/Ellipse — Filled Circle/Ellipse
Polygon — Filled Polygon

Several different
types of tools are
in the toolbox.

12

You use the *Scissors* and *Pick* tools to select objects in a drawing or to select areas within the drawing that contain several objects.

The *Airbrush, Paint Roller,* and *Brush* tools are for painting. The Airbrush tool splatters a transparent mist of paint. The Paint Roller tool fills a shape with paint. And the Brush tool paints a line of color. Before using any of these tools, make sure that the color or shade you want to paint with is selected in the palette.

With the *Text* tool, you can add text to a drawing. You use the Text menu to control the appearance of text.

The *Color Eraser* and *Eraser* tools enable you to change the colors in your painting or erase parts of the painting.

The *Curve* and *Line* tools are for drawing lines. The Curve tool draws curved lines, and the Line tool draws straight lines. Be sure to choose a line width from the line-width box before you draw a line.

The *Box* and *Rounded Box* tools draw boxes. The Box tools (filled and unfilled) draw boxes with right-angle corners; the Rounded Box tools (filled and unfilled) draw boxes with rounded corners. Before you draw any box, choose a line width to define the width of its borders. If you are drawing a filled box, select a fill color or shade from the palette.

Use the *Circle/Ellipse* tools (filled and unfilled) to draw circles and ovals. To draw a perfect circle, hold down the Shift key as you draw. Select a line width before you draw a circle or ellipse, and if you draw a filled shape, select a color or shade from the palette.

The *Polygon* tools (filled and unfilled) draw multisided objects with straight sides. Select a line width before you draw a polygon, and if you draw a filled polygon, select a color or shade from the palette.

Using the Line-Width Box

At the bottom left corner on-screen is the line-width box, containing eight lines of different widths.

An arrow points to the selected line width.

The selected line width controls the width of the lines you draw and the width of the borders around boxes, circles, and polygons. If, for example, you select the thin line width at the top of the box, the next line you draw will be thin. The selected line width also controls the width of some tools, such as the Airbrush, Brush, and Eraser tools. Note that selecting a line width doesn't change the width of lines already drawn.

To select a line width, follow these steps:

1. Move the pointer over the line width you want to select.
2. Click the left mouse button.

Using the Paintbrush Palette

At the bottom of the Paintbrush screen is a palette containing the colors or shades you use to draw, paint, and fill objects. If you have a color monitor, the palette shows colors; if you use a monochrome monitor, the palette shows shades of gray. You must select the colors or shades you want to use.

Note: Throughout this chapter, the term *color,* when referring to the palette, refers either to colors or to shades, depending on the monitor you have.

The palette at the bottom of the Paintbrush screen displays the colors (or shades, if you have a monochrome monitor) you can use in your painting.

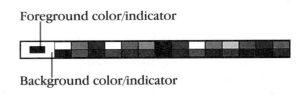

Foreground color/indicator

Background color/indicator

12

You actually get two choices in the palette: a *foreground* color and a *background* color. The foreground color is the color you draw with, using the line or shape tools, and it is the color you paint with whenever you use one of the painting tools (Airbrush, Paint Roller, or Brush). The foreground color also is the fill color that goes inside filled shapes. The *background* color is the color of the border around the edges of filled shapes and the background color of your screen whenever you start a new Paintbrush file.

If you look at the left end of the palette, you see a rectangle within a rectangle. These rectangles are foreground and background color indicators—they show you the colors currently selected. The inside rectangle shows the foreground color; the outside rectangle shows the background color. You choose foreground and background colors by clicking them with the mouse: click the *left* mouse button to select a foreground color; click the *right* mouse button to select a background color.

To select foreground and background colors, follow these steps:

1. Move the pointer on top of the foreground color you want to select, and click the *left* mouse button.

2. Move the pointer on top of the background color you want to select, and click the *right* mouse button.

Drawing Lines and Shapes

Paintbrush has two line tools, for straight and curved lines, and eight shape tools, for filled and unfilled boxes, circles and ellipses, and polygons. You use a similar process when you draw with each of these tools: select a tool, select a line width, select foreground and background colors, move the pointer into the drawing area (where the pointer becomes a cross hair), and draw the line or shape.

Lines and unfilled shapes are always drawn in the selected line width and selected foreground color. Filled shapes are filled with the selected foreground color and bordered with the selected background color. (If you want a filled shape with no border, select a background color that is the same color as the background of the drawing area—usually white.)

Note: Although you draw lines and shapes with the left mouse button, you use the right mouse button for a special purpose with the line tools. To undo the line you are drawing, click the right mouse button before you release the left mouse button.

Straight Lines

The Line tool draws a straight line in the foreground color and in the selected line width. While you're drawing the line, it appears as a thin black line. But when you release the mouse button to complete the line, it assumes the selected width and color.

To draw a straight line, follow these steps:

1. Select the Line tool from the toolbox.

2. Select a line width and foreground color.

3. Move the pointer into the drawing area, where the pointer becomes a cross hair.

4. Position the cross hair where you want the line to start.

5. Press and hold down the left mouse button.

6. While holding down the mouse button, drag the cross hair in any direction to draw a line.

7. Release the mouse button to complete the line.

Remember that you can press the right mouse button to cancel a line—as long as you do it *before* you release the left mouse button.

The Line tool draws straight lines. As you draw, hold down ⇧Shift to make the lines "snap to" an invisible vertical, horizontal, or 90-degree axis, whichever is closest to the line you draw.

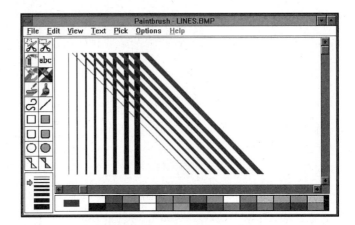

Curved Lines

The Curve tool doesn't draw "free-form" curves; instead, it draws precise C-shaped or S-shaped curves. Using the Curve tool requires a series of three drag movements with the mouse.

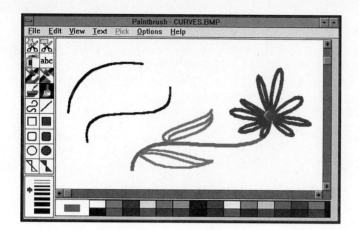

The line you draw shows the selected width and color only after you complete the line.

12

To use the Curve tool, follow these steps:

1. Select the Curve tool from the toolbox.

2. If you want, select a line width and foreground color.

3. Move the pointer into the drawing area, where the pointer becomes a cross hair. Position the cross hair where you want the line to start.

4. Press and hold down the left mouse button, drag the mouse to draw a straight line, and then release the mouse button. The line appears as a thin black line.

5. Move the cross hair to one side of the line you drew.

6. Press and hold down the left mouse button, and drag the cross hair away from the line to pull it into a C-shaped curve. Release the mouse button when you're done.

7. If you want the line to remain C-shaped, click the end of the curve to complete the operation.

   If you want to change the line to an S-shaped curve, press and hold down the left mouse button on the opposite side of the line, and then drag the cross hair away from the line to pull the line in the opposite direction. The line is complete when you release the mouse button.

12

You can cancel your line by clicking the right mouse button before you are finished drawing the line.

A second method of using the Curve tool enables you to draw petal shapes. Select the curve tool and click once where you want the pointed end of the petal. Then click a second time where you want the rounded end of the petal. Then click a third time to the side to indicate the width of the petal.

Boxes

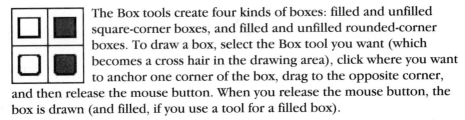 The Box tools create four kinds of boxes: filled and unfilled square-corner boxes, and filled and unfilled rounded-corner boxes. To draw a box, select the Box tool you want (which becomes a cross hair in the drawing area), click where you want to anchor one corner of the box, drag to the opposite corner, and then release the mouse button. When you release the mouse button, the box is drawn (and filled, if you use a tool for a filled box).

Note: Be sure that you select the line width, foreground color, and background color before you start.

To draw a box, follow these steps:

1. From the toolbox, select the filled or unfilled Box tool, or the filled or unfilled Rounded Box tool.
2. Move the pointer into the drawing area of the screen, where the pointer becomes a cross hair.
3. Position the cross hair where you want to anchor one corner of the box.
4. Press and hold down the left mouse button.
5. Drag the cross hair in any direction to draw the box. Until you release the mouse button, the box appears as a thin black line.
6. Release the mouse button when the box is the shape you want. The box assumes the selected line width and color.

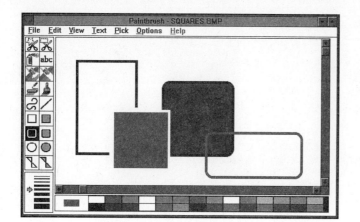

12

If you want to draw a square box, hold down ⌖Shift as you draw.

Circles and Ovals

 The Circle/Ellipse tools draw circles and ovals, either filled or unfilled. Both of the Circle/Ellipse tools draw oval shapes by default; if you want a perfect circle, hold down the Shift key as you draw the shape.

To draw a circle or oval, follow these steps:

1. Select the filled or unfilled Circle/Ellipse tool from the toolbox.
2. Move the pointer to the drawing area, where the pointer becomes a cross hair.
3. Position the cross hair where you want to start the circle or oval.
4. Press and hold down the left mouse button.
5. Drag the cross hair away from the starting point in any direction.
6. Release the mouse button to complete the circle or oval.

12

The circle or oval appears as a thin black line until you release the mouse button.

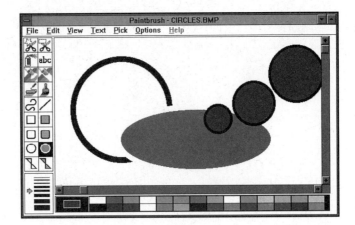

Polygons

A polygon is a multisided shape with straight edges. The most familiar example of a polygon is a stop sign—an eight-sided polygon. A stop sign is symmetrical, but the polygons you create with Paintbrush can be much more exciting, in any shape and with as many sides as you want.

Drawing a polygon is different from drawing a line or box. First, you draw one side of the polygon just as though you were drawing a line. Second, you click to define each of the polygon's remaining corners. Finally, you double-click to close the polygon by connecting the first point to the last point.

To draw an unfilled or filled polygon, follow these steps:

1. Select the filled or unfilled Polygon tool from the toolbox.
2. Move the pointer into the drawing area, where the pointer becomes a cross hair.
3. Press and hold down the left mouse button to start the polygon.
4. Drag the cross hair to draw one side of the polygon, and release the mouse button when the line is finished.
5. Position the cross hair where you want the polygon's next corner to appear, and then click the mouse button.
6. Create the polygon's remaining corners by positioning the cross hair where you want them and clicking the mouse button. Each time you click, you add a side to the polygon.
7. To complete the polygon, double-click the mouse button to connect the first point to the last point.

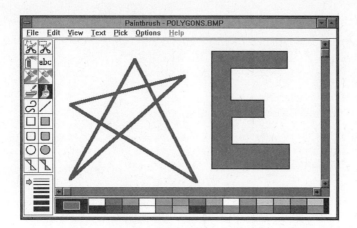

If you want perfectly horizontal, vertical, or diagonal sides, hold down ⇧Shift as you draw.

12

Using the Painting Tools

The Paintbrush drawing tools are rather constraining. You can draw straight lines, precise curves, and obedient shapes, but you cannot draw free-form images. If your nature is a little freer, you will appreciate Paintbrush's painting tools, which you can use to draw more imaginative shapes. All the painting tools "paint" in the selected foreground color. Before you start, remember to select the color you want by pointing to it and clicking the left mouse button.

The Airbrush Tool

 The Airbrush tool is a lot like a can of spray paint—it sprays a transparent mist of color instead of painting a solid color. If you select the Airbrush tool and click the left mouse button once, you get a round dot of misty color. If you drag the mouse, you get a misty line.

You control the diameter of an airbrush dot or line by selecting the line width you want from the line-width box: a thin line produces a small dot or thin line; a thicker line produces a larger dot or thicker line. You control the density of the mist by the speed with which you drag the mouse: a fast drag produces a light line; a slow drag produces a much denser airbrushed line.

To use the Airbrush tool, follow these steps:

1. Select the Airbrush tool.

2. Move the pointer into the drawing area, where the pointer becomes a cross hair.

3. Position the cross hair where you want to start the airbrush stroke.

12

4. Press and hold down the left mouse button.

5. Drag the cross hair to paint the airbrush stroke. Drag slowly for a dense line; drag quickly for a light line.

6. Release the mouse button.

Unlike other painting tools, the Airbrush tool sprays a transparent mist of color.

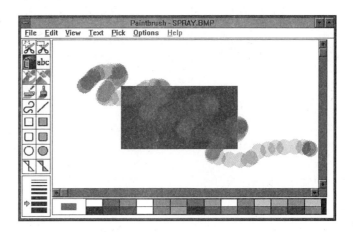

The Paint Roller Tool

 The Paint Roller tool fills a shape with a color. The shape you fill can be an open shape or one already filled with a solid color (but not with a pattern). In either case, the Paint Roller tool fills the shape with the selected foreground color.

When you select the Paint Roller tool and move the pointer into the drawing area, the pointer turns into a tool that looks like a paint roller spreading paint. The pointed tip of this tool is where paint flows out to fill a shape. Because the tip is pointed, you can use this tool to fill a very small shape.

Be careful when you fill a shape with the Paint Roller tool. If the shape is not completely closed, the paint leaks out, filling the entire screen. If that happens, choose the Edit menu and select the Undo command (or press Ctrl-Z); then close the shape and try again. If you can't see the leak clearly, use the View Zoom In command to "blow up" the painting so that you can patch the leak. (The View Zoom In command is explained in the section "Editing a Drawing," further in this chapter.)

To fill a shape with the Paint Roller tool, follow these steps:

1. Select the Paint Roller tool from the toolbox.

2. Select a foreground color from the palette by clicking the color you want with the left mouse button.

3. Position the pointed tip of the Paint Roller tool inside the shape you want to fill.

4. Click the left mouse button.

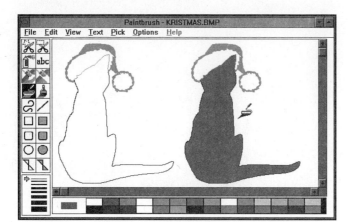

Use the Paint Roller tool to fill any shape with the selected foreground color.

You also can use the Paint Roller to fill a solid shape or liner—position the tip of the Paint Roller tool on the shape or line and then click. You cannot use the Paint Roller to fill a blended color made up of dots. You can fill a solid red box with blue, for example, but you cannot fill a blended green shape with blue.

The Brush Tool

The Brush tool paints an opaque stroke of the selected foreground color. You can modify this versatile tool in two ways: by selecting a line width and by selecting a different brush shape. (Six brush shapes are available; if you don't choose one, you get the default square brush shape.) Like the other painting tools, the Brush tool enables you to paint free-form shapes.

To use the Brush tool, follow these steps:

1. Select the Brush tool from the toolbox.

2. Select a foreground color from the palette.

3. Select a line width from the line-width box.

4. Move the pointer into the drawing area, where it assumes the shape of the brush you selected. The default brush shape is square.

12

5. Position the Brush tool where you want the brush stroke to begin.

6. Press and hold the left mouse button, and drag the brush to paint a brush stroke.

7. Release the mouse button.

Using a line-shaped Brush tool, you can draw a line of variable width.

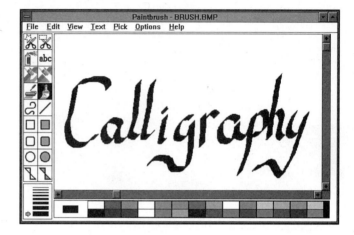

To change the brush shape, follow these steps:

1. Choose the O ptions menu and select the B rush Shapes command.

The Brush Shapes dialog box shows six different brush shapes.

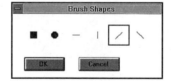

2. Select a brush shape: either click the brush shape you want, or press Tab⁺ to select the brush shapes group and then press the arrow keys to select the brush shape you want.

3. Choose OK or press ⏎Enter .

To quickly change the brush shape, double-click the Brush tool to display the Brush Shapes dialog box, and then double-click the brush shape you want to select.

Adding Text

 A picture may be worth a thousand words, but sometimes words can help clarify your message. Using the Text tool, you can type text in your drawing by using any of several fonts, styles, sizes, and colors.

12

Typing with Paintbrush has some limitations. Unlike a word processing program, Paintbrush doesn't enable you to edit your text after you finish typing it. You can press the Backspace key to correct typing errors *while* you are typing, but after you click the mouse button, you can no longer use the Text tool to edit your text. Paintbrush also lacks a word-wrap feature; when you reach the edge of the screen, you must press Enter to move the insertion point to the next line.

To type text, follow these steps:

1. Select the Text tool from the toolbox.

2. Move the pointer into the drawing area, where the pointer becomes an I-beam.

3. Position the I-beam where you want to start typing, and then click the left mouse button. The I-beam becomes a blinking cursor, or insertion point.

4. Type the text (press ⏎Enter when you want to start a new line). If you make a mistake, press ⬅Backspace to erase it.

5. Click the mouse button to "set" the text into your painting, after which you cannot edit the text.

When you type, text appears in the selected font, style, size, and foreground color. You can change any font and color selections *before* you start typing or *while* you type—any time before you click the mouse button. The changes apply to all the text you have typed.

You can type text in black or in any color or shade—whatever you select as the foreground color.

Enhancing Text

A text enhancement is a variation of the selected font. Paintbrush offers several text enhancements: Regular, Bold, Italic, Underline, Outline, and Shadow. You can use as many enhancements as you like, at the same time. For example, you can type a title that is both bold and underlined. Select Regular to return to plain, unenhanced text.

Typed text appears in the selected foreground color, with one exception: shadow text adds a shadow in the selected background color.

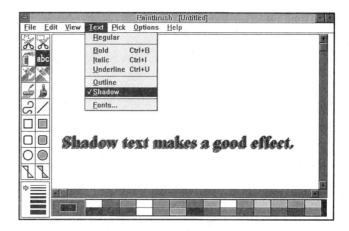

To select a text enhancement, follow these steps:

1. Choose the Text menu.

2. Select one of the following enhancements:

    > Regular
    >
    > Bold
    >
    > Italic
    >
    > Underline
    >
    > Outline
    >
    > Shadow

3. Repeat the process to select additional enhancements for the same text.

You can select a text enhancement before you begin typing or while you are typing, but after you click the mouse button to "set" your text into the

12

painting, you cannot change the text enhancement. (You can, however, erase the text and type new text; see the upcoming section on "Editing a Drawing.")

Selecting a Font, Style, and Size

A font is an alphabet of characters that have the same appearance. Common fonts include Times New Roman, Arial, and Courier New. Using the Fonts command, you can change the font, font style, and font size all at once (font styles are the same as the font enhancements listed in the Text menu). You also can add one of two special effects—strikeout and underlining.

To select a font, style, size, and special effects, follow these steps:

1. Choose the Text menu.
2. Select the Fonts command.

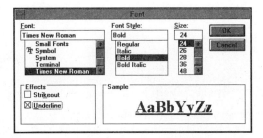

The Font dialog box appears, which enables you to change font, style, and size all at once. A sample box shows you how your font, style, and size will look.

3. From the Font list, select the font you want to use. TrueType fonts (those with a TT icon to their left) look better on-screen and when printed than fonts with no icon. Printer fonts (those with a printer icon to their left) also look good on-screen and when printed.

4. From the Font Style list, select the style you want.

5. From the Size list, select the text size you want.

6. In the Effects group, select Strikeout if you want a line through your text, or select Underline if you want the text underlined.

7. Choose OK or press ⏎Enter.

When you select a font, that font applies to any new text you type and to the text you currently are typing, if you haven't clicked the mouse button.

To learn more about TrueType and other fonts, refer to Chapter 9, "Managing Fonts and TrueType."

Editing a Drawing

12

You can modify a drawing in many ways. You can edit single objects, or you can change the whole picture. You can use the Undo command, which undoes your most recent action or series of actions. You can erase part of a drawing or change its colors. You can move or duplicate objects, and you can resize or tilt objects. For many editing procedures, you must first use either the Scissors or Pick tool to select the object or objects you want to modify.

Using the Undo Command

Everyone makes mistakes. When you do, you will find a useful ally in the Undo command. Undo erases everything you have done since the last time you selected the tool you're using, chose a menu command, used a scroll bar, opened another program, or resized the window. To avoid undoing something accidentally, reselect your tool each time you draw a line or shape you want to keep. That way, the next time you choose Undo, your work is undone only back to that point.

To undo your work, follow these steps:

1. Choose the Edit menu.
2. Select the Undo command, or press Ctrl + Z.

Erasing

 Paintbrush has two tools you can use to erase—or recolor—parts of a drawing. Use the Color Eraser tool (on the left) to change the colors in the drawing. Use the Eraser tool (on the right) to change everything to the background color. Selecting either tool produces a square "eraser." To erase, just drag the square eraser across the drawing. The size of the eraser depends on the selected line width; you get a small eraser with a thin line width, or a large eraser with a thick line width.

The Color Eraser Tool

The Color Eraser tool isn't really an eraser; it's a color switcher. It works two ways, and both ways depend on the foreground and background colors you select from the palette (this tool works only with colors, not shades):

- Drag the Color Eraser tool across an area in your drawing. Every occurrence of the *selected* foreground color changes to the selected background color.

- Double-click the Color Eraser tool in the toolbox. Every occurrence of the *selected* foreground color in the visible area of your drawing changes to the selected background color. (The Color Eraser tool changes only the *selected* foreground color, whereas the Eraser tool, described next, changes *all* colors.)

Remember that the foreground color is the color in the *center* of the rectangle at the left end of the palette. You select the foreground color by using the *left* mouse button to click the color you want. The background color is the *outer* color in the rectangle in the palette box. You select the background color by clicking the *right* mouse button.

To use the Color Eraser tool on part of your drawing, follow these steps:

1. Select the Color Eraser tool (the tool on the left side of the toolbox).

2. Select from the palette a foreground color (the color you want to change).

3. Select from the palette a background color (the color to which you want to change the foreground color).

4. Move the pointer into the drawing area, where the pointer becomes a square eraser.

5. Press and hold down the left mouse button.

6. Drag the Color Eraser tool across the part of the drawing that you want to change from the selected foreground color to the selected background color.

7. Release the mouse button.

The Eraser Tool

The Eraser tool "erases" by changing every part of your drawing that it touches to the selected background color. If the background color is white, passing the Eraser tool over an area turns it white. (If the background color is not white, the Eraser tool works more like a paintbrush than an eraser; everything you drag the tool over turns to the background color.)

To use the Eraser tool, follow these steps:

1. Select the Eraser tool from the toolbox (the tool on the right side of the toolbox).
2. If necessary, select a background color from the palette.
3. Move the pointer into the drawing area, where the pointer becomes a square eraser.
4. Press and hold down the left mouse button.
5. Drag the Eraser tool across the part of the drawing that you want to change to the background color.
6. Release the mouse button.

If the background color is white, passing the Eraser tool over an area turns it white.

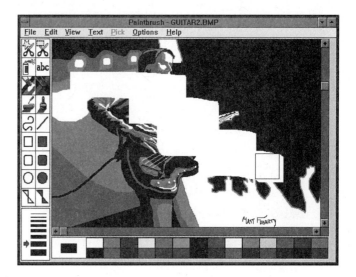

You can use the Eraser tool to erase your entire drawing by double-clicking the Eraser tool in the toolbox. When you do, Paintbrush closes the current file, but first prompts you to save your changes. Choose Yes if you want to save them; otherwise, choose No. When a new document opens, its entire background is the color of the currently selected background color.

Zooming In and Out

When you are doing detailed work, you can zoom in to get a close-up look at your drawing. To get an overview, you can zoom out to see the whole page.

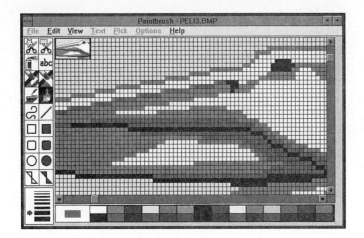

12

When you zoom in, you can edit a drawing dot by dot.

Click the *left* mouse button to draw a dot in the selected foreground color; click the *right* mouse button to draw a dot in the selected background color. You can use the Paint Roller tool in Zoom In mode if you want to fill an area with the foreground color.

To zoom in for a close-up view of a drawing, follow these steps:

1. Choose the View menu and select the Zoom In command. A Zoom box appears, to help you define where you want to zoom in.

2. Position the Zoom box over the spot where you want to zoom in.

3. Click the left mouse button to zoom in.

To zoom back out to the regular editing view, choose the View menu and select the Zoom Out command. If you're in the regular editing view, Zoom Out shows you a reduced picture of the entire page.

Viewing More of a Drawing

If your drawing is larger than your computer screen, you can see more of the drawing by hiding all toolboxes, menus, and scroll bars. You can only view in this mode; you cannot edit the drawing.

To view more of a drawing, follow these steps:

1. Choose the View menu and select the View Picture command.

2. To return to the regular editing view, click the mouse button or press Esc.

Selecting Objects in a Drawing

 With the two cutout tools, the Scissors (on the left) and the Pick (on the right), you can draw an enclosure around any part of your Paintbrush drawing. What's inside the enclosure is then "selected," enabling you to move, cut, copy (and then paste elsewhere), resize, tilt, flip, or invert it. The left cutout tool, the Scissors, draws a free-form enclosure. The right cutout tool, the Pick, draws a rectangular enclosure.

To draw an enclosure (select) with the Scissors tool, follow these steps:

1. Select the Scissors tool from the top *left* corner of the toolbox.
2. Move the pointer into the drawing area, where the pointer becomes a cross hair.
3. Press and hold down the left mouse button where you want to begin the enclosure.
4. Drag the mouse to draw a line around the area you want to select.
5. Release the mouse button at the same place you started drawing the line.

Press the left mouse button if you want to cancel the cutout. To cancel before you finish drawing an enclosure, click the right mouse button.

With the Scissors tool, you can select an irregular shape; in this example, one of the pelicans is selected.

To draw an enclosure (select) with the Pick tool, follow these steps:

1. Select the Pick tool from the top *right* corner of the toolbox.

12

2. Move the pointer into the drawing area, where the pointer becomes a cross hair.

3. Press and hold down the left mouse button where you want to begin the enclosure.

4. Drag the mouse to draw a rectangle around the area you want to select.

5. Release the mouse button.

With the Pick tool, you can select a rectangular shape; in this example, the entire drawing is selected.

Moving Objects

You can move an object, or group of objects, to a different place in the drawing. First, you must select the object or objects with the Scissors or Pick tool.

To move an object, follow these steps:

1. Select the Scissors or Pick tool.

2. Draw an enclosure around the object or objects you want to move.

3. Move the pointer inside the selection enclosure, where the pointer becomes an arrow.

4. Press and hold down the mouse button to "pick up" the selection.

5. Drag the selected object where you want it.

6. Release the mouse button.

To move the selection as a transparent object, drag it with the *left* mouse button. To move the selection as an opaque object, drag it with the *right* mouse button.

Duplicating Objects

12

After you select an object, you can use the Scissors or Pick tool to duplicate it. To duplicate an object, you simply copy and paste it. When you paste the object, it appears—selected—at the top left corner on-screen. You then can move the object, using the method described in steps 3 through 6 of the preceding section.

To duplicate an object, follow these steps:

1. Select the Scissors or Pick tool.
2. Draw a selection enclosure around the object you want to copy.
3. Choose the **Edit** menu and select the **Copy** command.
4. Choose the **Edit** menu and select the **Paste** command.

A quick way to duplicate an object is to select it, hold the Ctrl key, and drag the selected object somewhere else on-screen. The original object you selected is left in place.

Using Special Effects

Using the **Pick** menu, you can perform all kinds of tricks with objects you have selected with either of the cutout tools (Scissors or Pick). You can flip, invert, shrink, enlarge, or tilt your selection.

Flipping a Selection

You can flip a selection in two ways: horizontally—left to right—so that it faces the opposite direction; or vertically—top to bottom—so that it turns upside down. To flip a selection, follow these steps:

1. Use the Scissors or Pick tool to select the object you want to flip.
2. Choose the **Pick** menu and select either the Flip **Horizontal** command or the **Pick** Flip **Vertical** command.

Inverting Colors

You can invert the colors in your drawing, changing each one to the opposite color on the red/green/blue color wheel. If you invert a black-and-white drawing, for example, black becomes white, and white becomes black. If you invert a green-and-yellow drawing, green becomes purple, and yellow becomes blue.

To invert colors, follow these steps:

1. Use the Scissors or Pick tool to select the object or area you want to invert.

2. Choose the Pick menu and select the Inverse command.

Shrinking and Growing a Selection

You can use the Pick Shrink + Grow command to reduce or enlarge your selection. The procedure is a little unusual. After you select the object and choose the command, drag the mouse to draw a box that is the size you want the resized image to fit. When you release the mouse button, a duplicate of the object drops into the box you drew, and the box disappears.

To shrink or enlarge a selection, follow these steps:

1. Use the Scissors or Pick tool to select the object or area you want to shrink or grow.

2. Choose the Pick menu and select the Shrink + Grow command.

3. Move the cross hair where you want the resized image to appear.

4. Press and hold down the mouse button, and then drag the mouse to draw a box that is the size you want for the duplicate image.

5. Release the mouse button.

To keep the new image proportional to the original, hold down Shift as you press, hold, drag, and release the mouse button.

If you choose the Pick menu and then select the Clear command before you select the Shrink + Grow command, Paintbrush clears your original selection when you create the new, resized image. If you don't select Clear, you create a duplicate of your original.

Tilting a Selection

The Tilt command works a little like the Shrink + Grow command. After you select the object and choose the command, drag the mouse to draw a box that is the angle into which you want the tilted image to drop. When you release the mouse button, a duplicate of the object appears, tilted, in the box you drew. The box disappears.

12

To tilt a selection, follow these steps:

1. Use the Scissors or Pick tool to select the object or area you want to tilt.
2. Choose the Pick menu and select the Tilt command.
3. Move the cross hair where you want the tilted object to appear.
4. Press and hold down the mouse button (a dotted border appears), and then drag the cross hair left or right to tilt the box.
5. Release the mouse button.

If you choose the Pick menu and then select the Clear command before you select the Tilt command, Paintbrush clears your original selection when you create the new, tilted image.

If you don't select Clear, you create a duplicate of your original.

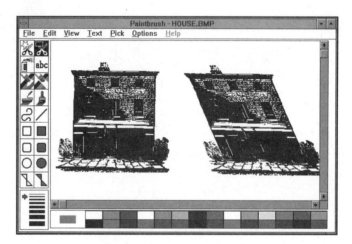

Changing Margins, Headers, and Footers

Before you print your masterpiece, you may want to adjust its margins, or add headers or footers. Paintbrush starts out with default margins of one-half inch (0.50) on each side. If you want your drawing positioned differently on the page, you can change the margins. Headers appear at the top of each printed page; footers appear at the bottom of each printed page. Headers and footers are centered between the left and right margins of the printed pages.

To change margins, headers, and footers, follow these steps:

1. Choose the File menu and select the Page Setup command.

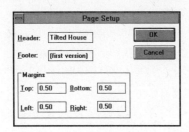

The Page Setup
dialog box
appears.

12

2. In the Header text box, type a header.

3. In the Footer text box, type a footer.

4. In the four Margins boxes (Top, Bottom, Left, and Right), type the margins you want (in decimal numbers).

5. Choose OK or press ⏎Enter.

Printing a Drawing

When you are ready to print your drawing, many options are available with Paintbrush. For example, you can print a draft copy of the drawing to see a rough version of it, or you can print a final proof. You can print the whole drawing, or you can print only part of it. You can print one or more copies of the drawing, and you can print the copies at a reduced or enlarged scale.

Paintbrush prints on the printer currently selected in Windows. If you have been printing with another Windows program, you probably do not have to select a printer in Paintbrush; however, if this is your first time to print or if you need to change printers, be sure to use the Print Setup command to select a printer.

To select a printer, complete these steps:

1. Choose the File menu and select the Print Setup command.

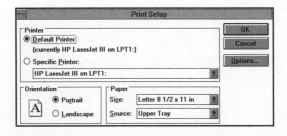

The Print Setup
dialog box
appears.

2. Select a printer from the Printer group. You can select the **Default Printer**, or you can select a printer from the Specific **Printer** list.

3. Select an option from the Orientation group: **Portrait** to print your drawing vertically on the page; **Landscape** to print horizontally.

4. If necessary, choose options from the Paper group: to change the paper size, select an option from the Size list; to change the paper source on your printer, select an option from the Source list.

5. Choose OK or press (⏎Enter).

To learn about installing and connecting a printer, see Chapter 8, "Controlling the Printer."

To print a Paintbrush drawing on the selected printer, follow these steps:

1. Choose the **File** menu and select the **Print** command.

The Print dialog box appears.

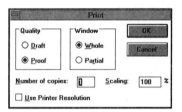

2. In the Quality group, select **Draft** to print a rough draft, or **Proof** to print a final version of the drawing.

3. In the Window group, select **Whole** to print the entire drawing, or **Partial** to print the portion you select.

4. In the **Number of copies** box, type the number of copies you want to print.

5. In the Scaling box, type a percent at which you want to print the drawing. For example, type **50** (for 50 percent) to print at half size.

6. Select the Use Printer Resolution check box to print at printer resolution rather than screen resolution.

   If your drawing appears out of proportion the first time you print it, select the Use Printer Resolution option and print the drawing again. This option may correct the problem.

7. Choose OK or press (⏎Enter).

If you select the option to print only part of the drawing and then choose OK to print, Paintbrush displays a reduced version of the drawing and gives you a cross hair. Use the cross hair to draw a box around the area of the drawing you want to print. As soon as you release the mouse button, printing begins.

If you print a *draft-quality* page, Paintbrush prints without printer enhancements, but at a faster speed. If you print a *proof-quality* page, Paintbrush prints more slowly, but uses all the printer's enhancements. On some printers, such as laser printers, no difference exists between draft- and proof-quality printing.

Saving a Drawing and Quitting Paintbrush

To avoid losing any of your work, you should save your files frequently. Saving several versions of your progressing drawing is often a good idea. If you're creating a chart, for example, you might name your successive files CHART01, CHART02, and so on. File names can contain up to eight characters.

Like most programs, Paintbrush saves files in its own native file format and assigns a three-letter extension to the end of each file (an extension is like a last name). The extension that Paintbrush assigns to file names is BMP. If, for instance, you assign the name PAINTING to a file, Paintbrush saves it as PAINTING.BMP.

If you want to save a drawing to use in a different program, you can save the drawing in a different format. Many graphics and desktop publishing programs are compatible with the PCX format, for example. If you save a Paintbrush drawing in PCX format, Paintbrush assigns the extension PCX to the file name.

To save a Paintbrush file, follow these steps:

1. Choose the **File** menu and select the Save **As** command.

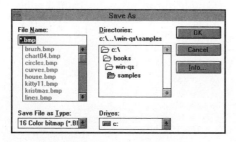

The Save As dialog box appears.

313

12

2. Type a file name in the File Name text box.

3. From the Drives list, select the drive on which you want to save the file.

4. From the Directories list box, select the directory in which you want to save the file.

5. If you want to save your picture in the PCX file format, select PCX file (*.PCX) from the Save File as Type list.

6. Choose OK or press ↵Enter.

To resave your file later, without changing its name, choose the Edit menu and select the Save command.

When you are finished working with Paintbrush, quit the program by choosing the File menu and selecting the Exit command.

Embedding and Linking Paintbrush Paintings

Besides being a stand-alone painting program, Paintbrush also is an *object linking and embedding* (OLE) server program. A *server* is a program you can use to create "objects" you can embed within or link to documents created in other programs. Paintbrush enables you to create objects you can embed within or link to documents created by programs like Windows Write and Word for Windows. For example, you can embed or link a Paintbrush painting (or part of one) inside a letter created in Windows Write or inside a report created in Word for Windows.

When you embed or link objects inside a document, the program you used to create that document functions as an OLE *client* program. Other programs besides Write and Word for Windows also can function as OLE clients.

When a Paintbrush object is embedded within or linked to a document, you can start Paintbrush—with the object displayed in its drawing window—from within that document. For example, if a bar chart you created in Paintbrush is embedded or linked in a letter you created in Write, you can start Paintbrush and edit the bar chart from within your Write document.

Embedding and linking differ in three ways: the way you get the embedded or linked object from the server document into the client document; the way the client program stores the object; and the way you update the object.

Embedding a Paintbrush Object

Two techniques enable you to embed a Paintbrush painting within a document created by a program that supports OLE. You can either copy it into the client program's document or use a command in the client program to insert the object. Each technique has its advantages. If you copy the painting, you can use an existing painting; or if you create a new painting, you can save it to a separate file that you can embed in other documents. If you embed a painting from within the client document, you cannot use an existing painting or save the painting as a stand-alone file, but you can create the painting without leaving the client document.

To embed a Paintbrush painting by copying, follow these steps:

1. Start both the client program (into which you want to embed your Paintbrush painting) and Paintbrush.

2. In the client program, open the document into which you want to embed the Paintbrush painting. Position the insertion point where you want to embed the painting in the document.

3. In Paintbrush, open the document containing the painting you want to embed in the client document, or create the painting (save the painting if you want to use it again later).

4. Select the Paintbrush painting (or part of it) that you want to embed.

5. Choose the Edit menu and select the Copy command.

6. Switch to the client program.

7. Choose the Edit menu and select the Paste command.

The commands for embedding a Paintbrush painting from within a client program vary from client to client. The following steps explain the commands you use to embed a painting into a Windows Write document. Using this technique, you must create the painting from within your Write document, and you cannot save the painting to use in any other document. (You also can use the same technique to embed many other types of objects, besides Paintbrush paintings.)

To embed a Paintbrush painting from within Windows Write, follow these steps:

1. Start Windows Write and open the document into which you want to embed a painting. Position the insertion point where you want the painting.

2. Choose the Edit menu and select the Insert Object command. The Insert Object dialog box appears.

12

3. From the Object Type list, select Paintbrush Painting. Choose OK or press ⏎Enter.

    Paintbrush appears on-screen with a new, blank painting window.

4. Create your painting.

5. To add your painting to your Write document without closing Paintbrush, choose the File menu and select the Update command. Choose the File menu and select Exit & Return command when you're ready to close Paintbrush and return to your document.

    To add your painting to your Write document and simultaneously close Paintbrush, choose the File menu and select the Exit & Return command. When a dialog box prompts you to update your Write document, choose Yes.

To embed a Paintbrush painting into a Word for Windows document, choose the Insert menu, select the Object command, and proceed with steps 3 through 5 of the preceding steps. If you have a different program, check the menus to see which command will work; although the command may not be exactly the same as the commands in Write or Word for Windows, it's likely to be similar.

To save your Paintbrush painting, be sure to save your Write or Word for Windows file.

After you embed a Paintbrush object within a client program's document, you can edit the object from within that document. In almost any program, you can modify the object by double-clicking the object to start Paintbrush. You also can use keyboard commands to edit embedded objects in most programs, but the commands vary. In Write, for example, select the object, choose the Edit menu, and select the Edit Paintbrush Picture Object command. In Word for Windows, select the object, choose the Edit menu, and select the Paintbrush Picture Object command. Look for a similar command if your program is different.

To update an embedded Paintbrush object, follow these steps:

1. Start Paintbrush from within the client document by double-clicking the Paintbrush picture or by choosing the appropriate command from the client program's menu.

2. Modify the Paintbrush object.

3. Choose the File menu and select the Update command.

4. Choose the File menu and select the Exit & Return command to exit Paintbrush and return to your document.

Linking a Paintbrush Object

Linking an object from Paintbrush into a client document is similar to embedding, except that only one technique is available, rather than two: you must use a special command to copy a saved object into the client document.

Unlike an embedded object, a linked object is not stored as a complete file inside the client document. Instead, the client document stores a link to the original file; thus, if you give someone a diskette with a Write file containing a linked Paintbrush object, you also should include the Paintbrush object on-disk.

The advantage to linking is that when you change the original object, the object in the client document updates to reflect your changes. Because the client document stores a link to the original instead of storing the original, you can create a single original object and link it to many client documents, even if you use different programs to create the documents. All the client documents update to reflect changes to the original.

To link a Paintbrush object to a client document, follow these steps:

1. In Paintbrush, create or open the object you want to link to the client document. If you make any changes, you must save the file.

2. Select the portion of the object you want to link, choose the Edit menu, and select the Copy command.

3. Start the client program and open the document in which you want to link the object. Position the insertion point where you want the object.

4. Choose the Edit menu and select the Paste Link command.

Most client documents link objects so that they update automatically when you change the original object. However, you can edit the link in many ways: you can set it for manual updating; you can update the link to reflect a new location for an original file you have moved; or you can link the object to a different original file.

Like an embedded object, you can edit a linked object from within the client document. The technique for starting the server program is the same as for embedding: you can double-click the linked object, or you can select it and choose an editing command. After the program starts, you can edit and save the object.

To learn more about OLE, read Chapter 10, "Using Object Linking and Embedding."

12

Summary

12

Paintbrush is a simple graphics program you can use to create illustrations for your work or to create computer drawings just for fun.

Paintbrush contains tools for drawing lines, boxes, circles, and polygons, as well as tools for drawing free-form lines and shapes. A line-width box offers a selection of line widths, and a palette displays an array of colors (if you have a color monitor) or a variety of gray shades (if you have a monochrome monitor).

You can type text in your drawing, selecting from a variety of fonts, sizes, and styles. You can perform many tricks with selected objects—tricks such as flipping, reducing, enlarging, and tilting them. To improve your drawing, you can erase and edit it.

In this chapter, you learned the following important points about the Paintbrush tools:

- You use the Scissors and Pick tools to select objects in a drawing. You can then change, copy, or move the selected objects.

- The Airbrush tool sprays a fine mist of the color you select from the palette.

- With the Text tool, you can type text in a drawing.

- The Color Eraser and Eraser tools change the colors in a drawing when you drag these tools across it. If you erase with white and the background of the drawing is also white, the Eraser tool erases the portion you drag across.

- The Paint Roller tool fills a shape with a color. The Brush tool paints a stroke of color.

- You use the Curve tool to draw precise C-shaped or S-shaped curves, and the Line tool to draw straight lines.

- The unfilled Box tool draws empty boxes with right-angle corners. The filled Box tool draws filled boxes with right-angle corners. The unfilled Rounded Box tool draws empty boxes with rounded corners, and the filled Rounded Box tool draws filled boxes with rounded corners.

- The unfilled Circle/Ellipse tool draws empty circles and ovals; the filled Circle/Ellipse tool draws filled circles and ovals.

- The unfilled Polygon tool draws empty polygons, and the filled Polygon tool draws filled polygons.

In Chapter 14, "Using Desktop Accessories," you learn about many more Windows accessory programs. Described in that chapter are Notepad, a text editing program that works like a simple word processing program; Cardfile, a computerized stack of name-and-address cards; Calendar, an automated appointment tracker; Calculator, a quick desktop calculator you can use side-by-side with your other programs; Terminal, an easy-to-use communications program to use with your modem; and Clock, a small but accurate desktop timepiece. In combination with Windows Write and Windows Paintbrush, the desktop accessories are valuable aids in your day-to-day work.

12

Creating Macros

With the Windows Recorder, you can automate many tasks that you now do repeatedly by hand. The Recorder keeps track of keystrokes you type, shortcut keys you press, and mouse actions you make—saving them all in a *macro* you can play back later. When you play back the macro, Windows repeats the keystrokes and mouse movements exactly as you made them the first time. Macros can therefore save you a great deal of work whenever you retype phrases, reuse a formatting sequence, or regularly copy data from one program and paste it into another program.

You can use the Windows Recorder with any Windows program or group of Windows programs. Even with such powerful programs as Microsoft Excel and Word for Windows, which have their own built-in macro recorders, you will find the Windows Recorder useful for integrating the work you do in multiple programs.

13

Recording a macro

Playing back a macro

Editing and changing a macro

Managing macros

Ideas for macros

13

Key Terms in This Chapter

Macro	A sequence of keystrokes or mouse actions that the Recorder repeats when requested.
Record	To create a sequence of keystrokes or mouse actions that the Recorder stores in a macro.
Recorder file	A file that contains one or more macros.

Recording a Macro

Before you begin recording a macro, you should have a good idea of what you want to do. You may find it helpful to practice the procedure you want to record, before you actually record it. During this practice, you often find shorter or better ways to complete the procedure.

The macro you create is stored in a *Recorder file* with the extension REC. Each Recorder file can contain multiple macros. After you start the Recorder and open a Recorder file, you see within the file the macros it contains.

Each of the macros available in a Recorder file shows a shortcut key and descriptive name.

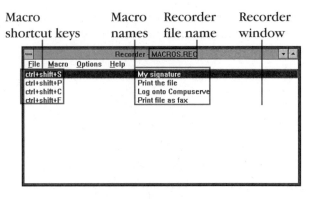

Macro shortcut keys | Macro names | Recorder file name | Recorder window

Note: Macros do not work with DOS programs. Also, when you use a macro with the Windows Terminal program, the macro works only until you are connected to another computer.

Preparing To Record a Macro

Before recording a macro, you need to prepare your Windows programs. (Your macro may involve one or more windows and programs.) To prepare your programs for a recording, follow these steps:

1. Open the programs and documents for the recording.
2. Practice the task you want to record.
3. Position the program and document windows as you want them for the recording.

If the procedure you want to record is long, divide it into segments and record each segment as a separate macro. Making small macros you can run separately is easier than making and repairing one large macro.

Note: If you want a macro to work on text or graphics you select before playing back the macro, select a representative piece of text or graphics before you start the Recorder. If you wait until after the Recorder is on to select the text or graphics, the Recorder always tries to select the same text or graphics you selected during the original recording.

To prepare the Recorder for recording, first start all the programs you want to use during the recording. Be sure to position the program windows the way you want them during the recording. Then follow these steps:

1. Open the Program Manager and open the Accessories group window.

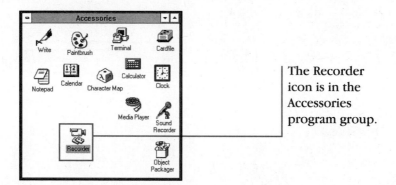

The Recorder icon is in the Accessories program group.

2. Start the Recorder program by double-clicking the Recorder icon, or by selecting the Recorder icon and then pressing ⏎Enter. (This action does not start recording your steps, but only opens the Recorder program.) Minimize the Program Manager so that it's out of the way.

13

The Recorder window appears, and the Program Manager is minimized to an icon at the bottom of the screen.

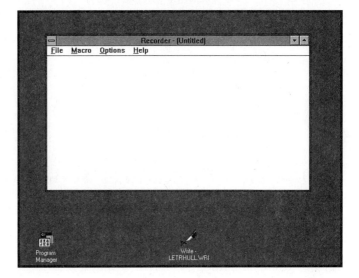

3. Activate the Windows program you want to use first in the recording.

4. Select text or graphics, or position the insertion point where you want it when you start the macro.

In this screen, the insertion point is positioned where it should be when the macro starts recording.

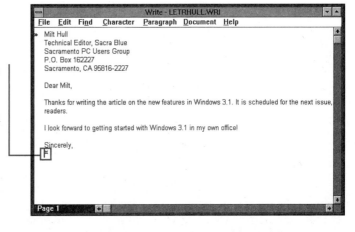

5. Press ⌈Alt⌉+⌈Tab⇥⌉ to activate the Recorder window.

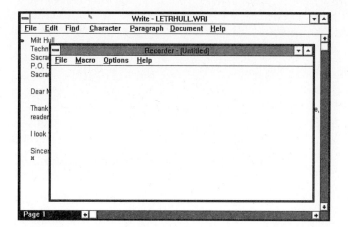

13

With the Recorder window active and the other windows positioned, you are ready to begin recording.

Recording a Macro

After you prepare your programs for recording a macro and start the Recorder, you are *almost* ready to start recording your macro. One very important task remains before you can start: practice the steps involved in creating the macro.

When you record a macro, you may find that many of your actions do not translate well into a macro. For example, your macro may involve opening a Paintbrush file that contains a scanned signature you will then select and copy into a Write document. When you open a file, you usually scroll through the list of available files, select the file you want, and then choose OK. But this method does not work well for a macro because the list may contain more or less files the next time you run the macro. Instead, you should type the name of the file you want to open in the File Name text box. You therefore need to know the exact file name.

In the same example, you will record not only keystrokes but also mouse movements because you must select the signature before you copy it. In addition, because programs open in different places on-screen (depending on how many programs you already have running, and how big their windows are), you must record mouse movements relative to the window, rather than the screen. To accurately repeat the mouse movement that selects the signature, the Recorder must know exactly where the signature is located. The Paintbrush window may open in different places on-screen, but the signature will always appear in the same place relative to the window. In this section, you learn how to make these choices.

Finally, you may be accustomed to using the mouse to select commands quickly. But in a macro, keystrokes are usually preferable because commands can move to different locations (for example, if you size a Write window so that it is very narrow, the menu bar wraps to two lines) and because dialog boxes often vary. Keystroke commands, however, rarely vary. So before you record your macro, practice using keystroke commands rather than the mouse whenever you can.

Follow these steps to record a macro:

1. Choose the **M** acro menu and select the Re**c** ord command.

The Record Macro dialog box appears. Use this dialog box to determine how keystrokes and mouse move- ments are re- corded, and how your macro plays back.

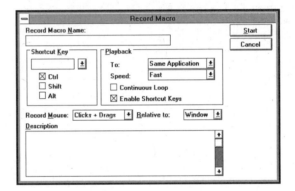

You cannot select options in the Record Macro dialog box by pressing Alt +*letter* because the options do not have underlined letters. To select an option, press Alt +*letter* to select the group enclosed by a box. To move between the options, press Tab ⁂ or ⇧Shift +Tab ⁂ . The active check box or option button appears with a surrounding dashed line; an active text box appears with a flashing insertion point; an active list appears highlighted. Select or deselect an option by pressing **space bar** . To make an entry in a text box, activate the text box so that an insertion point appears, and type the text. To open a drop-down list—indicated by a down arrow to the right of a text box—move to the text box and then press Alt +↓ .

2. Type a macro name of up to 40 characters in the Record Macro **N** ame text box. You use this name later to identify the macro you want to run.

3. To control how the macro plays back, select one of the options described in table 13.1.

Table 13.1
Options for Controlling Macro Play Back

Option	Description
Shortcut Key	Specifies the key you press to activate the macro. Type a single letter in the text box or choose a special key from the drop-down list. Select Ctrl, Shift, or Alt (or a combination) to indicate the key you want to use in combination with the letter you specified in the text box.
Playback To	Determines the programs in which the macro runs. Select Same Application to run the macro only in the program in which it was recorded. Select Any Application to run the macro in any program.
Playback Speed	Determines the speed of the macro. Select Fast to play back the macro at maximum speed. Select Recorded Speed to play back the macro at the speed at which you recorded it.
Playback Continuous Loop	Repeats the macro continuously. Useful for tutorials and demonstrations. Press Ctrl + Break to stop the macro.
Playback Enable Shortcut Keys	Enables you to press shortcut keys that run other macros while you record a new macro. You therefore can nest one macro inside another. If this option is deselected, you can run your macro, but it ignores any nested macros.

continues

13

327

13

Table 13.1 Continued

Option	Description
Record Mouse	Determines the type of mouse actions that you record:
Ignore Mouse	Records only keystrokes. Select this option if you want to use the macro across multiple programs with windows in varying positions, or if you want to copy the macro to computers with different graphics resolutions.
Everything	Records keystrokes and mouse actions. Press Ctrl + Break to stop the recording when this option is selected.
Clicks + Drags	Records keystrokes and those mouse actions that result when you click a mouse button or drag the mouse pointer, such as choosing a menu or selecting a command.
Relative to	Determines how mouse movements appear in the macro. Select Screen to make mouse movements relative to the screen position. Select Window to make mouse movements relative to the active window. This option is unavailable if you have selected Ignore Mouse in the Record Mouse list.
Description	Provides room for you to type a description of what the macro does and with which programs it works.

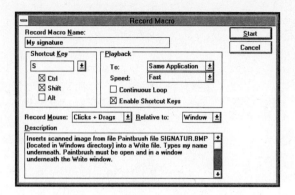

This filled-in dialog box describes the macro *My signature* and determines how it will play back when run.

13

4. Choose the **S**tart button.

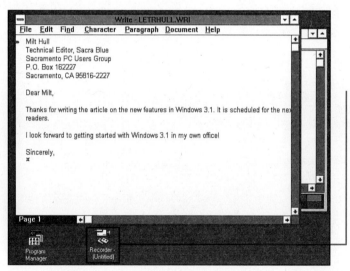

The Recorder becomes an icon at the bottom of the screen.

The Recorder icon flashes while the Recorder is recording. You may not be able to see this icon if it is behind a window.

5. Perform the steps you want to record in the macro.

Using keystrokes during recordings is usually preferable to using mouse actions. A recording of keystrokes plays back as expected, but mouse actions may not produce the same results produced in the original recording. A problem may arise because the Recorder repeats the exact screen location of the mouse pointer when you recorded a mouse action. (The mouse movements are measured in pixel units based on the current screen resolution.) During playback, if the windows are in different locations or the screen has a different resolution than in the original recording, the mouse pointer may be incorrectly positioned to make the selection or give the command you want. You should therefore use keystrokes to give commands, change windows, and select text or objects during the recording.

If you make a mistake during a recording, correct the mistake and continue. The macro records your correction. If you make selected text italic, for instance, but you wanted the text to be bold, simply change the italic to bold while the Recorder is on.

If one of your Recorder macros includes a nested macro with a shortcut key that conflicts with a key combination in another program, change the conflicting shortcut key for the nested macro.

Stopping or Pausing the Recorder

To stop or pause the recording, follow these steps:

1. Click the Recorder icon or press Ctrl + Break. (Break is usually located on the same key as Pause or PrtSc, depending on your keyboard.)

The Recorder dialog box appears.

2. Choose one of the following buttons from the Recorder dialog box:

Button	Description
Save Macro	Saves the macro you recorded.
Resume Recording	Continues recording from where you stopped.
Cancel Recording	Cancels the macro without recording what you did.

3. Choose OK or press ⏎Enter.

Recording Additional Macros

The macro you recorded and saved with the procedures just described should now appear as a line item within the Recorder window. Each macro in the Recorder window shows as a line containing the macro shortcut key and the macro name.

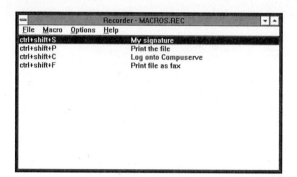

You can record and store multiple macros in one file. The file in this example is named MACROS.REC.

You can record additional macros by repeating the same procedures. The new macros are added to the current file. The section "Saving Macros," further in this chapter, explains how to save the Recorder file containing your recordings, and the section "Recording a Macro in an Existing Recorder File" teaches you how to open existing Recorder files that contain other macros. Although you can have many different Recorder files, each containing many macros, you can open only one Recorder file at a time in the Recorder.

An easy way to look at Recorder files is to think of them as libraries that contain collections of similar macros. For example, you might have one file for typing letters in Windows Write, another file for copying and deleting files in the File Manager, and another file for transferring data between Microsoft Excel and Word for Windows.

Saving Macros

When you record a new macro, the recording is placed with the other macros in the current Recorder file. If you do not save this file, you will lose the macros you have recorded. A Recorder file can contain many macros.

To save your macros, follow these steps:

1. Choose the File menu and select the Save As command.

2. In the Drives list, select the drive where you want to save your Recorder file.

3. In the Directories list, select the directory where you want to save your Recorder file.

4. In the File Name box, type a name for your Recorder file. You can use as many as eight characters in the file name.

5. Choose OK or press ⏎Enter.

You can use the File Manager to see the macro files on-disk. Files containing macros have the default extension REC, although you choose any extension you want.

Recording a Macro in an Existing Recorder File

You can have more than one Recorder file on-disk, and each file can contain multiple macros. Suppose that you already have a Recorder file that contains macros, and you want to add a new macro recording to the existing file. Follow these steps:

1. Start the Recorder program as described at the beginning of this chapter.

2. Choose the File menu and select the Open command.

The Open dialog box appears.

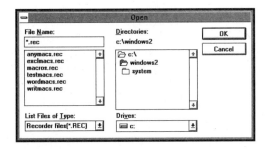

3. If necessary, select the drive containing your macro file in the Drives list, and select the directory in the Directories list.

4. Select a Recorder file from the File Name list and choose OK or press ⏎Enter. When the file opens, the Recorder window displays a list of the macros contained in the file.

5. Proceed with the steps outlined in "Recording a Macro," a previous section in this chapter, for recording a macro. The macro you create is stored in the file you opened in step 4.

When you add new macros to an existing Recorder file, you can save the Recorder file without changing its name, by choosing the File menu and selecting the Save command.

13

Playing Back a Macro

You can play back any of the macros stored in the current Recorder file. From within your program, press the appropriate shortcut key to run a macro; or from the Recorder, select the macro's name from the list in the Recorder window and choose the Run command from the Macro menu.

Running a Macro

You can run a macro by pressing the appropriate shortcut key or choosing the macro name from the list in the Recorder window. When you run a macro, it reacts with the currently loaded programs in Windows in one of two ways:

- If the macro is the type that runs with any program, the macro will play back.
- If the macro is the type that runs in a specific program, the Recorder activates that program's window when the macro runs. If you have not yet started the program or if the program is an icon, the macro does not play back. (If the Recorder Playback Aborted dialog box appears, choose OK or press Enter to continue.)

To run a macro with a shortcut key, follow these steps:

1. Start the Recorder program and open the file containing the macro you want to run.

2. Activate the program in which you want the macro to run; then position the insertion point where you want to run the macro, or select the appropriate text or graphics.

3. Press the shortcut key or keys assigned to the macro.

If you want the Recorder to reduce to an icon during playback, choose the Options Minimize on Use command from the Recorder before you play back the macro (this option is selected by default).

You also can play back a macro by choosing its name, which is especially useful when you have a lot of macros—too many to assign shortcut keys to conveniently—or when the macros are so complex that you cannot remember their actions.

To run a macro by choosing its name, follow these steps:

1. Start the Recorder program, choose the File menu, and select the Open command.

2. Choose the file containing the macro you want to run.

3. Activate the program in which you want to run the macro, and then position the insertion point or select the appropriate text or graphics.

4. Click the Recorder window to activate the Recorder so that it is the topmost window, or press [Alt] + [Tab⇥] until the Recorder is on top.

5. Choose the macro you want to run by double-clicking its name, or select the name by using the arrow keys and then selecting the Run command from the Macro menu.

When the macro runs, the Recorder window shrinks to an icon or moves to the background so that it is out of the way.

Stopping a Running Macro

To stop a currently running macro, press Ctrl+Break. You can prevent a macro from being stopped with Ctrl+Break by choosing the Options menu and selecting the Control+Break Checking command. If no check mark appears next to the command, pressing Ctrl+Break does not turn off the macro; you must wait for the macro to finish.

If Control+Break Checking is turned off and you want to stop a continuously running macro, press Ctrl+Alt+Del to stop the macro. A screen appears, offering you three options. You can press Esc to return to Windows, but your macro will still run continuously. You can press Ctrl+Alt+Del again to restart your computer, but you will lose any unsaved data in any open program. Or you can press Enter—your best option—which closes the program in which the macro is running, causing you to lose unsaved data in only that program. (If pressing Enter does not work—and occasionally it doesn't—you must press Ctrl+Alt+Del to reboot your computer.)

In short, when you create a continuously running macro, make sure that the Control+Break Checking option is selected (with a check mark to its left) so that you can press Ctrl+Break to stop the macro.

Editing and Changing a Macro

You cannot change the steps a recorded macro performs, but you can change some of its properties, such as its shortcut key, whether the macro works with a specific program or any program, and whether the macro plays back continuously.

The Macro Properties dialog box enables you to change the way in which a previously recorded macro works. For example, you can change the shortcut key combination that runs the macro, and you can change a property that causes the macro to run with any program rather than with only a specific program. The following procedure does not enable you to change or edit previously recorded keystrokes or mouse actions.

To change a macro's properties, follow these steps:

1. Activate the Recorder and open the Recorder file containing the macro you want to change.

2. Select the macro name whose properties you want to change by clicking the macro name or by pressing the arrow keys.

3. Choose the Macro menu and select the Properties command.

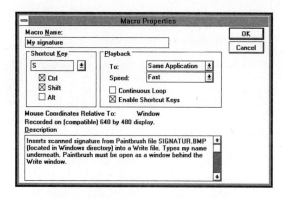

The Macro Properties dialog box appears.

Notice that the Macro Properties dialog box looks similar to the Macro Record dialog box. Many of the same items are changeable.

4. Select and change each property you want to modify in the dialog box. For example, you can change the shortcut key by replacing the current one.

5. Choose OK or press ⏎Enter.

13

The properties in the Macro Properties dialog box are described in detail in "Recording a Macro," a previous section in this chapter. You cannot change the Mouse Coordinates Relative To property, nor can you change the video display characteristics for the recording hardware. If you used the mouse in the original recording, the screen resolution is shown underneath the text `Mouse Coordinates Relative To`.

Note: To change the default settings of the Record Macro dialog box, choose the **Options** menu and select the **Preferences** command. The Default Preferences dialog box appears. You can change the default settings for **Playback To**, **Playback Speed**, **Record Mouse**, and **Relative To** options.

Managing Macros

Macros, like files, seem to expand and grow on their own. One moment, you have only two macros on-disk; the next time you look, you have 159. Although so many macros can seem overwhelming, you can learn to manage them.

Deleting a Macro from a File

If your macros become too numerous, sometimes the best way to manage them is simply to delete them. Especially useful is deleting early versions of macros you have rerecorded several times.

Delete a macro from its file in the Recorder by following these steps:

1. Activate the Recorder.
2. Choose the **File** menu and select the **Open** command.
3. Select the file containing the macro you want to delete, and choose OK or press ⏎Enter. After the file is loaded into the Recorder, the list of macros in that file appears in the Recorder window.
4. Select the macro name you want to delete.
5. Choose the **Macro** menu and select the **Delete** command.
6. When prompted to confirm that you want to delete the macro, choose OK or press ⏎Enter.

Merging Macros in Recorder Files

If you want to use one macro in multiple files, you can merge the files. Suppose, for example, that you have created one file of macros to use with invoices, another file of macros for memo writing, and another file of macros for worksheets. You previously created a macro that enters your name and signature, and you want to use the macro in all of these files. Merging the files enables you to use the macro in all of them.

Merging files brings the macros from a file on-disk into the active file in the Recorder. If an incoming macro contains a shortcut key that already is in use, the macro merges anyway, but the shortcut key for the active file in the Recorder takes precedence.

To merge the macros in two files, follow these steps:

1. Open a file in the Recorder, or create a new file by making a new macro.

2. Delete unwanted or duplicate macros from the current file in the Recorder.

3. Choose the File menu and select the Merge command.

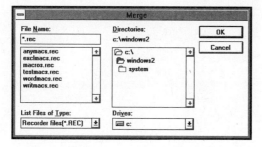

The Merge dialog box appears.

4. Type the name of the file you want to merge, or select the file name from the list of files.

5. Choose OK or press ↵Enter. The file in the Recorder now has the combined set of macros.

You can save the file containing the old and merged macros to the same name by choosing the File menu and selecting the Save command, or you can save the file to a new name by choosing the File menu and selecting the Save As command.

Troubleshooting Macros

If you run a macro that cannot properly carry out its recorded instructions, the macro stops and you see the dialog box named Recorder Playback Aborted! In that dialog box, the Error text box indicates why the macro stopped.

The Recorder Playback Aborted! dialog box indicates that the macro cannot play back because the Write program's window is not active.

The most common causes of macro failure are as follows:

- You were not running the correct programs when you played back the macro. Note which programs are used by the macro. During macro operation, these programs must be running in windows. The first program the macro uses does not need to be in the active window; the macro activates windows as needed.

- The macro you played back contains mouse actions, but the windows are not in the same location they were in when you recorded the macro. Check to see whether it will run when you correctly position the windows involved. If the macro continues to fail, re-record the macro with keystrokes.

Ideas for Macros

After you start creating macros, you find that it is hard to stop. To help you get started, here are some ideas for some simple and complex macros. Many of them take advantage of the fact that most Windows programs use the same keystrokes for the same types of commands.

- Record a macro that quickly prints a document. Use the File Print command, and press the Enter key. Assign a shortcut key to this macro so that you can print the current document with one keystroke, no matter which Windows program you are running. Set the macro's Playback To option to Any Application.

- Record a macro that sets up a common header or footer for your document.

- Record a macro that pauses the printer (through the Print Manager) and another macro that restarts it.

- Record a macro that starts your communications program by logging on to your favorite Bulletin Board System (BBS). You can create a group of macros that have start-up commands for different BBSs. (You might want to store this group of macros in a file with an extension other than REC if you share your computer with others or if your Recorder files are stored in a common directory on your network.)

- Record a macro that prints pending faxes from your fax board.

- Record a complex start-up macro that uses several subroutine macros. Set up a macro to check your electronic mail and another to print your calendar page for the current day. Then combine these macros into a master macro that performs each macro subroutine.

13

Summary

After you become familiar with Windows and with running several Windows programs or accessories, you will want to make your work easier by creating macros to handle repetitive tasks. You can create macros by recording your keystrokes or mouse actions with the Recorder program, located in the Accessories group window. Macros can involve operations with one or more Windows programs, but do not work with DOS programs.

The following important points were covered in this chapter:

- A Recorder file with the default extension REC can contain more than one macro. The macros do not work until you load the file in the Recorder.

- You can record macros so that they work with only a specific program.

- After you load a Recorder file, you can run a macro by activating the Windows program in which you want to run the macro, positioning the insertion point, and then pressing the shortcut key assigned to the macro.

- You will have the best success with macros if you record keystroke actions. Mouse actions, which are recorded relative to screen resolution and window position, may not play back correctly when run on a different display or with window locations other than those used during the original recording.

Now that you're familiar with creating and running macros, refer to Chapter 11, "Using Windows Write," and Chapter 12, "Using Windows Paintbrush," for ideas about creating macros for those two Windows accessory programs. Then look ahead to Chapter 14, "Using Desktop Accessories," to see how you can use macros with Terminal, Cardfile, Notepad, Calendar, and other Windows accessory programs.

13

The Windows environment adds a great deal of power to both Windows and DOS programs. To learn how to get the most from running one or more DOS programs in Windows, read Chapter 20, "Running DOS Programs." To learn how to pass data between programs and how to integrate Windows programs so that they act as one program, read Chapter 19, "Integrating Multiple Programs."

Using Desktop Accessories

One of the greatest advantages to using Windows is that you can run several programs at the same time. Instead of using your major programs side by side, however, you may want to work with only one of those programs and keep small accessory programs close at hand. That's where the Windows accessory programs shine. Suppose, for example, that you are working in Microsoft Excel and want to jot down an idea in a quick memo. The Notepad accessory is perfect for the task. Or you may be working in Word for Windows and need to do a quick calculation. Open the Calculator accessory, add up your figures, and copy the total back into Word for Windows. Use Character Map to insert special characters or symbols into a document. At the end of the day, you may want to relax with a game. Challenge yourself with Solitaire.

The Windows accessory programs Notepad, Character Map, Calendar, Cardfile, Calculator, and Clock are small, so they don't use much of your computer's memory. And they're simple, so they don't take much of *your* memory! These accessories programs, located in the Accessories group window, are good, useful companions to your primary programs.

14

Key Terms in This Chapter

Insertion point	The flashing vertical line where text appears when you type (sometimes called a cursor).
Scroll	To move horizontally or vertically in a document. Most programs have scroll bars to make scrolling easy.
Select	To highlight text for editing.
Cut/copy and paste	To move or copy text from one part of a document to another, or to move or copy text between programs.
Clipboard	The temporary file in Windows that stores any text you select and then cut or copy. You can paste the contents of the Clipboard wherever you move the insertion point.
Search or find	To look through a document for a specific word or phrase.
View	To look at a document in a different way; for example, you can look at Calendar in the Day view or Month view.

The Accessories group also contains the two accessories Media Player and Sound Recorder. These two accessories can liven up an otherwise dull computer session. To learn more about the Media Player and Sound Recorder, please refer to Chapter 18, "Using Multimedia."

Four other Windows programs—Write, Paintbrush, Recorder, and PIF Editor—also are considered Windows accessory programs. Because they are powerful enough to be used as primary programs, the first three are discussed in separate chapters, and the PIF Editor is explained in Chapter 20, "Running DOS Programs." This chapter examines seven accessory programs and two games:

- Notepad—a miniature word processing program you can use to type quick notes and memos. Notepad is excellent for creating batch files like those described in Chapter 20, "Running DOS Programs."

- Character Map—a table of the characters and symbols contained in each font available to your system. Copy these characters and symbols from the table into your Windows documents.

- Calendar—an "alarming" appointment calendar that enables you to see daily or monthly views of your schedule. You can set an alarm to remind you of something important.

- Cardfile—a computerized "stack of cards" you can use to store names, addresses, phone numbers, and other information. You can quickly find the cards containing a specific word or phrase.

- Terminal—a communications program that enables your computer to "talk" with another computer over a telephone line. (You must have a modem to take advantage of Terminal.)

- Calculator—a program that works just like a calculator, except that you don't need batteries.

- Clock—a clock that enables you to be a clock-watcher as you stare at the screen. Even as an icon, Clock shows the time.

- Solitaire—the classic card game to help you get tense about something other than work.

- Minesweeper—a game that keeps you on edge as you risk your life with each step across a deadly minefield.

14

Starting the Windows Accessory Programs

Windows accessory programs are located inside the Accessories group window. Each accessory program appears as an icon with its name below it. To start any program, just double-click its icon. Alternatively, select the Accessories window, press an arrow key to select the program item icon, and press Enter.

When the Accessories group icon is open as a window, you can see the programs it contains.

After you start the accessory programs, you may want to minimize them as icons at the bottom of the screen until you need to use them.

Writing in Notepad

The Notepad program is like a miniature word processing program. Although Notepad has limited functions compared to Windows Write or Word for Windows, Notepad is ideal for many purposes. Just as you use a notepad on your desk, you can use Notepad to take notes on-screen alongside other Windows programs, such as Microsoft Excel. Notepad is also useful for creating batch files to start your computer, to load DOS programs, or to configure networks. One of your first uses for Notepad should be to read the TXT files Windows stores in the Windows directory during installation. These files contain information more current than the manual.

As a bonus, Notepad includes a feature for logging time. You can use Notepad as a time clock to let you know when you opened a file or to monitor the time you spend on a project.

Notepad retrieves and saves files in text format, which is a computer's most basic file format. For this reason, you can read Notepad files into almost any word processing program.

Opening Notepad and Typing Text

Open the Notepad program just as you open any Windows program—by double-clicking the Notepad icon in the Accessories group window, or by pressing the arrow keys to select the icon and then pressing Enter.

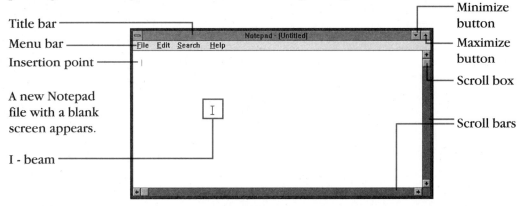

Title bar

Menu bar

Insertion point

A new Notepad file with a blank screen appears.

I - beam

Minimize button

Maximize button

Scroll box

Scroll bars

As soon as you open a Notepad file, you can begin typing. Each character you type appears to the left of a blinking vertical line called the *insertion point*. Unlike most word processing programs, Notepad does not automatically wrap text to the next line. If you want text to wrap (so that you don't have to press Enter each time you reach the end of a line), choose the Edit menu and select the Word Wrap command.

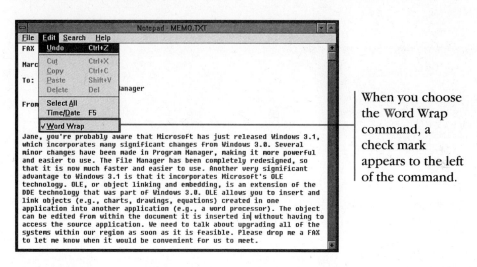

When you choose the Word Wrap command, a check mark appears to the left of the command.

With Word Wrap selected, text wraps to fit the width of the Notepad window, no matter how wide the window is. If you make the window wider, the text rewraps to fit it. With Word Wrap turned off, lines can be as long as 160 characters.

Moving and Scrolling on the Notepad Page

To edit text in a Notepad file or to add new text, you must learn to scroll the page and move the insertion point. The Notepad page scrolls just like other Windows programs. The horizontal and vertical scroll bars represent the entire Notepad document; a gray box, the *scroll box*, represents your current position within the document. With the mouse, scroll the Notepad page line-by-line by clicking the up and down arrows in the vertical scroll bar, or scroll horizontally by clicking the left and right arrows in the horizontal scroll bar. You can move to a new position in the document by dragging the scroll box to a new position on the scroll bar. You can move one screen at a time, up or down, by clicking the scroll bar either above or below the scroll box. With the keyboard, scroll the page by pressing the PgUp and PgDn keys, or the up- and down-arrow keys.

14

Another way to move around on the Notepad page is to move the insertion point, using either the mouse or the keyboard. As in any word processing program, you cannot move the insertion point beyond where you have already typed.

To move the insertion point with the mouse, position the I-beam where you want the insertion point, and then click the mouse button. To move the insertion point with the keyboard, use the keystrokes described in table 14.1.

14

Table 14.1
Keystrokes for Moving the Insertion Point

Keystroke(s)	Action
↑	Moves the insertion point up one line.
↓	Moves the insertion point down one line.
←	Moves the insertion point left one character.
→	Moves the insertion point right one character.
End	Moves the insertion point to the end of a line.
Home	Moves the insertion point to the beginning of a line.
Ctrl + Home	Moves the insertion point to the beginning of the document.
Ctrl + End	Moves the insertion point to the end of the document.
Ctrl + ←	Moves the insertion point left one word.
Ctrl + →	Moves the insertion point right one word.

Opening an Existing or New Notepad File

If you have already opened the Notepad program, you can open an existing Notepad file—one you created earlier. When you open an existing Notepad file, the Notepad file you are currently working on closes, offering you the option to save your changes.

To open an existing Notepad file, follow these steps:

1. Choose the File menu and select the Open command.

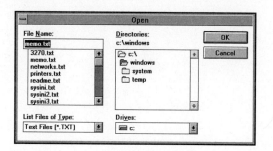

The Open dialog
box appears.

14

2. From the Drives or Directories list, select the drive and directory
    containing the file you want to open.

3. From the File Name list, select the file you want to open.

4. Choose OK or press ⏎Enter.

If you want to open a new Notepad file, choose the File menu and select the
New command. If you haven't saved the Notepad document you're currently
working on, Notepad asks whether you want to save the document. Choose
Yes if you want to save the file, No if you don't, or Cancel to return to the
document. Refer to the section "Saving and Printing Notepad Files," further in
this chapter, to learn more about saving a file.

Selecting and Editing Text in Notepad

Selecting and editing text in Notepad is similar to selecting and editing text in
Write and other word processing programs.

The simplest way to edit is to insert and delete text one character at a time. To
insert text, move the insertion point to the new text location and start typing.
Delete a single character by moving the insertion point to the left of the
character and pressing Del, or by moving to the right of the character and
pressing Backspace.

To make more extensive edits, you must first select text. To select text with
the mouse, drag the I-beam across the text you want to select. To select text
with the keyboard, hold down the Shift key and then press any arrow key. You
can select all the text at once in your Notepad document by choosing the Edit
menu and selecting the Select All command.

To delete text, select the text you want to delete, choose the Edit menu, and
select the Delete command. Alternatively, select the text to you want to delete
and press the Del key.

347

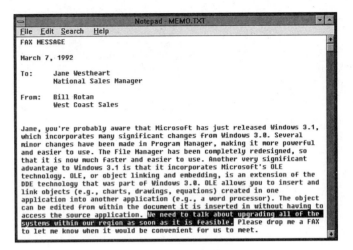

14

You can replace selected text by simply typing the new text.

If you make a typing error, you can correct it by choosing the Edit menu and selecting the Undo command. You can quickly undo an action by pressing Ctrl+Z. Remember that you can undo only the most recent action.

Copying and Moving Text in Notepad

Notepad's Edit commands enable you to copy or move selected text from one place to another. As in any Windows program, text that you copy or cut is stored in the Clipboard, a temporary file that holds only one selection. You then paste text from the Clipboard into the document at the insertion point.

To copy or move text, follow these steps:

1. Select the text you want to copy or move.

2. Choose the Edit menu and select the Copy command to copy text. To move text, choose the Edit menu and select the Cut command.

3. Move the insertion point to the place where you want to copy or move the text.

4. Choose the Edit menu and select the Paste command.

You can paste text from the Clipboard as many times as you like. Because the Clipboard holds only one item at a time, though, be sure to paste text soon after you copy or cut it; the next item you copy or cut replaces what is currently in the Clipboard.

Searching through a Notepad Document

Notepad's Search menu contains commands for finding and selecting any word or phrase. When Notepad finds the first occurrence of the word or phrase you are looking for, the program selects that word or phrase; the dialog box remains open so that you can continue the search if you want.

To search for text, follow these steps:

1. Choose the Search menu and select the Find command.

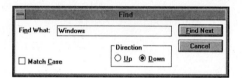

The Find dialog box appears.

2. In the Find What text box, type the text you want to find.
3. Select the Match Case box (so that an X appears in it) if you want to find text that matches the upper- and lowercase letters you typed.
4. Select Down to search forward from the insertion point; select Up to search backward from the insertion point.
5. Choose the Find Next button.

The program selects the first occurrence of the word or phrase. The dialog box remains open, enabling you to continue the search by choosing Find Next again. To return to the document, choose Cancel. If Notepad cannot find the word or phrase, it displays a message box to tell you so. Choose OK to acknowledge the message, and then choose Cancel in the Find dialog box to return to the document. To continue the search after you close the dialog box, choose the Search menu and select the Find Next command (or press F3).

Sometimes Notepad finds text that is hidden underneath the Find dialog box. You can move the dialog box by positioning the tip of the mouse pointer on the title bar, pressing and holding down the left mouse button, dragging the dialog box to a new location, and releasing the mouse button.

Creating a Time Log File with Notepad

Using a special but simple code, Notepad automatically enters the time and date at the end of a document each time you open it. This feature is convenient if you need to monitor your time or calculate the amount of time you spend on a project.

To create an automatic time log in your document, follow these steps:

1. Move the insertion point to the left margin of the first line in your Notepad document.

2. Type the command **.LOG** in uppercase letters.

3. Choose the **E**dit menu and select the Time/**D**ate command to insert the starting time and date.

4. Make notes about your work, if you want, choose the **F**ile menu, and select the Save **A**s command. Type a file name in the File **N**ame text box, and choose OK or press ⏎Enter.

5. Close your time log file by opening a different Notepad file or by exiting Notepad.

6. Reopen the file.

   When you reopen the Notepad file, the time and date are inserted automatically. Now you can type a note describing your project. Entering notes after each time and date listing enables you to keep an accurate log of how you are spending your time.

7. Make additional work notes and save the file again.

   Each time you reopen the file, the time and date are entered.

Each time you open a file that has .LOG as its first line, Notepad logs the current time and date.

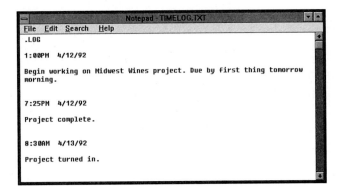

Another way to create a time log is to insert the current time and date manually.

To insert the time and date in your document, follow these steps:

1. Move the insertion point where you want the time and date entered.

2. Choose the **E**dit menu and select the Time/**D**ate command.

14

Note: The time and date are controlled by an internal clock. You can reset this clock using the Date/Time program in the Control Panel. See Chapter 7, "Customizing Your Work Area."

Setting Up the Page for Printing

You can choose the File menu and select the Page Setup command to set the margins for your document and to add a header or footer to your document. Headers and footers print at the top and bottom, respectively, of each page of your document. You can choose from several codes to enhance your headers and footers.

To set the margins for your document, follow these steps:

1. Choose the File menu and select the Page Setup command. The Page Setup dialog box appears.

2. Select the Left, Right, Top, or Bottom option in the Margins group, and type a margin in decimal inches. For example, type .5 for a half-inch margin.

3. Choose OK or press ⏎Enter.

To add a header or footer to your document, follow these steps:

1. Choose the File menu and select the Page Setup command. The Page Setup dialog box appears.

2. Select the Header text box or the Footer text box, and type the text you want to appear in the header or footer.

   You can type any of the following codes in your header or footer:

Code	Result
&d	Inserts current date.
&p	Inserts page number.
&f	Inserts file name.
&l	Left-justifies text following code.
&r	Right-justifies text following code.
&c	Centers text following code.
&t	Inserts the current time.

Saving and Printing Notepad Files

To save a Notepad file and give it a name, follow these steps:

1. Choose the File menu and select the Save As command.

14

The Save As
dialog box
appears.

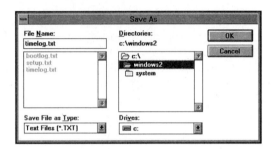

2. From the Drives list, select the disk drive where you want to save your file. From the Directories list box, select the directory in which you want to save the file.

3. Type a name (up to eight characters) in the File Name text box.

4. Choose OK or press [↵Enter].

Notepad adds the extension TXT to the file name. For example, if you call the file MEMO, Notepad names it MEMO.TXT.

To save a file with the name it already has, choose the File menu and select the Save command. The current file replaces the original version.

You can print a Notepad file on the currently selected printer.

To select a printer, follow these steps:

1. Choose the File menu and select the Print Setup command. The Print Setup dialog box appears.

2. From the Printer group, either select Default Printer or select any other printer from the Specific Printer list.

3. Choose OK or press [↵Enter].

To print a Notepad file, follow these steps:

1. Make sure that the Notepad file you want to print is displayed on-screen, and that your printer is on.

2. Choose the File menu and select the Print command.

When you print the file, a message box appears on-screen, telling you that the document is printing. To cancel the print job, choose the Cancel button.

Closing a File and Exiting Notepad

You can close a Notepad file in two ways: open another file (or a new file) or exit the Notepad program. To open a file, choose the File menu and select the Open command. (You can even use this technique to reopen the currently open file—for example, to log the current time and date.) To create a new file, choose the File menu and select the New command. To exit the Notepad program, choose the File menu and select the Exit command.

14

Using Character Map

The Character Map accessory gives you access to *symbol fonts* and *ANSI characters*. A symbol font, Symbol, is included with Windows. Others may be built into your printer; for example, most PostScript printers include Zapf Dingbats. ANSI characters are the regular characters that you see on your keyboard, plus more than one hundred other characters, including a copyright symbol, a registered trademark symbol, and many foreign language characters.

To use the Character Map accessory, you must first start it from the Program Manager. You can then select any characters or symbols from the Character Map dialog box and insert them into any Windows program, using the Clipboard.

Note: Windows programs, such as Notebook, that do not have font formatting capabilities may not be able to show the special characters from Character Map.

Open Character Map by double-clicking the Character Map icon in the Accessories window, or by pressing arrow keys to select the icon and then pressing Enter.

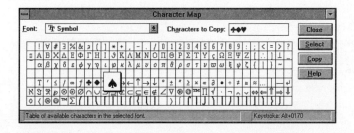

The Character Map dialog box appears. When you click a character, it enlarges.

353

The Character Map dialog box includes a drop-down list box from which you can select any of the available fonts on your system. After you select a font, the characters and symbols for that font appear in the Character Map table.

To insert characters and symbols into a Windows program, copy to the Clipboard the characters you selected from the Character Map dialog box, and then paste the characters into your program, using the normal Windows copy-and-paste procedures.

To insert a character from Character Map into a Windows program, follow these steps:

1. Open the Character Map accessory from the Program Manager.

2. Select the font you want to use from the Font list.

   Character Map displays the characters for the selected font.

3. View characters by clicking them and holding the mouse button; or press [Tab⇥] until you select the character display area, and then press the arrow keys to view the characters.

4. Double-click the character you want to insert, or choose the Select button to place the current character in the Characters to Copy text box.

5. Repeat steps 2 through 4 to select as many characters as desired.

6. Choose the Copy button to copy to the Clipboard the characters appearing in the Characters to Copy text box. Choose the Close button to close Character Map.

7. Open or switch to the program to which you want to copy the characters.

8. Place the insertion point where you want to insert the characters, choose the Edit menu, and select the Paste command.

   If the characters do not appear as they did in Character Map, you probably need to select characters and select the same font you selected in Character Map. You can change the font before you insert the characters; or you can select the characters after you insert them, and then change the font.

Note: If you plan on using Character Map frequently, you may want to include it in the StartUp program group so that it automatically opens when you start Windows. (See Chapter 5, "Grouping Programs and Documents," for more information on using the StartUp program group.) By including Character Map in the StartUp program group, you can quickly access Character Map from within any Windows program.

Tracking Appointments with Calendar

The Windows Calendar program is a computerized appointment book you can use to record appointments, mark special dates, and even set an alarm to remind you of an important event. Calendar operates in two views: Day and Month.

Opening Calendar

Open the Calendar program as you open any Windows program—by double-clicking the Calendar icon in the Accessories group window, or by pressing the arrow keys to select the icon and then pressing Enter. A new Calendar file appears, displayed in the Day view.

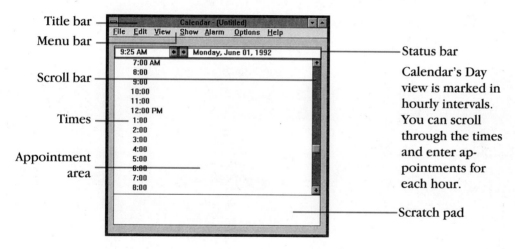

Below the Calendar window's menu bar is a status bar showing the current time and date. (If the time and date are wrong, refer to Chapter 7, "Customizing Your Work Area," to learn how to reset them through the Date/Time program in the Control Panel.) Calendar's two views, Day and Month, both share the status bar.

Typing Appointments in the Day View

When you open the Calendar window, you see the Day view for the current time and date. Times are listed on the left side of the Calendar window; you

355

14

can type appointments next to each time. To type an appointment, move the insertion point to the correct time, and then type the text. You can type 80 characters on each line.

To move the insertion point with the mouse, position the I-beam where you want to type, and then click the mouse button. To move the insertion point with the keyboard, press the up- or down-arrow key.

Although only part of the day is displayed in the Calendar window, 24 hours are available. To enter an appointment for a time not displayed, use the scroll bar on the right side of the Calendar window to scroll up or down to the time you want. Alternatively, with the keyboard, use the up- and down-arrow keys or the PgUp and PgDn keys to scroll respectively up and down.

To type an appointment in a Calendar file, follow these steps:

1. Scroll the Calendar window to display the time you want.

2. Move the insertion point to the time of your appointment.

3. Type the appointment.

In this example, a 9:00 a.m. appointment is entered in the Calendar file.

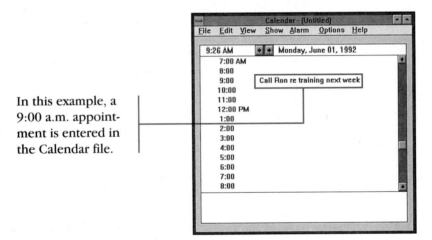

4. Press ⏎Enter to move the insertion point to the next line.

At the bottom of each daily or monthly Calendar window is a three-line scratch pad in which you can type notes. A note stays attached to its date; whenever you turn to that date, the note appears in the scratch pad.

To type a note in the scratch pad, follow these steps:

1. Move to the scratch pad by clicking it or pressing Tab⇆.

2. Type the text of your note.

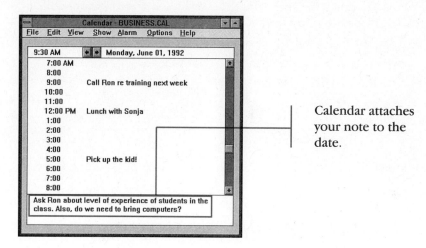

Calendar attaches
your note to the
date.

14

3. Move back to the appointment area by clicking it or pressing Tab⁺.

Opening an Existing Calendar File

Calendar, like any other program, creates and stores files. You can create as
many different Calendar files as you want. For example, you may want to
create a separate Calendar file for individual projects. You can open each
Calendar file as you need it.

To open an existing Calendar file, follow these steps:

1. Choose the File menu and select the Open command.

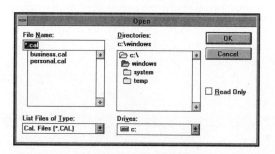

The Open dialog
box appears.

14

2. In the Drives list, select the drive containing the calendar file you want to open. In the Directories list, select the directory containing the Calendar file you want to open.

3. In the File Name list, select the Calendar file you want to open.

4. Choose OK or press ⏎Enter.

Editing and Moving Calendar Appointments

You can edit text in the appointment area and the scratch pad, just as you edit text in any Windows program. For example, you can select text and then press Backspace or Del to delete the text. To add text, position the insertion point where you want the new text, and then type. You also can copy or move appointments from one time or date to another time or date.

To copy or move appointments or notes, follow these steps:

1. Select the text you want to copy or move.

2. Choose the Edit menu and select the Copy command to copy the text. Or choose the Cut command to move the text.

3. Move the insertion point to the new time or date.

4. Choose the Edit menu and select the Paste command.

Removing Appointments from a Calendar File

Old appointments take up disk space, and you probably don't want them cluttering your Calendar files. Fortunately, you can remove appointments for an individual day or for a range of days. (You can remove appointments only in the currently open Calendar file.)

To remove appointments from the currently open Calendar file, follow these steps:

1. Choose the Edit menu and select the Remove command.

The Remove dialog box appears, enabling you to specify a range of dates to remove.

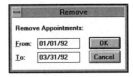

2. In the From text box, type the first date you want to remove, using the format suggested in the box (for example, type **01/01/92**).

3. In the To text box, type the last date you want to remove, using the suggested format.

4. Choose OK or press ⏎Enter.

If you want to remove appointments from just one date, type the date in the From text box and leave the To text box empty.

Changing the Time Intervals and Starting Time

The starting calendar displays the time in hours, but you can change the intervals on your calendar, and you can change the starting time. You also can add special times.

To change the time intervals and starting time, follow these steps:

1. Choose the Options menu and select the Day Settings command. The Day Settings dialog box appears.

2. From the Interval group, select 15, 30, or 60 minute intervals.

3. In the Starting Time box, type a different starting time.

4. Choose OK or press ⏎Enter.

To add a special time, follow these steps:

1. Choose the Options menu and select the Special Time command. The Special Time dialog box appears.

2. In the Special Time box, type the time you want to enter.

3. Select the AM or PM option.

4. Choose Insert or press ⏎Enter.

Setting an Alarm

To remind yourself of an important appointment, you can set an alarm that alerts you when the time for the appointment arrives. You can set alarms for as many appointments in a Calendar file as you want.

To turn on the alarm, follow these steps:

1. Move the insertion point to the time when you want the alarm to sound.

2. Choose the **Alarm** menu and select the **Set** command.

To turn off the alarm, follow the same procedure.

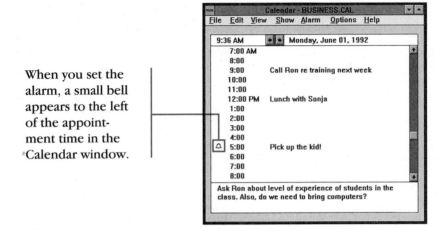

14

When you set the alarm, a small bell appears to the left of the appointment time in the Calendar window.

When the appointed time arrives, an alarm sounds a beep (unless you have turned off the sound), and the Alarm dialog box flashes to remind you of your appointment.

If you want, you can set the alarm to ring from 1 to 10 minutes early. To turn off the alarm sound or to set the alarm to ring early, follow these steps:

1. Choose the **Alarm** menu and select the **Controls** command.

The Alarm Controls dialog box appears.

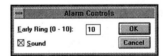

2. To set an early ring, select the **Early Ring** option and type a number from **1** to **10**.

3. To turn off the sound, deselect the **Sound** option. To turn on the sound, select the **Sound** option.

4. Choose OK or press ↵Enter.

When the Alarm dialog box displays to remind you of your appointment, you must respond to continue working.

14

If Calendar isn't active when the alarm goes off, the Calendar title bar or icon flashes in a background window. You must activate Calendar so that you can respond to the Alarm dialog box. To turn off the Alarm dialog box, choose OK in the dialog box.

Using Calendar's Two Views

As indicated previously, Calendar has two views: Day and Month. The Day view shows the details of each day's appointments. The Month view shows an overview of an entire month.

Switching between the views is easy. To switch to the Month view, choose the View menu and select the Month command. To switch to the Day view, choose the View menu and select the Day command.

If you have a mouse, you can double-click the date in the status bar to switch between the Month and Day views. In the Month view, you can double-click any date (or select the date and press Enter) to switch to the Day view for that date.

Viewing Calendar by the Month

Like the Day view, Calendar's Month view shows the current time and date in the status bar below the menus. The day selected in Calendar's Month view is the same day displayed when you switched from the Day view.

14

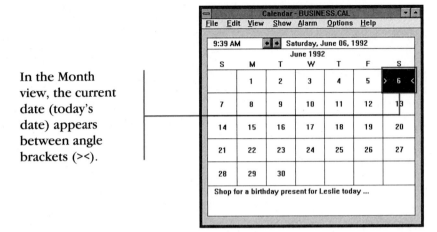

In the Month view, the current date (today's date) appears between angle brackets (><).

Notice that the scratch pad for the selected day in the Month view is the same as the scratch pad for that day in the Day view. You can move into the scratch pad to type or edit text by either pressing the Tab key or clicking the mouse button in the scratch pad.

To select a different day in the Month view, press an arrow key to move one day in that direction, or click the day you want to select. You can move in the monthly calendar just as you move in the daily calendar; these movement techniques are listed in table 14.2 in the upcoming section "Displaying Different Dates and Times."

Marking Important Days

In the Month view, you can mark a date to remind yourself of a special event, such as a report due date, a project completion date, or your sister's birthday. (As a reminder, you should make a note in the scratch pad area to specify *why* you marked the occasion.)

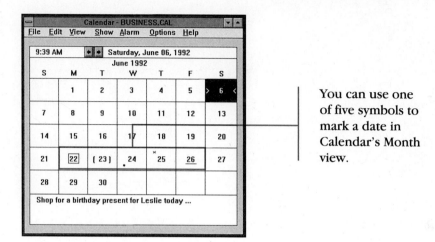

You can use one of five symbols to mark a date in Calendar's Month view.

To mark a date in Calendar's Month view, follow these steps:

1. Select the date you want to mark by clicking it or pressing the arrow keys.

2. Choose the Options menu and select the Mark command.

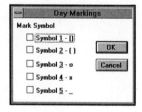

The Day Markings dialog box appears.

3. Select one of the following options:

       Symbol 1 - [ ]

       Symbol 2 - ( )

       Symbol 3 - o

       Symbol 4 - x

       Symbol 5 - _

4. Choose OK or press ⏎Enter.

Displaying Different Dates and Times

Whenever you open a new or existing Calendar file, you will always see the current date in the Day view, or the current month in the Month view. You can move between different dates and times by using the techniques listed in table 14.2. Many of the techniques include commands in the Show menu.

Table 14.2
Moving in a Calendar File

Action	To
Choose the Show menu and select the Previous command	Move to the previous day or month.
Click the left arrow in the status bar	Move to the previous day or month.
Choose the Show menu and select the Next command	Move to the next day or month.
Click the right arrow in the status bar	Move to the next day or month.
Choose the Show menu and select the Today command	Move to the current date.
Choose the Show menu, select the Date command, type the date (such as 9/1/92), and press ⏎Enter	Move to a specific date.
Press ↑ or ↓	Move to a different time (Day view) or month (Month view).
Press PgUp or PgDn	Move to a different time (Day view) or month (Month view).
Click the scroll bar arrows	Move to a different time (only Day view).
Press Tab⇥	Move between the scratch pad and the appointment area (Day view) or date (Month view).

Saving a Calendar File

You can save as many different Calendar files as you want—for different projects, resources, clients, and so on. The first time you save a Calendar file, you must name it.

To save a new Calendar file, follow these steps:

1. Choose the File menu and select the Save As command.

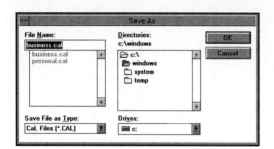

The Save As dialog box appears.

2. In the File Name text box, type a file name (up to eight characters).

3. From the Drives list box, select the drive in which you want to save the file. From the Directories list box, select the directory in which you want to save the file.

4. Choose OK or press ↵Enter.

To save an existing Calendar file without changing its name, choose the File menu and select the Save command.

Printing Appointments from a Calendar File

You can print appointments for a day or a range of days from the currently open Calendar file. Pages are printed on the currently selected printer.

Before you can print, you must set up the printer. To set it up, follow these steps:

1. Choose the File menu and select the Print Setup command. The Print Setup dialog box appears.

2. In the Printer group, select either Default Printer, or select a printer from the Specific Printer list.

3. Choose OK or press ↵Enter.

To print a range of appointments, follow these steps:

1. Choose the File menu and select the Print command.

The Print dialog
box appears.

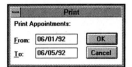

14

2. In the From text box, type the first appointment day you want to print.
3. In the To text box, type the last day you want to print, using the format suggested.
4. Choose OK or press ⏎Enter.

If you want to print only a single date, type the date in the From text box and leave the To text box empty.

Closing a Calendar File and Exiting the Program

You can close a Calendar file in two ways: open another file or close the Calendar program. To open a new or existing file, choose the File menu and select the New or Open command. To close the Calendar program, choose the File menu and select the Exit command.

Storing and Retrieving Information in Cardfile

The Cardfile program is a good place to store names, addresses, phone numbers, and even graphics—any information you want to access quickly. Each "card" in a Cardfile file has two parts: an index line at the top and an area for text (or graphics) below. Cardfile always arranges cards alphabetically by index line and displays the active card on top of the stack.

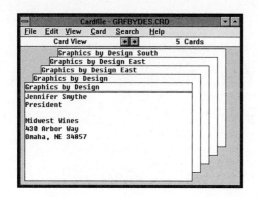

Cardfile is like a computerized stack of 3-by-5-inch index cards.

You can create as many separate Cardfile files as you want. For example, you may want a separate file for each of your major clients or projects, or you may want separate files for home and office.

Starting Cardfile

You open the Cardfile program the way you open any Windows program—by double-clicking the Cardfile icon in the Accessories group window, or by pressing the arrow keys to select the icon and then pressing Enter.

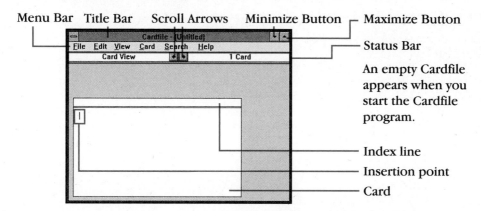

Menu Bar   Title Bar   Scroll Arrows   Minimize Button   Maximize Button

Status Bar

An empty Cardfile appears when you start the Cardfile program.

Index line

Insertion point

Card

When the Cardfile program is running, you can open an existing Cardfile. When you open an existing Cardfile, the file you are using closes. If necessary, a dialog box asks whether you want to save the current changes. Choose Yes to save the current changes, No to discard them, or Cancel to return to your file.

14

To open an existing Cardfile, follow these steps:

1. Choose the File menu and select the Open command.

The Open dialog
box appears.

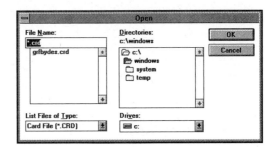

2. From the Drives list, select the drive containing the file you want to open. From the Directories list, select the directory containing the file you want to open.

3. From the File Name list, select the file you want to open.

4. Choose OK or press ⏎Enter.

After you start the program, you can create a new Cardfile by choosing the File menu and selecting the New command.

Entering Information into a Cardfile Card

When you open a new Cardfile, you see a single blank card. The card's index line is at the top of the card, and the card's body is below the index line. The insertion point flashes in the top left corner of the body of the card, just below a double line. You type information—such as a name, address, and phone number—in the body of the card. To enter the information, simply begin typing. When you reach the right edge of the card, text automatically wraps to the next line.

The index line at the top of the card is important because Cardfile arranges cards alphabetically by index lines. Creating an index line is different from typing text in the body of the card. You must choose a menu command before you can type an index line.

To create an index line and type text in it, follow these steps:

1. Choose the Edit menu and select the Index command.

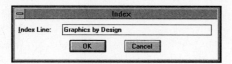

The Index dialog
box appears.

2. In the Index Line text box, type the text for the index line.

3. Choose OK or press ⏎Enter.

Using the Index dialog box is the only way to enter—or change—an index line
in an existing card. (To change an existing index line, follow the same steps
for creating a new index line. Instead of typing new text, edit the existing text
in the index line.) A shortcut for displaying the top card's index line is to
double-click the index line or press the F6 key.

Adding a Card

Adding new cards to an existing Cardfile is easy, but the procedure is a little
different from starting with a brand new Cardfile. When you add a new card,
you type the index line before you type the text on the card.

To add a new card to an existing Cardfile, follow these steps:

1. Choose the Card menu and select the Add command.

The Add dialog
box appears.

2. In the Add text box, type an index line for the new card.

3. Choose OK or press ⏎Enter.

The new card with the index line you just typed is displayed on top of the
stack of cards. The insertion point is at the top left of the card, ready for you
to type the card's contents.

Scrolling through the Cards

After you add many cards to a Cardfile, you need a way to display the card you
want to see by bringing it to the top of the stack. The Cardfile program
provides several ways to scroll through your cards to display the one you
want.

14

369

You can scroll through the cards one by one. At the top of the Cardfile window is a pair of arrows, one facing left and one facing right. Click the left arrow to scroll backward one card; click the right arrow to scroll forward one card. The PgUp and PgDn keys perform the same tasks. Perhaps the easiest way to display a card, however, is to click its index line. These and additional methods of scrolling in a Cardfile are summarized in table 14.3.

Table 14.3
Scrolling in a Cardfile

Action	*To*
Click the left arrow in the Cardfile window, or press PgUp	Scroll backward one card.
Click the right arrow in the Cardfile window, or press PgDn	Scroll forward one card.
Click the card's index line	Scroll to a specific card.
Press Ctrl + Home	Scroll to the first card.
Press Ctrl + End	Scroll to the last card.
Press Ctrl + Shift + *letter*	Scroll to the card whose index begins with *letter*.

Searching through the Cards

Another way to find a specific card, besides scrolling, is to search for a card containing a certain word or phrase. You can search through text in the body of the cards, or you can search the index lines—you use a different command for each type of search. An additional command enables you to repeat your most recent search quickly.

To search through index lines in a Cardfile, follow these steps:

1. Choose the Search menu and select the Go To command.

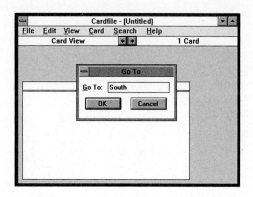

The Go To dialog box appears.

14

2. In the Go To text box, type any portion of the index line you want to find. (You can type a partial word.) It doesn't matter whether you use upper- or lowercase letters.

3. Choose OK or press ⏎Enter.

When you choose OK, the next card whose index line contains the text you're searching for jumps to the top of the stack. If no index line has the text you're searching for, you get a dialog box advising you that Cardfile cannot find the text. Choose OK and try again.

To search through text in the body of the cards, follow these steps:

1. Choose the Search menu and select the Find command.

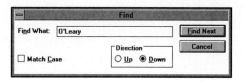

The Find dialog box appears.

2. In the Find What text box, type any portion of the information you want to find. (You can type a partial word.)

3. Select a Direction option (Up or Down), and select the Match Case option if you want the search to match your upper- and lowercase letters exactly.

4. Choose the Find Next button.

Cardfile finds and selects the first occurrence of the word. To continue the search, choose Find Next again. To close the dialog box, choose Cancel. To repeat the most recent search after closing the dialog box, choose the Search menu and select the Find Next command (or press F3).

Editing and Moving Text

You can change, add, or delete text from a card or its index line. And you can move text or graphics from one card to another. You even can transfer data between cards or to other programs.

To edit the text in the body of a card, follow these steps:

1. Display the card you want to change.
2. Use normal editing techniques to edit the text in the body of a card: move the insertion point where you want to make a change by positioning the I-beam and clicking the mouse button, or by pressing the arrow keys.
3. Press ⟨◆Backspace⟩ or ⟨Del⟩ to delete text, or type to insert text.

To edit text, you can select longer blocks of text by pressing the mouse button and dragging across the text, or by holding down the Shift key and pressing the arrow keys. Type new text to replace the selected text, or press Del or Backspace to remove the text.

To edit an index line, follow these steps:

1. Display the card containing the index line you want to edit.
2. Choose the Edit menu and select the Index command. Alternatively, double-click the index line of the top card. This command displays the Index dialog box, where you can make changes.

To copy or move text between cards or to other programs, follow these steps:

1. Display the card containing the text you want to copy or move.
2. Select the text.
3. Choose the Edit menu, and then select either the Copy command to copy text or the Cut command to move text.
4. Position the insertion point where you want to copy or move the selected text.
5. Choose the Edit menu and select the Paste command.

Two additional editing features are the Undo and the Restore commands. Cardfile "remembers" your most recent single edit and will undo it—as long as you use Undo before you make another change. Cardfile also remembers the information that was on the displayed card before you began editing it, and will restore the card to its original condition as long as you have not turned to another card since you began editing.

To undo your most recent edit, follow these steps:

1. Choose the Edit menu.
2. Select the Undo command.

To restore a card to its original condition, follow these steps:

1. Choose the Edit menu.
2. Select the Restore command.

Duplicating and Deleting Cards

Sometimes the information on two cards is so similar that duplicating the current card and making minor edits to it are faster than typing a whole new card. For example, you may want to create two separate cards for two people in the same company—the names and phone numbers are different, but the company name and address are the same.

To duplicate a card, follow these steps:

1. Bring the card you want to duplicate to the top of the stack.
2. Choose the Card menu and select the Duplicate command.

Edit the text on the duplicated card with the usual Windows text-editing procedures. If you want to edit the index line, choose the Edit menu and select the Index command.

To delete a card, follow these steps:

1. Bring the card you want to delete to the top of the stack.
2. Choose the Card menu and select the Delete command.

A message box prompts you to confirm that you want to delete the card.

3. Choose OK or press ⏎Enter.

Viewing a List of Index Lines

When you look at a Cardfile on-screen, you can see the top card in its entirety, and you can see the index lines for several more cards. To more easily see *all* the index lines in a Cardfile, you can use a special List view.

To view a list of the index lines, follow these steps:

1. Choose the View menu.
2. Select the List command.

You can edit an index line in the List view, just as you edit an index line in the Card view.

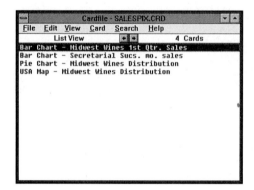

Double-click the line you want to edit. The Index dialog box appears, and you can edit the index line.

To restore a full view of the cards, choose the View menu and select the Card command.

Dialing a Phone Number with Cardfile

If your computer is connected to a modem and you include phone numbers on your cards, you can use Cardfile to dial the phone numbers for you.

When you choose the command for automatic dialing, Cardfile dials the *first* number listed on the top card in the stack. Unfortunately, that number may be a ZIP code, or it may be a phone number that is different from the one you want to dial. If the number you want to dial isn't listed first on the card, select the phone number before choosing the automatic dialing command, or type the correct phone number in the Autodial dialog box.

When you type a phone number on a card, be sure to include the area code (if it's different from your own). Don't use spaces or parentheses; Cardfile doesn't understand them. Hyphens do not interfere with autodialing, so a good format for phone numbers might be 707-538-1737.

To dial a phone number automatically, follow these steps:

1. Display the card containing the phone number you want to dial. If that number is not the first one listed on the card, select the number you want to dial.

2. Choose the Card menu and select the Autodial command.

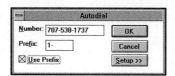

The Autodial dialog box appears.

3. If the correct number is not shown in the Number text box, type the phone number you want to dial.

4. Select Prefix and type a dialing prefix if necessary (a prefix is useful for long-distance calls).

5. Select Use Prefix if you want to begin dialing with the prefix (you do not need a prefix for local calls).

6. Choose OK or press ↵Enter. A Cardfile dialog box instructs you to pick up the phone.

7. Pick up your phone receiver as instructed by the dialog box that appears.

8. Choose OK or press ↵Enter to complete the connection.

The first time you dial automatically, check the available dial settings—dial type, port, and baud rate. After you establish these settings, they stay set and you shouldn't have to change them.

To change the automatic dialing settings, follow these steps:

1. Choose the Card menu and select the Autodial command.

2. Choose the Setup button.

The Autodial
dialog box
expands to
display Dial Type,
Port, and Baud
Rate settings.

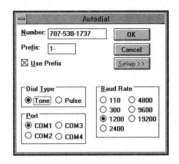

14

3. Make the appropriate dialog box selections:
   - In the Dial Type box, select Tone or Pulse, depending on which type of phone you have. (If you hear tones while dialing, you probably have a touch-tone phone; to be sure check with a telephone operator.)
   - In the Port box, select COM1, COM2, COM3, or COM4, depending on the port to which your modem is connected.
   - In the Baud Rate box, select 110, 300, 1200, 2400, 4800, 9600, or 19200, depending on your modem's baud rate.
4. Choose OK or press Enter.

Printing a Cardfile

Printing a Cardfile is simple. You just choose a print command, and your cards are printed on the selected printer. You can choose one command to print only the top card, or a different command to print all your cards. Printed cards from a Cardfile look like real cards, and they are the right size to cut out and paste onto a rotary card file.

Before you can print, you must set up the printer. To set it up, follow these steps:

1. Choose the File menu and select the Print Setup command. The Print Setup dialog box appears.
2. In the Printer group, either select Default Printer or select a printer from the Specific Printer list.
3. Choose OK or press Enter.

To print the top card in the stack, follow these steps:

1. Choose the File menu.
2. Select the Print command.

To print all the cards in a Cardfile, follow these steps:

1. Choose the File menu.
2. Select the Print All command.

Saving and Naming a Cardfile

When you save Cardfile files, Cardfile automatically assigns them the extension CRD. You can create as many different Cardfile files as you want.

To save and name a Cardfile, follow these steps:

1. Choose the File menu and select the Save As command.

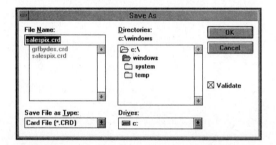

The Save As dialog box appears.

2. Type a file name (up to eight characters) in the File Name text box.
3. From the Drives list, select the drive in which you want to save the file. From the Directories list box, select the directory in which you want to save the file.
4. Choose OK or press ⏎Enter.

To save an existing Cardfile, choose the File menu and select the Save command. The new version of the file replaces the old version.

Closing a Cardfile and Exiting the Program

You can close a Cardfile in two ways: open a new or existing Cardfile or exit the Cardfile program. To open a new Cardfile, choose the File menu and select the New or Open command. To exit the Cardfile program, choose the File menu and select the Exit command.

Using Terminal

Personal computers give a great deal of power to the individual; however, sometimes individual power isn't enough. People need to be able to communicate with other people and with other computers. You can use your computer to exchange files with other computers; to get data from corporate mainframe computers; or to "talk" with on-line services (such as CompuServe) that offer free software, databases of publicly available information, and "conversation" with other computer users.

Terminal is a communications program that controls a modem, which connects your computer—by telephone line—to another computer. Terminal has several jobs. First, it establishes the settings that ensure that the computers on both ends of the phone line can understand one another. Second, it dials the telephone to make the connection. Third, it transfers or receives data over the open communication line.

To establish the settings that enable your computer to communicate with other computers, you must know quite a bit about your computer, your modem, and your communications package—for instance, the baud rate, or speed at which data is transferred. You need similar information about the computers you plan to communicate with, and you need to know their phone numbers. The good news is that you need to learn these settings only once, because Terminal saves the information as files you can open later. (The better news is that your company's personal computer coordinator probably can create these settings for you.) The Terminal settings are not included in this book; if you need to learn more about them, refer to the more comprehensive Que book, *Using Windows 3.1*, Special Edition.

Starting Terminal

You start the Terminal program the same way you start any other Windows program—by double-clicking the Terminal icon in the Accessories group window, or by pressing the arrow keys to select the icon and then pressing Enter. If this is the first time you have ever used Terminal, a message box named Default Serial Port appears, prompting you to specify which port your modem is connected to (it proposes a port). Select a different port, if necessary, and then choose OK or press Enter. (Use the Windows Control Panel to change the serial port settings after you have used Terminal the first time.)

14

Opening a Terminal Settings File

If someone has set up your computer for you, some *settings files* probably have been created and are available for you to use. These settings files contain the information you need to communicate with other computers. For example, if you regularly send files by modem to your San Francisco office, you might have a settings file called SF.TRM (TRM is the extension Terminal assigns to files).

To open an existing Terminal settings file, follow these steps:

1. Choose the File menu and select the Open command.

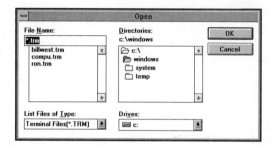

The Open dialog box appears.

2. From the File Name list box, select the settings file you want to open. (Change to a new drive, if necessary, by choosing a drive from the Drives list, and to a new directory by selecting a directory from the Directories list.)

3. Choose OK or press ⏎Enter.

After you open a settings file, your screen does not look any different, but the settings are in place.

Creating and Saving a New Settings File

When you first start the Terminal program, you see a new, untitled file. At that time, you can create your own settings file. The Settings menu contains many commands for establishing settings. After your settings files are in place, the most frequent change you will make is to the phone numbers.

To set a phone number in a new or existing Terminal settings file, follow these steps:

1. Choose the Settings menu and select the Phone Number command.

The Phone
Number dialog
box appears.

2. Select the Dial box and type the phone number (include the access number and area code for a long-distance number).

3. Choose OK or press ⏎Enter.

After you enter a phone number (and establish any other needed settings), save your settings file and give it a descriptive name. Terminal automatically assigns the extension TRM.

To save a Terminal settings file, follow these steps:

1. Choose the File menu and select the Save As command.

2. If you want the file placed in a different drive or directory, select the drive or directory from the Drives or Directories list.

3. Select the File Name text box and type a file name (up to eight characters).

4. Choose OK or press ⏎Enter.

Dialing the Phone

After you open a settings file, you are ready to make the connection to a remote computer. Because the settings file already contains the phone number for the computer you want to "talk" to, all you have to do is instruct your computer to dial. To dial a remote computer, choose the Phone menu and select the Dial command.

The screen
displays a mes-
sage box telling
you that the
remote computer
is being dialed.

Making the Connection

Dialing the phone opens the pathway for communicating with another computer; what you do after you dial depends on the type of communication

14

you want. In many cases, the computer you connect with will control the session. For example, after you dial CompuServe, a message tells you the number of rings that have occurred. When a connection is made, the word Connect appears on-screen. At that point, you press the Enter key. When the on-screen prompt Host: appears, type CIS. CompuServe Information Services then prompts you for your user ID number and password. Press Enter after you enter each. Other remote communications programs behave in much the same way; simply respond to the directions you see on-screen. Because telephone communication may have delays, wait for a response before pressing keys multiple times.

14

Sending a File

Your Terminal session may include sending previously created files to a remote computer. You can send two types of files: text and binary. The process is similar for both.

To send a text or binary file, ensure that Terminal is connected to the computer bulletin board system (BBS) or information service. Normally you need to enter a choice from a menu or type a command to prepare this service to accept the file you are sending. After the BBS or service prompts you that it is ready to receive data, continue with the following steps:

1. Choose the Transfers menu and select either the Send Text File command or the Send Binary File command.

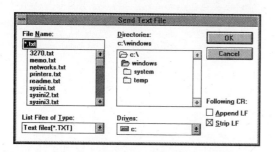

The Send Text (or Binary) File dialog box appears.

2. From the File Name list box, select the file you want to send. (Change to a new drive, if necessary, by choosing a drive from the Drives list, and to a new directory by selecting a directory from the Directories list.)

3. Choose OK or press ⏎Enter.

Note: Use the text-file mode to send and receive text-only files, such as those created by Notepad. Use the binary-file mode to send or receive files created by most programs, such as Windows Write, Microsoft Excel, or Word for Windows. Use the binary-file mode to send or receive files compressed by programs such as PKZIP.

Receiving a File

If you want to receive a file from a remote computer, you must select the directory into which you want to receieve the file, and you must give the file a name. As with sending files, you can receive either text or binary files, and the process for both is the same. Most systems specify whether a file is text or binary. If the file ends with TXT, assume that it is text; otherwise, it probably is a binary file.

To receive a text or binary file, follow these steps:

1. Choose the Transfers menu and select either the Receive Text File command or the Receive Binary File command.

The Receive
Binary (or Text)
File dialog box
appears.

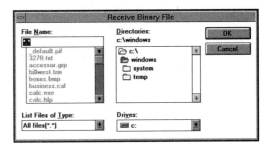

2. Change to a new drive, if necessary, by choosing a drive from the Drives list, and to a new directory by selecting a directory from the Directories list.

3. In the File Name text box, type a file name (up to eight letters) and file extension (a period and up to three letters), such as MEMO.TXT or BUDGET.ZIP.

4. Choose OK or press ⏎Enter.

Hanging Up (Disconnecting)

After your communications session is complete, be sure to disconnect from the remote computer you are connected with, and then hang up the phone to avoid excess on-line or long-distance phone charges. Each remote system has its own method of disconnecting. In CompuServe, for example, type **BYE** at any ! prompt, and then press Enter. Hanging up doesn't happen automatically—you must use the **H**angup command to disconnect the modem.

To hang up (disconnect), choose the **P**hone menu and select the **H**angup command.

Exiting Terminal

When your Terminal session is complete, you can exit the Terminal program. If you have established or changed settings, Terminal asks whether you want to save them. Choose **Y**es if you want to save the settings; otherwise, choose **N**o.

To exit the Terminal program, choose the **F**ile menu and select the E**x**it command.

Making Calculations with the Calculator

Like the calculator you may keep in your desk drawer, the Windows Calculator is small, but it can save you much time (and help prevent mistakes, too). The Calculator performs all the math of a standard calculator—addition, subtraction, multiplication, and division—but has some added advantages. For example, you can keep the Calculator on-screen alongside other programs, and you can copy numbers between the Calculator and other programs.

The standard Windows Calculator works so much like a pocket calculator that you need little help getting started.

383

The Calculator's "keypad" contains familiar number keys, along with memory and math keys. A display window just above the keypad shows the numbers you enter and the results of calculations. The Scientific view of the Calculator (described in an upcoming section) performs more advanced calculations.

Although you cannot change the size of the Calculator, as you can other Windows programs, you can minimize the Calculator to an icon so that it's easily available as you work in another program.

Opening and Closing the Calculator

Open the Calculator program just as you open any Windows program—by double-clicking the Calculator icon in the Accessories group window, or by pressing the arrow keys to select the icon and then pressing Enter. The Calculator opens in whichever view (Standard or Scientific) it was displayed in the last time you used it.

To close the Calculator program, choose the Control menu (with the mouse, click the square to the left of the title bar; with the keyboard, press Alt and then the space bar) and select the Close command. If you plan to use the Calculator frequently, minimize it to an icon instead of closing it; that way, you can access it quickly when you need it.

Using the Calculator

Operating the Windows Calculator is nearly the same as operating a desk calculator—you "press" the appropriate buttons (by selecting them), and the result displays at the top of the Calculator.

To use the mouse to select numbers and math functions on the Calculator, click the appropriate number and math keys, just as you press buttons on a desk calculator. Numbers appear in the display window as you select them, and results appear after you perform calculations.

Operating the Calculator with the keyboard is just as easy. Enter numbers with either the numeric keypad or the numbers across the top of your keyboard. To calculate, press the keys on the keyboard that match the Calculator's keys. For example, if the Calculator button reads +, press the + key on your keyboard.

The basic math functions are easy to perform. For instance, to add two plus two, select 2, select +, select 2, and then select =. These selections produce the formula $2+2=$.

To use the Calculator to add (+), subtract (-), multiply (*), or divide (/), follow these steps:

1. Select the first number on which you want to perform a calculation. The number appears in the display area at the top of the Calculator.

2. Select a mathematical function (+, -, *, or /).

3. Select the second number you want to calculate. This number now appears in the display area.

4. Select the = button on the Calculator, or press ⌷=⌷ on the keyboard. The result appears in the display.

   The other three math functions—finding a square root, calculating a percentage, and inverting a number (the 1/x button on the Calculator)—operate differently.

To find a square root, follow these steps:

1. Select the number for which you want to find a square root.

2. Select the sqrt button or press ⌷@⌷.

To calculate a percentage, follow these steps:

1. Select the number for which you want to calculate a percent.

2. Select the * button (for multiply) or press ⌷*⌷.

3. Select the percentage amount.

4. Select the % button or press ⌷%⌷ to display the result.

For example, to find 15% of 80, select 80*15%. The result, 12, is displayed in the Calculator's display area.

Note: Be sure to press the C button to clear all numbers and functions after calculating a percentage.

Inverting a number means dividing that number into the number 1.

To invert a number, follow these steps:

1. Select the number you want to invert.

2. Select the 1/x button or press ⌷R⌷.

The Calculator can work with positive or negative numbers. A negative number is indicated with a minus (-) sign to its left. To change any number's sign, select the number to display it, and then select the +/- button or press the F9 key.

14

Editing Numbers in the Calculator Display

Three buttons on the Calculator—C, CE, and Back—are used for editing a number or function. These buttons (and their keystroke alternatives) carry out the following operations:

Calculator Button	Keystroke Alternative	Function
C	Esc	Clears (erases) the Calculator of all numbers and functions.
CE	Del	Deletes the displayed value.
Back	◆Backspace	Deletes the last number in the displayed value.

Working with the Calculator's Memory

You can use the Calculator's memory to store numbers. The memory holds a single number, which starts as zero. You can add to, display, or clear that number; or you can store a different number in memory. You can display the number in memory at any time and perform calculations on the number, just as you can on any other number. Any time a number is stored in memory, the letter M appears in the box above the sqrt button on the Calculator.

The Calculator's memory functions are as follows:

Calculator Button	Keystroke Alternative	Function
MC	Ctrl+L	Clears (erases) the memory.
MR	Ctrl+R	Reveals (displays) the value in memory.
MS	Ctrl+M	Stores the displayed value in memory.
M+	Ctrl+P	Adds the displayed value to memory.

One use for the Calculator's memory is to sum a series of subtotals. For example, you can sum the first series of numbers and then add that sum to the memory by clicking the M+ button or pressing Ctrl+P. Then clear the display and calculate the second subtotal. Add the subtotal to memory. Continue until you have added all the subtotals to memory; then display the value in memory by clicking the MR button or pressing Ctrl+R.

Copying a Number from the Calculator into Another Program

When working with many numbers or complex numbers, you are less likely to make mistakes if you copy the Calculator results into another program instead of retyping the results. The Calculator is easy to use with other Windows programs and DOS programs.

To copy a number from the Calculator into another program, follow these steps:

1. Perform the math calculations required to display the number in the Calculator's display area.
2. Choose the Edit menu and select the Copy command to copy the displayed value (or press Ctrl + C).
3. Activate the program in which you want to copy the number.
4. Position the insertion point where you want to copy the number.
5. Choose the Edit menu and select the Paste command (or its equivalent in the new program).

Copying a Number from Another Program into the Calculator

You can copy a number from another program and paste it into the Calculator. When the number is in the Calculator, you can perform calculations with the number and then copy the result back into the other program.

To copy a number from another program into the Calculator, follow these steps:

1. Select the number in the other program.
2. Choose the Edit menu and select the Copy command (or its equivalent for that program).

3. Activate the Calculator, choose the Edit menu, and select the Paste command.

Using the Scientific Calculator

If you have ever written an equation wider than a sheet of paper, you're a good candidate for using the Scientific Calculator. This special version of the Calculator offers many scientific functions.

To display the Scientific Calculator, follow these steps:

1. Activate the Calculator.
2. Choose the View menu and select the Scientific command.

The Scientific Calculator works the same as the Standard Calculator, but contains many advanced functions.

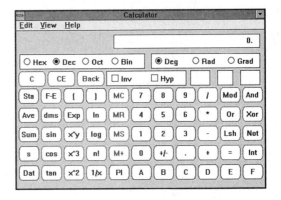

The advanced functions of the Scientific Calculator aren't described here, but they're well documented in the Calculator's Help command. To learn more about using the Help feature, refer to "Getting Help" in Chapter 3 of this book.

Watching the Clock

Windows comes equipped with a standard clock, which you can display on the computer screen in almost any size by simply resizing the clock's window. When you minimize the Clock program to an icon at the bottom of the screen, you can still read the hands or digital readout.

The Clock, even when reduced to a small icon, tells you the time.

14

The Clock program has one menu—the Settings menu. From this menu you can choose whether to display the clock in Analog or Digital view. The Analog view shows a round clock face with ticking hands; the Digital view shows a numerical readout of the time. You can change the font used in the Digital view. In either view, you can remove the title bar and choose whether or not you want to display seconds and the date (in the title bar). Windows remembers the settings you choose and uses those settings the next time you start the Clock program.

To change the settings for the Clock, follow these simple steps:

1. Choose the Settings menu.

2. Select the Analog command to display a clock with hands. Select the Digital command to display a clock with numbers.

3. Select Set Font to change the font used in Digital view.

4. Select No Title to remove the title bar from the clock display.

5. Select Seconds to display seconds (or deselect Seconds to remove seconds from the display).

6. Select Date to display the date (or deselect Date to remove the date from the display).

The time displayed by the clock is based on either your computer's internal clock (if you have one) or the time you specified when you started your computer. If the time on the clock is inaccurate, use the Control Panel to reset the clock. (To learn more about the Control Panel, refer to Chapter 7, "Customizing Your Work Area.")

Developing Your Strategic Skills with Minesweeper and Solitaire

14

The discussion of the games Minesweeper and Solitaire is included at the *end* of the chapter for a good reason: many Windows users stay up until the wee hours of the morning trying to beat their computer at a challenging game! You have a good excuse for playing these games: you can claim that you're developing your strategic skills and learning how to use the mouse adeptly.

Opening and Closing Minesweeper and Solitaire

Open either game by double-clicking its icon in the Program Manager. Both games are included in a group window called Games, rather than in the Accessories group window, which contains the other Windows accessory programs. Close either game by choosing Exit from the Game menu.

Playing Solitaire

When you start the Solitaire game, you see a screen with three active areas: the *deck* in the upper left corner of the playing area, four *suit stacks* in the upper right corner of the playing area (the stacks start out empty), and seven *row stacks* in the bottom half of the screen.

The object of the game is to move all the cards out of the deck, onto the row stacks in the middle of the playing field, and from there into the suit stacks at the top right corner of the screen. You build the row stacks downward, in alternating colors; you build the suit stacks upward, in sequential order, from Ace to King, one suit per stack. To start a suit stack, you need an Ace.

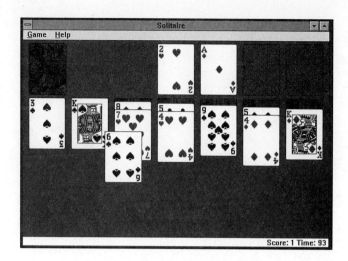

This Solitaire window shows a game in progress.

14

To move a card between the stacks or from the deck to the stacks, drag the card you want to move. When you release a card over a valid position, the card stays in that position. In the lower stacks, you can move either a single card at a time or a group of cards.

To get new cards, click the deck to turn over the top card, or move cards off of facedown cards in the lower stacks. Click facedown cards to turn them over.

Solitaire offers several options. Choose the Game menu and select the Deck command to choose a different deck illustration. Choose the Game menu and select the Options command to select the Draw (one or three cards) and Scoring options. Solitaire even has an Undo command in the Game menu to undo your last action.

When you're finished playing and want to start a new game, choose the Game menu and select the Deal command. To learn the rules of Solitaire, browse through the information in the Help command.

Playing Minesweeper

When you open Minesweeper, you are faced with a grid of squares that represents a mine field. The goal of the game is to mark all the mines; if you step on a mine, the game is over.

14

When you step on a square, three outcomes are possible: the square contains a mine and the game therefore ends; the square does not contain a mine and your minesweeper indicates that no mines are in the surrounding eight squares; or the square does not contain a mine and your minesweeper indicates that a certain number of mines are in the surrounding eight squares (displaying the number in the square).

As you successfully uncover squares without stepping on a mine, the information provided by minesweeper helps you deduce which squares contain mines. When you know a square contains a mine, you can mark that square, which effectively deactivates that mine. The idea is to mark all the mines before you step on any of them.

This Minesweeper window shows the outcome of stepping on a mine.

To uncover a square, click it. If the square does not contain a mine, either a number appears in the square, indicating the number of mines in the surrounding eight squares, or a blank space appears. If the square contains a number, you can then try to deduce which of the surrounding squares contain mines, and mark those squares. To mark a mine, click the square with the right mouse button.

You can clear the squares around an uncovered square if you have marked all the mines around that square. To clear the squares, point to the uncovered square and click both mouse buttons. If you try to clear the squares and you have not marked enough mines, nothing happens. For example, if the number 3 appears in the square, but you have marked only two squares, you cannot clear the surrounding squares. If you have incorrectly marked the surrounding mines, the game ends when you attempt to clear the squares. For example, if you know two mines are surrounding a square, but you mark the wrong ones, the game ends when you attempt to uncover the surrounding squares. For this reason, haphazardly marking squares does not pay.

From the Game menu, you can choose from three predefined skill levels of Minesweeper: Beginner, Intermediate, and Expert. The difference between the levels is the size of the minefield (and, therefore, the total number of mines). You can use the Game Customize command to define your own minefield. For additional information on the rules of Minesweeper and some strategic hints on playing the game, choose the Help command.

Summary

The Windows desktop accessories are so convenient to use that they can quickly become a part of your daily business tools. Calendar and Cardfile are useful every day. After checking appointments and a To Do list, you can minimize these accessories to icons or close them if you need maximum memory. Notepad is a great way to keep track of telephone conversations or to make notes as you work on various projects. Terminal links your computer to other computers so that you can exchange files or send and receive messages. The Calculator is a handy tool for quick mathematical functions, and the Clock, even when minimized as an icon, specifies the time. Minesweeper and Solitaire can challenge you to a little fun at the end of the day.

In this chapter, you learned the following information about the Windows accessories:

- The Notepad program is a simple text processor you can use to type quick notes and memos. Notepad saves files in text format, which most programs can understand.

- Calendar displays daily or monthly views of your appointment schedule. You can use this accessory to keep track of appointments and to remind yourself of important deadlines.

- Cardfile is a computerized "stack of cards" for storing names, addresses, phone numbers, and other information. You can quickly flip through the cards to find the one containing the information you need, or even search through the cards automatically if you're looking for a specific name or number not listed at the top of a card. If your computer has a modem, you can use Cardfile to dial phone numbers for you.

- Character Map provides you with an easy way to copy symbols into your documents.

- Terminal is an easy-to-use communications program. With Terminal and a modem, you can exchange files or messages with other computers.

14

393

- The Calculator program works just like a pocket calculator, except that you don't need batteries. You use it to add, subtract, multiply, divide, calculate percentages, invert numbers, and compute square roots. You can copy results from the Calculator into other programs.

- The Clock program enables you to be a clock-watcher as you stare at the screen. The Clock has two views: Analog (showing hands) and Digital (showing numbers).

- Solitaire challenges you with the classic card game.

- With Minesweeper, you put your life on the line as you make your way across a field laced with deadly mines.

In the next few chapters, you learn how to use the *applets* (small programs) that come with many Windows programs. These applets enhance the capabilities of any Windows program that has object linking and embedding (OLE) capability. If you are using Word for Windows 2, for example, you can open the Microsoft Draw applet described in the next chapter and use its extensive drawing capabilities to edit or add drawings to your Word for Windows document. Similarly, you can use the Microsoft Graph applet to add 3-D charts to a Word for Windows or other document.

14

15

Using Microsoft Draw

Your memory often works with cues. You hear the first few notes of a favorite old song and you know what the song is. You smell a long-forgotten fragrance and recall the memory of someone who wore that scent. When you have misplaced something, you visualize the last place you used it—and sure enough, there it is.

A new concept from Microsoft works the way your memory does, storing compound files together—the way you use and remember them. The new concept is called *object linking and embedding,* or *OLE,* the underlying concept behind the program Microsoft Draw. Microsoft Draw is a drawing *applet* that comes free with several Windows programs, including Word for Windows and Publisher.

Key Terms in This Chapter

Applet	A mini-application, or small program, that works only within a client program.
Object linking and embedding (OLE)	The technology that enables you to embed an object (such as a picture created in Draw) within a client program.
Client	A program or document in which you can embed objects, such as pictures created in Draw.
Server	A program or applet that creates objects you can embed in a client document.
Object	In the client document, the embedded Draw picture (or object created by other applet); in Draw, any shape you draw.
Cross hair	Tool you use to draw shapes in Draw.
Color palette	Palette of colors you use to drawing objects.

An applet is a mini-program that works from within another program. For example, you may be using Word for Windows to create a simple newsletter, and you want to include an illustration. From within Word for Windows, you choose a command to insert an object, and you specify that the object is a Microsoft Draw object.

15

The Draw window appears on-screen, over your Word for Windows document.

You use Draw to create your illustration, and then you add it to your document. Later you can edit your drawing from within Word for Windows.

Because Draw is an applet, you cannot start it from the Windows Program Manager, the way you can other programs (even though you may see an icon for it in the Program Manager). You can use Draw, or any other applet such as Graph or WordArt, only from within a program that supports object linking and embedding.

The Microsoft Draw applet is a good complement to Windows Paintbrush, which comes with Windows at no extra charge. Two general varieties of graphics programs are available: *object-oriented drawing programs* and *bit-mapped painting programs*. Microsoft Draw is an object-oriented drawing program. It creates objects on-screen, including squares, circles, lines, and freeform shapes, which can be edited, moved around, and layered on-screen. In contrast, a bit-mapped painting program, such as Microsoft Paintbrush, works in a single, flat layer on-screen; you can erase and redraw shapes you create using Paintbrush, but you cannot edit them. Each type of program has its benefits.

Note: In this chapter, the step-by-step instructions are specific to Word for Windows. Other programs use similar—but not identical—commands. Where appropriate, a chart describing the commands you need to use Microsoft Draw in other programs follows the steps.

Starting Microsoft Draw

As an OLE-based accessory program, Microsoft Draw works only from within a document created in your client program. To start Microsoft Draw, you first must start Word for Windows or some other program that supports object linking and embedding, and open a new or existing document.

To start Microsoft Draw, follow these steps:

1. Open a Word for Windows document or create a new document.
2. Position the insertion point where you want to insert your drawing.
3. Choose the Insert menu and select the Object command.

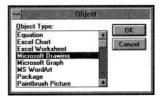

The Object dialog
box appears.

4. In the Object Type list, select Microsoft Drawing.
5. Choose OK or press ⏎Enter. Microsoft Draw appears in a new window on-screen.

To start Microsoft Draw from other programs, use the following procedures:

Program	Procedure
PowerPoint	Choose the File menu and select the Insert command. Select Microsoft Drawing from the list of programs.
Publisher	Choose the Edit menu and select the Insert Object command. Select Microsoft Drawing from the Object Type list.
Microsoft Excel	Choose the Edit menu and select the Insert Object command. Select Microsoft Drawing from the Object Type list.

Program	Procedure
Ami Pro	Choose the Edit menu, select the Insert command, and then select New Object.
Write	Choose the Edit menu and select the Insert Object command. Select Microsoft Drawing from the Object Type list.

Because the Windows applets are not stand-alone programs, you cannot save as stand-alone files the objects they create. To save Draw objects, you must use a command to *update* the client document and save that file. When Word for Windows is your client program, for example, you add the Draw picture to your Word for Windows document, and then save the Word for Windows file. To add a Draw object to a document, you must update the client document. To learn how to update the client document, refer to the section "Updating the Client Document," further in this chapter.

Understanding the Microsoft Draw Screen

If you have ever used a graphics program before, you probably will find that the Microsoft Draw screen looks familiar.

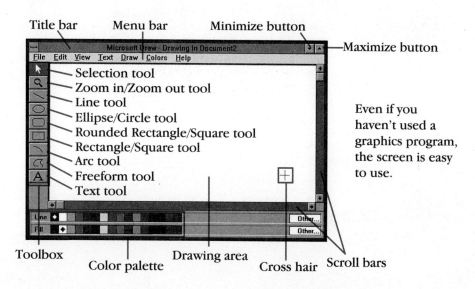

Title bar   Menu bar   Minimize button

Maximize button

Selection tool
Zoom in/Zoom out tool
Line tool
Ellipse/Circle tool
Rounded Rectangle/Square tool
Rectangle/Square tool
Arc tool
Freeform tool
Text tool

Even if you haven't used a graphics program, the screen is easy to use.

Toolbox   Color palette   Drawing area   Cross hair   Scroll bars

399

Along the top of the Microsoft Draw window are the title and menu bars, as in every Windows program. On the left side is the *toolbox*, containing the tools you use to create your drawing. On the bottom is the *color palette:* you use the top half of the palette, the *Line palette,* to choose the line color, and you use the bottom half of the palette, the *Fill palette,* to choose the fill color. On the right and bottom sides of the screen are the familiar scroll bars that enable you to scroll the drawing area horizontally and vertically. (To hide the palette and give yourself more drawing room, choose the Colors menu and select the Show Palette command. To display the palette, choose the command again.)

The general process for creating a drawing involves selecting menu options to set frame and fill defaults, selecting the tool you want to use, selecting colors from the palette, and drawing your picture in the drawing area. You can edit any object after you create it. The following sections in this chapter provide details about using the tools, palette, and menu options.

Note: Although you can operate most Windows programs with both a mouse and a keyboard, you must use a mouse to use Microsoft Draw. Some keyboard techniques and shortcuts are available in the program, but most operations depend on a mouse.

Choosing a Frame, Fill, Pattern, and Line Style

Each object you draw with Microsoft Draw is either a line or a shape. Lines have only one component: a line style. You can draw a line in any of several line styles. Shapes have two components: a frame (the line around the shape's edges) and a fill (the color or pattern inside the shape). A shape can be framed or unframed and filled or not filled. You can choose any line style for a framed shape, and you can choose from several patterns to fill a shape.

You make all these choices from a menu, and you choose them either *before* you draw an object, so that your choices become defaults and apply to any subsequent shapes you draw; or *after* you draw and select an object or objects, so that your choices apply only to the selection.

Note: If no object is selected, choices you make about frame, fill, pattern, and line style become defaults and apply to future objects you draw. If an object is

400

selected, however, your frame, fill, pattern, and line style choices apply only to the selection. Notice that when you first start Draw, some defaults are already selected. You can change those defaults for your drawing by selecting new defaults; for example, you can change the default line style or fill color.

You make frame, fill, pattern, and line style choices through the Draw menu. The Framed and Filled commands toggle on and off: the command is on if a diamond or check mark appears to its left; the command is off if nothing appears to its left. A diamond indicates that the command is selected as a default; a check mark indicates that the command is selected for the currently selected object in your drawing. (Some commands, such as Snap to Grid and Show Guides, are global—they cannot apply to only a single object. When selected, they have a check mark to the left.)

15

The diamond indicates that Filled is toggled on as the default for this drawing.

If two objects with conflicting frames or fills are selected, no mark appears to the left of the Framed or Filled command.

Patterns (which you can add to an object's fill) and line styles (which apply to lines and frames) also are commands you can choose either as defaults or as attributes for a selected object. The Pattern and Line Style commands have cascading submenus.

From the **Pattern** list, you can choose a pattern, which fills any filled shape.

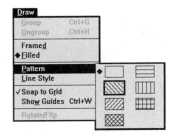

From the **Line** Style list, you can select a line style, which frames any framed shape.

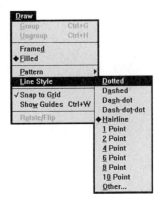

The **Pattern** and **Line Style** commands also toggle on and off, with a diamond indicating a default choice and a check mark indicating the status of the currently selected object or objects.

To specify a frame, fill, pattern, or line style, follow these steps:

1. Select the object or objects for which you want a frame, fill, pattern, or line style. If you want to set a default, thus affecting all objects you draw in the future, do not select any objects.

2. Choose the **Draw** menu.

3. Select one of the following options:

Option	Description
Frame**d**	Frames an object or objects with a line around the outside edge; uses the selected line style and color.

Option	Description
Filled	Fills an object or objects with the selected pattern and color.
Pattern	Fills an object or objects with the pattern you select from the **P**attern list.
Line Style	Frames an object or objects with the line style you select from the **L**ine Style list.

Color is another important component in the drawings you create with Microsoft Draw. Lines and the borders around framed shapes are drawn in the color you select from the Line palette. Fills and patterns appear in the color you select from the Fill palette. To select a Line or Fill color, click the color you want. Like other choices you make in Draw, you can choose colors *before* you begin your drawing so that the colors become the defaults for any subsequent lines or shapes you draw, or *after* you draw and select a line or shape so that the colors apply only to the current selection. In the color palette, default colors contain a diamond; colors for the currently selected object contain a check mark. To learn more about using colors, see "Working with Colors," further in this chapter.

15

Using the Drawing Tools

Each of the tools in the Microsoft Draw toolbox has a specific function. Some tools have more than one function: for example, the Ellipse/Circle tool can draw an oval or a perfect circle; the Rectangle/Square tool can draw a rectangle or a perfect square; the Freeform tool can draw a line or a closed polygon. To use a tool, you first must select it.

To select a tool from the toolbox, click the tool icon in the toolbox. After you select a tool, move the pointer into the drawing area, where the pointer changes from an arrow into some other shape. For drawing most objects, the pointer turns into a cross hair. You can use your drawing tool (or the Text tool, if you have selected it from the toolbox) to create your drawing, as explained in the following sections.

You can choose the **E**dit menu and select the **U**ndo command to undo your most recent screen action, or you can press Ctrl+Z.

Selecting with the Selection Tool

With the Selection tool, you select text and objects in your drawing, usually to edit them in some way. You can use the Selection tool in one of two ways: you can point to the object you want to select and click the left mouse button; or, to select multiple objects, you can draw a box—or *marquee*—around the group of objects you want to select.

The Selection tool is particularly important because of a guiding principle that applies in nearly every Windows program: *select and then do.* You first must select an object before you can do anything to it. Selecting an object (or objects, or text) tells Microsoft Draw where to apply the changes you want to make.

To select an object or objects, follow these steps:

1. Click the Selection tool in the toolbox.

2. Point to the object you want to select, and click the mouse button (hold ⇧Shift to select several objects).

   To select a group of objects, drag the Selection tool in a box around the group of objects you want to select. The box appears as a dotted line until you release the mouse button, at which point it disappears. Be sure that you completely enclose each object you want to select.

Selected objects, such as the building on the left, have selection handles on each corner or end.

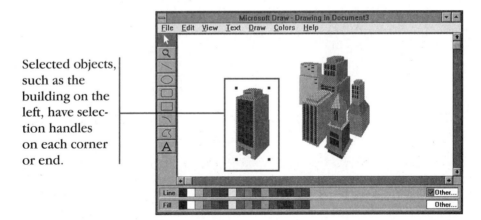

Many tools in the toolbox revert to the Selection tool after you use them. After you draw a box and click somewhere else in the drawing area, for example, the cross hair turns into the Selection arrow.

15

Zooming In and Out

When you first start Microsoft Draw, your drawings are actual size—the same size they will be when printed. You may want to zoom out, however, to see more of your page, especially if your drawing is larger than the drawing area.

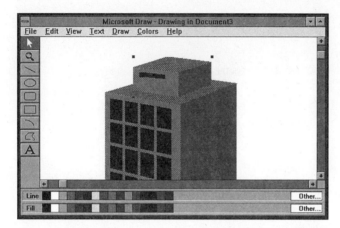

You can zoom in to edit details in your drawing, which is especially helpful when your drawing is made up of many small objects.

Microsoft Draw offers seven magnification levels for viewing a picture: 25%, 50%, 75%, Full size, 200%, 400%, and 800%. You can draw and edit at any magnification. The available magnifications are listed in the View menu. The same choices also are available through the Zoom in/Zoom out tool, which is easier to use because you just point and click.

To use the Zoom in/Zoom out tool to magnify or reduce your drawing, follow these steps:

1. Select the Zoom in/Zoom out tool from the toolbox.

2. Position the Zoom in/Zoom out tool over the place in your drawing where you want to zoom in or zoom out.

3. To zoom in to the next higher magnification, click the left mouse button. To zoom out to the next lower magnification, hold ⇧Shift and click the left mouse button.

4. Click repeatedly to continue zooming in or out.

To use the menu to magnify or reduce your drawing, choose the View menu and select 25% Size, 50%, 75%, Full Size, 200%, 400%, or 800%. To zoom in to see a particular object, first select the object.

Drawing Lines

The Line tool enables you to draw straight lines. Your line appears in the default line color (the color containing a diamond in the Line palette) and in the default line style (the Line Style option with a diamond next to it in the Draw menu).

To draw a line, follow these steps:

1. Select the Line tool from the toolbox.
2. Move the pointer into the drawing area, where the pointer becomes a cross hair.
3. Position the cross hair where you want to start your line.
4. Click and hold the mouse button.
5. Drag the cross hair to the point at which you want to end your line.
6. Release the mouse button.

Drawing a line is a simple process: click, drag, and release.

A newly drawn line has selection handles at each end, as shown on the bottom line in this example. The selection handles enable you to edit the line, as explained in "Editing Text and Objects," further in this chapter.

To draw a line at a 45- or 90-degree angle (useful when you want a perfectly horizontal or vertical line), hold the Shift key as you draw the line. To draw your line from the cross hair outward in both directions, hold the Ctrl key as you draw.

Drawing Ellipses, Circles, Rectangles, and Squares

Three tools enable you to draw round and square shapes. If the shapes are framed, their borders are in the default line style (the Line Style option with a diamond next to it in the Draw menu) and the default line color (the color containing a diamond in the Line palette). If the shapes are filled, they contain the default fill color (the color containing a diamond in the Fill palette). You also can fill shapes with any pattern you select with the Pattern command in the Draw menu.

The process for drawing ellipses, circles, rectangles, and squares is the same. To draw an ellipse, circle, rounded rectangle, rounded square, rectangle, or square, follow these steps:

1. Select one of the following tools from the toolbox:

Tool	Function
Ellipse/Circle	Draws an ellipse or a circle; hold ⇧Shift to draw a circle.
Rounded Rectangle/Square	Draws a rounded rectangle or square; hold ⇧Shift to draw a square.
Rectangle/Square	Draws a rectangle or square; hold ⇧Shift to draw a square.

2. Move the tool into the drawing area, where it becomes a cross hair.
3. Position the cross hair where you want your shape to start.
4. Click and hold the mouse button, and drag to draw your shape.
5. Release the mouse button when your shape is correct.

15

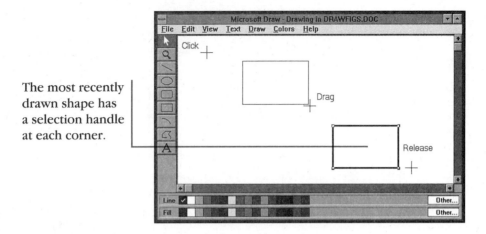

The most recently drawn shape has a selection handle at each corner.

You can use the selection handles to edit the shape, as described in "Editing Text and Objects," further in this chapter.

To draw a perfect circle or a perfect square, hold down the Shift key as you draw. To draw from the center outward, hold down the Ctrl key as you draw.

Drawing Arcs and Wedges

An *arc* is one quarter of an ellipse or circle. If your arc is framed, its border is in the default line style (the Line Style option with a diamond next to it in the Draw menu) and the default line color (the color containing a diamond in the Line palette). If the arc is filled, it becomes a *wedge* that contains the default fill color (the color containing a diamond in the Fill palette). You also can fill arcs with any pattern you select with the Pattern command in the Draw menu.

The process of drawing an arc or a filled wedge is similar to that of drawing an ellipse or rectangle in Microsoft Draw. To draw an arc, follow these steps:

1. Select the Arc tool from the toolbox.
2. Move the tool into the drawing area, where it becomes a cross hair.
3. Position the cross hair where you want to start your arc.
4. Click where you want to start the arc, and drag to the point at which you want to end the arc.
5. Release the mouse button.

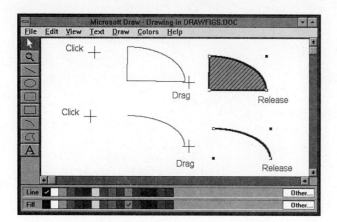

As with all tools, you can drag the cross hair in any direction as you draw.

To draw a quarter of a perfect circle instead of a quarter of an ellipse, hold down the Shift key as you draw. To draw your arc from the center rather than from one corner to another, hold down the Ctrl key as you draw.

Drawing Freeform Lines and Polygons

The Freeform tool is one of the most versatile tools in the toolbox. With the Freeform tool, you can draw a curved line, a jagged line, or a closed polygon. Freeform lines, as well as the borders surrounding closed and framed freeform shapes, appear in the default line style (the **Line Style** option with a diamond next to it in the **Draw** menu) and the selected line color (the color containing a diamond in the Line palette). Closed and filled freeform shapes contain the default fill color (the color containing a diamond in the Fill palette). You can fill closed freeform shapes with any pattern you select with the **Pattern** command in the **Draw** menu.

You can change the shape, size, frame, fill, pattern, and line style for any freeform object, as discussed in "Editing Text and Objects," further in this chapter. You use a special technique to change each individual segment of a polygon.

To draw a jagged line or a closed polygon with the Freeform tool, follow these steps:

1. Select the Freeform tool from the toolbox.
2. Move the tool into the drawing area and position the cross hair where you want your jagged line or polygon to begin.

3. Click the mouse button to anchor the first end of the line or polygon.

4. Position the cross hair where you want the second point on your line or polygon, and click again.

5. Continue positioning the cross hair and clicking the mouse button to define each point on your line or polygon.

6. To complete a jagged line, double-click the last point of the line. To close and complete a polygon, double-click the first point of your polygon, joining the last point with the first point.

15

You can use the Freeform tool to draw jagged lines or closed polygons.

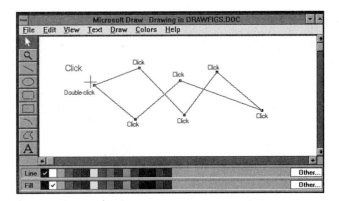

To draw a curved line or closed curved freeform shape, follow these steps:

1. Select the Freeform tool from the toolbox.

2. Move the tool into the drawing area and position the cross hair where you want to begin your curved line or freeform shape.

3. Click and hold the mouse button, and wait until the cross hair turns into a pencil.

4. Still holding down the mouse button, drag the pencil around in the drawing area to draw your line or shape.

5. If you are drawing a curved line, double-click the mouse button when you reach the end of your line. If you are drawing a curved freeform shape, double-click the line's beginning point to close the shape.

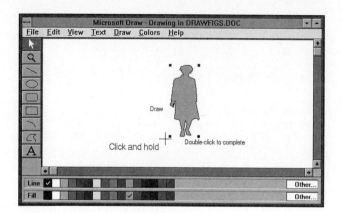

The Freeform tool
draws curved
lines and shapes,
which you can fill.

To draw line segments along a horizontal, vertical, or 45-degree axis, hold down the Shift key as you draw.

Adding Text

Although Draw is primarily an illustration program, you can easily add text to your Microsoft Draw drawing, selecting its font, style, and size. Later, you can select and edit your text as needed.

You can type only a single line of text in Microsoft Draw. If you reach the end of the screen, text does not wrap and you cannot press Enter to start a new line. To stack lines of text, you must type each line separately and use the Selection tool to drag each line into place, as explained in "Editing Text and Objects," further in this chapter.

Typing Text

When you type text, it appears in the color selected in the Line palette. Text also includes all the options selected as defaults in the Text menu. You can select a text style, alignment, font, and size. Each default setting has a diamond next to it in the menu.

After you finish typing text and clicking the mouse button or pressing Enter, the text is selected. It appears in a *text block* that has selection handles on each corner. Before you type text, select your defaults as follows:

1. From the Text menu, select any of these style or alignment commands:

Command	Description
Plain	Removes bold, italic, and underline formatting.
Bold	Boldfaces the text.
Italic	Italicizes the text.
Underline	Underlines the text.
Left	Left aligns the text in the text block.
Center	Centers the text in the text block.
Right	Right aligns the text in the text block.

2. To change the font, choose the Font command from the Text menu, and then select the font that you want.

A cascading font menu appears, listing all available fonts.

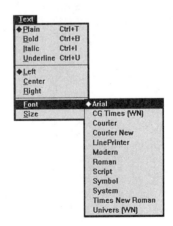

412

3. To change the size of your text, choose the Size command from the Text menu, and select the size you want.

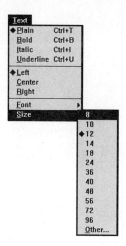

A cascading menu appears, listing all the sizes available for the font you selected.

4. From the Line palette at the bottom of the screen, select a color for your text. (If the color palette is not visible, choose the Colors menu and select the Show Palette command to display it.)

Three of the choices in the Text menu—Bold, Italic, and Underline—are style choices, which you can combine. You can type text that is both bold and italic, for example, or that is both underlined and bold. Each style choice selected for the current text has a check mark next to it. To remove all style choices at once, select the Plain style.

After you select options that indicate how you want your text to appear, type the text by following these steps:

1. Select the Text tool from the toolbox.

2. Move the tool into the drawing area, where it becomes an I-beam. Position the I-beam where you want the left margin of your block of text.

3. Click the mouse button to insert the cursor where you want your text to start.

4. Type the text.

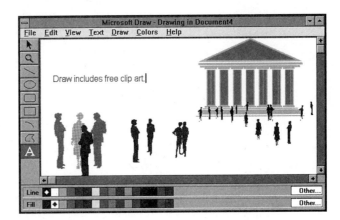

Before you end
the text block,
you can press
⎣←Backspace⎦ to
erase characters.

5. To end the text block, press ⎣←Enter⎦ or click the mouse button somewhere outside of the text. This step selects the text block and the
   Selection tool.

Changing Text

Although you *first* specify how you want your text to appear, before you even
type it, you can go back later and change its appearance. To change text, you
first must select it.

To select text so that you can change its style, alignment, font, or size, follow
these steps:

1. Select the Selection tool from the toolbox.

2. Point at the text you want to change, and click the mouse button.

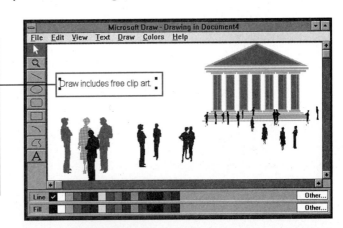

Like any selected
object, selected
text has a selec-
tion handle at
each of its four
corners. The
selection handles
indicate that you
can move or edit
the text.

When text is selected, you can change its style, alignment, font, or size by choosing commands from the Text menu. To change the color of the text, select a new color from the Line palette at the bottom of your screen.

Alternatively, you can change the words by deleting, inserting, or retyping characters. To change the words in a text block, you first must move the insertion point inside the selected text.

To place the insertion point inside the text and then edit the text, follow these steps:

1. Select the text block by clicking it with the Selection tool.
2. Choose the Edit menu and select the Edit Text command, or double-click the text box.

   The Edit Text command places the insertion point at the beginning of the text inside the text block. Double-clicking places the insertion point exactly where you double-clicked.
3. Edit the text using standard editing techniques.

   You can press ⟨◆Backspace⟩ to erase characters to the left and ⟨Del⟩ to erase characters to the right; you can select text and retype it; or you can cut, copy, and paste text using commands from the Edit menu.
4. Press ⟨↵Enter⟩ or click outside the text block to complete the editing process.

Working with Colors

If you have a color monitor, you will enjoy Microsoft Draw's colors. The Line and Fill palettes contain as many as 16 solid colors (Windows' limit) and seemingly limitless "dithered" colors blended from the available solid colors. You can apply these colors to any object you create—text or shapes. (If you see less than 16 colors, your PC supports fewer colors.)

You can change the color palette in two ways. One way is to click the Other button at the right end of the Line or Fill palette. The other way is to use the Colors menu. You can add new colors to your palette or change existing colors. You can even save palettes and use them in future drawings.

Remember that to enlarge your drawing space, you can hide the color palette. If the palette is displayed and you want to hide it, choose the Colors menu and select the Show Palette command. To display the palette, choose the command a second time. The Show Palette command toggles on and off; you see a check mark to its left when it's on.

15

415

Coloring Text and Objects

The default color in the Line palette is applied automatically to text, lines, the frame around framed objects, and the foreground in any patterned fill. The default color in the Fill palette is applied automatically to the fill in any filled shape and to the background in any patterned fill.

Although default color choices apply to any object you create, you can just as easily change the Line or Fill color of a previously created object or text. Select the object (or objects) and choose the Line or Fill color you want. Colors change only for the selected object or objects.

To select a Line or Fill color as a default, or to change the Line or Fill color for a selected object, follow these steps:

1. To change the default line or fill color, make sure that no object is selected (an easy way to do that is to select the Selection tool, which cancels all selections).

   To change the line or fill color for one or more specific objects, select the objects.

2. In the Line palette, click the line color you want. Alternatively, in the Fill palette, click the fill color you want.

Using Blended Colors

Although your initial color palette contains no more than 16 solid colors, you can paint your objects with a rainbow of blended colors. Working with blended colors requires that you use the most colorful dialog box in Microsoft Draw—the Other Color dialog box. The Other Color dialog box offers a rainbow of colors you can add to your palette or apply to the selected objects. (If you access this dialog box through the Colors menu, its title instead is Add Color.)

Before you blend colors, you should understand how computers work with color. Computers understand color in terms of light, not pigment. So forget what you have learned about color wheels. To a computer, for example, pure red and pure green combine to make yellow; and pure red, pure green, and pure blue combine to make white. Computers use an additive system for blending colors, whereas pigments use a subtractive system.

In the following section, you learn how you can add blended colors to your palette.

To blend a color for a selected object, follow these steps:

1. Select the objects whose line or fill colors you want to change. Choose the Other button from the right end of the Line or Fill palette.

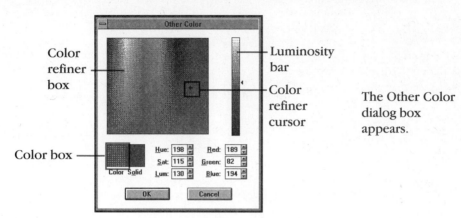

The Other Color dialog box appears.

15

2. Select a color from the Color refiner box: click the color you like; or drag the Color refiner cursor (black diamond) until the color in the Color box is satisfactory, at which point you release the mouse button.

3. To set your selected color's luminosity (how light or dark it is), use the Luminosity bar: click the brightness you like; or drag the Color refiner cursor upward to select a lighter color or downward to select a darker color.

    The Color box indicates what your color looks like.

4. To select a color by hue (color), saturation (amount of color), and luminosity (brightness), select values from 0 to 240 in the Hue, Sat, and Lum boxes, respectively. (You can type the value in the text box or select the up or down arrow to increase or decrease the value.)

    Values range from 0 (red hue; black or no saturation; and black or no luminosity) to 240 (red hue; full saturation, or pure color; and full luminosity, or pure white).

5. Choose OK or press ⏎Enter.

Editing the Palette

You can add blended colors to your initial palette, and you can change the existing colors. You also can delete colors in your palette. To edit the palette, you use the Colors menu, which accesses the Other Color dialog box, described in the preceding section.

When you edit your palette using the Colors menu, you change the Line and Fill palettes simultaneously.

To change, add to, or delete colors from the palette, follow these steps:

1. Choose the Colors menu and select the Edit Palette command.

The Edit Palette dialog box appears, displaying the colors in the current palette and many blank spaces where you can add new colors.

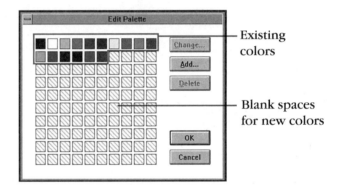

Existing colors

Blank spaces for new colors

2. Select the existing color you want to change or delete.

3. Choose Change to change the color you have selected, choose Add to add a color to the next available blank space, or choose Delete to delete the selected color.

    If you add or change a color, you advance to the Add Color dialog box (which is the same as the Other Color dialog box).

4. Make your choices in the Add Color dialog box (as explained in the preceding section), and choose OK or press ⏎Enter. You return to the Edit Palette dialog box.

5. Choose OK or press ⏎Enter.

You can display up to 100 colors on your palette. If your palette contains more colors than can fit on-screen, you see scrolling arrows at the left and right ends of your on-screen palette. Click those arrows to display the other colors.

Saving and Opening Palettes

When you first start Microsoft Draw, a color palette is displayed at the bottom of the drawing area, but you can retrieve a different palette (Microsoft Draw includes several). You also can save the palettes you create, which makes them available the next time you use Microsoft Draw and which enables you to share colors among drawings.

To save your custom palette, follow these steps:

1. Choose the Colors menu and select the Save Palette command.
2. Enter an eight-character file name. Microsoft Draw supplies the extension PAL.
3. Choose OK or press ⏎Enter.

To open an existing palette, follow these steps:

1. Choose the Colors menu and select the Get Palette command. The Get Palette dialog box appears.
2. In the Files list box, select the palette you want to open.
3. Choose OK or press ⏎Enter to display the new palette on-screen.

Editing Text and Objects

After you draw objects and type text in Microsoft Draw, you can manipulate your drawing in many ways. Everything you create—even text—is an object you can move, layer, or group with other objects. You can resize, reshape, rotate, and flip shapes or grouped shapes (but not text). You can choose the Edit menu and select the Undo command to undo your most recent screen action.

Because your Draw picture is part of your client document, to edit your picture you must first open the client program, and then open the client document containing your Draw picture. If your Draw picture is embedded in a Word for Windows document, for example, you must open the Word for Windows document to edit the picture. After you finish editing, update your client document as described in "Updating the Client Document," further in this chapter.

15

To edit a Draw picture in a Word for Windows document:

1. Locate the Draw picture in your document.
2. Using the mouse, double-click the picture to start Draw with your picture in its drawing window.

   Using the keyboard, select the picture by positioning the insertion point next to it, holding down ⌜⇧Shift⌟, and pressing the appropriate arrow key to pass the insertion point over the drawing. Then choose the Edit menu and select the Microsoft Drawing Object command. Draw starts, with your picture in the drawing window.
3. Edit your drawing.
4. Update your Word for Windows document.

To edit a Draw object in other programs, use the following procedures:

Program	Procedure
PowerPoint	Double-click the object, or select the object, choose the Edit menu, and select the Edit Microsoft Drawing command.
Publisher	Double-click the object.
Microsoft Excel	Double-click the object.
Ami Pro	Double-click the object.
Write	Double-click the object; or select it, choose the Edit menu, and select the Edit Microsoft Drawing Object command.

Scrolling the Drawing Page

Although you can see only a portion of it, the full Microsoft Draw page measures 22 inches by 22 inches. Use the horizontal scroll bar at the bottom of the screen to scroll left and right on the page, and use the vertical scroll bar at the right to scroll up and down on the page.

15

Selecting Text and Objects

Remember that before you can edit any object, you first must select it. When selected, an object has a selection handle on each of its four corners—even non-rectangular shapes have four selection handles arranged in a rectangle around the outside of the object. You can drag these handles to resize or reshape the selected object.

You can select an object by selecting the Selection tool and clicking the object, or by drawing a selection marquee around a group of objects you want to select. You can select all the objects in your drawing by choosing the Edit menu and selecting the Select All command.

Resizing and Reshaping Objects

You can change the shape and size of any selected object, with the exception of text, by dragging the selection handles. Holding down the Shift while you resize keeps the object in proportion; holding down the Ctrl key resizes and reshapes from the center outward. As you're resizing or reshaping the object, a dotted-line bounding box shows you the object's new size or shape.

To change an object's size or shape, follow these steps:

1. Select the object.

   You cannot resize or reshape multiple objects simultaneously unless you first group them (see the upcoming section "Grouping and Ungrouping Text and Objects").

2. To reshape the object, drag any corner handle to a new shape; release the mouse button when the bounding box shows the shape you want.

   To resize the object, keeping it proportional, hold Shift while you drag a corner handle.

Copying, Moving, and Deleting Text and Objects

You can easily move an object or a text block by dragging it to its new location. Because you can drag only as far as the edge of the window, you may want to zoom out so that you can move on a larger area of the page. You can move a selected group of objects simultaneously by dragging one of the objects. As you're dragging an object to move it, you see a dotted-line bounding box that represents the position of your moving object (the object reappears when you release the mouse button).

If you prefer, you can choose the Edit menu and use the standard Windows Cut, Copy, and Paste commands to copy and move selected objects using the Clipboard. This technique is useful when you want to copy or move objects between drawings or between distant spots on the same large drawing. Because you can switch between programs in Windows by sharing the Clipboard, you also can use this technique to copy or move a drawing from Microsoft Draw into another program besides Word for Windows.

To copy, move, or delete objects, follow these steps:

1. Select the object or objects you want to copy, move, or delete.
2. To copy an object, choose the Edit menu and select the Copy command. To move an object, choose the Edit menu and select the Cut command. To delete an object, press `◆Backspace` or `Del`.
3. Move to where you want the object moved or copied.
4. Choose the Edit menu and select the Paste command.

When you copy or move an object, it is stored in the Clipboard until you use the Copy or Cut command to copy or move another object (or until you turn off your computer). You can use the Paste command to paste the Clipboard's object as many times as you want, enabling you to create duplicates of an object.

Working with Layers

Like most drawing programs, Microsoft Draw enables you to work in layers; that is, you can create two or more objects and stack them on top of one another. Menu commands (and keyboard shortcuts) enable you to bring a selected object to the front or send it to the back of other objects.

Classic examples of layering include shadow boxes (usually a white box overlapping a darker box of the same size) and text on a background of a different color.

To move an object to a different layer in your drawing, follow these steps:

1. Select the object or objects you want to send to the back or bring to the front of other objects.
2. To bring the object to the top layer, choose the Edit menu and select the Bring to Front command.

    To send the object to the bottom layer, choose the Edit menu and select the Send to Back command.

Editing a Freeform Shape

You can edit a freeform shape in one of two ways. One way is to resize or reshape it as described in the previous section "Resizing and Reshaping Objects." This technique leaves the freeform object in the same general shape (although by dragging its corner handles, you may condense or expand the shape if you don't hold down the Shift key to keep it proportional).

A second and rather unique way to edit a freeform shape is to edit the segments that make up the shape. You use the Selection tool and then a menu command to display control handles you can use to reshape the freeform shape. Note that as you edit a freeform object, it appears on-screen as an empty shape with a thin black frame.

To edit a freeform shape, follow these steps:

1. Select the shape by clicking it with the Selection tool. Four selection handles appear, one on each corner.

2. Choose the Edit menu and select the Edit Freeform command.

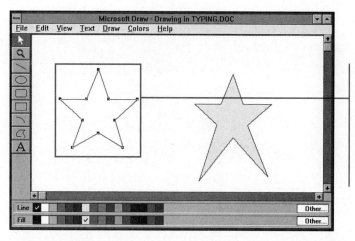

Control handles appear at the end of each segment of the freeform shape, and the selection arrow turns into a black arrowhead.

3. Drag any control handle to change the freeform's shape.

   To add a control handle, hold Ctrl (the arrowhead turns into a plus sign inside a circle) and click anywhere on the edge of the shape.

   To remove a control handle, hold Ctrl + Shift (the arrowhead turns into a minus sign inside a square) and click any existing control handle.

4. Press Enter or click anywhere outside the freeform shape to hide the control handles.

Note: As an alternative to selecting the freeform shape and then choosing the Edit Freeform command, you can double-click the freeform shape to display the control handles.

Editing an Arc or Wedge

Like a freeform shape, you can edit an arc or wedge in two ways. You can select it with the Selection tool and resize or reshape the arc by dragging the corner handles (hold the Shift key as you drag to keep the arc proportional); or you can change the arc's degree by first selecting it with the Selection tool, and then choosing a menu command to display special control handles.

To change the degree of an arc or a wedge, follow these steps:

1. Select the arc or wedge by clicking it with the Selection tool. Four corner handles appear.
2. Choose the Edit menu and select the Edit Arc command. Two control handles appear—one at each end of the arc or wedge.
3. Drag either control handle clockwise or counterclockwise to change the degree.
4. Click outside the arc or wedge to deselect it.

Note: As an alternative to selecting the arc, choosing the Edit menu, and then selecting the Edit Arc command, you can double-click the arc to display the control handles.

Grouping and Ungrouping Text and Objects

If you want to turn several objects into one (such as to copy, reshape, or move them together), you can select and group them. You then can edit the objects as a single object; however, you cannot resize, reshape, rotate, or flip any text included in the group. Later, you can ungroup grouped objects.

To group objects, follow these steps:

1. Select all the objects you want to group (hold ⇧Shift while you click each object you want to select, or draw a selection marquee around a group of objects).
2. Choose the Draw menu and select the Group command, or press Ctrl+G.

To Draw, the grouped objects are now one object.

To ungroup a grouped object, follow these steps:

1. Select the grouped object.

2. Choose the **D**raw menu and select the **U**ngroup command, or press Ctrl + H.

Rotating and Flipping Objects

You can rotate a selected object or group in 90-degree increments to the left (counterclockwise) or right (clockwise), and you can flip an object vertically or horizontally. You cannot rotate or flip text.

To rotate or flip an object, follow these steps:

1. Select the object.

2. Choose the **D**raw menu, select the **R**otate/Flip command, and select Rotate **L**eft, Rotate **R**ight, Flip **H**orizontal, or Flip **V**ertical.

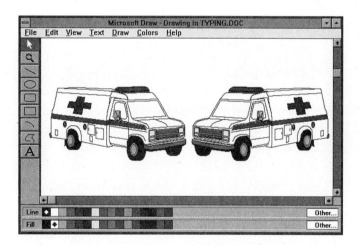

You can create mirrored objects by first copying and pasting the object and then horizontally flipping the pasted object.

Importing and Editing Clip Art and Other Pictures

You can import many types of graphics into Microsoft Draw. Among the most interesting graphics are a series of clip art images that come with Microsoft Draw, which you can import and disassemble to use in whole or in part. Browse through the various clip art files to see what is available.

To import a picture, follow these steps:

1. Choose the File menu and select the Import Picture command. The Import Picture dialog box appears.
2. Select the file you want to import from the Files box, changing the directory if necessary.

Clip art files are located in the subdirectory CLIPART, located inside your Word for Windows directory. These files have the extension WMF. (Note that if you did not install CLIPART when you installed your client program, these files are not listed.)

You also can import BMP, PCX, and TIF files. If you import object-oriented images, you edit them the same way you edit any Microsoft Draw object. You also can import bit-mapped files, such as those created in Microsoft Paint-brush. Microsoft Draw converts the bit maps into objects, which you can then resize, reshape, or recolor.

Updating the Client Document

You transfer your Draw object back into the client document in either of two ways: you can update the document without closing Microsoft Draw; or you can simultaneously close Microsoft Draw and update your client document. To save your drawing, you must be sure to save your client document after you update the drawing.

To update your client document without closing Draw, choose the File menu and select the Update command in Draw.

To update your client document and simultaneously close Microsoft Draw, choose the File menu and select the Exit and Return to Document command. A dialog box appears, prompting you to update your client document. Choose Yes.

To exit Draw without updating the client document, choose the File menu and select the Exit and Return to Document command. When a dialog box appears to prompt you update your client document, choose No.

Note: Updating your client document does not save your drawing. To save your drawing, you must save the client document that contains your drawing. Your drawing exists only as part of your client document.

Summary

Microsoft Draw is a simple but very powerful program you can use to create original works of art to illustrate your Windows program document or to edit existing art. You can even use the clip art that comes with Microsoft Draw as the basis for your own drawings. Using Draw is much like using other graphics programs: you select the tool you want to use; select the color you want; select options for lines and borders; and draw your shapes.

To learn more about Draw, refer either to the documentation accompanying the client program that came with Draw or to Que's book *Using Word for Windows 2.* To learn more about object linking and embedding, refer to Chapter 10, "Using Object Linking and Embedding," a previous chapter in this book.

15

In this chapter, you learned the following important points about Draw:

- Draw comes free with Word for Windows, Publisher, and other programs from Microsoft.

- Because Draw is an applet, the only way to start it is from within another program that supports applets. The drawing you create becomes part of the document in which you create the drawing.

- Draw comes with free clip art you can use as the basis of your own drawings.

- To edit a drawing, you first open the document that contains the drawing, locate the drawing, and double-click it. Draw opens and displays the drawing.

- Because Draw is an object-oriented program, each of the shapes you create is an editable object.

- After you edit your drawing, you should update the document to reflect the changes.

- The only way to save a drawing is to save the document containing the drawing.

In the next chapter, "Using Microsoft Graph," you learn about another applet—one you can use to transform numbers into charts. The colorful charts you create can appear in many forms: bar charts, pie charts, line charts, and more. Graph enables you to add legends to your chart, change the fonts and colors, and add text.

16

Using Microsoft Graph

With Microsoft Graph you can create informative and impressive charts (graphs) you can incorporate into any Windows program that supports object linking and embedding, or OLE (see Chapter 10 for a discussion of OLE). Microsoft Graph is an *applet*, which is a small program designed to work with Windows programs that have OLE capability. Applets add additional features to OLE-capable programs. Microsoft Graph is a separate program that embeds charts and their data into Windows programs such as Microsoft Word for Windows.

Using Microsoft Graph, you can turn an overwhelming table of numbers into a chart that shows important trends and changes. You can then relegate the detailed numeric table to a location where it doesn't slow down communication.

Key Terms in This Chapter

Applet	A mini-application (small program) that works only within a client program.
Object linking and embedding	The technology that enables you to embed an object (such as a chart created in Graph) within a client document.
Client	A document or program in which you can embed objects.
Object	A chart you create in Graph and embed within a client document (or anything you create using some other applet).
Data sheet	A worksheet made up of intersecting horizontal rows and vertical columns, in which you enter the numbers that serve as the basis for your chart.
Chart	A graph, or a graphical depiction of numbers; can be a bar, column, pie, line, scatter, combination, or 3-D chart.
Data point	Data from the data sheet that is plotted on the chart.
Axes	Intersecting vertical and horizontal lines on which data points or categories are plotted; one axis carries the values, and the other carries the categories.
Series	A group of related data; on a chart, a series may be all the data points on the green line, for example, or all the blue columns, or the red wedge in a pie chart.

16

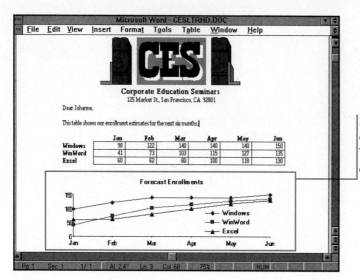

In this example, a chart enhances a Word for Windows document.

16

Microsoft Graph is not just a small graphing program; it has all the capability of Microsoft Excel, the powerful Windows spreadsheet, graphics, and database program.

Charts embedded into a Windows program contain the chart and the data that creates the chart. When you activate Microsoft Graph, it loads the selected chart and its data so that you can make changes. You cannot save the chart or data separately, because they are embedded into the Windows program.

Creating a Chart

You create charts from data you enter into a *data sheet*. A data sheet contains rows and columns that intersect to form cells, much like a spreadsheet. With Microsoft Graph, you can create a new chart in a Windows program in a number of ways. You can select the text and numbers from a table in a word processing document and insert them into the data sheet; you can type the text and numbers into Microsoft Graph directly; you can copy them from any Windows program; you can import them from Microsoft Excel, Lotus 1-2-3, or a text file; or you can read them in from an existing Microsoft Excel chart.

To create a chart within a Windows program, select the place in your document where you want the chart to appear, and then insert a chart with the commands in the particular program you are using. For example, in Write— the word processing program included with Windows—you choose the Edit menu and select the Insert Object command. You then select Microsoft Graph from the Object Type list. In Word for Windows (version 2.0), you choose the Insert menu, select the Object command, and select Microsoft Graph from the Object Type list. Microsoft Graph opens in a program window on top of your program.

16

Data sheet —

Microsoft Graph opens with default data in the data sheet and chart.

Chart —

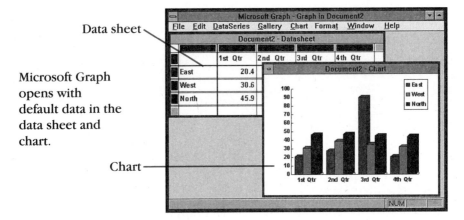

The chart reflects the data in the sample data sheet, which appears in the chart worksheet by default. (If you select data in a Windows program before starting Microsoft Graph, the selected data appears in the data sheet.) If you change the data in the data sheet, you change the chart. When you exit Microsoft Graph, you embed the chart and its related data into your program.

In Microsoft Graph, you can change the data in the data sheet in many ways. You also can choose different types of charts from the Gallery menu. The Chart menu enables you to add items such as legends, arrows, and titles to your chart, and you can remove them. You can change the appearance or position of selected chart items or data in the data sheet by using the commands in the Format menu.

Understanding the Data Sheet Layout

Graph consists of a data sheet and a chart. The data sheet contains horizontal rows and vertical columns. The top row and leftmost column are often used to specify labels for your chart. The chart graphically displays the labels and numbers contained in the data sheet.

Microsoft Graph plots the data from the data sheet as *markers* in the chart. Markers can appear as lines, bars, columns, data points (in X-Y charts), or wedges (in pie charts). A row of data in the data sheet, therefore, appears as a series of markers in the chart. A series of values appears in the chart either connected by a line or as bars or columns that have the same color.

Column of data   Row of data

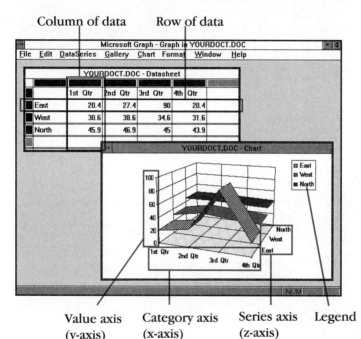

The data sheet row labeled *East*, for example, corresponds to one line in the 3-D line chart.

16

Value axis   Category axis   Series axis   Legend
(y-axis)   (x-axis)   (z-axis)

By default each row of data in the data sheet translates to a series of data points in the chart. If the series are to appear in rows (as is Graph's default), the text in the top row of the data sheet becomes the *category labels* that appear below the *category axis* (the x-axis, or horizontal axis). The text in the leftmost column becomes the *series labels*, which Microsoft Graph uses as labels for the *legend*. (The legend is the box that indicates the different colors or patterns used by each series of markers.) To reverse this placement, choose the **D**ata Series menu and select the Series in **C**olumns command.

If your data on the data sheet uses the reverse orientation, so that each data series is listed in a column, you must choose the **D**ataSeries menu and select the Series in **C**olumns command.

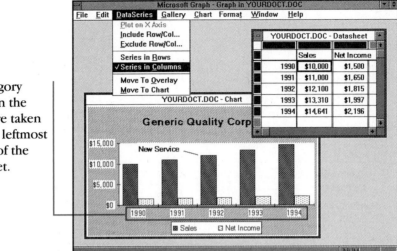

The category labels (on the x-axis) are taken from the leftmost column of the data sheet.

16

In this example, the series labels (legend labels) are taken from the top row of data. When you create a Microsoft Graph chart, be sure that you have text for each series label (legend label), text for each category label (x-axis), and a number for each marker.

Typing Data for a New Chart

To manually create a chart, type over the numbers and text that appear in the default data sheet. When you change the default data sheet, you update the chart.

If you change numbers or text in the data sheet, the chart correspondingly reflects your changes. Rows or columns of data you add to the data sheet are added to the chart. Ensuing sections in this chapter describe methods of editing data.

Copying Data from Windows Programs

You can copy data from programs and paste it into the data sheet to create a chart. You can create a chart, for example, from a series of text and numbers aligned at tabs in Word for Windows or Write, or you can copy a range of cells from a Microsoft Excel worksheet. (The section "Importing a Microsoft Excel Chart," later in this chapter, describes how to import a range from Microsoft Excel or use a Microsoft Excel chart as a basis for a Microsoft Graph chart.)

In a word processing document, you must use tabs or a table to separate data and text for the information to copy into separate data sheet cells. You must arrange data and text as you want it to appear in the Microsoft Graph data sheet.

To create a chart by copying data from a document or a Microsoft Excel worksheet, follow these steps:

1. Select the tabbed or table data or range of Microsoft Excel cells that you want to copy, choose the Edit menu, and select the Copy command.

2. Move the insertion point to the place where you want the chart in your document, and then follow the instructions of your particular program for inserting a chart. For example, in Word for Windows (version 2.0), choose the Insert menu, select the Object command, select Microsoft Graph from the Object Type list, and choose OK.

3. Activate the data sheet and erase all existing data by choosing the Edit menu and selecting the Select All command. Then choose the Edit menu and select the Clear command or press `Del`. When the Clear dialog box displays, choose OK or press `⏎Enter`.

4. Ensure that the top left cell in the data sheet is selected, and then choose the Edit menu and select the Paste command.

   The data is pasted into the data sheet, and the chart updates.

5. Format, modify, or size the chart and data sheet as necessary.

6. Choose the File menu and select the Exit Return to Document command.

7. Choose Yes when prompted to update the chart in the document.

   Microsoft Graph inserts the chart at the insertion point.

Importing Worksheet or Text Data

When creating a chart, you may want to use data you have in an ASCII text file or in a Microsoft Excel or Lotus 1-2-3 worksheet. You can save time by importing this data directly into the Microsoft Graph data sheet.

To import data into the data sheet, follow these steps:

1. Erase all unwanted data from the Microsoft Graph data sheet, and then select the cell where you want the top left corner of the imported data. If you are importing an entire data sheet, select the top left cell of the data sheet.

16

2. Choose the File menu and select the Import Data command.

The Import Data
dialog box
appears.

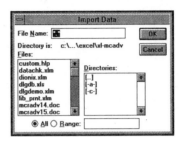

3. From the Files list, select the file containing the data you want to import (change the directory, if necessary, in the Directories list). Or type the file name in the File Name text box.

4. Specify the amount of data you want to import. To import all data, choose the All button. To import a range of data, choose the Range button and specify the range in the text box. Use a range format such as A12:D36.

5. Choose OK or press ⏎Enter.

Importing a Microsoft Excel Chart

With Microsoft Excel, you can create mathematical models that generate charts you can link to Windows client programs, such as Word for Windows. If you change the worksheet, you change the chart. These changes are reflected in the client program. Importing a Microsoft Excel chart into Microsoft Graph so that the chart can be embedded, rather than linked, into a Windows client program has other advantages. Embedding keeps the data with the chart so that another person can update the chart without needing Microsoft Excel or the original Microsoft Excel worksheet. Links are not broken if the source worksheet or chart in Microsoft Excel is renamed or moved to a different directory. Object linking and embedding are described in Chapter 10.

To import a Microsoft Excel chart and the chart's related data, follow these steps:

1. Move the insertion point to the place where you want the chart, and then start Microsoft Graph by following the instructions for your particular program.

16

2. Choose the File menu and select the Open Microsoft Excel Chart command. To overwrite existing data in the data sheet, choose OK or press ⏎Enter when prompted.

3. Select the drive, directory, and file name of the Microsoft Excel chart, and then choose OK or press ⏎Enter. Microsoft Excel charts use the file extension XLC.

The chart opens in Microsoft Graph, and the associated data appears in the data sheet. Data series that were in rows in Microsoft Excel are in columns in the Microsoft Graph data sheet, but the chart will be correct.

Editing Existing Charts

Updating an existing Microsoft Graph chart embedded in a Windows program is easy. With a mouse, double-click the chart. With the keyboard, select the chart by moving the insertion point next to the chart and then holding down the Shift key while you press the appropriate arrow key to move the insertion point over the chart. After you select the chart, follow the instructions of your particular program for editing an embedded object. For example, in Word for Windows (version 2.0), choose the Edit menu and select the Microsoft Graph Object command.

Microsoft Graph opens and loads the data and chart. You then can use any of the procedures described in this chapter to modify your chart or data.

Editing the Data Sheet

Working in the data sheet is similar to working in a Word for Windows table or a Microsoft Excel worksheet. However, unlike working in an Excel worksheet, you can edit cellular data directly in a cell or within an editing box.

Selecting Data

Moving and selecting data in the data sheet requires many of the same techniques you use in Microsoft Excel. If you are using a mouse, you can use the scroll bars to scroll to any location on the data sheet. To select a cell, click it. To select multiple cells, drag the mouse across them. To select a row or column, click its header. To select multiple rows or columns, drag across the headers. To select all cells in the data sheet, click the blank rectangle at the top left corner where the row and column headings intersect. (Selecting the entire worksheet and pressing Del erases the entire worksheet.)

If you are using the keyboard, use the following keys to move the insertion point:

Press	To move
← → ↑ ↓	One cell, in the direction of the arrow
Home	To first data cell in row
End	To last data cell in row
Ctrl + Home	To top left data cell
Ctrl + End	To lower right data cell
PgUp PgDn	One screen up or down, respectively
Ctrl + PgUp or Ctrl + PgDn	One screen right or left, respectively

Use the following keys to select cells and the cells' contents:

Press	To select
← → ↑ ↓	One cell, in the direction of the arrow
Shift + ← → ↑ ↓ or F8, ← → ↑ ↓, F8	A range (rectangle) of cells, in the direction of the arrow. (Pressing F8 toggles Extend mode on and off.)
Shift + space bar	One row
Ctrl + space bar	One column
Shift + Ctrl + space bar or Ctrl + A or Edit Select All	The entire data sheet

If you have selected multiple cells, you can deselect them by pressing Shift+Backspace.

16

Replacing or Editing Existing Data

The easiest way to replace the contents of a cell is to select the cell by moving to it or clicking it, and then typing directly over the cell's contents. When you press Enter or select a different cell, the change takes effect.

To edit the contents of a cell, select the cell by moving to it or clicking it. Type the new data and press Enter. Alternatively, press F2, which is the Edit key, or double-click the cell. An *edit box* appears, showing the contents of the cell. Type the new data, or edit existing data. After you finish editing, choose OK or press Enter.

Inserting or Deleting Rows and Columns

Microsoft Graph expands the chart to include data or text you add to rows or columns in the data sheet. If you add rows or columns of data and leave blank rows or columns, Microsoft Graph does not include the blank rows or columns as part of the chart.

To insert or delete rows or columns in the data sheet, select the rows or columns where you want to insert or delete, and then choose the Edit menu and select the Insert Row/Col or the Delete Row/Col command. The shortcut keys for inserting and deleting are Ctrl+ + and Ctrl+ - , respectively. A dialog box appears if you do not select an entire row or column, prompting you to select whether you want to affect the rows or columns that pass through the selected cells.

Copying or Moving Data

Copy or move data in the data sheet using normal Windows techniques. Select the cells you want to copy or move, and then choose the Edit menu and select the Copy or Cut command. (The shortcut keys are Ctrl+C to copy, and Ctrl+X to cut.) Select the cell at the top left corner of the area in which you want to paste the data, choose the Edit menu, and select the Paste command, or press Ctrl+V. The pasted data replaces the data it covers. To undo the paste operation, choose the Edit menu and select the Undo command, or press Ctrl+Z.

16

439

Changing the Chart Type

When Microsoft Graph first opens, the chart appears as a *three-dimensional column* chart. Many different chart types are available, but you have to select the appropriate one.

You should choose the appropriate chart type before you begin changing and formatting your chart. (If you choose a different chart type after you change your chart, you may lose your changes.) To change the chart type after you customize, follow the procedures described in the section, "Customizing an Existing Chart Type," further in this chapter.

Selecting the Original Chart Type

16

When you build charts, you can use any of the 81 predefined chart formats. The easiest way to create charts is to select the predefined chart closest to the type you want. You then can customize the predefined chart until it fits your needs. To use a predefined chart, follow these steps:

1. Select the Gallery menu.
2. From the menu, choose one of the chart types, each of which is described in table 16.1.

Table 16.1
Chart Types

Option	Description
Area	An *area chart* compares the continuous change in volume of a series of data. This type of chart adds the data from all the individual series to create the top line that encloses the area, showing the viewer how different series contribute to the total volume.
Bar	A *bar chart* compares distinct (noncontinuous), unrelated items over time. This chart type uses horizontal bars to show positive or negative variation from a center point.
Column	*Column charts* often compare separate (noncontinuous) items as they vary over time. This chart type uses vertical columns to indicate distinct measurements made at different intervals.

Option	Description
Line	A *line chart* compares trends over even time or measurement intervals plotted on the category axis. Use the line chart in production, sales, or stock-market charts to show the trend of revenue or sales over time.
Pie	A *pie chart* compares the size of each of the pieces making up a whole unit. Use this type of chart when the parts total 100 percent for a single series of data. Only the first data series in a worksheet selection is plotted.
XY (Scatter)	A *scatter chart* or *XY chart* compares trends over uneven time or measurement intervals plotted on the category axis. Use scatter charts when you must plot data in which the independent variable is recorded at uneven intervals or the category data points are not specified in even increments.
Combination	A *combination chart* lays one chart over another. This type of chart is helpful when you're comparing data of different types or data requiring different axis scales.
3-D Area	*3-D area charts* are similar to regular (2-D) area charts, but 3-D versions enable you to compare series without adding them together.
3-D Bar	*3-D bar charts* are horizontal bars that show variation between discrete items.
3-D Column	*3-D column charts* are vertical bars that show variation between discrete items.
3-D Line	*3-D line charts* also are known as *ribbon charts*. Use 3-D line charts for the same types of data as those used in regular (2-D) line charts.
3-D Pie	*3-D pie charts* work well for marketing materials or presentations in which an overall impression is required.

After you make your choice, the Chart Gallery dialog box appears, displaying the different predefined types of charts.

16

441

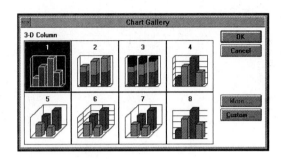

This Chart Gallery
dialog box shows
the gallery of
predefined
formats for 3-D
Column charts.

3. To select a chart type, click its square or type its number.

4. If you do not see the type you want and the More button is not grayed, choose the More button to see additional formats of this type.

5. Choose OK or press ⏎Enter.

16

Note: Alternatively, to select the chart type you want, double-click the box in the Gallery containing the chart. This technique selects the type and chooses OK.

Customizing an Existing Chart Type

You can save yourself work by deciding on the type of chart you want *before* you customize it. Use the Gallery menu to try different types of charts, and then customize the one you decide to use. If you use the Gallery menu to change the chart type *after* you customize a chart, the new chart type may override some of your custom selections.

To change a chart type without losing custom formatting, choose the Format menu, select the Chart command, and select a new type from the Chart Type drop-down list. Format Chart changes the basic chart type or customizes the main chart.

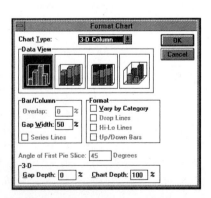

The Format Chart
dialog box
enables you to
customize a chart.

442

In the Format Chart dialog box, you can choose from a limited selection of views in the Data View group. If you have selected a bar or column chart, you may be able to specify Overlap of bars or columns within a category, or the Gap Width between clusters, or whether to include Series Lines. In other types of charts, especially line charts, you can make format selections, such as Vary by Category to give different colors to each data marker, and you can select Drop Lines, Hi-Lo Lines, and Up/Down Bars for charts that track stock prices. In a pie chart, you can select the Angle of the first pie wedge, and in 3-D charts you can select the Gap Depth (or distance between data series) and the Chart Depth (or depth of the chart as a percentage of its width).

Formatting the Data Sheet

Formatting the data sheet is important for more reasons than making data entry easier and more accurate. The format of the numbers and dates in the data sheet also controls the appearance of numbers and dates in your chart and, therefore, in your document.

Adjusting Column Widths in the Data Sheet

When you enter numbers in unformatted cells, they appear in General format (without commas, decimals, dollar signs, and so forth). If the column is not wide enough to display the full general-format number, the number changes to scientific format. The number 6,000,000, for example, changes to 6E+6. When a scientific number is too large to fit in a cell, or if a formatted number is too wide for a cell, the cell fills with # signs.

To change the column width with the mouse, follow these steps:

1. Move the pointer onto the vertical line to the right of the column heading that you want to widen. The pointer changes to a two-headed horizontal arrow.

2. Drag the arrow left or right until the column border is where you want it, and then release the mouse button.

To change the column width with the keyboard, follow these steps:

1. Select a cell in the column you want to change. You can change multiple columns by selecting a cell in each column you want to change.

2. Choose the Format menu and select the Column Width command.

3. In the Column Width box, enter the number of characters you want the column to contain, or select the Standard Width option for a column that is nine characters wide.

4. Choose OK or press ⏎Enter.

Formatting Numbers

Microsoft Graph has many predefined numeric formats. When you enter data in a formatted cell, the data assumes the cell's formatting. For example, if a cell contains date formatting and you enter a number in the cell, the number is formatted to look like a date. You can choose from many formats to format the data sheet and chart.

The format of the first data cell in a series defines the numeric format for that series in the chart.

To format data cells, follow these steps:

1. Select the data cell or range you want to format.

2. Choose the Format menu and select the Number command.

   If you selected a row or column, you will see a dialog box telling you that only cells containing data will be formatted. Choose OK or press ⏎Enter.

The Number dialog box appears, displaying a list of different numeric and date formats.

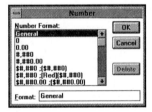

3. From the Number Format list, select the numeric or date format you want to apply to the selected data cells. (See table 16.2 for a list of formats.)

4. Choose OK or press ⏎Enter.

The items in the list may appear strange until you understand the symbols that represent the different numeric and date formats. The characters in the list are as follows:

Table 16.2
Formatting Options for Numbers

Option	Example	Explanation
General	3000	Graph's default; no formatting
0	3000	Displays all numbers, even zeros
0.00	3000.00	Displays two decimal points
#,##0	3,000	Displays commas
#,##0.00	3,000.00	Displays commas and two decimal points
$#,##0	$3,000	Displays dollar signs and commas
$#,##0.00	$3,000.00	Displays dollar signs, commas, and two decimal points
0%	3000%	Displays percent sign
0.00%	3000.00%	Displays two decimal points and percent sign
m/d/yy	4/12/92	Displays numeric date
d-mmm-yy	12-April-92	Displays date with month spelled
d-mmm	12-April	Displays day and month
h:mm AM/PM	10:00 AM	Displays time and AM or PM
m/d/yy h:mm	4/12/92 10:00	Displays date and time

Adding Items to a Chart

You can add to your Microsoft Graph charts many items that make them more informative and easier to read. For example, you can add titles, floating text, and arrows. Some of the items you add are movable; others are fixed. Items fixed in position appear with white handles at their corners when selected. You cannot move or resize them. You can move or resize items that display black handles when selected.

Adding Titles

You can use the Chart menu to add or delete most items from a chart. To add a title to a fixed location on a chart, for example, follow these steps:

1. Select the chart by clicking it or pressing [Ctrl]+[F6].
2. Choose the Chart menu and select the Titles command.

The Attach Title dialog box appears. Note that the contents of the dialog box vary according to the type of chart you selected.

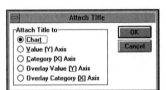

16

3. Select one of the following option buttons:

Option	Description
Chart	Attaches Title at the top of the chart.
Value (Y) Axis	Attaches title Y to value axis. Uses title 2 on 3-D chart.
Category (X) Axis	Attaches title X to category axis.
Series (Y) Axis	Attaches title Y on series axis in 3-D chart.
Overlay Value (Y) Axis	Attaches title Y on overlay value axis on 2-D chart with overlay.
Overlay Value (X) Axis	Attaches title X on overlay value axis on 2-D chart with overlay.

If you choose Chart or one of the axis options, a default title of Title, X, Y, or Z appears at the appropriate location in the chart, depending on the type of chart you selected.

4. Choose OK or press [↵Enter].
5. While that default title is selected, type the text you want. Press [↵Enter] to move to a second line. Use normal editing keys to edit the text.
6. To finish the text, press [Esc] or click outside the text.

To remove a title, select the title by clicking it or pressing an arrow key until the title is selected, and then either press the Del key or choose the Edit menu and select the Clear command.

Adding Floating Text

A title attaches to a specific location on a chart, but you can add floating text to any location on a chart.

To add floating text, make sure that no other text is selected and then type the text. To complete the box, click outside it or press Esc. Your text appears in a floating box in the center of the chart, surrounded by black selection handles.

The black handles on selected text indicate that you can resize and move the floating text box by dragging the box to a new location or dragging a handle to resize the box. You can format floating text boxes to include colors and patterns. (See the section "Formatting the Chart and Chart Items," further in this chapter.)

To edit the text in a floating text box, click the text to select it, click where you want to locate the insertion point, and then edit the text. If you are using a keyboard, you must retype the text. To delete a floating text box, select the text and then press the Del key, or choose the Edit menu and select Clear.

Adding Legends and Arrows

Microsoft Graph's default chart includes a legend. To delete the legend, choose the Chart menu and select the Delete Legend command. To add a legend, choose the Chart menu and select the Add Legend command. The legend appears. Notice that the legend is enclosed with black handles. To move a legend, select it, choose the Format menu, select the Legend command, select Bottom, Corner, Top, Right, or Left, and then choose OK. Alternatively, drag the legend to a new location and release it.

To change the labels in the legend, change the series labels in the data sheet. You cannot resize a legend.

An arrow on your chart can highlight important information by pointing to a specific bar or line. To add arrows to your charts, make sure that an arrow is not selected, and then choose the Chart menu and select the Add Arrow command. If you do select an arrow, however, the Delete Arrow command replaces the Add Arrow command. Notice that arrows have black handles at either end so that you can resize them. To move an arrow, position the

16

447

pointer on the arrow's shaft and then drag it. You also can format arrows to display different heads, thicknesses, or as a line.

Formatting the Chart and Chart Items

After you select a predefined chart format and add chart items, you can customize your chart. You can change the colors, patterns, and borders of chart items; the type and color of the fonts; the position and size of some chart items; and you can add lines, arrows, titles, legends, and floating text. By selecting an axis and then a format command, you can change the scale and the appearance of tick marks and labels. You also can rotate three-dimensional charts and create picture charts, in which pictures take the place of columns, bars, or lines.

Formatting Fonts and Text

The data sheet uses only one font, type size, and type style; however, each text item in the chart, such as titles and floating text, can have a different font, size, or style.

To change an item's font, size, or style, follow these steps:

1. Select any cell in the data sheet, or select the item whose font you want to change in the chart.

2. Choose the Format menu and select the Font command.

The Chart Fonts dialog box appears.

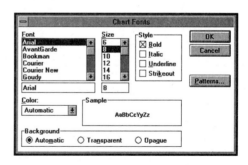

3. Select a font from the Font list, a size from the Size list, and Bold, Italic, Underline, or Strikeout from the Style group.

4. If you want, select a color from the Color list.

5. From the Background group, select Transparent for a see-through background, or Opaque for a solid background. The default selection is Automatic.

6. Choose OK or press ⏎Enter.

To rotate or align a title, floating text, or the text on an axis, follow these steps:

1. Select the text or axis.

2. Choose the Format menu and select the Text command.

3. If you are formatting text on an axis, select Left, Center, or Right from the Horizontal Text Alignment group, and select Top, Center, or Bottom from the Vertical Text Alignment group. (Alignment is not available for floating text or titles.)

4. Select a text orientation from the Orientation group.

5. For floating text, you can select Automatic Size to fit the border to the text. For a title, select Automatic Text to revert to the original title text (such as *Title*).

6. Choose OK or press ⏎Enter.

Changing Patterns and Colors

You can alter the graphic appearance of a chart in many ways. You can change the color or weight of an axis, and vary its tick marks. For legends, text, and titles, you can add a border in any color or weight—with or without a shadow—and you can include color or a pattern in the background. Bars and columns in a chart can display in reverse color if the value is negative.

The choices available in the Patterns dialog box vary according to what you select before you choose the command.

To change patterns and colors, follow these steps:

1. Select the axis, legend, floating text, title, bar, or column for which you want to change the pattern or color.

2. Choose the Format menu and select the Pattern command. The Area Patterns or Axis Patterns dialog box appears.

3. Select the patterns, colors, and other options you want.

4. Choose OK or press ⏎Enter.

As a shortcut, you can display the Patterns dialog box by double-clicking the object for which you want to change the patterns or colors.

16

You can return to the default colors, patterns, and borders by selecting the chart items you want to change, choosing the Format menu, selecting the Patterns command, and then selecting the Automatic option.

Sizing the Chart

When resizing your chart, you get the best results if you resize it in Microsoft Graph rather than in the program in which the chart is embedded. Resizing the chart in the program changes the size, but does not correct the text placement, readjust the scale, and so on. By sizing the chart in Microsoft Graph, before you update it in your program, you take advantage of Microsoft Graph's capability to reposition and resize elements in the chart.

In Microsoft Graph, you change the size of the chart as you would the size of any window. With a mouse, drag the chart's borders or corners. With the keyboard, press Alt + - to open the Document Control menu, choose the Size command, and then use the arrow keys to resize the window. Make sure that the chart's window is the size you want the chart to be when you paste it into your program.

Although you can change the magnification of the chart, changing the magnification does not change the size of the chart in your document. Magnifying is useful when you format or position text or arrows. To magnify or shrink your view of the chart, select the Window menu and choose one of the percentage options.

Formatting Axes

Microsoft Graph automatically scales and labels the axes, but you can select any axis and change its scale, the number of labels or tick marks that appear, and the orientation and font of the text.

To rescale a chart (vertical or horizontal) follow these steps:

1. Select the vertical or horizontal axis.
2. Choose the Format menu and select the Scale command.

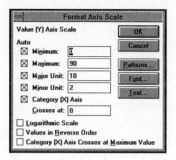

The Format Axis
Scale dialog box
appears.

3. Select options from the Format Axis Scale dialog box (the options vary
    according to the axis you selected and the type of chart you have).

    Options for the value (Y) axis include Minimum, or lowest number on
    the vertical axis; Maximum, or highest number on the vertical axis;
    Major unit, for the increments between major tick mark units; and
    Category (X) Axis Crosses at, to specify where the vertical axis inter-
    sects with the horizontal axis.

    Options for the category (X) axis include Number of Categories
    Between Tick Labels, to indicate how many categories will have labels;
    and Number of Categories Between Tick Marks, to indicate which
    categories will have tick marks (for both options, enter 1 for labels or
    tick marks for each category, 2 for labels or tick marks for every other
    category, and so on). Other options are Value (Y) Axis Crosses at
    Category Number, to indicate at which value axis the category axis will
    cross; and Value (Y) Axis Crosses at Maximum Category, to cross the
    value axis at the last category.

4. Choose OK or press ⏎Enter.

Exiting or Updating Charts

You can keep Microsoft Graph open and update the chart in your client
document, or close Microsoft Graph and update the chart. Updating the chart
embeds the chart and its data into the document. You cannot save the chart
and data separately; and you must save them as embedded objects within a
program's document.

16

To see how your chart or its changes will appear in your program, you do not need to close Microsoft Graph. To keep Microsoft Graph open and update the new or existing chart in the document, choose the File menu and select the Update command.

When you exit Microsoft Graph, you are given a chance to update the new or existing chart in your program. To exit Microsoft Graph, choose the File menu and select the Exit and Return to document command. If you made changes since the last update, you are prompted to update the chart in the document. Choose Yes to update the chart.

Summary

16

If you are familiar with graphing in Microsoft Excel, you can use what you learned in Microsoft Excel to learn about Microsoft Graph. For more detailed information on Microsoft Excel, refer to *Using Excel 4 for Windows,* Special Edition, published by Que Corporation. Many of the descriptions, tips, and tricks discussed in this special edition apply to Microsoft Graph.

■ Microsoft Graph is an applet, or mini-application, you can use only from within a program that supports object linking and embedding (OLE). You cannot start Microsoft Graph as a stand-alone program. Graph comes free with programs such as Word for Windows, Publisher, and PowerPoint, all from Microsoft.

■ Although Microsoft Graph comes free with only a few select programs, it is available to any program that supports OLE.

■ To embed a chart in your document, you must use a command to insert an object (the command varies from program to program). You then select Microsoft Graph from a list of applets.

■ To edit a chart, you can double-click it or, in some (but not all) programs, you can select the chart and choose a command. The command varies from program to program.

■ You can copy or import data into Graph from a variety of programs; thus, you can use existing data to create a chart.

■ The Microsoft Graph program is powerful: you can select from a wide variety of chart types, including bar, column, pie, line, and scatter (and select from several styles for each type); you can format the text in your chart; you can customize patterns and colors; and you can add titles, legends, and floating text.

■ After you edit a chart, you must update your document to transfer your changes to the document.

■ To save your chart, you must save your document. You cannot save a Microsoft Graph chart as a separate file; it exists as part of your document.

In the next chapter, you learn about other useful applets that come free with Windows programs. You can use WordArt, for example, to create logos and decorative text. Equation Editor is a wonderful tool for anyone producing scientific journals or mathematical papers that include symbols.

To learn more about handling the chart as an embedded object, read Chapter 10, "Using Object Linking and Embedding," which discusses OLE in detail.

16

Using
Windows
Applets

17

Sometimes characters in a document play a special role. In scientific and mathematical documents, for example, you often need to include equations made up of a special type of character: mathematical symbols not commonly found on a computer keyboard. Microsoft's Equation Editor enables you to use many scientific and mathematical symbols to make such documents look more professional.

Equation Editor and WordArt come free with some Microsoft programs, including Word for Windows. After you install these programs, they are available to all programs that support object linking and embedding (OLE), such as Windows Write.

Sometimes characters play a whimsical role. In publications, for example, you may want to use special characters that add spice to brochures, ads, newsletters, memos, stationery, forms, or cards. Microsoft WordArt enables you to produce special effects by twisting and turning your words into more interesting shapes.

Like Microsoft Draw and Microsoft Graph, discussed in the two preceding chapters of this book, Equation Editor and WordArt are *applets,* or mini-applications, that work from within *client* programs. Applets don't exist independently—you can start and use them only from within the client program. To include an equation or WordArt logo in a Word for Windows document, for example, you must first start Word for Windows and then choose the **I**nsert **O**bject command to activate the applet. You can use applets in any program that supports OLE, including Word for Windows, Publisher, PowerPoint, Ami Pro, Microsoft Excel, and others.

Applets offer a big advantage in file management: you can always find the objects you create using Equation Editor and WordArt in the same document where you created them. Because the objects are already located where you use them, you have much less chance of not being able to find them later.

17

Key Terms in This Chapter

Slots	Small boxes into which you enter text or insert symbols and templates. When you first open the Equation Editor, the insertion point is located in an empty slot. Templates can also contain slots.
Templates	Ready-made sets of symbols and empty slots that simplify the task of building an equation. Templates for creating fractions, square roots, and matrices are examples. You access templates through drop-down palettes located at the top of the Equation Editor window.
Symbols	Special characters, such as Greek letters and mathematical operators, used in creating equations. You access symbols through drop-down palettes located at the top of the Equation Editor window.
Applet	A mini-application (small program) that works only within a client program.
Object	Anything you create using an applet such as Equation Editor or WordArt. Objects are embedded in the client document.
Object linking and embedding	The technology that enables you to embed an object, such as an equation created in Equation Editor or a logo created in WordArt, within a client program.

Client	A document or program that contains an object you created using an applet such as Equation Editor or WordArt.
Server	The applet you used to create an object embedded within the client document.
Font	The style of type you used to create a WordArt image. WordArt uses its own set of decorative fonts; they are different from the fonts installed in Windows.

Note: Throughout this chapter, instructions for accessing Equation Editor and WordArt assume that you are using Word for Windows. The commands for using these applets with other programs are similar; they are listed in a box below the Word for Windows commands. (If your program is not listed, find a command similar to one listed for another, similar program.) The procedures for using the applets themselves are identical, no matter what your client program.

To learn more about object linking and embedding, refer to Chapter 10, "Using Object Linking and Embedding."

Using the Equation Editor

If you are a scientist or engineer, you may appreciate an easy way to enter equations into a document so that you do not have to hand-draw equations into an otherwise polished-looking document. With the Equation Editor, you can quickly and efficiently produce professional looking equations you can include in any program that supports object linking and embedding.

To open the Equation Editor, you need to follow the instructions for your Windows program. After you create an equation, you can insert it in your program wherever the insertion point is located when you open the Equation Editor. To insert an equation into a document, follow these steps:

1. Position the insertion point where you want to insert the equation in your program.
2. In Word for Windows, choose the Insert Object command. Select Equation from the list of applets, and choose OK.

17

457

Slot   Title bar   Menu bar   Symbol palettes   Template palettes

When you choose OK, the Equation Editor opens.

3. Create the equation in the Equation Editor (see the following sections for detailed instructions on creating an equation).

4. To close the Equation Editor and return to your program, choose the File menu and select the Exit and Return to document command. You are asked whether you want to save the equation in the program; choose Yes.

   To insert the equation into the program without closing the Equation Editor window, choose the File menu and select the Update command. You can return to your document as you would switch to any other program: press Ctrl + Esc to use the Task List or press Alt + Tab⁒ until the document window is active.

To start the Equation Editor from other programs, use the appropriate procedure from the following list:

Program	Procedure
PowerPoint	Choose the File menu and select the Insert command. Select Equation from the list of programs.
Publisher	Choose the Edit menu and select the Insert Object command. Select Equation from the Object Type list.
Microsoft Excel	Choose the Edit menu and select the Insert Object command. Select Equation from the Object Type list.
Ami Pro	Choose the Edit menu, select the Insert command, and then select New Object.
Write	Choose the Edit menu and select the Insert Object command. Select Equation from the Object Type list.

17

When you first open the Equation Editor, you are presented with a screen containing a single *slot*. Slots demarcate the different components of an equation. If you are entering a fraction, for example, you will see one slot for the numerator and a second slot for the denominator. You move from slot to slot by clicking the slot you want or by pressing the arrow keys or Tab, filling in the slots with text, templates, and symbols to create your equation.

The Equation Editor has several tools for simplifying the task of creating an equation. Just below the menu bar are two rows of buttons. The top row includes symbol palettes; the bottom row includes template palettes. To access these palettes, you point to the button and press and hold down the mouse button. The *symbol palettes* include scientific and mathematical symbols. The *template palettes* contain collections of ready-made templates that enable you to create the different components in an equation easily.

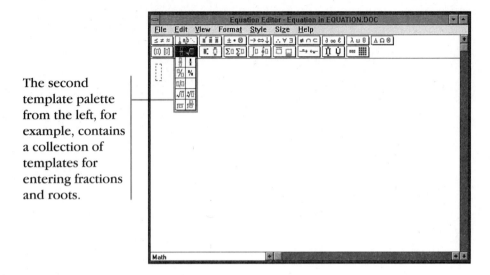

The second template palette from the left, for example, contains a collection of templates for entering fractions and roots.

17

The dotted areas within a template represent the empty slots into which you enter symbols and numbers. The template palettes contain a variety of templates for creating fractions, roots, summations, matrices, integrals, and many other mathematical expressions.

The Equation Editor also has symbol palettes, which you use to enter symbols such as math operators, Greek symbols, arrows, and so on. The best way to become familiar with both the template and symbol palettes is to experiment with them, running through them one-by-one and inserting either the template or symbol to see what it looks like.

Constructing an equation consists largely of using the template palette to insert slots, the symbol palette to insert symbols, and the keyboard to insert text.

You assemble an equation piece by piece. You enter text and symbols into slots, which are either stand-alone—such as the slot that appears on-screen when you first open the Equation Editor—or part of a template. You can add slots by selecting them from the template palette. The Equation Editor enters text or symbols into whichever slot contains the insertion point. (Use the arrow keys or the Tab key to move the insertion point from slot to slot.)

The templates take care of most of the positioning and spacing aspects of equation building, although commands are available for fine-tuning spacing and alignment of the components of an equation. Commands also are available for controlling the font and font size of the various elements in an equation.

460

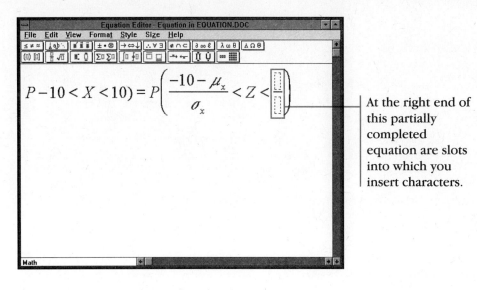

At the right end of this partially completed equation are slots into which you insert characters.

Typing in the Equation Editor

Typing in the Equation Editor is much like typing in any Windows program, such as Word for Windows, although with some important differences. Whenever you type in the Equation Editor, text is entered into the slot containing the insertion point. You can use the Backspace and Del keys to delete characters as you would in a word processing program.

Unless you choose the Text style from the Style menu, the space bar has no effect. The Equation Editor takes care of the spacing in an equation. When you type an equal sign, for example, the Equation Editor adds spacing before and after the equal sign. If you press the Enter key, you start a new line.

If you want to type regular text, choose the Text style from the Style menu or press Ctrl+Shift+E. You then can enter text as you normally would, using the space bar to insert spaces. Choose the Math style from the Style menu or press Ctrl+Shift+= to return to the Math style—the style you normally work with when creating an equation.

Entering Equation Templates

A template includes empty slots and mathematical symbols that combine to form a mathematical unit such as a fraction or a partial or complete equation. Generally, you build your equation by inserting templates and symbols and filling in the slots with numbers. The insertion point flashes inside a slot or next to a symbol or template.

461

To enter a template in an equation, follow these steps:

1. Place the insertion point where you want to insert the template (the insertion point should not be inside a slot).

2. Use the mouse to choose a template from one of the template palettes.

   The Equation Editor inserts the template immediately to the right of the insertion point.

3. Before you enter text or symbols, you must position the insertion point in the slot. To position the insertion point, click the desired slot or press the arrow keys or $\boxed{\text{Tab}\ ^{\cdot}_{\cdot}}$.

4. Type text or enter symbols into each slot in the template.

Entering Symbols

Many fields of mathematics, science, and medicine use symbols to represent concepts or physical structures. To insert symbols into slots, follow this procedure:

1. Position the insertion point where you want to insert the symbol.

2. Click the desired symbol from one of the symbol templates.

Adding Embellishments

The Equation Editor has several embellishments you can add to characters or symbols, such as prime signs, arrows, tildes, and dots. You add an embellishment by typing the character or inserting the symbol and then selecting the appropriate embellishment from the Embellishment symbol palette. To add an embellishment, follow these steps:

1. Position the insertion point to the right of the character you want to embellish.

2. Click the Embellishment symbol palette (the third symbol palette from the left) and hold down the mouse button. The embellishment palette drops down.

3. Drag the mouse pointer down the palette to select the embellishment you want to use, and then release the mouse button. The embellishment is added to the character to the left of the insertion point.

Controlling Spacing

With the Format Spacing command, you can modify spacing parameters, such as line spacing and row and column spacing in matrices. To modify the spacing setting that the Equation Editor uses, follow these steps:

1. Choose the Format menu and Select the Spacing command. The Spacing dialog box appears.

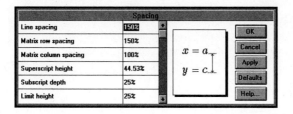

The Spacing dialog box displays a list of dimensions.

2. Select the text box next to the dimension you want to modify. Use the scroll bar to move through the list of dimensions.

    The dimension you select is illustrated in the diagram at the right side of the dialog box.

3. Type a new measurement. To increase line spacing, for example, replace the default measurement (150%) by typing **200%**.

    Many dimensions are expressed as percentages; others have specific values. You can use either type of measurement. The default unit of measure is points. You can specify other units by typing the appropriate abbreviation from the following list:

Unit of measure	Abbreviation
Inches	in
Centimeters	cm
Millimeters	mm
Points	pt
Picas	pi

17

463

4. Choose the Apply button to apply the new dimensions without closing the Spacing dialog box. Choose OK or press `⏎Enter` to accept your changes and close the dialog box.

   Choosing Apply applies the modified dimension to the current equation and leaves the dialog box open, enabling you to continue making modifications. Pressing `⏎Enter` applies your modifications and closes the dialog box.

Note: In practice, you probably should specify the spacing dimensions as a percentage of the point size specified for Full size type, which you set using the Size Define command. The advantage to this approach is that if you change the type size, you don't have to redefine your spacing dimensions; spacing will always be proportional to the type size.

Aligning Equations

With the Equation Editor, you can horizontally align the lines in an equation, or lines of multiple equations, using the Format commands. You can align lines to the left, center, or right, or you can align them around equal signs or decimal points.

To align equation lines, follow these steps:

1. Position the insertion point in the line you want to align, or select the lines you want to align.

2. Choose the Format menu and select one of the following commands:

   Align Left

   Align Center

   Align Right

   Align at =

   Align at . (decimal point)

Selecting Font Styles

Font styles are simply a combination of font and character formatting you assign to selected characters or to characters you are going to type. The available styles include Math, Text, Function, Variable, Greek, Matrix-Vector, and Other. Choose the style you want to use from the Style menu. You can modify the font and character formatting (that is, make the font bold or italic) of these styles using the Styles dialog box.

To define the font and character attributes for a style, follow these steps:

1. Choose the Style menu and select the Define command.

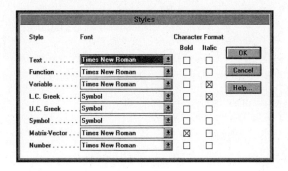

The Styles dialog box appears.

2. Select the style you want to define.
3. Select the desired font from the list of available fonts.
4. Select the Bold or Italic boxes, if desired.
5. Choose OK or press ↵Enter.

Use the Text style to type regular text. Selecting this style applies the Text style to the text you type and also enables the space bar so that you can enter spaces manually. With the other styles, spacing is handled automatically by the Equation Editor.

When you work in the Equation Editor, you normally use the Math style found in the Style menu. When you use the Math style, the Equation Editor automatically recognizes standard functions and applies the Function style (typeface and character formatting, for example) to such functions. The Variable style is applied otherwise.

If the Equation Editor fails to recognize a function, you can select the function and manually apply the Function style. Other styles also are available, such as Text, Greek, and Matrix-Vector.

Selecting Font Sizes

Just as the Equation Editor provides several predefined font styles, it also provides several predefined font sizes. Full size is the choice you normally work with when building equations. You also have selections for Subscripts, Sub-subscripts, Symbols, and Sub-symbols. You can use the Other size option for those cases in which you want to specify a size not defined by one of the standard sizes just listed.

17

To apply a font size to an equation, follow these steps:

1. Select the characters whose point size you want to modify.

    If you do not select any characters, the size you choose applies to characters you type subsequently.

2. Choose the Size menu.

3. Select the desired size from the Size menu. If none of the defined sizes match your needs, select Other and specify a size (in points) in the Other Size dialog box.

You can modify the default settings for each of the sizes listed in the Size menu by using the Define command, as in the following steps:

1. Choose the Size menu and select the Define command.

The Sizes dialog box appears.

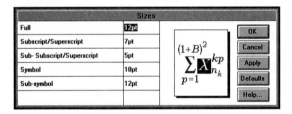

2. Select the box to the right of the size you want to define.

    When you select a box, the element you are defining is highlighted in the diagram on the right side of the dialog box.

3. Type a new size.

4. Choose OK or press ⏎Enter.

To apply a size before you begin typing, select the size from the Size menu and then type the characters to which you want to apply the size. To apply a size to characters you already have typed, select the characters and then choose a size.

Working with Matrices

The Matrix template palette (the last palette in the second row) includes several matrices of predefined size. (A *matrix* is a structure of slots containing no symbols or characters.) To insert a matrix template, click the Matrix template palette and drag the pointer to the desired template. Release the

17

mouse button. If you select a template from the bottom row of icons, the Matrix dialog box appears, enabling you to select the size and alignment of the matrix.

After you insert a matrix, you also can format it. To format a matrix, select the entire matrix, choose the Format menu, and select the Matrix command.

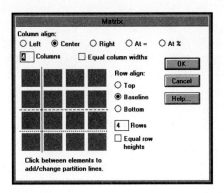

The Matrix dialog box appears, enabling you to specify the dimensions of the matrix and to make several other selections.

17

You can specify how you want to align the elements in your matrix's rows and columns, and whether or not the column widths and row heights are equal (if the rows and columns are not equal, their width and height are based on the widest or highest entry).

To align the columns, select the Left, Center, Right, At =, or At % option from the Column Align group. To change the number of columns in the matrix, select the Columns box and type a new number. If you want all the columns to be the same width (rather than having each column as wide as its widest slot), select Equal column widths.

To align the rows, select Top, Baseline, or Bottom from the Row align group. To change the number of rows, select the Rows box and type a new number. If you want all the rows to be the same height (rather than having each row as high as its highest slot), select Equal row heights.

The Matrix dialog box displays a gray square for each slot. By clicking the space between the gray squares in the dialog box, you can select one of three types of partition lines: solid, dashed, or dotted lines. As you click the space, you cycle through the three types of lines and then back to no line: click one time to insert a solid line, a second time to insert a dashed line, a third time to insert a dotted line, and a fourth time to remove the line.

Make the desired selections from the dialog box. Choose OK or press Enter.

Editing an Equation

To edit an equation, you must return to the Equation Editor from within the client document. To open the Equation Editor from Word for Windows, follow these steps:

1. Double-click the equation you want to edit, or select the equation and choose the Edit Equation Object command.

2. Make the desired editing changes.

3. To update the equation without closing the Equation Editor, choose the File menu and select the Update command. To close the Equation Editor and return to your program, choose the File menu, select the Exit and Return to document command, and then choose Yes when you are prompted to save the equation in the document.

To edit an Equation Editor object in other programs, use the appropriate procedure from the following list:

Program	Procedure
PowerPoint	Double-click the object, or select the object and choose the Edit Edit Equation command.
Publisher	Double-click the equation.
Microsoft Excel	Double-click the equation.
Ami Pro	Double-click the object.
Write	Double-click the object, or select the object and choose the Edit Edit Equation Object command.

Printing Equations

In general, to print an equation, you print the document containing the equation (you cannot print from the Equation Editor). To print equations, you need to have a PostScript printer, an HP LaserJet printer that supports downloadable fonts, or a dot-matrix or HP DeskJet printer in conjunction with a font-scaling utility, such as TrueType or Adobe Type Manager. Although the details of printing equations created in the Equation Editor are not covered in this book, the Help facility in the Equation Editor contains extensive information on using printers and fonts with the Equation Editor. To access these help screens, follow these steps:

17

468

1. Choose the **H**elp command in the Equation Editor.
2. Choose **I**ndex.
3. Select one of the topics under the Printers & fonts category.

You can obtain a printout of the help screen by choosing the **F**ile menu and selecting the **P**rint Topic command.

Turning Words into Pictures with WordArt

Although Equation Editor is an important tool for scientists and mathematicians, Microsoft WordArt is useful for people whose interests are more graphics oriented. This applet enables you to use special effects to turn words into pictures.

Words don't always function strictly as abstract symbols that you read for meaning. Words sometimes work as graphics, not only conveying meaning, but also attracting attention and creating memorable images. Every day you see examples of words used as graphics: logos incorporate words into symbols you recognize without even reading; decorated words embellish the mastheads in newsletters; special text effects add interest to album covers.

17

These three logos, shown in a Word for Windows document, were created using WordArt.

You can use WordArt to add shadows and colored backgrounds, stretch and condense letters, angle text, turn words on end, and arrange words in a circle.

Starting and Exiting WordArt

WordArt is a program you run from within Word for Windows or another program that supports object linking and embedding. With WordArt, you can embed a WordArt object into your document. In the section "Editing a WordArt Image," further in this chapter, you learn how to change your image after you embed it into your document.

To embed a WordArt image into a Word for Windows document, follow these steps:

1. Position the insertion point where you want to embed the WordArt image.

2. Choose the Insert menu and select the Object command.

The Object dialog box appears.

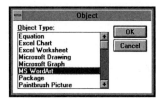

17

3. Select MS WordArt from the Object Type list, and choose OK or press ⏎Enter.

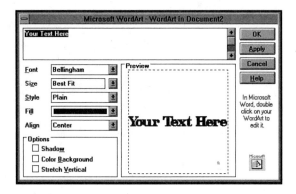

The Microsoft WordArt dialog box appears.

4. Create your WordArt image, as explained in the sections "Entering Text" and "Applying Special Effects," further in this chapter.

5. Choose the Apply button to insert your image or update an existing image in your Word for Windows document without exiting WordArt. Alternatively, if you want to exit WordArt, choose OK to insert your image or update an existing image in your document.

To start Microsoft WordArt from other programs, use the appropriate procedure from the following list:

Program	Procedure
PowerPoint	Choose the File menu and select the Insert command. Select MS WordArt from the list of programs.
Publisher	Choose the Edit menu and select the Insert Object command. Select MS WordArt from the Object Type list.
Microsoft Excel	Choose the Edit menu and select the Insert Object command. Select MS WordArt from the Object Type list.
Ami Pro	Choose the Edit menu, select the Insert command, and then select New Object.
Write	Choose the Edit menu and select the Insert Object command. Select MS WordArt from the Object Type list.

Because your WordArt image exists only as part of the client document, you cannot save the image by itself. To save your WordArt image, you must save your client document.

Understanding the WordArt Dialog Box

Although WordArt is a separate program, it appears in a dialog box. Most other programs appear in windows you can resize; however, you cannot resize the WordArt dialog box.

17

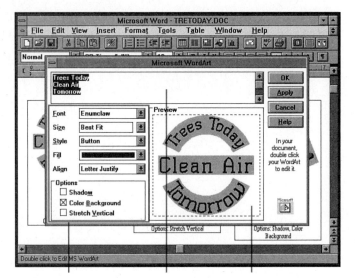

WordArt appears
in a dialog box
instead of in a
window.

Text options   Text entry area   Preview screen

17

In the *text entry area*, you type the text for your WordArt picture. The *Preview screen* displays a preview of the choices you make. Use the text options to manipulate your text. The Font, Size, and Fill lists enable you to set the appearance of your text; the Style list enables you to stretch, tilt, flip, arch, and stand text on end; and the Align list sets the alignment of text within the text frame. The Options box is below these lists. By selecting choices from the Options box, you can enhance text.

Entering Text

When creating a new WordArt image, you first must enter the text. When you start the program to create a new image, the text entry area contains the sample text Your Text Here. Type your own text to replace the selected sample text. Press Enter to start a new line of text.

After you insert your text into the text entry area, you can modify it using any standard Windows text-editing procedures. You can select several words or lines by dragging the mouse across the text, for example, or you can select a single word by double-clicking. You can click the mouse button to position the insertion point, press Backspace to delete text to the left of the insertion point, or press Del to delete text to the right of the insertion point. Pressing Enter ends a line.

The text you enter appears in the font selected in the Font list box. The Font list contains 19 different fonts, from Anacortes to Wenatchee. These fonts are graphic fonts specific to WordArt and are not the same as the fonts built into your printer.

The text you enter appears in the font size selected in the Size box. To enable WordArt to select the size that best fits the WordArt frame, select Best Fit from the Size list.

To change the font or size, follow these steps:

1. Type the text in the text entry area.

2. To change the font, choose the Font list and select the font you want from the drop-down list that appears. You can press ↑ or ↓ to cycle through the fonts, watching the Preview screen to see how each font looks.

3. To change the size, choose the Size list and select the size you want from the drop-down list, or type the size you want in the Size box.

Applying Special Effects

WordArt offers many ways to enhance words graphically. You can change the style by arching or flipping the words; you can change the fill or color; and you can align the words to fit the frame in many different ways. You also can add a drop shadow to words, add a colored background, or stretch the words vertically.

You must choose the Apply button to see your special effects in the Preview screen.

To apply special effects to text, follow these steps:

1. Type the text in the text entry area.

2. From the Style list, select a style.

    The choices in the Style list release you from the typical text baseline. The Style choices include the following:

Option	Description
Top to Bottom	Stands text vertically, with the first letter on top.
Bottom to Top	Stands text vertically, with the first letter on bottom.
Plain	Removes all styles.
Upside Down	Inverts text.
Arch Up	Fits text to the top of a circle.
Arch Down	Fits text to the bottom of a circle.
Button	Arches up the first line of text, leaves the second line of text horizontal, and arches down the third line of text.
Slant Up (Less)	Slants text slightly upward.
Slant Up (More)	Slants text upward approximately 45 degrees.
Slant Down (Less)	Slants text slightly downward.
Slant Down (More)	Slants tex downward approximately 45 degrees.

3. From the Fill list, select a color for your text.

   If your PC supports the full Windows palette, the list displays 16 colors, including black, white, and two shades of gray. If your PC supports fewer colors, however, the list displays fewer colors.

4. From the Align list, select one of the following text alignment options:

Option	Description
Left	Aligns text at the left edge of the frame.
Center	Aligns text in the center of the frame.
Right	Aligns text at the right edge of the frame.
Letter Justify	Spaces the letters to fill the frame.

17

Option	Description
Word Justify	Spaces words equally from the left to right edges of the frame.
Fit Horizontally	Stretches the text to fill the frame.

Letter Justify and Word Justify change the spacing of the text, not its appearance. Fit Horizontally, in contrast, stretches the actual characters, distorting those letters smaller than the frame. To see the effects of Fit Horizontally, select a small point size for a short line of text.

5. From the Options group, select from the following options to design your WordArt image further (an X indicates a selected option).

Option	Description
Shadow	Adds a black drop-shadow to text (or a white shadow if the background color is black).
Color Background	Adds a colored background (adds a black background if your text is white; adds a light gray background if your text is not white).
Stretch Vertical	Stretches the text vertically to fit the frame (similar to the Fit Horizontally alignment option, except that Stretch Vertical stretches text vertically instead of horizontally).

6. Choose Apply to see your changes in the Preview screen.

Editing a WordArt Image

You can edit your WordArt image in two ways: start WordArt and modify the image itself, using any of the techniques previously described in this chapter; or edit the image in the client program. In Word for Windows, for example, you can resize a WordArt image by selecting it and dragging its corner handles.

17

475

To edit a WordArt image in Word for Windows, follow these steps:

1. Double-click the image to start WordArt, or select the WordArt image and choose the Edit MS WordArt Object command.
2. Make changes in the Microsoft WordArt dialog box.
3. Choose Apply to apply your changes to the Preview screen and the Word for Windows document, or choose OK to apply your changes and exit WordArt.

To edit a Microsoft WordArt object in another program, use the appropriate procedure from the following list:

Program	Procedure
PowerPoint	Double-click the object, or select the object and choose the Edit Edit Equation command.
Publisher	Double-click the object.
Microsoft Excel	Double-click the object.
Ami Pro	Double-click the object.
Write	Double-click the object, or select the object and choose the Edit Edit Equation Object command.

Summary

The Equation Editor applet enables you to produce publication-quality equations you can insert into any Windows program that supports object linking and embedding (OLE). What used to be a tedious and usually unsatisfying task can now be accomplished with ease using this powerful applet.

Many features of the Equation Editor make creating equations easy—features such as templates, which serve as the framework for building equations, and symbol palettes, which contain a complete collection of all the characters you need to create polished equations. You have complete control over the fonts, font sizes, alignment, and spacing in your equations.

17

Microsoft WordArt is an applet that enables you to change words into pictures. You can rotate, flip, bend, stretch, and tilt words, and you can choose from a wide selection of fonts and styles. You can add a shadow or a colored background to words. WordArt images are great for logos, business cards, signs, and much more.

The equations and logos you create using Equation Editor and WordArt exist only as part of your client document. Thus, you start these applets, or miniprograms, from within another program, and you save the images as part of that program's document. You cannot start an applet from the desktop, as you can other programs.

Some of the important concepts and procedures covered in this chapter are:

- You can use Equation Editor to create scientific and mathematical equations in a document.

- You can use the template and symbol palettes to assemble an equation quickly and easily.

- Unless you specify otherwise, the Equation Editor automatically spaces the elements in an equation.

- You use the Format, Style, and Size menu commands to control font sizes and styles, the alignment, and the positioning of the elements in an equation.

- You can select from a long list of special fonts for your WordArt words.

- Choose the Apply button to see the effect of the changes you make to your WordArt image.

- Experiment with WordArt styles, alignments, colors, and options to see how they look. It's fun!

In the next chapter, "Using Multimedia," you learn how to use multimedia tools to produce and deliver sound and visual effects.

17

Using Multimedia

As computers edge their way into more and more aspects of our lives, they take on new roles. Consider these: computer as musician; computer as storyteller; computer as a presentation delivery medium; computer as educational tool; computer as research assistant.

Multimedia—the presentation of information through multiple media—plays a part in each of these roles, because it combines into a single package two communication media we're already familiar with—sound and sight. It also gives computer users control over both producing and delivering sound and visual effects.

You can use multimedia in several ways. With the right equipment, you can play any of the many multimedia packages available commercially. Included are games, stories, full encyclopedias, complete reference texts, and much more. You can record simple messages and embed them into documents you create in Windows. If you get adventurous, you can move beyond the simple programs that come with Windows and into a multimedia authoring program to create your own multimedia presentations.

Using multimedia requires that you have the right equipment. You need a CD-ROM player, speakers, and a sound board. All must be compliant to the Multimedia

Installing multimedia drivers

Playing sounds, video, and CD-ROMs

Operating multimedia equipment

Personal Computer (MPC) standard developed by Microsoft. You can get the equipment you need in one of two ways: by upgrading your present PC or by buying a special multimedia PC that comes equipped with everything you need.

Key Terms in This Chapter

Multimedia	The presentation of information on a computer, using graphics, sound, animation, and text. Multimedia components include sound and video, often played on a CD-ROM device.
MPC	Multimedia Personal Computer—a standard in multimedia computing, which most vendors agree to support. This standard means that anything you buy labeled *MPC* is compatible with your MPC system.
CD-ROM	Compact Disk Read-Only Memory. *CD-ROM* most accurately refers to a plastic disk (CD) that uses optical storage techniques to store digital data; however, *CD-ROM* also can refer to the disk drive, or player, that reads CD-ROM disks. A CD-ROM disk is similar to a music CD, but can contain sound, video, graphics, and text.
Sound board	A board you install in your PC to produce sound. Although your PC contains a speaker, it is adequate for little more than producing a beep. If you add a sound board, plan on adding speakers too.
Driver	Software that "drives" external devices like sound boards, CD-ROM players, synthesizers, and printers.
Media	The hardware on which files are stored. In a multimedia environment, the medium is often a CD-ROM disk.
MIDI	Musical Instrumental Digital Interface. A standard communications protocol for the exchange of information between computers and musical synthesizers, often used with multimedia.

18

Adding Multimedia Drivers

Before you can use a multimedia device, such as a sound board or a CD-ROM player, you must first physically plug the device into your PC, then you must install its device driver in Windows, and finally you must set it up. The process is much like installing a new printer on your system: plugging it in establishes the physical connection; installing the driver tells Windows it's there; setting up the device tells Windows how to communicate with it.

Plugging in the device—whether it's a sound board or a CD-ROM player—isn't as difficult as it may sound. If the device is internal, like a sound board, you can turn off your PC's power, remove a few screws from the sides of your PC, and slide the cover off fairly easily. (You may also have to remove a port cover from the back of the PC to provide external access to the new board's ports.) Boards plug into an area of your PC reserved for boards; to see how they attach, take a look at boards already in your PC. Then look at your new board: you can see that the board has ports at one end that must point toward the back of the PC for external access, and you can see a wide "tab" on one side of the board that pushes into any of the available slots inside the PC. Though it takes firm pressure to push the tab into the slot, it's not complex or danger-ous. When you're finished, slide the cover back on the PC and replace the screws. (And just think how impressed your friends will be when you casually mention that you installed a new board in your PC today.)

CD-ROM players may be internal, such as a board, or external, like a printer. Either way, you usually connect them to your PC with a cable.

Read the documentation that comes with your device for details about attach-ing multimedia equipment to your PC. You may also need to attach the device to other equipment. A sound board, for example, requires speakers or head-phones. The documentation explains how to make that connection.

Some multimedia devices include a test program; after you attach the device to your PC, you can run this program to check the connection. After you plug in a Sound Blaster board, for example, you can run a test to determine whether it's successfully connected to both your PC and your speakers. If the test is successful, you're rewarded with music you never thought you would hear from a computer. You learn two things from the test: that the speakers are correctly attached, and that the PC and the board are communicating.

Note: Make sure that you write down any information that the test program gives you about the installation. For example, the Sound Blaster test may tell you that the board is currently using I/O address #220 and Interrupt #7. You will need this information later when you install the driver in Windows.

18

To install the driver, you also need to have on-hand both the original Windows diskettes and the diskettes that come with the device. The Windows diskettes are likely to contain the driver you need for the device; if not, the driver probably is on the diskettes that come with the device. If you have a choice between using the Windows driver or one that comes with the device, choose the Windows driver unless the device documentation gives you good reason not to. The Windows driver is sure to be compatible with Windows. If the driver you need is on neither set of diskettes, call the device manufacturer to see whether they have a Windows driver. If they don't, install the device with the generic driver contained in Windows.

Installing a Device Driver

When you have successfully attached your multimedia device, follow these steps to install the driver and set it up in Windows:

1. In the Windows Program Manager, open the Main Window, and then choose the Control Panel.

18

The Control Panel window appears.

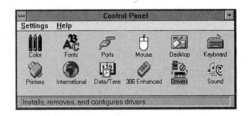

2. Choose the Drivers icon. (Double-click the Drivers icon with the mouse; or press the arrow keys to select it, and then press ⏎Enter.)

The Drivers dialog box appears, display-ing a list of the drivers already installed.

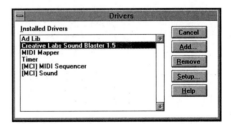

3. Choose the Add button.

482

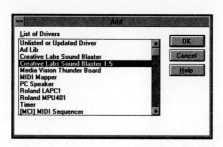

The Add dialog box appears, listing the drivers that Windows supplies.

4. Select your equipment's name in the List of Drivers, and choose OK or press ↵Enter. If your equipment is not listed, select Unlisted or Updated Driver.

The Install Driver dialog box appears, prompting you to insert the diskette containing the device driver. The message tells you exactly which diskette to insert.

18

5. Insert into drive A the diskette containing the driver. If your driver is located on a different drive or directory in your PC, type the drive and directory names (but not the driver file name).

If you don't know where the driver is located, choose Browse. In the Browse dialog box, select the drive and directory containing the device driver, and then choose OK or press ↵Enter.

483

6. When you return to the Add dialog box, choose OK or press ⏎Enter.

Depending on the driver, a setup dialog box appears, requesting configuration information. This example shows the Sound Blaster Setup dialog box.

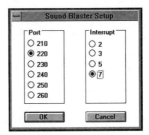

7. Referring to the notes you took when you tested your device (if the device has a test), select the necessary setup information, and choose OK or press ⏎Enter.

8. If Windows requires additional drivers to go with the one you installed, the program installs them automatically and may ask you for additional setup information. Respond to any dialog box that appears, and choose OK or press ⏎Enter.

18

If the installation is complete, a dialog box advises you that you must restart Windows for your installation to take effect.

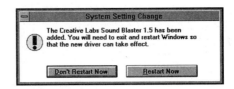

9. Choose **R**estart Now to restart Windows so that you can use your driver.

Setting Up a Device Driver

Windows has only a limited number of channels through which it can communicate with devices such as sound boards and CD-ROM players. When you install and set up your new device, you must make sure that the settings you choose don't conflict with any settings already in use by other devices. Testing the equipment after you connect it to your PC is the best way to be sure that no conflict exists; however, a conflict may exist if you have trouble using your device after you connect it, install it, and set it up. Refer to the device's documentation to determine where the conflict lies, contact the manufacturer, or call the Microsoft support line (the telephone number is included in Appendix C, "Help, Support, and Resources").

To make changes to the driver setup, follow these steps:

1. Choose the Drivers icon in the Control Panel. The Drivers dialog box appears.
2. Select the driver you want to set up from the Installed Drivers list.
3. Choose the Setup button. (The Setup button is dimmed if your driver requires no settings.) The Setup dialog box appears.
4. Select the setup options you need, referring to the device's documentation.
5. Choose OK or press ↵Enter.
6. When the System Setting Change dialog box appears, choose Restart Now if you want your changes to take effect immediately.

Removing a Device Driver

If you no longer are using a driver, you can remove it from the Installed Drivers list. Doing so doesn't remove it from your hard disk, so you can easily reconnect it later. Do not remove the drivers that Windows installed automatically (just to be safe, don't remove any drivers you don't recognize).

To remove a driver, follow these steps:

1. Choose the Drivers icon in the Control Panel. The Drivers dialog box appears.
2. Select the driver you want to remove from the Installed Drivers list.
3. Choose the Remove button.

The Remove dialog box appears, prompting you to confirm the removal of the driver.

4. Choose Yes to remove the driver.
5. Choose Restart Now if you want the removal to take effect immediately.

Installing a MIDI Driver

When you install some devices, like the Sound Blaster sound board, a Musical Instrument Digital Interface (MIDI) driver is automatically added. The driver appears as a new icon in the Control Panel, named MIDI Mapper.

When you install Windows, it includes some predefined MIDI settings. Your new device conforms to those settings and therefore should work flawlessly with Windows. You can change the settings, however, using the MIDI Mapper program in the Control Panel. You may need to change these settings if you're using a nonstandard MIDI setup or if your sound board doesn't include a MIDI setup.

To alter a MIDI setting, follow these steps:

1. In the Program Manager, select the Main window and choose the Control Panel.

If you have installed a MIDI device, MIDI Mapper is among the icons.

2. Choose the MIDI Mapper icon.

   The MIDI Mapper dialog box appears.

3. Make sure that the Show Setups option is selected; then from the Name list, select the setup you want to use.

4. Choose Close.

Creating a new MIDI setup is a complicated procedure that assumes you have a good understanding of MIDI concepts. Refer to Que's *Using Windows 3.1, Special Edition,* for details.

Operating Sound Recorder

To use sound on your PC, you should add a sound board that conforms to the Multimedia Personal Computer specifications for your PC. After adding the board, you must install it as described in the previous section "Adding Multimedia Drivers." If you are using high-level MIDI sound or a synthesizer, you also must install the drivers for those devices.

After you install your sound board, you can use the Windows accessory program, Sound Recorder, to record and play sound files that include music and voice (to record voice, you need a microphone). You also can edit and mix sound files and add special effects. Sound Recorder comes free with Windows 3.1, like all accessories, and was available as an optional "multimedia extension" with previous Windows versions.

Using Sound Recorder, you can play, record, and edit sounds with the WAVE format (Sound Recorder's file format). You can assign these sounds to events or use them in programs that support object linking and embedding (OLE). For example, you can embed a spoken message inside a Microsoft Excel spreadsheet file or a Word for Windows document. (Chapter 10 provides a detailed explanation of OLE.)

The Sound Recorder program appears on-screen as a small window with a menu across the top, buttons on the bottom, and an oscilloscope-like display in between. You use the menus to open, edit, and save sound files. You use the buttons to start and stop the recorder, just like a tape recorder. You watch the wave-like display to monitor your sound file's progress.

18

Starting Sound Recorder

To start Sound Recorder, follow these steps:

1. In the Program Manager, open the Accessories window.

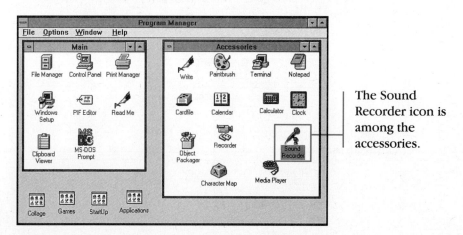

The Sound Recorder icon is among the accessories.

2. Choose Sound Recorder. (Double-click the Sound Recorder icon with the mouse; or press the arrow keys to select it, and then press ⏎Enter.)

The Sound
Recorder window
appears.

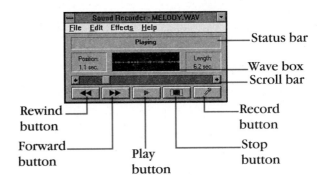

Status bar

Wave box
Scroll bar

Rewind
button

Record
button

Forward
button

Play
button

Stop
button

Opening and Playing Sounds

On a PC, sound is stored as a file, just like any other document. To play a sound, you must first start Sound Recorder (see the preceding section) and open the sound file.

To open and play a sound file, follow these steps:

1. Choose the File menu and select the Open command.

The Open dialog
box appears.

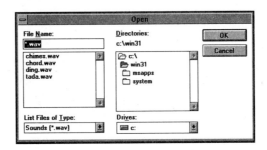

2. Choose the drive containing your file in the Drives list, if necessary, and select the directory in the Directories list. Select the file you want to open in the File Name list.

3. Choose OK or press ⏎Enter.

4. Choose the Play button.

488

In *Playing mode*, Sound Recorder displays sound waves in the Wave box.

The status bar reads Playing, and the Wave box shows a visual representation of the sound waves. The scroll box moves to the right as the file progresses.

Each time you choose the Play button, the sound plays from beginning to end. When the file is finished, the word Stopped appears in the status bar.

You can manually stop the file by choosing the Stop button (and resume it by choosing Play again). You also can move around in a sound file. To move forward 1/10 second, click the right arrow (to move backward, click the left arrow). To move in one-second increments, click the shaded part of the scroll bar in the direction you want to move. With the keyboard, press Tab to select the scroll bar and press the left- or right-arrow keys to move forward or backward 1/10 second.

Note: You can quickly move to the end of a sound file by choosing the Forward button or pressing the End key; you can move to the beginning by choosing the Rewind button or pressing Home.

Creating a Sound File

You can create a sound file by recording it from scratch, by adding to an existing sound file, by inserting one sound file into another, or by mixing two sound files together. To record, you must attach, install, and set up a microphone. Check your device documentation to learn how.

You can record up to one minute of sound.

To record a new sound file, follow these steps:

1. Choose the File menu and select the New command.
2. Choose the Record button.
3. Talk into the microphone to record your message.
4. Choose the Stop button when you're finished.

To record into an existing file, open the file and use the Play and Stop buttons to get to where you want to add more dialog. Choose the Record button and talk into the microphone. Choose Stop when you're finished, and save the file (see the section "Saving a Sound File," further in this chapter).

18

To insert one sound file into another, open the sound file into which you want to add another sound file, and use the Play and Stop buttons to get to the place where you want to add another sound file. Choose the Edit menu and select the Insert File command. Select the file you want to insert, and choose OK or press Enter. Save your new file.

Another alternative is to mix two files so that their sounds play simultaneously. One file might be music; the other voice. Open one of the files, and use Play and Stop to move to the place where you want to mix in another file. Choose the Edit menu and select the Mix With File command. Select the file you want to mix in, and choose OK. Save your new file. When you play the new mixed file, you hear both sounds at the same time. Mixing files is a good way to create a "voice over" with a musical background.

To delete part of a sound file, move to the position before or after which you want to delete the sound, and choose the Edit menu. Select either Delete Before Current Position or Delete After Current Position.

You can undo your changes any time before you save your sound file by choosing the File menu and selecting the Revert command.

18   Editing a Sound File

After you create a sound file, you can edit it by adding special effects. You can make it louder or softer, faster or slower, and you can add an echo or reverse the sound.

To edit your sound file, follow these steps:

1. Choose the File menu and select the Open command.
2. Select the file you want to edit and choose OK or press ⏎Enter.
3. Choose the Effects menu, and select one of the following options:

Option	Description
Increase Volume (by 25%)	Makes the sound file 25 percent louder.
Decrease Volume	Makes the sound file 25 percent softer.
Increase speed (by 100%)	Doubles the speed of the sound file.
Decrease Speed	Halves the speed of the sound file.
Add Echo	Adds an echo to the sound file.
Reverse	Plays the sound file backward.

You can undo your changes any time before you save your sound file by choosing the File menu and selecting the Revert command.

Saving a Sound File

After you create or edit a sound file, be sure to save it.

To save a sound file, follow these steps:

1. Choose the File menu and select the Save As command.
2. In the Drives list, select the drive where you want to save your file.
3. In the Directories list, select the directory where you want to save your file.
4. Type a file name in the File Name box. Include the file extension WAV to make the file easier to open later.
5. Choose OK or press ⏎Enter.

To save a file that already has a name, choose the File menu and select the Save command instead of the Save As command.

Assigning Sounds to Events

The simplest form of sound on your computer is the sound you can assign to events such as pressing the asterisk key or question mark and starting or stopping Windows. Windows comes equipped with several sound files you can assign to these events, or you can use Sound Recorder to create your own. You also can turn off system sounds so that your PC operates more discreetly. For details about assigning sounds to events and turning off system sounds, refer to the section "Turning Sound On or Off" in Chapter 7.

Exiting Sound Recorder

When you're finished playing your sound file, choose the File menu and select the Exit command.

Operating Media Player

Like Sound Recorder, Media Player is an accessory program that comes free with Windows 3.1 (it was available as an optional multimedia extension with previous versions of Windows). You can use Media Player to play multimedia devices installed on your MPC, including CD-ROM drives and videodisc players. You can play sound, animation, and MIDI music files designed for multimedia—or, if you have a CD-ROM player, you can play music CDs.

Using the Media Player program, you can play multimedia programs you have created or purchased. Many educational programs, stories, and games are now available for multimedia PCs.

Before you use Media Player, you must connect your multimedia device (usually a CD-ROM player, a VCR, or a synthesizer) to your PC, and you must install it in Windows and set it up to run with Windows. Refer to the previous section on "Adding Multimedia Drivers" to learn how.

Media Player displays in a small window containing menus, a scroll bar, and buttons. The menus enable you to open files, select the device on which to play the files, and switch between time and tracks. The scroll bar follows the progress of the file you play. The buttons play, pause, stop, and eject the media, just like a VCR or CD-ROM player.

Unlike Sound Recorder, you cannot use Media Player to create your own files. To create multimedia files, you must purchase a multimedia authoring kit such as Multimedia ToolBook from Asymetrix or Guide Media Extensions from Owl International.

18

Starting Media Player

Because Media Player is a Windows accessory, it is located in the Accessories window.

To start Media Player, follow these steps:

1. Activate the Accessories window in the Program Manager.

The Media Player icon is among the accessories.

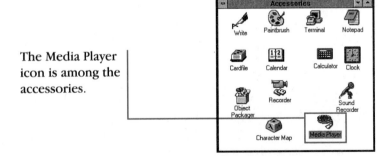

492

2. Choose Media Player. (Double-click the Media Player icon with the mouse; or press the arrow keys to select it, and then press ⏎Enter.)

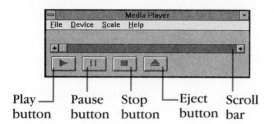

The Media Player window appears.

Play button   Pause button   Stop button   Eject button   Scroll bar

Choosing a Media Player Device

Before you can play your multimedia program, game, or story, you must specify the device on which you are going to play it. Two types of devices are available: *simple* and *compound.* A simple device plays whatever you physically load into the device; for example, you can load a music CD or CD-ROM disk into a CD-ROM player and use Media Player to play it. A compound device, on the other hand, consists of two components: the physical device and the computer file you want to play on that device; for example, you can use a sound board to play a computer file such as a MIDI file.

To choose a media device, follow these steps:

1. Choose the Device menu.

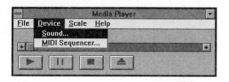

The devices listed in the Device menu depend on what's installed on your system.

2. Select the device you want to play.

   Note that simple devices are not followed by a dialog box. Compound devices, such as Sound and MIDI Sequencer in this example, are followed by a dialog box.

3. If you select a compound device, select in the dialog box the file you want to play, and choose OK or press ⏎Enter.

493

Opening a File

After you specify a compound device and open a file, you can open a different file without choosing the device again (unless you want to switch to a different device).

To open a file, follow these steps:

1. Choose the File menu and select the Open command. The Open dialog box appears.
2. In the Drives list, select the drive where your file is located.
3. In the Directories list, select the directory containing your file.
4. In the File Name list, select the file you want to open.
5. Choose OK or press ⏎Enter.

Windows includes two two-minute music files you can play on a compound device such as a sound board. These files are CANYON.MID and PASSPORT.MID and are located in your Windows directory.

Playing a Media Player File

After you select a device and either insert the medium, such as a CD-ROM disk, (if you selected a simple device) or open a file (if you selected a compound device), Media Player is ready to play. The buttons in the Media Player window enable you to play, pause, stop, and eject (if your device supports ejecting) the medium:

Button	Description
Play	Plays the medium in your simple device, or plays the file in your compound device.
Pause	Pauses the medium (choose either Pause or Play to restart).
Stop	Stops the medium (choose Play to restart).
Eject	Ejects the medium.

The scroll box in the scroll bar moves to the right as the medium or file plays.

.18

Changing the Scale and Moving to a Different Position

As Media Player plays, you can see its progress in the scroll bar. By default, no scale appears above the scroll bar in Media Player; however, two scales are available: time and tracks. These scales are similar to the display on a compact disc player: the *time scale* displays the playing time of the medium or file (the units depend on the length of the medium or file); the *track scale* displays the number of tracks on the medium or file. Because the scales appear above the scroll bar, you can move to a specific position in your file by watching the scale as you move the scroll box in the scroll bar.

To change the scale, follow these steps:

1. Choose the Scale menu.
2. Select the Time command.

The time scale appears.

Alternatively, select the Tracks command.

The tracks scale appears.

You can move to a different spot in your file by clicking the left or right arrow in the scroll bar; dragging the scroll box; clicking the scroll bar; or pressing the left-arrow, right-arrow, PgUp, or PgDn keys.

Exiting Media Player

When you finish playing your medium or file, choose the File menu and select the Exit command. If you are playing a simple device when you exit, that device continues to play; to stop play, you must turn off the device itself. If you are playing the "Complete Beatles Greatest Hits" in your CD-ROM player, for example, it continues to play after you exit Media Player, until you turn off the CD-ROM player.

18

Summary

Multimedia is an exciting new technology that turns your PC into a sound-and-video-equipped teacher, research assistant, storyteller, or musician. Your PC can look up information in a CD-ROM encyclopedia, read you a story, play you a tune, or any combination. You not only can hear what your PC has to say, but you can see what it has to show.

In this chapter you learned these important points:

- To operate multimedia, you need a CD-ROM player, speakers, and a sound board, all of which must conform to MPC standards so that they operate well with Windows.
- Before you can use your multimedia devices, you must connect, install, and set them up.
- You can use Sound Recorder to play existing sounds and record your own sounds.
- You can record up to a minute of speech, and you can combine sound files. For example, you can mix a music file with a voice file.
- You can use Media Player to play a CD or a file.
- Media Player works with simple devices, such as VCRs, to play whatever media you insert into the device. Media Player also works with compound devices to play a computerized music, animation, or voice file.

In the next chapter, "Integrating Multiple Programs," you learn how to share information between Windows programs.

18

Integrating Multiple Programs

One of the most useful features of Windows is its capability to run multiple programs—both Windows and DOS programs—at the same time and to transfer data between those programs. Windows enables you to use different Windows programs as though they were parts of a single program. By integrating programs, you multiply their power, making your work more efficient and your result more professional.

19

Key Terms in This Chapter

Data
Text, numbers, or graphics. Windows enables you to transfer data between documents and programs by copying and pasting, reading and saving other file formats, linking, and embedding. (Some forms of linking transfer both formats and data.)

Dynamic Data Exchange (DDE)
A feature of many Windows programs that enables those programs to pass data to documents in other Windows programs that support DDE. When you change data in the server document, Windows sends those changes to each client document.

Embedding
Stores data from one document from a Windows applet or program within another document from a Windows program. When you double-click embedded data, Windows loads the data into its original program so that you can change or update it.

Linking
Shares data in a document in one Windows program (the server) with a document in another Windows program (the client) through Dynamic Data Exchange (DDE).

Client
A document or program that receives embedded data.

Server
A document or program that supplies embedded data.

Macro
A program written in a special language built into a program. For example, Ami Pro, Microsoft Excel, and Microsoft Word for Windows all have macro languages. Many Windows programs, such as Polaris PackRat, come with macro programs that add commands to menus. You can use macros to make program integration easier.

Personal information manager (PIM)
A program that stores and manages personal information, such as personal contact lists, agendas, calendars, to-do lists, phone numbers, and names and addresses.

When you integrate multiple Windows programs, you can work in many new ways; the following are just a few examples:

- You can use PackRat, a personal information manager designed for Windows, to enter an address in a letter by selecting the name in the letter and then choosing a custom command from one of the word processing program's menus. PackRat finds the correct address and inserts it in the letter. You never see PackRat working. The macros that perform these tasks come with PackRat.

- Many corporations use Windows to link Microsoft Excel (a graphics-oriented spreadsheet program) to databases on a PC hard disk, on an SQL Server, or on a mainframe computer. Microsoft Excel includes the program Q+E, which enables you to link areas of a worksheet to a database. This feature is very useful for companies that want to write reports quickly or to analyze or chart database information: for example, as a user enters sales data into a mainframe or network database, another user can use Microsoft Excel to read that information and to create reports and charts that show changes against forecast sales. You can operate Q+E by using commands on a Microsoft Excel menu or control Q+E automatically by using macros.

- If you use Windows at home, in a small business, or in a corporate division, you may want to integrate Quicken and Microsoft Excel. Quicken is a popular personal financial manager that tracks multiple check books, credit cards, and personal investments. By linking data in a Quicken document to a Microsoft Excel worksheet, you can perform financial calculations and create charts beyond the capabilities of Quicken alone.

- You can update end-of-the-month budget and financial reports automatically by linking numbers and charts from Microsoft Excel to a professional word processing program such as Microsoft Word for Windows or Ami Pro or a presentation program such as Microsoft PowerPoint. When you change numbers in the worksheets, Windows also changes the numbers and charts in the report or presentation.

- Windows also makes DOS programs more productive. For example, you can use DOS programs under Windows to copy budget and report information from Lotus 1-2-3 for DOS or a DOS accounting program, and then paste that information into another DOS or Windows program. This procedure also can be helpful if you want to copy a column of numbers from Lotus 1-2-3 for DOS and paste them into the DOS accounting program. (Remember, however, that DOS programs can copy and paste data, but cannot link or embed data.)

19

Understanding Types of Integration

You can use the following types of integration with DOS and Windows programs:

- Copying and pasting data between DOS and Windows programs. DOS programs can receive only alphanumeric data (text and numbers).
- Transferring data by saving a file in one DOS or Windows program and then reading and converting the file into another DOS or Windows program.
- Linking data from one Windows program to another Windows program by using the Copy and Paste Link commands.
- Embedding data from one Windows program into another Windows program (actually storing the data from the server document within the client document).
- Linking data between Windows programs through Dynamic Data Exchange (DDE) under the control of a macro program.

One of the easiest ways to transfer data between programs is to use the copy and paste procedures common to all Windows programs. You select the data you want to copy from one Windows program, choose the Edit menu, select the Copy command, switch to the other Windows program, position the insertion point where you want to place that data, and then choose the Edit menu and select the Paste command. (If you are working with DOS programs, however, you must perform additional steps, and you can copy and paste only characters.)

The most common way to exchange data between DOS programs is to save the file in one program, exit that program, use a second program to convert the file's data and format, exit that program, and finally retrieve the file into a third program. You are using this method when you use 1-2-3 for DOS with its Translate program or WordPerfect for DOS with its Convert utility.

Windows programs significantly improve this method of exchanging data. Most Windows programs can read or save other file formats, automatically converting or translating the file at the same time that they open the file. Microsoft Excel, for example, reads and writes text files, Lotus 1-2-3 files, and dBASE files. Word for Windows reads and writes files for common word processing programs such as WordPerfect, WordStar, MultiMate, and the IBM standard DCA (RFT). Aldus PageMaker reads and saves files from Word for DOS, WordPerfect, and other word processing programs. With Windows

19

500

programs, the translation process is invisible to you. Thus, you can conveniently use different Windows programs in the same office.

Some Windows programs also have the capability to include in their documents all or part of files created in other Windows programs. In many Windows word processing programs, for example, you can create a document that contains not only its own text, but also all or part of documents from other word processing programs, worksheets or charts from various spreadsheet programs, and graphics from different graphics file formats. You can *link* this data to a file on-disk or *embed* it in the document. If you link the data to a file on-disk, you can update the client document to reflect changes you make to the server document (the file containing the original object).

Linking and embedding provide the greatest level of integration between Windows programs. *Linking* enables Windows to transfer any updated data from the server document to the client document. Windows can transfer the changes automatically or when you request an update. *Embedding* "buries" one program's data within another program's document. You do not have to worry about copying multiple files or keeping track of where the data came from—the information is all in one document, even though the data retains its original format and you can edit it by using its original Windows program.

If you are unfamiliar with the concepts or procedures of copying and pasting, linking, or embedding, you may want to read Chapter 4 to learn about basic copying and pasting in Windows programs, Chapter 10 to learn about linking and embedding with Windows programs, and Chapter 20 to learn about copying and pasting operations that involve DOS programs.

19

Integrating Windows Programs

The capability of Windows programs to operate together makes the power of multiple programs available for any task. You can use one program to enhance or analyze data from another program—Windows programs do not limit you to using the features of the program you use most frequently or the program you choose for the general task. Because Windows programs use similar menus and similar procedures, you can use multiple Windows programs without spending days to learn each one.

The following sections demonstrate some of the ways in which you can use Windows programs together to work more efficiently or to produce a more polished result than you could by using a single program.

Updating Word Processing Letters
with a Personal Information Manager

One way in which Windows can improve productivity is to link a *personal information manager* (PIM), such as PackRat, to a word processing program, such as Word for Windows or Ami Pro. Because you are using Windows programs, you can have PackRat pass the name, address, and client data to your word processing letter as you type that letter.

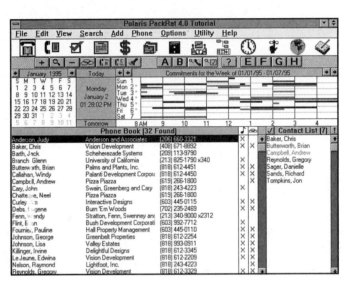

Linking PackRat
to Word for
Windows or Ami
Pro enables you
to look up and
enter names,
addresses, and
client data.

19

PIMs such as PackRat store names, addresses, contact dates, priority lists, agendas, phone books, and so on. Such programs also can contain many notes that you retrieve by searching for key words within the notes.

PackRat comes with a set of macros you can load into Word for Windows or Ami Pro. After you load the macros, they automatically appear as new commands on the word processing program's menus. These commands enable you to remain in the word processing program, but retrieve information from PackRat. After you type a name, for example, you can choose a command that looks up the appropriate address in PackRat and inserts that address below the name you typed. You also can generate form letters from a group of names and addresses you select in PackRat.

To retrieve a forgotten address for a name stored in PackRat and automatically insert that information into a letter you are typing in Word for Windows, follow these steps:

1. Position the insertion point in the Word for Windows letter where you want the name and address to appear.

2. Type the name for which you want to find the address. If you want to find Brian Butterworth's address, for example, type **Butterworth.**

3. Select the name you typed (or position the insertion point directly to the right of the name).

4. Choose the Insert menu and select the Find Name in PackRat command. (Find Name in PackRat is a custom Word for Windows command that PackRat adds to the Word for Windows Insert menu.)

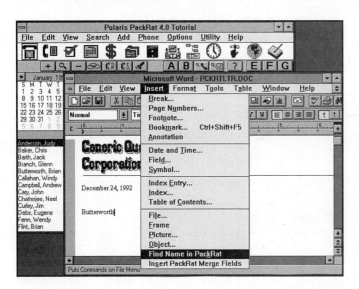

Some Windows programs provide custom commands to make integration with other Windows programs easy.

19

5. If PackRat finds a single name that matches the name you typed, it inserts and formats the corresponding address.

   If PackRat cannot find a single name that matches the name you typed, it displays a dialog box from which you can choose the correct name. When you select a name and choose OK, PackRat inserts and formats the address.

PackRat uses its phone and address lists to fill in the address in the Word for Windows document.

Pasting Worksheet Data and Charts into a Word Processing Program

One of the more frequent uses of copying and pasting data between Windows programs is to transfer tables of numbers and charts from a spreadsheet program such as Microsoft Excel to a word processing program such as Word for Windows, Ami Pro, or WordPerfect for Windows. Copying and pasting numeric data prevents wasted effort by retyping existing data, eliminates the possibility of typing incorrect numbers, and produces a more professional report with tables, charts, and illustrations integrated into the text body.

When you paste worksheet data and charts into a word processing document, the pasted data does not change when you change the related worksheet.

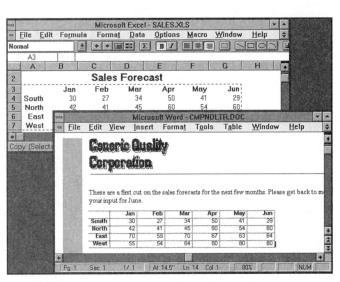

When you paste Microsoft Excel data into Word for Windows, Word builds a table to hold the data. You can format the cells, cell contents, and borders in the Word for Windows table by adding single or double outlines or shading, and even by making each cell a different width.

Follow these steps to copy worksheet data from Microsoft Excel and paste it into Word for Windows to produce a table of data that is not linked to the worksheet:

1. Activate the Microsoft Excel worksheet from which you want to copy data.

2. Select the cells you want to copy.

3. Choose the Edit menu and select the Copy command.

   Microsoft Excel copies the data to the Clipboard.

4. Activate the Word for Windows document into which you want to paste the copied data.

5. Position the insertion point in the document where you want the copied data to appear.

6. Choose the Edit menu and select the Paste command.

   Word for Windows pastes the data from the Clipboard.

The Microsoft Excel worksheet data appears as a table in Word for Windows. This table contains numbers and text just as though you typed the data directly into the Word for Windows document. Because you selected the Paste command instead of the Paste Special command from the Edit menu, Windows did not link the data to the Microsoft Excel file.

You can display the edges of cells as nonprinting gray lines on-screen by choosing the Table menu and selecting the Gridlines command. You also can use the Format Border command to format tables with single and double outlines. To apply shading to selected cells in the table, choose the Shading button in the Format Border dialog box.

When you paste Microsoft Excel worksheet data into some Windows programs, the program pastes each worksheet cell as a cell in a table. In other Windows programs, such as Windows Write, the program pastes each cell as data separated by tabs. To align data separated by tabs, select all the rows of data and then create new decimal or right tab settings.

Linking or Embedding Microsoft Excel Data and Charts into Word for Windows

You also can link or embed Microsoft Excel worksheet data and charts into a Word for Windows document. Windows provides two types of linking: you can copy and paste to create a link between an active worksheet and word processing document, or you can link the Word for Windows document to a Microsoft Excel file.

19

When you link or embed worksheet data and charts into a word processing document, you can update the linked or embedded data to reflect changes to the worksheet or chart.

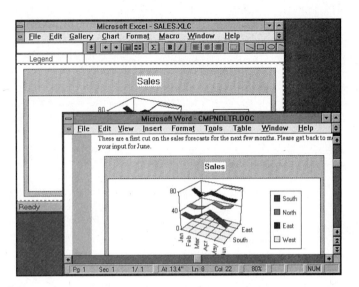

To link or embed Microsoft Excel worksheet data or a chart into a Word for Windows 2 document, follow these steps:

1. Activate the Microsoft Excel worksheet or chart you want to link or embed.

2. Save the worksheet or chart.

   Windows uses the file name to link the worksheet or chart; thus, you must save and name your original file to link it to a client document. To embed worksheet data or a chart, however, you do not need to save the original file.

3. To link or embed worksheet data, select the worksheet cells you want to link.

   To link or embed a chart, choose the Chart menu and select the Select Chart command.

4. Choose the Edit menu and select the Copy command.

   Microsoft Excel copies the data or chart to the Clipboard.

5. Activate the Word for Windows document in which you want to link or embed the data or chart.

19

6. Position the insertion point in the Word for Windows document where you want the data or chart to appear.

7. Choose the Edit menu and select the Paste Special command.

   Word for Windows displays the Paste Special dialog box.

8. To embed the data or chart, select Excel Worksheet Object or Excel Chart Object from the Data Type list, and then choose the Paste button.

   To link the data or chart, select one of the other alternatives (Formatted Text, Unformatted Text, Picture, or Bitmap), and then choose the Paste Link button.

The data or chart appears in the Word document. Chapter 10, "Using Object Linking and Embedding," describes how to update linked or embedded data.

If you later change the file name of the server worksheet or chart in Microsoft Excel, you must also change the linked file name in the Word for Windows document. To change or update the links, choose the Edit menu and select the Links command, as described in the section "Editing Links When Server File Names or Locations Change" in Chapter 10.

Linking Microsoft Excel to Databases

Windows' capability to integrate programs enables computer users to combine existing programs and use the combination for new purposes. For example, many corporations link Microsoft Excel and Q+E to personal-computer, SQL Server, or mainframe databases that hold accounting, sales, manufacturing, and inventory information. These corporations link selected Excel worksheets to corresponding portions of the databases and perform analysis as the data changes. Rather than waiting until the end of the month to learn how their business is changing, these corporations can examine the changes every day. For complex analyses and reports, the corporations can run this work at night by using a Microsoft Excel macro that automates the process.

19

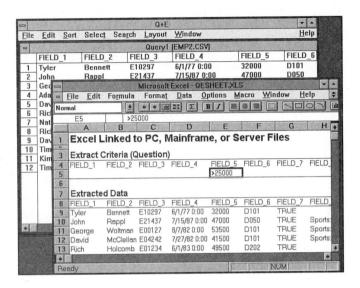

Linking a worksheet to local or mainframe databases means more responsive business analyses.

Microsoft Excel includes a free copy of Q+E. Pioneer Software, the manufacturer of Q+E, also sells a more comprehensive version of the program.

Microsoft Excel also includes add-in macros (QE.XLA and QESTART.XLA, stored in the EXCEL\XLSTART\QE directory) that add Q+E commands to Microsoft Excel's Data menu. The new commands enable you to link to a local or remote database manually and to extract selected data into your worksheet. This procedure uses the same steps you use to extract data from a Microsoft Excel database. You also can use Q+E by itself to query or edit the connected databases.

To automate the process of linking worksheets to databases, you can use Microsoft Excel's macro language to control the Q+E command language. This technique enables you to download and analyze database information during the night so that an updated report filled with charts and tables is waiting for you in the morning.

Enhancing Charts with a Graphics Program

You can copy and paste charts or graphics from one Windows program into other Windows programs for graphic enhancement or changes. For example, you can copy and paste a chart from Microsoft Excel into CorelDRAW!, Aldus Freehand, or another high-end drawing program and add artistic enhancements such as logos, symbols, or gradient shaded backgrounds.

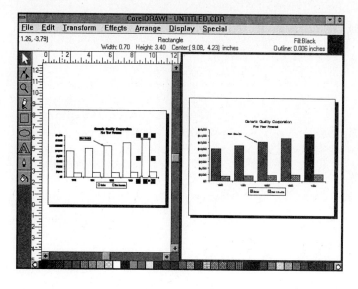

Copy a chart into a drawing program to add high-quality enhancements.

To copy a Microsoft Excel chart and paste it into CorelDRAW! for enhancement, follow these steps:

1. Activate the Microsoft Excel chart you want to copy.
2. Choose the Chart menu and select the Select Chart command.
3. Choose the Edit menu and select the Copy command.

    Microsoft Excel copies the chart to the Clipboard.
4. Start or activate CorelDRAW!. A new CorelDRAW! drawing opens automatically.
5. Choose the Edit menu and select the Paste command.

    CorelDRAW! pastes the chart from the Clipboard.

When you paste the Microsoft Excel chart into CorelDRAW!, each element of the chart (each column, arrow, string of text, and so on) becomes a separate object you can stretch, rotate, resize, or color individually. (In some drawing programs, you may need to select an *ungroup* command to convert the chart from a single entity into its component objects.)

Now you can use the professional art capabilities of CorelDRAW! to select and change any object on the chart. In the active window of the preceding illustration, the square handles at the corners of the rightmost column indicate that this object is selected. You also can paste in your corporate logo, add clip art, or add a shaded and colored background.

19

Copying and Linking between DOS and Windows Programs

Windows programs and DOS programs can exchange data in two ways: you can copy and paste data between the programs manually, or you can use a common file format that both programs understand. Copying and pasting data between Windows and DOS programs is easier when Windows is operating in 386-enhanced mode. If you run Windows in 386-enhanced mode, you can switch between programs easily and select portions of the screen to copy and paste into another program. If you run Windows in standard mode, Windows can copy only the entire screen of data, not portions of the screen.

Different DOS programs paste multiple lines of data differently, depending on how the program deals with the end of a line. If you paste multiple lines of data into 1-2-3 for DOS, for example, the program pastes all lines of data from the Clipboard into one worksheet cell, entering each line on top of the preceding line. (To transfer data into 1-2-3 for DOS, therefore, you should copy and paste one cell at a time.) DOS word processing programs paste multiple lines of copied data onto separate lines, but end each line with a hard return.

Capturing DOS and Windows Screens for Documentation

Windows includes excellent tools for creating training materials and documentation. Windows makes it easy to create software documentation because you can simultaneously run the software you want to document and the Windows software you are using to create the documentation.

When a DOS program is running full screen, you can capture a screen as characters. When a DOS program is running in a window, you can capture a screen as a graphic. To switch between full screen and window modes, press Alt+Enter (remember, however, that you can run a DOS program in a window only in 386-enhanced mode).

The following steps describe how to capture a 1-2-3 for DOS screen and paste it into Windows composition software, such as PageMaker, Word for Windows, or Ami Pro. You also can use this technique to capture screens of Windows programs:

1. Start Lotus 1-2-3 for DOS and retrieve the worksheet you want to document.

19

2. Start the Windows software you are using to write the documentation. (This example uses PageMaker.)

3. Activate the 1-2-3 worksheet. Run 1-2-3 full screen if you want to capture the worksheet as characters. Run 1-2-3 in a window if you want to capture the worksheet as a graphic. (Press [Alt]+[↵Enter] to switch between full screen and windows modes.)

4. Capture an image of the 1-2-3 screen by pressing [PrtSc]. (On some computers, you may need to press [Alt]+[PrtSc].)

   Windows stores the screen text in the Clipboard. If you were capturing a screen of a Windows program, Windows would store the screen as a graphic (for more information, see Chapter 4, "Editing, Copying, and Moving in Windows").

5. Activate the PageMaker window and position the insertion point where you want the captured screen to appear.

6. Choose the **E**dit menu and select the **P**aste command.

   If you captured the 1-2-3 screen as characters, it appears in PageMaker as though you typed the screen text. If you captured the screen as a graphic, it appears in PageMaker as a graphic.

7. If you captured the 1-2-3 screen as characters and the pasted text is not aligned correctly, select the text and change the font to Courier (a nonproportional typeface) or insert tabs to align the columns. If you captured the screen as a graphic, you can use PageMaker techniques to move or resize the image.

19

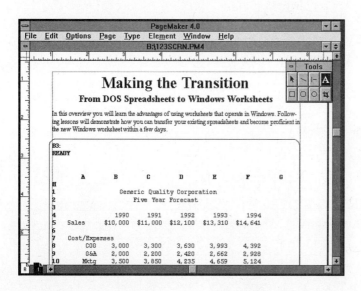

Press the [PrtSc] key to capture screens and paste them into Windows programs.

If you paste a graphics screen image into PageMaker, Word for Windows, or Ami Pro, the image appears as a picture that you can resize or crop. These Windows programs also enable you to draw lines and borders around screen images. You can print the resulting documentation with a personal computer printer or print the documentation to a file for typesetting on a Linotronic typesetter.

Linking DOS Word Processing Files into Word for Windows Documents

Word for Windows and some other Windows word processing programs (such as WordPerfect for Windows) also can link to DOS word processing, spreadsheet, and database files on-disk. To link a Word for Windows document to a WordPerfect document, for example, follow these steps:

1. Start Word for Windows and open the file (or create a new file) in which you want to insert the WordPerfect document.

2. Position the insertion point in the Word for Windows document where you want to insert the WordPerfect document.

3. Choose the Insert menu and select the File command.

4. Select All Files (*.*) from the List Files of Type list so that you can see WordPerfect file names (by default, Word for Windows displays only Word for Windows file names).

5. If necessary, select the drive containing the WordPerfect file from the Drives list, and select the directory containing the WordPerfect file from the Directories list.

6. From the File Name list, select the WordPerfect file you want to insert in the Word document.

7. Select the Link to File check box.

    Word for Windows links the data in Word for Windows to the WordPerfect file on-disk.

8. Choose OK or press Enter.

Word for Windows reads the file from disk and displays it on-screen with its original WordPerfect format, tables, and pictures. If you later change the WordPerfect file, you can update the Word document to reflect those changes by selecting the inserted data and pressing the F9 key.

19

Linking 1-2-3 Worksheets to Microsoft Excel Worksheets

If you use Microsoft Excel, but work with others who use Lotus 1-2-3 for DOS, you may want to link your Microsoft Excel worksheets to their 1-2-3 for DOS worksheets. Because Microsoft Excel can read and write 1-2-3 for DOS worksheets and read 1-2-3 for DOS charts, you also can use Microsoft Excel to consolidate 1-2-3 for DOS worksheets or to enhance 1-2-3 for DOS reports or charts.

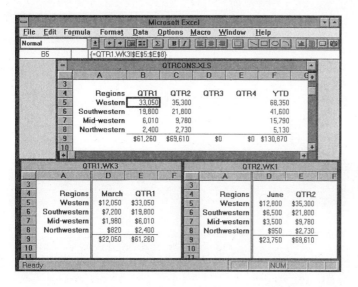

Microsoft Excel can link to, consolidate, and enhance Lotus 1-2-3 for DOS worksheets.

19

To open 1-2-3 worksheets in Microsoft Excel, follow these steps:

1. Activate Microsoft Excel.

2. Choose the File menu and select the Open command.

3. Change the File Name pattern to *.WK? and choose OK so that you can see the 1-2-3 file names (by default, Microsoft Excel displays only Excel file names).

   Alternatively, in the List Files of Type list, select a Lotus 1-2-3 format.

4. If necessary, select the drive containing the 1-2-3 worksheet from the Drives list, and select the directory containing the 1-2-3 worksheet from the Directories list.

5. In the File Name list, select the first 1-2-3 worksheet you want to link to Microsoft Excel. If the 1-2-3 worksheet has attached graphs, Microsoft Excel asks whether you want to convert them.

   Microsoft Excel reads and opens the 1-2-3 worksheet in Microsoft Excel; you do not have to perform any conversion.

6. Choose OK or press ⏎Enter.

7. Repeat steps 2 through 6 until all the 1-2-3 worksheets you want to link are open in Microsoft Excel.

After you open the 1-2-3 worksheets in Microsoft Excel, you can link them to Microsoft Excel worksheets. To link an open 1-2-3 worksheet to a Microsoft Excel worksheet, follow these steps:

1. Activate the 1-2-3 worksheet you want to link to a Microsoft Excel worksheet.

2. Select the cell or range of cells you want to link.

3. In Microsoft Excel, choose the Edit menu and select the Copy command.

4. Activate the Microsoft Excel worksheet you want to receive the linked data.

5. In the Microsoft Excel worksheet, select the top left cell of the area where you want the linked data to appear.

6. Choose the Edit menu and select the Paste Link command.

The 1-2-3 worksheet cells are now linked to the Excel worksheet. If someone changes data in the 1-2-3 worksheet, the change appears in the Microsoft Excel worksheet the next time you open the Microsoft Excel worksheet.

Note: To update the 1-2-3 worksheet while it is open in Microsoft Excel, use the File Save As command to save the worksheet in 1-2-3 format.

You also can use Microsoft Excel to consolidate or "roll up" data from 1-2-3 for DOS and Microsoft Excel worksheets. You can use Microsoft Excel's Data Consolidate command to consolidate data located anywhere on the server worksheets, even when the data has different row or column headings and a different order on each worksheet. For more information on consolidating data, see Que's *Using Excel 4 for Windows,* Special Edition.

If you rename or move the 1-2-3 worksheets that you link to Microsoft Excel, however, you must choose the File menu and select the Links command to update the links. Also, if you create a chart or use an Excel feature that Lotus 1-2-3 does not recognize, you lose those changes and additions when you save the 1-2-3 worksheet. (Microsoft Excel automatically saves linked 1-2-3 worksheets in 1-2-3 format.)

19

Copying from DOS Programs into DOS and Windows Programs

You can copy text or numbers from any DOS program and paste what you copy into a Windows program or another DOS program. Suppose, for example, that you want to copy tabbed data from a memo in WordPerfect for DOS and paste that data into a Microsoft Excel worksheet.

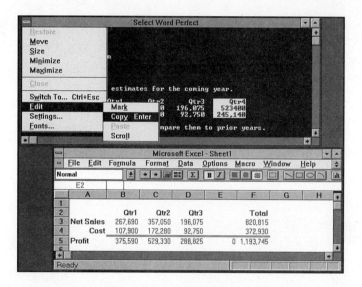

When you copy tabbed data, Microsoft Excel separates the data into cells in the worksheet.

19

Usually, copying from DOS programs is efficient only when Windows is operating in 386-enhanced mode. When Windows is in 386-enhanced mode, you can copy selected portions of the DOS program screen to the Clipboard. When Windows is in standard mode, however, you must copy the entire screen and edit the data after you paste it into another program.

To copy data from a document in a DOS program and paste it into a document in a Windows program or another DOS program (when Windows is operating in 386-enhanced mode), follow these steps:

1. Activate the DOS program and open the file from which you want to copy text or numbers.

2. Press Alt + ↵Enter until the DOS program displays in a window.

3. Use the DOS program's movement keys to display the text or numbers you want to copy.

4. Choose the Program Control menu by clicking the hyphen icon at the top left corner of the window or by pressing Alt + **space bar**.

515

5. Select the **Edit** command and select **Mark** from the cascading menu.

6. With the mouse, select the text or numbers you want to copy. Alternatively, with the keyboard, move the square cursor to a corner of the text or numbers you want to copy, press and hold (⇧Shift), and then press the arrow keys to select the information.

   The program highlights the selected text or numbers.

7. Choose the Program Control menu again.

8. Select the **Edit** command and select Copy Enter from the cascading menu.

   The program copies the selected text or numbers to the Clipboard.

To paste the copied text or numbers into another program, follow these steps:

1. Activate the program and open the file into which you want to paste the copied text or numbers.

2. Move the insertion point or cursor to the place where you want to paste the text or numbers.

3. If you are pasting the text or numbers into a Windows program, choose the **Edit** menu and select the **Paste** command.

   If you are pasting the text or numbers into a DOS program, press (Alt)+(↵Enter) to put the DOS program into a window. Choose the Program Control menu, select the **Edit** command, and then select **Paste** from the cascading menu.

Windows pastes text or numbers copied from DOS programs as lines of text.

Summary

An important feature of Windows is that multiple Windows and DOS programs can work together and share data. You can link Windows programs so that data passes between them automatically or under the control of the user. You (or a consultant) can build integrated business systems that were never before possible.

The most important points covered in this chapter are the following:

■ You can use Windows to copy and paste text and numbers between any Windows programs. Use the **Edit Copy** command to copy the selected data and the **Edit Paste** command to insert the data.

■ You easily can link many Windows programs so that they pass data automatically. To copy selected data, choose the Edit menu and select the Copy command; to insert the data, choose the Edit menu and select the Paste Link or Paste Special command. Remember, though, that if you change the file name of the server data file, the Windows program no longer knows where to find the data for updating.

■ You can embed data created in one Windows program into the document of another Windows program. After you embed data in a document, you can conveniently pass files to another person without worrying about breaking links between data.

■ You can use macro commands to link many Windows programs so that they share data when needed. Some programs, such as Q+E or PackRat, come with macros that add commands to the menus of other Windows programs. You can integrate the programs by choosing these commands.

In the next chapter, you learn more about running DOS programs under Windows. Depending on whether your computer is operating in standard mode or 386-enhanced mode, you can run DOS programs full screen or in windows. When you run DOS programs in windows, you can take advantage of some Windows commands as you work in the DOS programs.

19

Running DOS Programs

Windows gives DOS programs, such as Lotus 1-2-3 for DOS and WordPerfect for DOS, more capabilities than they have running under DOS. With Windows, you can run more than one DOS program at a time, as well as copy and paste text or numbers to other DOS or Windows programs.

Although DOS programs gain features under Windows, DOS programs running under Windows do not have all the features of programs designed for Windows. Windows features not available to DOS programs include standardized menus, dialog boxes for quick access to options, better memory use, linking to pass data between programs, and embedding of one program's data into another program's document.

In addition, DOS programs use their own screen and printer drivers. Even if you run a DOS program under Windows, the program cannot use the screens or print drivers shared by Windows programs. DOS programs also cannot take advantage of the Print Manager's capability to queue printing jobs so that you can go back to work while the Print Manager controls printing.

Loading and running DOS programs

Controlling DOS programs

Setting up DOS programs for 386-enhanced mode

Why Windows uses PIFs

How Windows sets up PIFs

Creating a PIF

Editing a PIF

Managing PIFs

Key Terms in This Chapter

DOS program	A program that does not take full advantage of Windows capabilities. You can run these programs in DOS without using Windows. DOS programs include Lotus 1-2-3 Release 2.x, 1-2-3 Release 3.x, WordPerfect for DOS, and dBASE IV.
Device contention	A conflict that occurs when two or more DOS programs need to use the same printer or modem at the same time.
PIF Editor	A program that enables you to control how a specific DOS program runs under Windows.
PIF	Program information file. A file containing the characteristics that determine how Windows works when a specific DOS program runs.
Standard mode	The normal mode for running Windows on an 80286, 80386, or 80486 machine.
386-enhanced mode	An advanced Windows operating mode for 80386 and 80486 machines. 386-enhanced mode has better memory management features for running DOS programs.

20

Running DOS Programs in Different Modes

DOS programs running under Windows operate somewhat differently depending on whether Windows is in standard mode or 386-enhanced mode. The current mode depends on the computer processor, the available memory, and the mode you specified upon start-up.

You can learn whether Windows is running in standard mode or 386-enhanced mode by choosing the Help menu from the Program Manager and selecting the About Program Manager command. The About Program Manager dialog box indicates whether you are in standard mode or 386-enhanced mode, how much memory is available (including virtual memory), and what percentage of system resources is free.

Running DOS Programs in Standard Mode

Standard mode is the normal mode for running Windows on a 286, 386, or 486 machine. In standard mode, DOS programs run full screen rather than in windows. Full-screen display of one DOS program does not prevent you from running multiple DOS programs, but you can see and work with only one program at a time. The inactive programs (the programs not currently on-screen) appear as icons. The active program appears on-screen just as it appears when it runs in DOS without Windows.

When you run DOS programs under Windows in standard mode, you can start more DOS programs than otherwise would fit in the computer memory. Each time you start a DOS program, Windows creates on your hard disk a temporary storage area, called the *application swap file*. When the program and data are active, they remain in memory. When the program and data are inactive and Windows needs extra memory, Windows switches them to the application swap file. This capability makes your computer's available memory seem larger, but if your hard disk is cluttered, slow, or has little free space, Windows may run more slowly. You also may not be able to run as many DOS programs at one time. When you exit the DOS program, Windows deletes the temporary application swap file.

You also can run more than one copy of many DOS programs.

Running DOS Programs in 386-Enhanced Mode

386-enhanced mode is an advanced Windows operating mode for 386 and 486 machines. 386-enhanced mode has better memory management features for running DOS programs. In 386-enhanced mode, you can run DOS programs full screen or display them in windows. Displaying DOS programs in windows is convenient when you are copying and pasting between programs or comparing results from two programs.

20

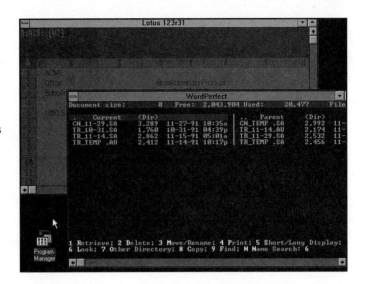

In 386-enhanced mode, you can run multiple DOS programs (such as Lotus 1-2-3 Release 3.1 and WordPerfect 5.1) in separate windows.

When you run DOS programs under Windows in 386-enhanced mode, however, Windows does not use application swap files; you must have sufficient memory to hold all the programs you want to run simultaneously.

Starting and Running DOS Programs

You can start DOS programs the same way you start Windows programs—from an icon in the Program Manager or from a file in the File Manager. You also can start DOS programs in other ways—you can choose the program's *program information file* (PIF) from the File Manager or open a DOS command window and run the program from the DOS prompt.

A PIF determines how Windows works when you run a specific DOS program. During the Windows installation process, the Windows Setup program automatically creates PIFs for the DOS programs you choose. If Windows did not create a PIF for a DOS program, Windows runs that program using the settings in a default PIF.

Note: When running Windows, do not run DOS utilities or programs that modify files or the file allocation table. When running, these programs may modify the temporary files that Windows leaves open for its use. If the utilities and programs destroy or modify the temporary files, Windows may freeze, you may lose data, and you may need to reinstall Windows. These programs include Mace Utilities, Norton Utilities, PC Tools, and Vopt, as well as the DOS

20

CHKDSK command when used with the /F switch. You use these utilities and programs to unerase or undelete files and to defragment or compact your disk. Such programs are extremely useful, but you should not use them while Windows is running.

Starting a DOS Program from the Program Manager

When you installed Windows, you had the option to make Windows find your DOS programs, create program item icons and PIFs for your DOS programs, and put those icons in a program group. If you did not have Windows set up your DOS programs when you installed Windows, you can accomplish the same thing by running the Windows Setup program from the Main program window at any time.

You can start a DOS program from a program group window in the Program Manager by double-clicking the program item icon or by pressing an arrow key to select the icon and then pressing Enter (just as you start a Windows program). Chapter 5, "Grouping Programs and Documents," describes starting a program from the program item icon.

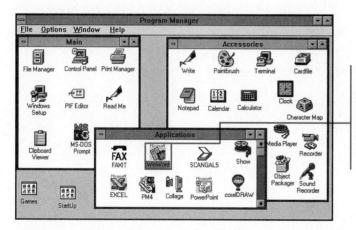

In this example, the program item icon for Word for Windows (in the Applications group) is selected.

20

Starting a DOS Program from the File Manager

You also can start a DOS program from the File Manager. Open the File Manager and then open a directory window for the directory that contains the program file or the PIF for the program. Program file names have the extension COM, EXE, or BAT. When you find the program file or its PIF (which has the same file name, but the extension PIF), double-click the file name or PIF or select the file or PIF, and then press Enter.

523

To learn more about the File Manager, see Chapter 6, "Managing Files." In a few cases, Windows cannot run a DOS program with the default PIF settings. For these programs, you must create a custom PIF (see the section "Editing a PIF," further in this chapter).

Running Multiple DOS Programs

To run multiple DOS (or Windows) programs, start the first program with the Program Manager or File Manager. Start the other programs by activating the Task List (by double-clicking the desktop or pressing Ctrl+Esc), choosing the Program Manager, and then starting the other programs from their program item icons.

If the computer's memory or hard disk storage is not sufficient to start all the programs you need, Windows displays a warning dialog box. To increase available memory, close unneeded documents or programs. To increase available hard disk space, erase or remove unneeded files.

You can switch between running programs by double-clicking the desktop (if it's visible) or pressing Ctrl+Esc to open the Task List and then choosing the desired program, or by pressing Alt+Tab until the desired program's name appears (and then releasing both keys).

If you are running DOS programs in 386-enhanced mode, you can toggle between full-screen and window display of the current program by pressing Alt+Enter.

20

Running DOS from Windows

As the Windows Setup program installs program groups, it also installs an MS-DOS Prompt program item icon in the Main program group. Starting the MS-DOS Prompt program runs COMMAND.COM full screen. From the DOS prompt (for example, C:\>), you can run DOS internal and external commands—such as DIR, COPY, and FORMAT—just as you run these commands using DOS. To quit the MS-DOS Prompt program, type EXIT and press Enter.

When you start the MS-DOS Prompt program, DOS appears full screen. You can run DOS in a window by pressing Alt+Enter, but the Windows Setup program does not create a PIF for the MS-DOS Prompt program during the Windows installation process. If you always want to run the MS-DOS Prompt program in a window (in 386-enhanced mode), you must create a PIF for COMMAND.COM and make the MS-DOS Prompt program execute this PIF rather than COMMAND.COM. To learn how to create a PIF, refer to the section "Creating a PIF Manually," further in this chapter.

Running DOS Memory-Resident Programs

Some DOS programs are designed to be loaded into memory with other DOS programs. Programs that "co-reside" in memory are called *terminate-and-stay-resident* (TSR) programs. A well-known TSR program is SideKick.

You can start a TSR program as you would any program—by installing it in the Program Manager and then double-clicking the program item icon. When the TSR program is running, treat it as you would any other DOS program.

You can switch to a TSR program by double-clicking the desktop or pressing Ctrl+Esc to open the Task List, and then choosing the TSR; or by pressing Alt+Tab until the TSR's name appears, and then releasing both keys. You also can press the key combination that usually activates the program.

Controlling DOS Programs

Windows enables you to run multiple DOS programs, switch from one program to another, and copy and paste text and numbers between programs.

Switching between Full Screen and a Window

20

If you are operating in 386-enhanced mode, you can toggle between running a DOS program full screen or in a window by pressing Alt+ Enter.

Switching between Programs

Windows uses the same key combinations to switch between programs, regardless of whether they are Windows or DOS programs. To switch from an active DOS program to another program, press Alt+Tab until you see the window or name of the program you want to activate.

Another way to switch between programs is to use the Task List. To minimize a full-screen DOS program to an icon and display the Task List so that you can activate a different program, press Ctrl+Esc.

Some DOS programs prevent keyboard use in some operating modes; therefore, Alt+Tab (to switch between programs) and Ctrl+Esc (to activate the Task List) may not work. To switch back to Windows, return to the program's normal operating mode and then press Alt+Tab or Ctrl+Esc. If, for example, you are displaying a graph in 1-2-3 Release 2.2, press Esc to return to the spreadsheet or menu, and then press Alt+Tab or Ctrl+Esc. After you return to Windows, you can switch between programs by using the keyboard or mouse techniques described in Chapter 3, "Operating Windows."

Using the Control Menu

DOS programs running in 386-enhanced mode have a Program Control menu similar to that of Windows programs. You use the Program Control menu to copy and paste information and to move the icon when the running DOS program is minimized. In 386-enhanced mode, the Program Control menu controls whether the program runs full screen or in a window, and it determines the window size and temporary operating settings.

To activate the Program Control menu, press Alt+space bar. If the program is in a window, you also can click the Program Control menu at the top left corner of the window.

The Program Control menu contains the commands to Restore, Move, Size, Minimize, or Maximize a DOS program window. You also can use the Program Control menu to Switch To the Task List, copy and paste data, change the DOS operation settings, or change the size of fonts in the window.

A DOS program that you reduce to an icon also has a Program Control menu. The Minimize command shrinks the program to an icon, and the Maximize command expands the program to a window or full screen.

This example shows the Program Control menu for a DOS program.

Using a Mouse with DOS Programs

When a DOS program is full screen, you can use the mouse just as if you were running that program in DOS—to choose menus, select objects, and so on (if the program supports a mouse and you installed the mouse driver).

When a DOS program is in a window, the mouse operates under Windows control. You can use the mouse to select areas you want to copy and paste or to choose commands from the Program Control menu, but not to choose program menus or select graphics objects.

A DOS program that does not support a mouse gains Windows mouse utility when the program is in a window, but has no mouse utility when the program is full screen.

Sizing and Scrolling DOS Programs

When a DOS program is in a window (in 386-enhanced mode), you can use the mouse to restore, move, size, maximize, or minimize the window. To resize a window, you drag the appropriate edge of the window (you cannot, however, resize a maximized window). To minimize or maximize a window, you click the minimize or maximize button at the top right corner of the window. To move a window, you drag its title bar.

You also can use the keyboard to restore, move, size, maximize, or minimize a window. Press Alt+space bar to display the Program Control menu and then press the underlined letter for the Restore, Move, Size, Minimize, or Maximize command. If you choose Move, you then press the arrow keys to move the window, and press Enter to fix its location. If you choose Size, press the arrow key that points toward the edge you want to change, press the arrow keys to move that edge in or out, and then press Enter to fix its size.

When you reduce the size of a DOS program's window, portions of the program remain outside the window, and vertical and horizontal scroll bars appear at the side and bottom of the window. To see the portions of the program that are outside the window, you must scroll the window. Note, however, that you cannot scroll the window to see more information than normally appears on one screen.

To scroll a window by using the mouse, click the up or down arrow on the vertical scroll bar to scroll up or down, or click the left or right arrow on the horizontal scroll bar to scroll left or right.

To scroll a window by using the keyboard, choose the Program Control menu by pressing Alt+space bar, select the Edit command, and then select the Scroll

20

command from the cascading menu. The window's title bar changes to indicate that the program is in Scroll mode (for example, Lotus 1-2-3 becomes Scroll Lotus 1-2-3). Press the arrow keys, PgUp, PgDn, Home, or End to scroll the window. When you finish scrolling, press Esc or Enter to exit Scroll mode.

Copying and Pasting Information between Programs

DOS programs running under Windows can use the Windows Clipboard. Because Windows uses the same Clipboard for all programs, you can copy and paste data from a DOS program to a Windows program, from a Windows program to a DOS program, or to copy text between two DOS programs. (You cannot, however, use the more powerful features of Windows, such as the common menu system, linked data, or embedded objects.)

Copying or Capturing DOS or Windows Screens

In 386-enhanced mode, you can copy a full or partial screen from a DOS program; the screen can contain text or graphics. In standard mode, you can copy only a full screen of text or a full-screen graphic from a DOS program. All Windows programs can receive copied text, and Windows programs designed to work with graphics can receive copied graphics. DOS programs can receive only copied text.

Copying or Capturing a Full Screen

To capture a full screen of text or graphics, press the PrtSc (Print Screen) key. (Some keyboards, however, require you to press Alt+PrtSc to capture the entire screen.)

Windows copies a full screen from a DOS text program (such as a Lotus 1-2-3 worksheet or a WordPerfect document) to the Clipboard as text characters. Windows copies a screen from a DOS graphics program or a Windows program to the Clipboard as a bit-mapped graphic. From the Clipboard, you can paste the image into other programs or save the image by using the Clipboard Viewer.

Capturing an image of a Windows or DOS program screen with the PrtSc (or Alt+PrtSc) key and pasting that image into Word for Windows, Ami Pro, or PageMaker is a quick way to produce polished documentation or training materials. (A full screen usually contains too much data for normal copying and pasting.)

20

To view the screen that Windows copied to the Clipboard, start the Clipboard Viewer from the Main program group in the Program Manager. You can see the contents of the Clipboard in the Clipboard Viewer window.

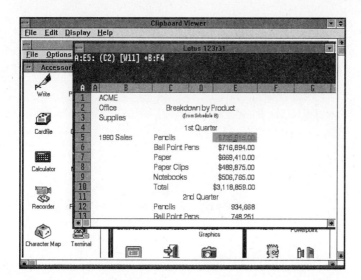

The Clipboard Viewer displays or saves screens you have captured.

Copying or Capturing a Partial Screen

In 386-enhanced mode, you can press Alt+PrtSc to capture only the active window. (In standard mode, you can capture or copy only the full screen.)

To use the mouse to copy a partial screen of text or graphics, follow these steps:

1. Activate the DOS program in which you want to copy or capture a partial screen. Press Alt+↵Enter until that program appears in a window.

2. Use your program's DOS techniques to scroll the document until the information you want to copy appears in the window.

3. Click the Program Control menu at the top left corner of the screen, select the Edit command, and then select the Mark command from the cascading menu.

4. Drag the mouse to select the text or graphic you want to copy. To scroll the window to the limit of the DOS screen, drag the mouse past the edge of the window.

   As soon as you start selecting, the window's title bar changes to indicate that the program is in Select mode. In this mode, you can only select text; you cannot use the program in any other way.

20

5. Click the Program Control menu again, select the **Edit** command, and then select the Copy Enter command from the cascading menu.

To use the keyboard to copy a partial screen of text or graphics, follow these steps:

1. Activate the DOS program in which you want to capture a partial screen. Press [Alt]+[⏎Enter] until that program appears in a window.

2. Position the program screen so that the information you want to copy appears in the window.

3. Press [Alt]+**space bar** to display the Program Control menu, select the **Edit** command, and then select the Mar**k** command from the cascading menu.

In this example, the Mar**k** command is selected.

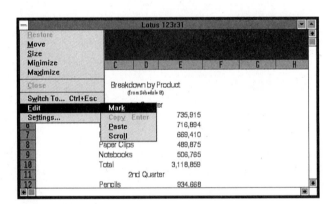

A rectangular cursor appears at the top left corner of the program screen. You use this cursor to select the screen area you want to copy.

4. Press [↑], [↓], [←], or [→] to move the cursor to the top left corner of the rectangular area you want to copy.

5. Hold down [⇧Shift] and press [↑], [↓], [←], or [→] to select a rectangular area that contains the information you want to copy.

20

530

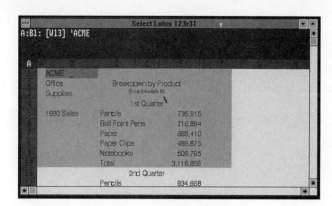

In this example, a
block of cells in a
Lotus 1-2-3
worksheet is
selected.

When you begin making a selection in the DOS program window, the
title bar changes to indicate that the program is in Select mode. While
in Select mode, you cannot paste, enter data, or use that program's
menu. To leave Select mode and return to normal program operation,
press Esc.

6. Press Alt+space bar to display the Program Control menu again,
   select the Edit command, and then select the Copy Enter command
   from the cascading menu.

Press Alt+Enter to switch a DOS program between full-screen and windowed
views while in 386-enhanced mode. When in full-screen view, the program
behaves as if it is running under DOS. When the program is in a window, you
can use the program as you use it in DOS, and you also can change the size of
the screen font and use the Program Control menu to copy and paste.

Pasting Data into DOS Programs

To paste the copied text or graphic from the Clipboard to a Windows or DOS
program, follow these steps:

1. Switch to the DOS or Windows program into which you want to paste
   the text or graphic from the Clipboard.

2. Move the program's cursor to where you want to place the top left
   corner of the pasted data.

3. If the program is a Windows program, choose the Edit menu and
   select the Paste command. If the program is a DOS program, press
   Alt+space bar to display the Program Control menu, select the Edit
   command, and then select the Paste command from the cascading
   menu.

20

531

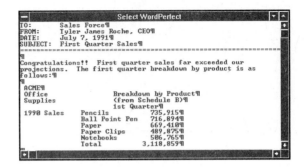

Windows pastes the 1-2-3 worksheet data into a WordPerfect document.

When pasting text into a DOS program such as WordPerfect, notice that the space between Lotus 1-2-3 columns contains space characters. If the receiving program uses proportional fonts, you may find that columns of text and numbers do not align correctly. To align the columns, you can insert tabs.

Changing Font Size in DOS Programs

You can make your DOS programs easier to read by changing the size of the font used in their display. To change the font size, follow these steps:

1. Choose the Program Control menu by clicking it or by pressing
   `Alt`+**space bar**.

2. Select the Fonts command.

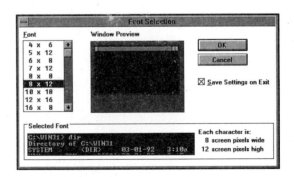

The Font Selection dialog box appears.

3. Select a font size from the Font list.

   The Window Preview box displays how large the window will become; the Selected Font box displays how that font will appear on-screen.

4. Select the Save Settings on Exit check box to use this size the next time you run this program (this check box may be selected already).

5. Choose OK or press ⏎Enter.

Closing DOS Programs

You quit a DOS program running under Windows the same way you exit that program in DOS. If the computer is connected to a network, disconnect from the network before you quit the DOS program.

Unlike Windows programs, each DOS program uses a different method of quitting. In a few cases, the screen does not return immediately to Windows; in this case, press Alt+space bar to display the Program Control menu, and then select the Close command.

When you close a DOS program, you return to Windows. If you try to close Windows before you close a DOS program, a message box warns you to return to the DOS program, close it, and then close Windows.

Setting Up DOS Programs for 386-Enhanced Mode

If you have an 80386 computer with more than 2M of memory and you run Windows in 386-enhanced mode, you can run a DOS program in a window. DOS programs in inactive windows can continue to run, enabling you to work on more than one program at a time (for example, you can type a letter while a long worksheet recalculates in an inactive window). Problems may arise, though, when you decide how DOS programs should share computer power and the same printer.

Setting Multitasking Options

If you run multiple DOS programs in 386-enhanced mode and each program uses part of the processor's calculating power, the performance of all the programs diminishes because processing takes longer. By using the Control Panel, you can specify how much processor time each program uses. This decision becomes important if, for example, you run a database report generator in the *background* (an inactive window) and calculate a worksheet in the *foreground* (the active window). If the two programs share processing power equally, the worksheet calculates more slowly than if it were running by itself. If you do not need to generate the database report quickly, you can schedule its processing for a smaller share of computing power. More calculating power is then available to the worksheet. (All Windows programs, however, share their processing time equally.)

20

533

To schedule different amounts of processing power for DOS programs, follow these steps:

1. Open the Control Panel from the Main group window in the Program Manager.

2. Open the 386 Enhanced program icon from the Control Panel. (This icon looks like a computer chip and is visible only when you are in 386-enhanced mode.)

The 386 Enhanced dialog box appears.

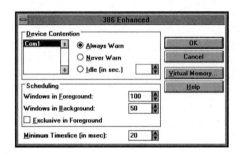

3. Select one of the following Scheduling options:

Option	Description
Windows in Foreground	To assign more processing power to the program in the active window, specify a number (from 1 to 10,000) larger than the number in the Windows in Background box. You usually make this number *much* larger so that the active program operates faster and does not keep you waiting.
Windows in Background	To assign more processing power to the programs in the inactive windows, specify a number (from 1 to 10,000) larger than the number in the Windows in Foreground box. This option slows down the performance in the active window.
Exclusive in Foreground	To give Windows programs 100 percent of the processing time when a Windows program is in the active window, select this box. This option puts DOS programs on hold when they are in inactive windows.

4. Choose OK or press ⏎Enter.

20

Managing Printing with Multiple DOS Programs

When Windows programs need the same printer or modem at the same time, Windows acts as a referee that decides which program is first. DOS programs are not so agreeable. If two or more DOS programs need the same printer or modem at the same time, you may lose data. This problem is called *device contention*. Using the Control Panel, you can control how Windows resolves device contention between DOS programs.

To control device contention, follow these steps:

1. Open the Control Panel from the Main group window in the Program Manager.

2. Open the 386 Enhanced program icon from the Control Panel.

3. From the Device Contention list, select the port that may have a problem—the port to which the printer or modem is attached.

4. Select the way you want Windows to resolve device contention:

Option	Description
Always Warn	Displays a message when a problem occurs, giving you the opportunity to select which program has priority. You usually select this option.
Never Warn	Enables any DOS program to use the port at any time. This option can cause contention problems.
Idle	Makes the port remain idle the specified number of seconds (1 to 999) before the next program can use that port without the warning message appearing. Select this option if you have a program that pauses between printing multiple pages (such as a 1-2-3 print macro that prints multiple but separate pages) or if you have a communications program that logs on to a database, downloads information, and then logs on a second time for additional information.

5. Choose OK or press ⏎Enter.

20

Creating a PIF

A program information file (PIF) defines how Windows works with a specific DOS program. A PIF, which is separate from the program file, contains characteristics that Windows uses when it starts the DOS program. These characteristics answer such questions as "Should this program run full screen or in a window?" and "How much memory should Windows reserve for this program?" In most cases, you do not have to create a PIF for a DOS program. When you install Windows, you can make Windows create PIFs for many popular DOS programs. If Windows does not have information about the DOS program you want to run, it uses a default PIF that works for most DOS programs.

Sometimes a DOS program does not run correctly or does not run the way you want. In this case, you may need to modify the program's PIF by using the PIF Editor. For instructions on using the PIF Editor, see "Editing a PIF," further in this chapter.

You can set up a PIF in three ways:

- Make the Windows Setup program create a PIF for your DOS programs.
- Use or modify the default PIF.
- Use the PIF that came with the DOS program.

The Windows Setup program can create a PIF for your DOS program when you first install Windows or after you install Windows. The Setup program searches your hard disk for all programs and creates PIFs for the DOS programs it recognizes.

Alternatively, many current DOS programs provide a PIF. For example, when you install Lotus 1-2-3 Release 3.1, you also install the 123.PIF file. Because the settings in this PIF are optimized, always use this PIF rather than the default PIF.

If the Windows Setup program does not create a PIF for a DOS program, and the program does not provide a PIF, Windows uses the default PIF. If you need to change settings in the default PIF so that the program works correctly with Windows, modify the default PIF with the PIF Editor. After you save the new PIF with the same name as the program file name (and the extension PIF), Windows uses that PIF whenever you start the DOS program.

20

Making Windows Create PIFs for Your DOS Programs

The simplest way to create a PIF is to use the Install program or the Windows Setup program to create a PIF for each DOS program on your hard disk. When you install Windows, the Install program asks whether or not you want Windows to look for programs on your hard disk and to set up those Windows and DOS programs. If you used this feature during installation, Windows created PIFs for the DOS programs you selected.

If you already installed Windows, but you want Windows to create one or more PIFs, you can run the Windows Setup program again. To run the Windows Setup program to create PIFs, follow these steps:

1. Open the Main group window in the Program Manager.

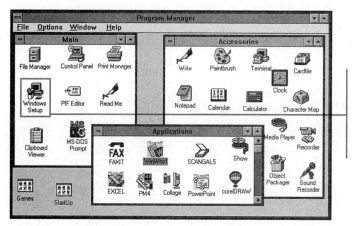

The Windows Setup program item icon looks like a personal computer with installation disks.

2. Open the Windows Setup program item icon.

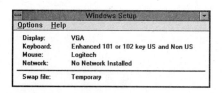

The Windows Setup dialog box appears.

3. Choose the Options menu and select the Set Up Applications command.

4. Select the Search For Applications option or the Ask You To Specify An Application option.

5. Choose OK or press ⏎Enter.

6. If you selected the Ask You To Specify An Application option, the Setup Applications dialog box appears. Type the program path and file name in the text box and then choose the name of the group window where you want to add the program item in the Add to Program Group list box. (If you do not know the name of the file or path, choose the Browse button and select the file name of the program.) Choose OK twice to complete the setup.

   If you selected the Search For Applications option, a different Setup Applications dialog box appears. Select the disk drive or path you want to search, and then choose the Search Now button. As Windows searches for DOS programs, it may ask you to identify a program—if Windows asks you to identify WP.EXE, for example, choose WordPerfect from the list.

When the search is complete, a third Setup Applications dialog box appears.

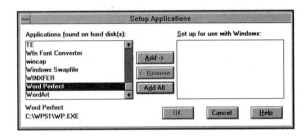

7. Select the programs you want to add to Windows from the list on the left side of the Setup Applications dialog box. You can click multiple programs or press ↑ or ↓ and **space bar** to select programs. Choose the Add button to add the programs to the list box on the right. Choose OK or press ⏎Enter.

Windows creates PIFs for the DOS programs about which it has information. Windows also creates program item icons for the DOS programs you selected, and it stores those icons in the Applications group window in the Program Manager.

If a DOS program runs incorrectly when you start it or if it does not run at all, check its PIF and its program item icon characteristics to ensure that they refer to the correct file name and directory. Chapter 5, "Grouping Programs and Documents," describes how to change the program item icon. The following sections describe how to edit a PIF. The Windows Setup program may be unable to create a PIF for a DOS program it does not recognize; if an unrecognized program does not run with the default PIF settings, you must create its PIF manually.

20

538

Creating a PIF Manually

If you need to create a new PIF manually, you use the PIF Editor. To create a new PIF, follow these steps:

1. Choose the PIF Editor from the Main group window in the Program Manager.

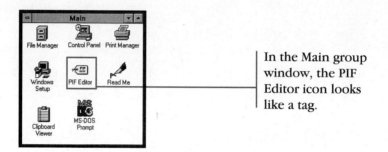

In the Main group window, the PIF Editor icon looks like a tag.

When you start the PIF Editor, a window displays a new, untitled PIF with the default settings. The PIF Editor window that appears depends on the current Windows mode (or the mode you select from the Mode menu).

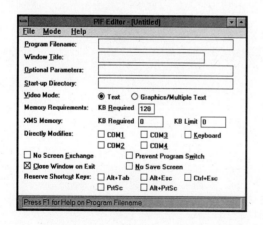

This PIF Editor window appears in standard mode.

20

This PIF Editor window appears in 386-enhanced mode.

```
┌──────────────────────────────────────────────────────────┐
│ ▬              PIF Editor - [Untitled]              ▼ ▲  │
│ File  Mode  Help                                           │
│ Program Filename:    [                              ]      │
│ Window Title:        [                              ]      │
│ Optional Parameters: [                              ]      │
│ Start-up Directory:  [                              ]      │
│ Video Memory:     ◉ Text   ○ Low Graphics   ○ High Graphics│
│ Memory Requirements:  KB Required  [128]  KB Desired  [640]│
│ EMS Memory:           KB Required  [0]    KB Limit  [1024] │
│ XMS Memory:           KB Required  [0]    KB Limit  [1024] │
│ Display Usage: ◉ Full Screen    Execution: ☐ Background    │
│                ○ Windowed                  ☐ Exclusive     │
│ ☒ Close Window on Exit          [Advanced...]             │
│ Press F1 for Help on Program Filename                      │
└──────────────────────────────────────────────────────────┘
```

2. Type information in the text boxes and select options.

   Most PIF options apply only to the mode in which you select them. The following options are common to the standard and 386-enhanced modes:

   > Program Filename
   >
   > Window Title
   >
   > Optional Parameters
   >
   > Start-up Directory
   >
   > Close Window on Exit
   >
   > Reserve Shortcut Keys

   Refer to the tables in "Editing a PIF," further in this chapter, for more information on these and other PIF options.

3. Choose the File menu, select the Save command, and then name and save the file.

4. Choose the File menu and select the New command to create another new PIF. To close the PIF Editor, choose the File menu and select the Exit command.

Before testing a PIF, close all other programs in Windows. If, for some reason, the program freezes the system, you can turn off and restart the computer without losing data in another program.

If you plan to start the program by choosing the program file name, the PIF must have the same name as the program file (WP.EXE and WP.PIF, for example). Then, when you choose the program file name, Windows executes the PIF. If you have several WordPerfect PIFs (for the same WordPerfect program) with different settings, start the program by choosing the PIF.

20

Editing a PIF

Windows can create predefined PIFs for many popular DOS programs. When you use the Windows Setup program to install a DOS program, you can make Windows create a PIF for the program and store the PIF in the Windows directory. If the program does not run correctly or as you want, you can edit its PIF with the PIF Editor.

You may have to edit a PIF in the following circumstances:

- The program is in a different directory from the one listed in the Program Filename text box of the PIF.

- The Start-up Directory, which specifies the data directory, is different from the directory you want or from the directory the program expects.

- You want to start a program by using a special parameter.

- You want to ensure that a program swaps to disk when not in use, freeing more memory for additional programs (the Prevent Program Switch option).

- An upgraded program requires more memory.

- You want to increase the memory available for a program to increase its performance.

Note: Before you edit a PIF, use the File Manager to make a backup copy of the original PIF. For example, a WordPerfect PIF such as WP.PIF might use the backup name WP.BCK. If your edited PIF causes problems, you can return to the preceding version by renaming the backup copy with the original name.

o edit a PIF, follow these steps:

1. Choose the PIF Editor program from the Main group window. (In the Main group window, the PIF Editor icon looks like a tag.)

   When you start the PIF Editor, a window displays a new, untitled PIF with the default settings. The PIF Editor window that appears depends on the current Windows mode (or the mode you select from the Mode menu).

2. Choose the File menu and select the Open command.

3. Change to the directory containing the PIF you want to edit. PIFs are usually in the Windows directory. Select and open the PIF you want to edit.

   The PIF Editor window displays the PIF for that program.

4. Choose the File Save As command and save a backup copy of the PIF (with the extension BCK).

20

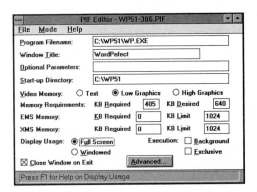

This PIF is for WordPerfect, running under Windows in 386-enhanced mode.

5. Make changes to the text boxes or selections in the PIF Editor window. (See tables 20.1, 20.2, 20.3, and 20.4, further in this chapter, for detailed descriptions of the available options.)

6. Choose the File Save As command and save the file under its original name (with the extension PIF). The PIF's root name must be the same as the program's root name—WP.EXE and WP.PIF, for example.

7. Choose OK or press ↵Enter.

8. Choose the File menu and select the Exit command to quit the PIF Editor.

Before you test an edited PIF, save the data in any other program running in Windows. If the DOS program freezes the system, you can turn off and restart the computer without losing data from other programs. Test the PIF by starting the program and checking whether your changes have solved the problem you hoped to fix by editing the PIF.

Before you edit your own PIFs, examine the upcoming tables to learn about the different parts of PIFs and the PIF Editor screens.

Overriding Default PIF Settings

When you start a DOS program for which Windows cannot find a PIF, Windows starts the program using the default PIF options for the current Windows mode. You can override the Windows default options by creating a PIF with the name _DEFAULT.PIF.

In 386-enhanced mode, for example, Windows starts DOS programs in full-screen mode. To start DOS programs in a window rather than in a full screen, you can create a _DEFAULT.PIF file and change the Display Usage option so that DOS programs start in a window. When you change _DEFAULT.PIF, leave the Window Title option blank. You must provide a Program Filename, though, because the PIF editor checks that this text box is filled before it enables you to save the PIF. You can use whatever program file name you want in the Program Filename box, but the file name must have the extension EXE, COM, or BAT. Type over this program file name when you make a new PIF.

Making Basic Changes to PIFs

The PIF Editor display for standard modes is nearly the same as for 386-enhanced mode—only a few check boxes and text boxes are different. Table 20.1 describes the PIF Editor text boxes that are the same in both modes.

Table 20.1
PIF Editor Text Boxes for Standard and 386-Enhanced Modes

Text Box	Description
Program Filename	Specifies the full path name and DOS program name, including the file extension. Most programs have the extension EXE or COM. Batch files that run commands or start programs have the extension BAT. For example, for WordPerfect 5.1, type C:\WP51\WP.EXE. For 1-2-3 Release 2.2, type C:\123\123.EXE.
Window Title	Specifies the name that will appear in the program window title bar and under the program item icon when you minimize the program.
Optional Parameters	Specifies the parameters that will be added to the program when it starts (the parameters or switches you type after the file name when you start the program from the DOS prompt).
	For example, if you type /m-macroname, the specified macro starts when you start WordPerfect 5.1, and typing /C puts Microsoft Word into character mode.
	If you frequently change program start-up parameters, type a question mark (?) in Optional Parameters. Windows prompts you for the parameters you want to use when it starts the program.

continues

20

Table 20.1 Continued

Text Box	Description
Start-up Directory	Specifies the full path name of the drive and directory where you want Windows to go when the program starts. If the program needs to locate additional files at start-up (as does Lotus 1-2-3), make sure that you indicate a start-up directory that is the same as the program's directory.

Editing Standard Mode PIFs

Table 20.2 describes some of the important PIF Editor options for standard mode *not* available in 386-enhanced mode.

Table 20.2
PIF Editor Options for Standard Mode

Option	Description
Video Mode Text	Select this option if the program uses only text. This option conserves memory.
Video Mode Graphics/Multiple Text	Select this option if the program displays graphics. You use this setting for most programs.
Memory Requirements KB Required	Type the number of kilobytes of memory recommended by the program's user's manual (without the approximately 40K that DOS uses). If you are unsure about the amount of memory, start with the default setting of 128 and raise the setting in increments of 64 until the program works.
Alt+Tab	Switches between programs.
Alt+Esc	Switches between programs.
Ctrl+Esc	Displays the Task List.
PrtSc	Copies the full screen to the Clipboard.
Alt+PrtSc	Copies the full screen to the Clipboard.
No Screen Exchange	Select this option to prevent copying and pasting between DOS programs. This option makes more memory available.

20

Option	Description
Prevent Program Switch	Select this option to conserve memory; however, you must quit the program to return to Windows. You usually do not select this option.
Close Window on Exit	Select this option to close the window when you exit the DOS program.

Note: Select the Reserve Shortcut Keys check boxes for the shortcut keys you want to use in the program. Windows reserves the selected keys for the program's use rather than for Windows' use.

Editing 386-Enhanced Mode PIFs

The PIF options for 386-enhanced mode appear in two dialog boxes: the PIF Editor dialog box (for basic options) and the Advanced Options dialog box. The basic PIF options are similar to those for standard mode. The advanced options fine-tune special features of the program for 386-enhanced mode. For more information on setting the advanced PIF features for 386-enhanced mode, see Que's *Using Windows 3.1*, Special Edition.

Table 20.3 describes some of the important PIF Editor options for 386-enhanced mode *not* available in standard mode.

Table 20.3
PIF Editor Options for 386-Enhanced Mode

Option	Description
Memory Requirements KB Required	Type the amount of conventional memory that must be free. Generally, you type 128; program manuals usually specify too much free memory because they must include memory for DOS and drivers. Windows does not start the program if the KB Required setting is not large enough. This option does not limit the amount of memory the program receives. Type -1 to give the program all available conventional memory.

continues

Table 20.3 Continued

Option	Description
Memory Requirements KB Desired	Type the maximum amount of memory you want the program to use, if memory is available. Usually, 640K is the maximum. Most programs use much less. Using a smaller setting conserves memory. Some programs run more efficiently with more memory. Type -1 to give the program as much memory as possible, but not more than 640K.
Display Usage Full Screen	Select this option to start the program full screen.
Display Usage Windowed	Select this option to start the program in a window.
Execution Background	Select this option to run the program while you are using another program. When this option is selected, programs running in the background share processing power with programs running in the foreground.
Execution Exclusive	Select this option to stop all other programs while this program is active. This option gives a program more computer power.
Close Window on Exit	Select this option to close the window when you exit the program.
Advanced	Choose the Advanced button to display the Advanced Options dialog box.

By using the advanced options in 386-enhanced mode, you can modify a PIF to get the best memory usage and performance from your DOS program. For a detailed discussion of the advanced options, see Que's *Using Windows 3.1*, Special Edition.

Changing Settings While Programs Are Running in 386-Enhanced Mode

In 386-enhanced mode, you can modify the way a DOS program operates, even while the program is running. To change settings for a running program, follow these steps:

20

1. Open the Program Control menu (by clicking the Program Control menu or by pressing Alt+space bar), and select the Settings command.

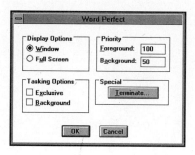

The Settings dialog box appears, displaying the program name in the title bar. This example shows the Settings dialog box for WordPerfect.

2. Select the option you want to change.

Table 20.4 describes the options you can change while the DOS program is running in 386-enhanced mode.

Table 20.4
Options You Can Change While Programs
Are Running in 386-Enhanced Mode

Option	Description
Window	Select this option to display the program in a window.
Full Screen	Select this option to display the program full screen.
Exclusive	Select this option to dedicate computer power to the active DOS program. If the DOS program is in a window, Windows programs continue to run.
Background	Select this option to run this program in the background when other programs are active.
Foreground	Increase this number (from 1 to 10,000) to give more computer power to the active program.
Background	Increase this number (from 1 to 10,000) to give more computer power to the inactive program and less power to the active program.

continues

20

Table 20.4 Continued

Option	Description
Terminate	Select this button when you cannot quit the program any other way. This button closes the program and gives you the opportunity to return to Windows and save open files in other programs. (You can, however, lose data in the program you are terminating.) You should close the other programs after saving their files, and then restart your computer.

Troubleshooting DOS Programs

As your computer environment changes or expands, you may encounter problems with PIFs. The following list describes some of the most common problems with PIFs, and suggests changes you can make in the PIF Editor to solve them:

Problem	Action
Program file not found	Check the program path name, file name, and extension in the Program Filename text box.
Associated files not found	Type the program's path name in the Start-up Directory text box.
Insufficient memory to start	Increase the KB Required.
Insufficient memory for documents	Increase the KB Desired or KB Limit.
Special keystrokes do not work	Use the Reserve Shortcut Keys options to reserve keystrokes for use in the DOS programs. (To see these options, choose the Advanced button in a 386 PIF Editor screen.)

Summary

In this chapter, you learned how to start, control, switch between, and fine-tune the operation of DOS programs. You also learned what a PIF is and how

20

Windows works with PIFs. You learned how to create, edit, and optimize PIFs and how to use the PIF Editor.

The following important points were covered in this chapter:

- In 386-enhanced mode, Windows can run multiple DOS programs simultaneously. In standard mode, Windows puts inactive DOS programs on hold.

- In 386-enhanced mode, you can press Alt+Enter to switch DOS programs between running full screen and in a window.

- You can switch between programs by pressing Ctrl+Esc and selecting a program from the Task List or by pressing Alt+Tab to cycle through the programs.

- Windows can run most DOS programs using default PIF settings.

- You can have multiple PIFs for a single program.

- To change operating settings while running DOS programs in 386-enhanced mode, press Alt+space bar, choose the Settings command, and then enter new settings in the dialog box.

20

549

Installing Windows 3.1

The Windows Setup program guides you through installing Windows. If you already have Windows 3.0 installed, you should install Windows 3.1 over the existing Windows. This procedure preserves your current settings, program groups, and custom drivers. New drivers for existing printers are upgraded. Installation should take no more than 30 minutes.

Two Setup modes are available: Express and Custom. If you are unfamiliar with computers, you should use Express Setup. It determines your hardware and software and makes appropriate selections for you. You are prompted to specify which type of printer your computer uses and where it is connected.

If you are familiar with computers and want to install only parts of Windows or make changes during installation, you should use Custom Setup. Custom Setup enables you to add additional printers and select hardware that may be different than what is automatically detected by the Setup program. If your hard disk is low on available storage, you may want to use Custom Setup to install parts of Windows rather than the full Windows and all accessories. You can run Setup at any time to add Windows features or accessories you did not install initially.

A

Before You Install Windows

For Windows to operate correctly, your hardware and software must meet the following requirements:

- IBM Personal System/2, Personal Computer AT, COMPAQ Deskpro 286, or a compatible computer that uses an 80286, 80386, 80386SX, or 80486 processor.
- 1M or more of memory on an 80286 PC, or 2M or more of memory on an 80386 or 80486 PC. (You should configure memory above 640K as extended memory. Refer to your hardware installation manual for this information.)
- Graphics adapter cards supported by Windows (usually VGA or EGA graphics).
- A hard disk with 5M to 10M of available storage.
- At least one 1.2M or 1.44M floppy disk drive.
- MS-DOS 3.1 or higher.

If you want to run multimedia programs in Windows, you need a Multimedia Personal Computer (MPC) or an MPC upgrade kit to upgrade your existing computer.

Optional equipment that Windows supports includes the following:

- One or more printers or plotters connected to the same PC. Windows supports over 250 printers.
- A mouse, which is highly recommended.
- Pen computer systems (add-in software available with handwriting-recognition system).
- A Hayes, MultiTech, TrailBlazer, or compatible modem for communications using Terminal.
- Major networks.

You can run Windows 3.1 in two different modes: standard mode and 386-enhanced mode. Use standard mode on all 80286 computers and on 80386 computers with less than 2M of memory. Use 386-enhanced mode on 80386 computers with more than 2M or more of memory. Both modes enable Windows and DOS programs to run. Standard mode enables you to switch between multiple programs, but DOS programs that are not active (full screen) do not run. They are suspended until you activate them again. 386-enhanced mode enables you to run multiple programs, and DOS programs in the background (in a window behind the foreground program) can continue to run. The computer and memory requirements for these modes are:

552

A

	Standard Mode	*386-Enhanced Mode*
Processor	80286 or higher	80386 or higher
Memory	1M (640K conventional and 256K extended)	2M (640K conventional and 1024K extended)
Storage	5M to 9M hard disk	5M to 10.5M hard disk

When you install Windows, it checks to see what equipment you have installed and tries to determine the equipment's manufacturer and type. Windows is usually correct, but if you want to confirm the list, use Custom Setup to review the hardware list. To speed the installation process, make a list of the following information before you install Windows. (If you are uncertain of the manufacturer or type of equipment you use, check your manuals or sales receipts, or call your dealer or corporate personal computer support line.)

- The name of the drive and directory in which you want to install Windows.

- Manufacturer and model number of your computer. If your computer has an MCA bus and you cannot determine your exact computer model, choose an equivalent IBM PS/2 model. If your computer has an EISA bus, choose an equivalent COMPAQ model. Most computers have an EISA bus.

- Type of display adapter. Most 80386 and 80386SX computers have VGA adapters.

- Manufacturer and model of your printer.

- Printer port for connecting your printer or printers. Most printers connect to the parallel ports: LPT1 or LPT2. Some older laser printers use a serial port: COM1 or COM2.

- Printer communication information, if you are using serial printers connected to a COM port or if you are connecting your computer to a phone line with a modem. Include baud rate, number of bits, stop bits, and parity. Find this information in your printer or modem manual, from your dealer, or from the manufacturer.

- Mouse manufacturer and type (if you have a mouse).

- Type of keyboard.

- Make and model of multimedia adapters (if you have multimedia capability).

553

- Type and version of the network to which you are connected (if you are connected to one). Your system administrator can help with this information.

Before you install Windows, you need to make sure that you have 5M to 10M of storage available on the hard disk on which you are installing Windows. Use the DIR command to find the available storage. You can install Windows on any hard drive; you do not have to install it on drive C.

Note: Windows runs faster and in some modes switches between programs faster if you properly prepare your hard disk before installing Windows. Because Windows frequently reads and writes information to disk as it operates, you should store the information on your disk as compactly as possible, without wasting space. Use a disk-defragmenting or disk-optimization program to rearrange files on-disk to increase your hard disk performance.

Installing Windows

After you make a list of your equipment, you are ready to install Windows. If you are unfamiliar with computers, you should use Express Setup. If you are familiar with computers or need to customize the installation, use Custom Setup.

Preparing for Installation

Before you install Windows, you may want to prepare for the installation by following these steps. Note, however, that these steps are not mandatory.

1. Protect your original diskettes from change. On 1.44M (3 1/2-inch) diskettes, slide open the write-protect tab (a square sliding button at the diskette's top edge). On 1.2M (5 1/4-inch) diskettes, put a write-protect tab (an adhesive patch) over the square notch on the diskette's edge. Copy the original diskettes onto backup diskettes, and store the originals at a separate site.

2. Complete the registration forms and mail them back to Microsoft while you are waiting for following segments of the installation to complete. Microsoft uses the registrations to send you special offers on related software, to send newsletters containing tips, and to inform you when updates to Windows are available. You may not get discount pricing on upgrades unless you are registered.

3. At the DOS prompt, such as C:\>, type **CHKDSK /F**. If lost clusters are found, respond Yes to collect them and store them.

   Note: Do not run the CHKDSK /F command while Windows is running.

4. Run a disk-defragmenting or disk-optimization program, if you have one, to make Windows run faster.

5. Remove any protected-mode memory-management programs, such as QEMM386, 386Max, or Blue Max, before installing Windows. Remove them by deleting their DEVICE= line from the CONFIG.SYS file, and then resave CONFIG.SYS as a text file. Restart your computer.

Controlling the Setup Options

Both Express Setup and Custom Setup begin with a "DOS segment," during which you use the keyboard to control the screen. The DOS segment displays only two colors, and characters appear as they do at the DOS prompt (C:\>, for example). After the Setup program installs the initial software, it changes to a Windows screen for the "Windows segment" of the installation. At that point you can use normal Windows keystrokes or mouse controls.

At almost any time during installation, you can get help by pressing F1, the Help key. This Help key is the same Help key used in Windows and Windows programs. To exit from a Help window, press the Esc key if you are in a DOS screen. If you are in a Windows screen and the Help window is on top, choose the File menu and select the Exit command.

During DOS segments of the installation, use the following controls. A status line at the bottom of the screen lists available controls.

Control	Result
↑ or ↓	Selects the next item, up or down.
↵Enter	Selects an option or moves to the next screen.
F1	Starts Help from a Setup screen.
←Backspace	Backs up in Help screens by one screen.
F3	Exits the Setup program.
Esc	Exits Help and returns to Setup.

During the Windows segments of the installation, use these controls:

Control	Result
F1	Starts Help from a screen or dialog box.
Tab⇄	Moves between areas in a dialog box.
space bar	Selects the current item in the dialog box.
Click	Chooses a button (such as OK or Cancel), selects a check box or option button, scrolls through a list (click the scroll arrows), or selects an item from a list.

The current item in a dialog box is surrounded by dashed lines. The current button, such as OK or Cancel, has a bold border.

To click something with the mouse, move the mouse so that the tip of the mouse pointer, usually an arrow, is on the item; then gently but quickly press and release the left mouse button.

Starting the Windows Setup

To install Windows, follow these steps:

1. Start your computer and, if necessary, return to a DOS prompt, such as C:\>.

2. Put Disk 1 of the Windows diskettes in a diskette drive and close the door.

3. Type the drive letter, followed by a colon (for example, type A: if the diskette is in drive A), and press ⏎Enter to switch to that diskette drive.

4. Type **SETUP** and press ⏎Enter.

5. Read and follow the directions on-screen.

6. You are given two alternatives for installation, Express Setup or Custom Setup. If you are unfamiliar with Windows or with computers, choose Express Setup. The differences between these choices are described later in this appendix.

If the Setup program detects that a previous version of Windows is already installed on your hard disk, you are given the option of either upgrading the older version in the same directory or installing Windows 3.1 in a new directory. Upgrading an older version of Windows preserves Windows settings, updates printer drivers when necessary, and preserves drivers it does not recognize. To upgrade, you need approximately 5M additional free space on the hard disk.

Note: If you choose to have Windows 3.1 and Windows 3.0 installed at the same time, make sure that the PATH in the AUTOEXEC.BAT does not list both directories at the same time, which causes improper operation and may corrupt system files.

At the beginning of the installation, you are prompted to enter your name and company name. You *must* enter a name. The program uses the name to notify anyone attempting to reinstall the software that it already is installed. Press Tab to move between the two edit boxes. Use the arrow keys, Backspace key, or Del key to edit what you type. You are given a chance to make corrections.

You are prompted to insert additional diskettes as you complete steps. Insert them as the Setup program requests, and then follow the instructions on-screen.

Note: If you have trouble installing Windows due to a terminate-and-stay-resident (TSR) program, remove the TSR load line from CONFIG.SYS and restart your computer so the TSR does not load. Then restart the Windows installation.

Note: If you are installing Windows on a network, or if you are installing Windows on a system connected to a network, check with your network administrator for the best method of installing it. The file NETWORKS.WRI contains information, in a Windows Write format, about installing Windows on a network.

When you finish installing Windows, three large buttons appear: Reboot, Restart Windows, and Return to MS-DOS. The selections you made during Setup do not take effect until you restart your computer by rebooting it. To reboot your computer, click the Reboot button or type R.

Rebooting restarts your computer without turning off the power. Restarting erases memory, reloads DOS, and rereads the AUTOEXEC.BAT and CONFIG.SYS files, which configures your computer with the selections you made during the setup. If you chose not to let Windows Setup modify AUTOEXEC.BAT and CONFIG.SYS, Windows may not run correctly, even after you reboot.

A

557

A

Installing Windows Using Express Setup

The Express Setup uses settings and hardware configuration that the installation program has determined will run on your system. If you need to, you can change these settings and installation configurations later (see the section "Changing the Setup after Installation," further in this appendix). Some of the things the Express Setup does are as follows:

- Modifies the AUTOEXEC.BAT and CONFIG.SYS files automatically.
- Installs Windows in C:\WINDOWS, unless drive C doesn't have enough room, in which case the installation program searches for a drive with enough room. If not enough room is available for a full version of Windows, Express Setup installs a smaller set of Windows and accessory programs.
- Reinstalls the printer drivers you installed in Windows 3.0, if Windows 3.0 is already installed. If Windows 3.0 is not already installed, it prompts you to specify which printer and connecting port you want to use.
- Searches your hard disks for programs, and creates icons and group windows for Windows programs and many DOS programs.
- Provides an optional short tutorial on using a mouse and Windows.

Note: In most cases you should use Express Setup. If the Express Setup does not work correctly, you can install or reinstall other items or features of Windows at a later time by rerunning Setup.

Installing Windows Using Custom Setup

The Custom Setup enables you to specify how you want to install Windows. You can see or select changes as they are made; for example, Express Setup changes the AUTOEXEC.BAT and CONFIG.SYS files automatically, whereas Custom Setup enables you to change those files yourself. Custom Setup enables you to cross-check the installation process or select hardware configurations different from those automatically selected. Some of the things Custom Setup does are:

- Displays a list of the hardware it detects. You can accept or change the detected hardware, which is useful if the type of mouse or video adapter has been incorrectly detected.

A

- Displays the changes it will make to AUTOEXEC.BAT and CONFIG.SYS, enabling you to edit the changes. You have the option to accept the modifications, reject the modifications, or make manual changes.

- Enables you to select the drive and directory name in which it will install Windows.

- Enables you to select the Windows components (such as games and screen savers) and accessory programs that you want to install.

- Gives you full control over installing printers.

- Enables you to select the Windows and DOS programs you want set up with icons and windows.

- Gives you the opportunity to take a short tutorial on the mouse and Windows.

In Custom Setup you make selections in dialog boxes that appear in the Windows screens. If you are familiar with Windows operations, use normal Windows selection techniques with the keyboard or mouse. For example, to select an item in a dialog box, press and hold Alt, and then press the under-lined letter of the item you want to select. Release both keys. In some Setup dialog boxes, you see a group of options with round buttons to the left; to select one of the options, press the arrow keys to cycle through the buttons. The button with the black center is the selected button.

To edit a name or text in a text box, hold down the Alt key and then press the underlined letter for that text box. A flashing cursor, called the *insertion point,* appears in the box. Move the insertion point with the left- or right-arrow keys; then use the Del key to delete characters to the right, use the Backspace key to delete characters to the left, or type to insert new characters at the insertion point.

During installation, you are asked where you want to install Windows. The default or automatic choice is

    C:\WINDOWS

You can edit this path name so that Windows is installed on a different hard drive or directory. To edit the path name, press the arrow keys to move from character to character, the Del key to delete to the right, the Backspace key to delete to the left, and the character keys to add text. For example, to install Windows on drive D in the directory WIN31, erase C:\WINDOWS and type **D:\WIN31.**

559

A

Windows also asks whether it can make changes to the AUTOEXEC.BAT and CONFIG.SYS files. The Setup program provides the changes that Windows needs in order to run your computer. You are given three choices for these files:

- You can accept all changes. Copies of the old files are saved to backup files.
- You can modify changes. A dialog box displays the original and proposed file. Use the Tab key to move into the top list and edit the proposed changes. You can move around in the proposed text by pressing the arrow keys; you can delete text by pressing Backspace or Del; you can add new text by typing at the insertion point.
- You can reject all changes.

You are given a chance to install Windows printer and plotter drivers. Drivers tell Windows how to interact with a printer or plotter. You do not have to install printer or plotter drivers at this point, although it is a convenient time. You can install drivers later, using the Control Panel, as described in Chapter 7, "Customizing Your Work Area."

From the list of printers on-screen, select the names that match your equipment and choose Install. Choose Connect to connect your printer to the port where it is physically attached. Choose Setup to change paper orientation (vertical or horizontal printing), paper size, number of copies, font cartridges, and so on. Choose Set as Default Printer if you want this printer to be the one on which Windows always proposes to print. You can change these settings later from a program's printer Setup command or from the Control Panel. Don't forget to use the help information available by pressing Help (F1).

Note: Each printer has different setup options, and if yours includes a memory option, be sure to specify how much memory your printer has. (The HP LaserJet III, for example, includes a memory option.)

When you finish installing printers, Windows asks whether you want it to search your hard disk for Windows and DOS programs. If you choose this option, Windows makes a list of all programs on your hard disk. You are given an opportunity to put the names of these programs into a special group window. Each program will be represented by a small picture. These pictures, called *icons,* make starting a program easy. At this point, you probably should select only the programs you recognize, to put them into a group. You can add or remove programs in a group window anytime after you install Windows. Procedures for using group windows are described in Chapter 5, "Grouping Programs and Documents."

Learning from the Setup Files

A

At the end of the Windows installation, you are given an opportunity to read the files that Setup copied into the WINDOWS directory. You can read the files from the installation program when it asks you to, or you can complete the installation of Windows and read the files with Write, a small word processing program that comes with Windows. The names of the Setup files are as follows:

Setup File	Contains
README.WRI	Current updates to the user manual.
PRINTERS.WRI	Additional information about configuring printers and fonts.
NETWORKS.WRI	Information about installing Windows on networks.
SYSINI.WRI	Information about modifying the SYSTEM.INI file.
WININI.WRI	Information about modifying the WIN.INI file.

Installing Unlisted Printers

If you cannot locate a printer driver from your printer's manufacturer, Windows offers a temporary solution. One of the choices for a printer driver is Generic/Text Only. Using the Generic/Text Only printer driver enables you to print text and numbers on most printers; however, you will not be able to print with special capabilities, such as underline, bold, or graphics.

Contact Microsoft or your printer manufacturer for a printer driver for your printer or for the name of a compatible driver. Windows supports hundreds of printer drivers. Microsoft maintains a Windows Driver Library (WDL) that contains device drivers supported by Windows 3.1. You can obtain a copy of this library through Microsoft forums on CompuServe, GEnie, ON-Line, or some public bulletin boards. You can receive a driver also by calling Microsoft. Refer to Appendix C in this book for Microsoft's telephone numbers.

When you receive a printer driver to match your equipment, you can install the driver without reinstalling Windows. Use the Control Panel to add the new printer driver. The procedure is described in Chapter 7, "Customizing Your Work Area."

A

Running Windows after Installation

After you install Windows and reboot, you can start Windows from the DOS prompt (such as C:\>) by typing **WIN** and pressing Enter. Windows starts in the most efficient mode for your processor and memory configuration.

You can force Windows to start in either of its two modes: standard mode or 386-enhanced mode. Refer to Chapter 2, "Getting Started," for details on starting Windows in its different modes.

If the screen goes blank when you start Windows, you may have installed Windows with an incorrect graphics adapter. To fix this problem, find out what kind of graphics adapter you have (you may need to call the manufacturer), and repeat the installation. Turn off your computer, restart it, and repeat the installation process, specifying a different graphics adapter.

Changing the Setup after Installation

After Windows is operating correctly, you can modify its setup without reinstalling the entire Windows system. You occasionally may want to change the setup. For example, you may have a portable computer running Windows. When you are on the road, you will need to use the portable's plasma or LCD screen, but when you are at the office, you will want to use a high-resolution color monitor. Instead of reinstalling Windows to get the new video driver, you can use the Windows Setup program to switch between the drivers you will be using. Windows Setup also is useful when you buy and attach a new keyboard or mouse, or when you attach your computer to a network.

The Windows Setup program is located in the Main group window of the Program Manager. To change the setup of the display, keyboard, mouse, or network after Windows is installed, follow these steps:

1. Activate the Program Manager and then activate the Main group window.

2. Choose the Windows Setup program item icon.

3. From the Windows Setup dialog box, choose the Options menu and select the Change System Settings command.

   From the Change System Settings dialog box, you can change installation settings for Display, Keyboard, Mouse, and Network without reinstalling Windows.

A

4. Select the pull-down list of the setting you want to change by clicking the related down-arrow icon. Or press Alt+*letter* to select the list, and then press ⬇ to display the list.

5. Select from the pull-down list the type of device you want to install, by clicking it or by pressing ⬆ or ⬇.

6. Choose OK or press ⏎Enter.

7. If a special driver is required, you may be prompted to insert one of the original Windows diskettes or a diskette from the manufacturer of your monitor, keyboard, mouse, or network.

8. After you create the new setup, you must restart Windows. You are given the choice of restarting Windows or returning to DOS. If you need to change hardware—such as attaching a new keyboard or mouse, or connecting a new monitor—return to DOS, make the new connection, and then restart Windows.

If Windows or a Windows program does not "behave" correctly after you change the setup, check the Windows Setup dialog box to see whether you have the correct settings. If necessary, return to the original settings or reinstall Windows.

Summary

This appendix teaches you how to install Windows and change your Windows installation when you change hardware. If you are a systems administrator and are installing Windows on a network, make sure that you read Que's *Using Windows 3.1*, Special Edition, and the notes in the NETWORK.WRI file that Windows installs. In *Using Windows 3.1*, Special Edition, you also learn performance and enhancement tips, as discussed in chapters 23 and 24. A list of Windows resources, such as computer bulletin boards, telephone hotlines, newsletters, and training can be found in Appendix C of this book.

After you install Windows, read chapters 1, 2, and 3 to get an overview of Windows and to learn why Windows is valuable to any personal computer user. In the early chapters, you also learn the fundamentals of operating all Windows programs, as well as how to start and exit Windows.

Summary of Windows Shortcuts

B

General Windows Shortcuts

This appendix provides a list of the shortcuts you can use in Windows programs. This section lists the general shortcuts. Ensuing sections list the shortcuts you can use in the Program Manager, File Manager, and in Windows accessory programs.

Windows Shortcuts

You can use the following shortcuts in any Windows program:

Press	To
F1	Start Help (if the program has Help).
Ctrl + Esc	Display the Task List.
Alt + Esc	Switch to the next program, if it is running in a window; select the next program, if it is running as an icon.

B

Press	To
Alt + Tab⇄	Switch to the next or previous program, restoring programs running as icons. Hold Alt while repeatedly pressing Tab⇄ to scroll through each active program. Release Tab⇄ when the program or program name you want appears.
PrtSc	Copy an image of the screen to the Clipboard. On some PCs, you press Alt + PrtSc. (This shortcut works for DOS programs only if they are running in text mode.)
Alt + PrtSc	Copy an image of the active window to the Clipboard.
Alt + space bar	Open the Control menu for a program window.
Alt + -	Open the Control menu for a document window.
Alt + F4	Quit a program.
Ctrl + F4	Close the active group window or document window.
Alt + ↵Enter	Switch a DOS program between a window and a full screen.
← → ↑ or ↓	Move a window after you choose the Move command from the Control menu.
	Or change the size of a window after you choose Size from the Control menu.

Menu Shortcuts

Use the following shortcuts to select menus and choose commands in any program or in the Program Manager:

Press	To
Alt or F10	Select or deselect the first menu on the menu bar.
letter	Choose the underlined letter or number in a menu or command.
← or →	Move between open menus.

Press	To
↑ or ↓	Move between commands in a menu.
↵Enter	Choose the selected menu name or command.
Esc	Cancel the selected menu name.
	Or close the open menu.

Dialog Box Shortcuts

Use the following shortcuts when you work in a dialog box:

Press	To
Tab⇄	Move from option to option or group to group, left to right and top to bottom.
⇧Shift + Tab⇄	Move from option to option or group to group in reverse order.
Alt + *letter*	Move to the option or group whose underlined letter or number you type.
← → ↑ or ↓	Move the selection from option to option within a group of options.
	Or move the cursor respectively left, right, up, or down within a list or text box.
Home	Move to the first item or character in a list or text box.
End	Move to the last item or character in a list or text box.
PgUp or PgDn	Scroll up or down in a list, one screen at a time.
Alt + ↓	Open a selected list.
space bar	Select an item or cancel a selection in a list.
	Or select or clear a check box.
Ctrl + /	Select all the items in a list box or window where multiple selections are allowed.
Ctrl + \	Cancel all selections except the current selection.

B

Press	To
⬆Shift + ← → ↑ or ↓	Extend or cancel the selection in a text box, one character at a time.
⬆Shift + Home	Extend or cancel the selection to the first character in a text box.
⬆Shift + End	Extend or cancel the selection to the last character in a text box.
↵Enter	Implement a command.
	Or choose the selected item in a list, and then implement the command.
Esc or Alt + F4	Close a dialog box without completing the command.

Insertion-Point Movement Shortcuts

These shortcuts move the cursor or insertion point in text boxes and in programs where you can type text, such as in Notepad or Write:

Press	To move the insertion point
↑	Up one line.
↓	Down one line.
→	Right one character.
←	Left one character.
Ctrl + →	Right one word.
Ctrl + ←	Left one word.
Home	To the beginning of the line.
End	To the end of the line.
PgUp	Up one screen.
PgDn	Down one screen.

B

Press	To move the insertion point
Ctrl + Home	To the beginning of the document.
Ctrl + End	To the end of the document.

Editing Shortcuts

Use these shortcuts to edit text in a dialog box or window:

Press	To
← Backspace	Delete the character to the left of the insertion point. Or delete selected text.
Del	Delete the character to the right of the insertion point. Or delete selected text.
⇧Shift + Del or Ctrl + X	Cut the selected text to the Clipboard.
⇧Shift + Ins or Ctrl + V	Paste text from the Clipboard to the active window.
Ctrl + Ins or Ctrl + C	Copy the selected text to the Clipboard.
Ctrl + Z or Alt + ← Backspace	Undo the last editing action.

Text Selection Shortcuts

When selecting text, you can use the following shortcuts in most Windows programs, but they may not work in all programs. All of the following selections begin at the insertion point. If text is already selected, the shortcuts instead may deselect the text.

B

Press	To select
⬆Shift + ← or →	One character at a time, left or right.
⬆Shift + ↑ or ↓	One line of text, up or down.
⬆Shift + PgUp	All text, one screen up.
⬆Shift + PgDn	All text, one screen down.
⬆Shift + Home	Text to the beginning of the line.
⬆Shift + End	Text to the end of the line.
Ctrl + ⬆Shift + ←	The preceding word.
Ctrl + ⬆Shift + →	The next word.
Ctrl + ⬆Shift + Home	Text to the beginning of the document.
Ctrl + ⬆Shift + End	Text to the end of the document.

Program Manager Shortcuts

Use these shortcuts in the Program Manager:

Press	To
← → ↑ or ↓	Move between items within a group window.
Ctrl + F6 or Ctrl + Tab⇆	Move between group windows and icons.
↵Enter	Start the selected program.
⬆Shift + F4	Arrange the open group windows side by side, or *tile* them.
⬆Shift + F5	Arrange the open group windows so that each title bar is displayed, or *cascade* them.
Ctrl + F4	Close the active group window.
Alt + F4	Quit Windows.

File Manager Shortcuts

This section lists the shortcuts you can use in the File Manager to make your work in the directory tree, contents lists, and drive area more efficient.

B

Directory Tree Shortcuts

When working with the directory tree, use the following shortcuts:

Press	To
Tab⇆	Move between the directory tree, the contents list, and the drive icons.
←	Select the directory listed above the current subdirectory.
→	Select the first subdirectory, if one exists, listed below the current directory.
↵Enter	Display or hide any subdirectories.
⇧Shift + ↵Enter	Open a new window displaying the contents of the selected directory.
↑ or ↓	Select a directory listed above or below the current directory.
Ctrl + ↑	Select the preceding directory at the same level, if one exists.
Ctrl + ↓	Select the next directory at the same level, if one exists.
PgUp	Select the directory one screen up from the current directory.
PgDn	Select the directory one screen down from the current directory.
Home	Select the root directory.
End	Select the last directory in the list.
letter	Select the next directory whose name begins with the letter or number you press.

B

Press	To
[+]	Expand the current directory.
[-]	Collapse the current directory.

Contents List Shortcuts

Use the following shortcuts when working with the list of files and subdirectories in the current directory:

Press	To
[Tab⇄]	Move between the directory tree, the contents list, and the drive icons.
[PgUp]	Select the file or directory one screen above the current selection.
[PgDn]	Select the file or directory one screen below the current selection.
[Home]	Select the first file or directory in the list.
[End]	Select the last file or directory in the list.
letter	Select the next file or directory whose name begins with the letter or number you press.
[⇧Shift] + [←] [→] [↑] or [↓]	Select or deselect multiple consecutive items.
[Ctrl]+[/]	Select all items in the list.
[Ctrl]+[\]	Cancel all selections in the list, except the current selection.
[Ctrl]+click	Select multiple nonconsecutive items.
[⇧Shift]+[F8]	Select or deselect nonconsecutive items. Press [⇧Shift]+[F8], and then press [←] [→] [↑] or [↓] and space bar.

B

Press	To
← → ↑ or ↓	Move the cursor or scroll to other items in the window.
↵Enter	Open a directory or start a program.
⇧Shift + ↵Enter	Open a new window displaying the contents of the selected directory.

Drive Area Shortcuts

Use these shortcuts in the drive area:

Press	To
Tab⇄	Move between the directory tree, the contents list, and the drive icons.
Click	Select a drive.
Ctrl + *letter*	Change to the drive icon that matches the drive letter you type.
← or →	Move between drive icons.
space bar	Change drives.
↵Enter	Open a new directory window.
Double-click	Open a new window.

Desktop Accessory Shortcuts

This section lists the shortcuts you can use in the Windows accessory programs, such as the Calculator, Calendar, Cardfile, Media Player, Notepad, Paintbrush, Write, and more.

Calculator Shortcuts

Use the following shortcuts for the Calculator:

Press	To
Esc	Clear (erase) the Calculator of all numbers and functions.
Del	Delete the displayed value.
←Backspace	Delete the last number in the displayed value.
Ctrl + M	Store the displayed value in memory.
Ctrl + P	Add the displayed value to memory.
Ctrl + R	Reveal (display) the value in memory.
Ctrl + L	Clear (erase) the memory.

Calendar Shortcuts

Use the following shortcuts in the Calendar's Day and Month views.

Day View Shortcuts

Press	To
↑	Move to the preceding time.
↓ or ↵Enter	Move to the following time.
PgUp	Move to the preceding screen.
PgDn	Move to the next screen.
Double-click status bar	Move to Month view.
Ctrl + Home	Move to the starting time.
Ctrl + End	Move to twelve hours after the starting time.
Tab⇆	Move between the appointment area and the scratch pad.

Press	To
⬆Shift + Del	Cut the selection to the Clipboard.
Ctrl + Ins	Copy the selection to the Clipboard.
⬆Shift + Ins	Paste the Clipboard contents to the appointment area or scratch pad.

Month View Shortcuts

Press	To
↑	Move to the preceding week.
↓	Move to the next week.
Double-click status bar	Move to Day view.
PgUp	Move to the preceding month.
PgDn	Move to the next month.
Double-click date	Move to Day view (that day).
Tab↹	Move between a date and the scratch pad.
↵Enter	Change to Day view.

Cardfile Shortcuts

You can use these shortcuts in the Cardfile:

Press	To
PgDn	Scroll forward one card in Card view.
	Or move forward one page of index lines in List view.
PgUp	Scroll backward one card in Card view.
	Or move back one page of index lines in List view.

B

Press	To
Ctrl + Home	Bring the first card in the file to the front.
Ctrl + End	Bring the last card in the file to the front.
⇧Shift + Ctrl + *letter*	Bring a card to the front of the file. Cardfile displays the first card whose index line begins with the letter or number you type.

Clipboard Viewer Shortcuts

Use the following shortcuts in the Clipboard:

Press	To
Del	Clear the Clipboard contents in the Clipboard Viewer.
⇧Shift + Del or Ctrl + X	In a document, cut a selection to the Clipboard.
Ctrl + Ins or Ctrl + C	In a document, copy a selection to the Clipboard.
⇧Shift + Ins or Ctrl + V	In a document, paste the Clipboard contents to a document.
PrtSc	In Windows, copy an image of the entire screen to the Clipboard. (This shortcut works for DOS programs only if they are running in text mode.)
Alt + PrtSc	In Windows, copy an image of the active window to the Clipboard.

Help Shortcuts

Use the following shortcuts to start Windows Help from a program:

Press	*To*
F1	Display the Help Contents for the program. If the Help window is already open, pressing F1 displays the Contents for How To Use Help. In some programs (such as Program Manager and File Manager), pressing F1 displays a Help topic about the selected command, dialog box option, or system message.
⇧Shift + F1	Add a question mark to the pointer. You can then click the command, click the screen region, or press the key or key combination about which you want to know more. This feature is available only in some programs.

Help Window Shortcuts

Use the following shortcuts after you start Help:

Press	*To*
Tab↹	Move clockwise among hot spots (where you can get further information) in the topic.
⇧Shift + Tab↹	Move counterclockwise among hot spots in the topic.
Ctrl + Tab↹	Select all the hot spots in a topic. Or deselect a hot spot.
Ctrl + Ins	Copy the current Help topic to the Clipboard without displaying the Copy dialog box. Or copy an entire annotation or a portion of it to the Clipboard.
⇧Shift + Ins	Paste the Clipboard contents into the Annotation dialog box.
Alt + F4	Quit Help.

Media Player Shortcuts

Use the following shortcuts in Media Player:

Press	To
Tab⇄	Move among buttons and the scroll bar, left to right.
⇧Shift + Tab⇄	Move among buttons and the scroll bar, right to left.
space bar	Choose a button.
←	Move back the playing position when the scroll bar is selected.
→	Move forward the playing position when the scroll bar is selected.
PgUp	Move back the playing position in large increments when the scroll bar is selected.
PgDn	Move forward the playing position in large increments when the scroll bar is selected.
Home	Move to the beginning of the sound when the scroll bar is selected.
End	Move to the end of the sound when the scroll bar is selected.

Notepad Shortcuts

See the cursor-movement, text selection, and Program Manager shortcuts in previous sections of this appendix.

Object Packager Shortcuts

Only one shortcut is available for the Object Packager:

Press	To
Tab⇄	Move the selection cursor between the Content and Appearance windows.

578

Paintbrush Shortcuts

Use the following shortcuts in Paintbrush.

Mouse Equivalent Shortcuts

Use these keys instead of using the mouse:

Pressing	Is equivalent to
Ins	Clicking the left mouse button.
Del	Clicking the right mouse button.
F9 + Ins	Double-clicking the left mouse button.
F9 + Del	Double-clicking the right mouse button.

Undo Shortcuts

Use the following shortcuts to undo your last editing action:

Press	To
◆Backspace	Undo all or part of what you have drawn since selecting a tool. Press ◆Backspace and then drag the eraser cursor over the part of the drawing you want to undo.
Alt + ◆Backspace or Ctrl + Z	Undo everything you have drawn or typed since selecting a tool.

Movement Shortcuts

Use these shortcuts for moving around the drawing area:

Press	To
Tab	Move the pointer among the Toolbox, Line-width box, Palette, and Drawing Area in a counterclockwise direction.

579

B

Press	To
⇧Shift+Tab⇄	Move the pointer among the Toolbox, Line-width box, Palette, and Drawing Area in a clockwise direction.
← → ↑ or ↓	Move the drawing tool within a window.
⇧Shift+Home	Jump to the left side of a drawing.
⇧Shift+End	Jump to the right side of a drawing.
PgUp	Move up one screen.
PgDn	Move down one screen.
Home	Jump to the top of a drawing.
End	Jump to the bottom of a drawing.
⇧Shift+←	Move the cursor to the left one space.
⇧Shift+→	Move the cursor to the right one space.
⇧Shift+↑	Move the cursor up one line.
⇧Shift+↓	Move the cursor down one line.

PIF Editor Shortcuts

Use the following shortcuts when you're working in PIF Editor:

Press	To
Tab⇄	Move from option to option, left to right and top to bottom.
⇧Shift+Tab⇄	Move from option to option in reverse order.
Alt+*letter*	Move to the option or group whose underlined letter matches the one you type. If the option is a check box, it also sets or clears the option.
← → ↑ or ↓	Move the selection cursor from option to option within a group of options.
space bar	Select or clear a check box.

Sound Recorder Shortcuts

Use the following shortcuts in Sound Recorder:

Press	To
Tab ⇥	Move among the buttons and the scroll bar, left to right.
⇧Shift + Tab ⇥	Move among the buttons and the scroll bar, right to left.
space bar	Choose a button.
← or →	Move backward or forward when the scroll bar is selected.
PgUp	Move back one second when the scroll bar is selected.
PgDn	Move forward one second when the scroll bar is selected.
Home	Move to the beginning of the sound when the scroll bar is selected.
End	Move to the end of the sound when the scroll bar is selected.

Write Shortcuts

The following shortcuts—movement and editing—help you work with Write. Note that when the key combination includes 5, it refers to 5 on the numeric keypad with Num Lock turned off. (Refer also to the insertion point movement, text selection, and Program Manager shortcuts in previous sections of this appendix.)

Movement Shortcuts

Use the following shortcuts to move the insertion point within a document:

Press	To
5 + →	Move to the next sentence.
5 + ←	Move to the preceding sentence.

B

Press	To
5 + ↓	Move to the next paragraph.
5 + ↑	Move to the preceding paragraph.
5 + PgDn	Move to the next page, according to the last repagination.
5 + PgUp	Move to the preceding page, according to the last repagination.

Editing Shortcuts

Use these shortcuts to edit text:

Press	To
Ctrl + ↵Enter	Insert a manual page break.
⇧Shift + Del or Ctrl + X	Cut a selection to the Clipboard.
Ctrl + Ins or Ctrl + C	Copy a selection to the Clipboard.
⇧Shift + Ins or Ctrl + V	Paste the Clipboard contents to a document.
Ctrl + Z or Alt + ⬦Backspace	Undo the last typing or editing action.
↓	Select a picture when the cursor is above the upper-left corner of the picture.
← → ↑ or ↓	Move the picture sizing cursor after you choose the Size Picture command from the Edit menu.
	Or move a selected picture after you choose the Move Picture command from the Edit menu.
Ctrl + ⇧Shift + -	Insert an optional hyphen.
Alt + F6	Switch between the document and the Find or Replace dialog box.
	Or switch between the document and the Page Header or Page Footer dialog box.

Help, Support, and Resources

Windows is one of the most popular software programs ever written, which means that a lot of support is available for it. The following resources will help you.

Telephone Support

Use the following telephone numbers to get technical support or product sales information about Windows or Windows programs.

For questions specific to Windows installation, the Program Manager, File Manager, or Accessories, call:

Microsoft Corporation   206-637-7098

For technical or sales information regarding a major product, call:

Manufacturer	Software	Telephone Support Line
Microsoft	Corporate	206-882-8080
	Technical (All software, Publisher, Money, and Project)	206-454-2030
	Windows	206-637-7098
	DOS (pay per call)	900-896-9000
	Microsoft Excel	206-635-7070
	Word for Windows	206-462-9673
Adobe	Corporate	415-961-4400
	Technical (Adobe Type Manager, Adobe Fonts)	415-961-4992
Aldus	Corporate	206-662-5500
	Technical (PageMaker, Persuasion, Freehand)	206-628-2040
Asymetrix	Corporate	206-462-0501
	Technical (ToolBook)	206-637-1600
Borland	Corporate	408-438-8400
	Technical (Object Vision)	408-438-5300
Corel	Corporate	613-728-8200
	Technical (CorelDRAW!)	613-728-1990
Intuit	Corporate	415-322-0573
	Technical (Quicken)	415-322-2800

C

Manufacturer	Software	Telephone Support Line
Lotus	Corporate	617-577-8500
	Technical (recordings) (1-2-3 for Windows, Ami Pro, Freelance)	617-253-9130
	Technical (pay per call)	900-454-9009
Polaris	Corporate	619-674-6500
	Technical (PackRat)	619-743-7800
Symantec	Corporate	310-449-4900
	Technical (Norton Desktop for Windows)	213-319-2020
WordPerfect	Corporate	801-225-5000
	Technical (WordPerfect 5.1 for Windows)	801-228-9907

C

Support Organizations

Most major cities in the United States have a computer club. A Windows special interest group (SIG) usually exists within this club. Clubs usually have monthly meetings, demonstrate new software, maintain a list of consultants, and have free or low-cost training. To contact your local computer club, check newspaper listings under *computer* or call local computer stores.

The Windows User Group Network (WUGNet) is a national organization devoted to supporting its members with information about Windows and Windows programs. It publishes a substantial bimonthly journal containing tips and articles written by members and consultants. Its staff is highly knowledgeable about Windows and Windows programs. Contact WUGNet for more information:

WUGNet Publications, Inc.
1295 N. Providence Rd.
Media, PA 19063
(215) 565-1861   Voice
(215) 565-7106   FAX

585

Computer Bulletin Board Forums

Computer bulletin boards are databases from which you can retrieve information over the telephone line using Terminal—the communications program that comes with Windows. Some bulletin boards contain a wealth of information about Windows and Windows programs. One of the largest public bulletin boards is CompuServe.

CompuServe contains forums in which its members can discuss Windows and Windows programs. You can submit questions to Microsoft operators who return answers within a day. CompuServe also contains libraries of sample files and new printer and device drivers. The Knowledgebase, available in Microsoft's region of CompuServe, has much of the same troubleshooting information used by Microsoft's telephone support representatives. You can use keywords to search through the Knowledgebase. The Microsoft region of CompuServe is divided into many different areas, such as Windows users, advanced Windows users, Microsoft Excel, Microsoft languages, and sections of each of the major Microsoft and non-Microsoft programs that run under Windows.

After you become a CompuServe member, you can access the Microsoft user forums, library files, and Knowledgebase. To gain access to one these areas, type one of the following GO commands at the CompuServe prompt symbol (!), and then press Enter.

Type	To access
GO MSOFT	Overall Microsoft area.
GO MSUSER	Overall applications and Windows areas.
GO MSAPP	Microsoft applications areas.
GO MSEXCEL	Microsoft Excel areas.
GO WINNEW	New Windows user areas.
GO WINADV	Advanced Windows user areas.
GO WINVEN	Overall non-Microsoft Windows applications areas.
GO WINAPA	Non-Microsoft Windows applications area.
GO WINAPB	Non-Microsoft Windows applications area.
GO WINAPC	Non-Microsoft Windows applications area.

Contact CompuServe for more information:

> CompuServe
> 5000 Arlington Centre Blvd.
> P.O. Box 20212
> Columbus, OH 43220
> (800) 848-8990

Consultants and Corporate Training

Microsoft Consulting Partners develop and support programs written using Microsoft products for the Windows environment. Microsoft Consulting Partners are independent consultants who have met strict qualifying requirements imposed by Microsoft.

Ron Person & Co., based in San Francisco, has attained Microsoft's highest rating for Microsoft Excel and Word for Windows consultants—Microsoft Consulting Partner. The firm helps corporations nationwide in consulting and developing in-house programming and support skills with the embedded macro languages in Microsoft Excel, Word for Windows, and other major Windows programs. The firm's macro developer's courses have enabled many corporations to develop their own powerful financial, marketing, and business analysis systems in a minimum amount of time. If your company plans to use Microsoft's embedded macro languages to develop programs, you will gain significantly from the courses taught by Ron Person & Co. For information on course content, on-site corporate classes, or consulting, contact:

> Ron Person & Co.
> PO Box 5647
> 3 Quixote Ct.
> Santa Rosa, CA 95409
> (415) 989-7508   Voice
> (707) 539-1525   Voice
> (707) 538-1485   FAX

Index

X-Y-Z

Computer Books from Que Mean PC Performance!

Spreadsheets

1-2-3 Beyond the Basics	$24.95
1-2-3 Database Techniques	$29.95
1-2-3 for DOS Release 2.3 Quick Reference	$ 9.95
1-2-3 for DOS Release 2.3 QuickStart	$19.95
1-2-3 for Windows Quick Reference	$ 9.95
1-2-3 for Windows QuickStart	$19.95
1-2-3 Graphics Techniques	$24.95
1-2-3 Macro Library, 3rd Edition	$39.95
1-2-3 Release 2.2 PC Tutor	$39.95
1-2-3 Release 2.2 QueCards	$19.95
1-2-3 Release 2.2 Workbook and Disk	$29.95
1-2-3 Release 3 Workbook and Disk	$29.95
1-2-3 Release 3.1 Quick Reference	$ 8.95
1-2-3 Release 3.1 + QuickStart, 2nd Edition	$19.95
Excel for Windows Quick Reference	$ 9.95
Quattro Pro Quick Reference	$ 8.95
Quattro Pro 3 QuickStart	$19.95
Using 1-2-3/G	$29.95
Using 1-2-3 for DOS Release 2.3, Special Edition	$29.95
Using 1-2-3 for Windows	$29.95
Using 1-2-3 Release 3.1, + 2nd Edition	$29.95
Using Excel 3 for Windows, Special Edition	$29.95
Using Quattro Pro 3, Special Edition	$24.95
Using SuperCalc5, 2nd Edition	$29.95

Databases

dBASE III Plus Handbook, 2nd Edition	$24.95
dBASE IV PC Tutor	$29.95
dBASE IV Programming Techniques	$29.95
dBASE IV Quick Reference	$ 8.95
dBASE IV 1.1 QuickStart	$19.95
dBASE IV Workbook and Disk	$29.95
Que's Using FoxPro	$29.95
Using Clipper, 2nd Edition	$29.95
Using DataEase	$24.95
Using dBASE IV	$29.95
Using ORACLE	$29.95
Using Paradox 3	$24.95
Using PC-File	$24.95
Using R:BASE	$29.95

Business Applications

Allways Quick Reference	$ 8.95
Introduction to Business Software	$14.95
Introduction to Personal Computers	$19.95
Norton Utilities Quick Reference	$ 8.95
PC Tools Quick Reference, 2nd Edition	$ 8.95
Q&A Quick Reference	$ 8.95
Que's Computer User's Dictionary, 2nd Edition	$10.95
Que's Using Enable	$29.95
Que's Wizard Book	$12.95
Quicken Quick Reference	$ 8.95
SmartWare Tips, Tricks, and Traps, 2nd Edition	$26.95
Using DacEasy, 2nd Edition	$24.95
Using Managing Your Money, 2nd Edition	$19.95
Using Microsoft Works: IBM Version	$22.95
Using Norton Utilities	$24.95
Using PC Tools Deluxe	$24.95
Using Peachtree	$27.95
Using PROCOMM PLUS, 2nd Edition	$24.95
Using Q&A 4	$27.95
Using Quicken: IBM Version, 2nd Edition	$19.95
Using SmartWare II	$29.95
Using Symphony, Special Edition	$29.95
Using TimeLine	$24.95
Using TimeSlips	$24.95

CAD

AutoCAD Quick Reference	$ 8.95
Que's Using Generic CADD	$29.95
Using AutoCAD, 3rd Edition	$29.95
Using Generic CADD	$24.95

Word Processing

Microsoft Word Quick Reference	$ 9.95
Using LetterPerfect	$22.95
Using Microsoft Word 5.5: IBM Version, 2nd Edition	$24.95
Using MultiMate	$24.95
Using PC-Write	$22.95
Using Professional Write	$22.95
Using Word for Windows	$24.95
Using WordPerfect 5	$27.95
Using WordPerfect 5.1, Special Edition	$27.95
Using WordStar, 3rd Edition	$27.95
WordPerfect PC Tutor	$39.95
WordPerfect Power Pack	$39.95
WordPerfect 5 Workbook and Disk	$29.95
WordPerfect 5.1 QueCards	$19.95
WordPerfect 5.1 Quick Reference	$ 8.95
WordPerfect 5.1 QuickStart	$19.95
WordPerfect 5.1 Tips, Tricks, and Traps	$24.95
WordPerfect 5.1 Workbook and Disk	$29.95

Hardware/Systems

DOS Tips, Tricks, and Traps	$24.95
DOS Workbook and Disk, 2nd Edition	$29.95
Fastback Quick Reference	$ 8.95
Hard Disk Quick Reference	$ 8.95
MS-DOS PC Tutor	$39.95
MS-DOS 5 Quick Reference	$ 9.95
MS-DOS 5 QuickStart, 2nd Edition	$19.95
MS-DOS 5 User's Guide, Special Edition	$29.95
Networking Personal Computers, 3rd Edition	$24.95
Understanding UNIX: A Conceptual Guide, 2nd Edition	$21.95
Upgrading and Repairing PCs	$29.95
Using Microsoft Windows 3, 2nd Edition	$24.95
Using MS-DOS 5	$24.95
Using Novell NetWare	$29.95
Using OS/2	$29.95
Using PC DOS, 3rd Edition	$27.95
Using Prodigy	$19.95
Using UNIX	$29.95
Using Your Hard Disk	$29.95
Windows 3 Quick Reference	$ 8.95

Desktop Publishing/Graphics

CorelDRAW! Quick Reference	$ 8.95
Harvard Graphics Quick Reference	$ 8.95
Que's Using Ventura Publisher	$29.95
Using Animator	$24.95
Using DrawPerfect	$24.95
Using Harvard Graphics, 2nd Edition	$24.95
Using Freelance Plus	$24.95
Using PageMaker 4 for Windows	$29.95
Using PFS: First Publisher, 2nd Edition	$24.95
Using PowerPoint	$24.95
Using Publish It!	$24.95

Macintosh/Apple II

The Big Mac Book, 2nd Edition	$29.95
The Little Mac Book	$12.95
Que's Macintosh Multimedia Handbook	$24.95
Using AppleWorks, 3rd Edition	$24.95
Using Excel 3 for the Macintosh	$24.95
Using FileMaker	$24.95
Using MacDraw	$24.95
Using MacroMind Director	$29.95
Using MacWrite	$24.95
Using Microsoft Word 4: Macintosh Version	$24.95
Using Microsoft Works: Macintosh Version, 2nd Edition	$24.95
Using PageMaker: Macintosh Version, 2nd Edition	$24.95

Programming/Technical

C Programmer'sToolkit	$39.95
DOS Programmer's Reference, 2nd Edition	$29.95
Network Programming in C	$49.95
Oracle Programmer's Guide	$29.95
QuickC Programmer's Guide	$29.95
UNIX Programmer's Quick Reference	$ 8.95
UNIX Programmer's Reference	$29.95
UNIX Shell Commands Quick Reference	$ 8.95
Using Assembly Language, 2nd Edition	$29.95
Using BASIC	$24.95
Using Borland C++	$29.95
Using C	$29.95
Using QuickBASIC 4	$24.95
Using Turbo Pascal	$29.95

For More Information, Call Toll Free!

1-800-428-5331

All prices and titles subject to change without notice.
Non-U.S. prices may be higher. Printed in the U.S.A.

Teach Yourself
With QuickStarts From Que!

The ideal tutorials for beginners, Que's QuickStart books use graphic illustrations and step-by-step instructions to get you up and running fast. Packed with examples, QuickStarts are the perfect beginner's guides to your favorite software applications.

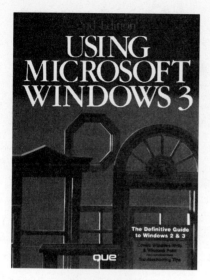

Find It Fast With Que's Quick References!

Que's Quick References are the compact, easy-to-use guides to essential application information. Written for all users, Quick References include vital command information under easy-to-find alphabetical listings. Quick References are a must for anyone who needs command information fast!

Complete Computer Coverage From A To Z!

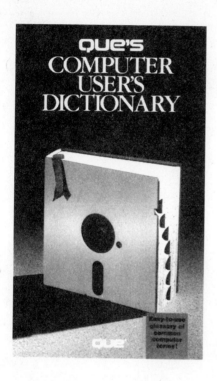

Que's Computer User's Dictionary, 2nd Edition

Que Development Group

This compact, practical reference contains hundreds of definitions, explanations, examples, and illustrations on topics from programming to desktop publishing. You can master the "language" of computers and learn how to make your personal computers more efficient and more powerful. Filled with tips and cautions, *Que's Computer User's Dictionary* is the perfect resource for anyone who uses a computer.

IBM, Macintosh, Apple, & Programming

$10.95 USA

0-88022-697-8, 550 pp., 4 3/4 x 8

The Ultimate Glossary Of Computer Terms— Over 200,000 In Print!

"Dictionary indeed. This whammer is a mini-encyclopedia...an absolute joy to use...a must for your computer library...."

Southwest Computer & Business Equipment Review

To Order, Call: (800) 428-5331 OR (317) 573-2500

Word Processing Is Easy
When You're Using Que!

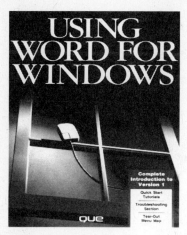

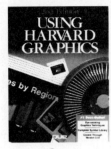
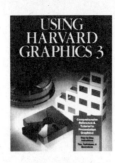

Count on Que for the Most Up-to-Date Information on Integrated Packages

Using Q&A
David Ewing & Bill Langenes

This best-seller covers all of Q&A's enhancements, including the database, word processor, and utilities. A comprehensive reference and tutorial, this book will give you everything you need to know about Q&A.

Version 4

$27.95 USA

0-88022-643-9, 550 pp., 7 3/8 x 9 1/4

Using Microsoft Works: IBM Version
Douglas Wolf
Through Version 2
$22.95 USA
0-88022-467-3, 444 pp., 7 3/8 x 9 1/4

Using Symphony, Special Edition
Geoffrey LeBlond & David Ewing
Through Version 2.2
$29.95 USA
0-88022-553-X, 160 pp., 7 3/8 x 9 1/4

**Microsoft Works
Quick Reference**
Que Development Group
Through IBM Version 2.0
$9.95 USA
0-88022-694-3, 160 pp., 4 3/4 x 8

Q&A QueCards
Que Development Group
Latest Version
$19.95 USA
0-88022-669-2, 60 cards, 7 3/8 x 9 1/4

Q&A 4 Quick Reference
Que Development Group
Latest Version
$8.95 USA
0-88022-828-8, 160 pp., 4 3/4 x 8

Q&A 4 QuickStart
Que Development Group
Version 4
$19.95 USA
0-88022-653-6, 400 pp., 7 3/8 x 9 1/4

SmartWare Tips, Tricks, and Traps, 2nd Edition
Andrew N. Schwartz
*SmartWare II Version 1.02 &
Smart Version 3.10*
$26.95 USA
0-88022-543-2, 550 pp., 7 3/8 x 9 1/4

Using SmartWare II
Andrew N. Schwartz
Version 1.02
$29.95 USA
0-88022-405-3, 650 pp., 7 3/8 x 9 1/4

To Order, Call: (800) 428-5331 OR (317) 573-2500